Critique

Omni-Science
and the Human Destiny

The following quotes, and those on the book cover, are from reviews written by highly respected scholars who have heard Anthony Marr's lectures, but have not read this version of the book *Omni-Science and the Human Destiny*. Also, the comments refer to the Omniscientific Cosmology only, and not to the background story in the book, nor to the book itself.

University of California, Berkeley

Biology, Professor **Richard W. Holms**:
"I have listened to a presentation by Anthony S. Marr. His synthesis of ideas from a remarkably broad perspective of sciences truly deserves the name OMNI-SCIENCE. His presentation was precise and clear, and I believe he would be an effective speaker for groups at varying levels of expertise…This is a person of great depth who speaks and writes both with confidence and ease. I am happy to recommend him as a speaker and a writer."

Astronomy and **Physics**, Professor **Marc Davis**:
"As one who actually specializes in cosmology as a research endeavour, I was at first very skeptical that Mr. Marr would be yet another crackpot of the type that seems to congregate in this field. However, after only a few minutes of listening to his explanation of his viewpoint, my fears were allayed…His ultimate goal appears to be to provide a forward-looking moral framework for progress in human social evolution, one that is consistent with empirical science and which is not based on historical writings…and important contribution to society…."

Anthropology, Professor **Tim White**:
"I have not seen a draft of the book, but I can say that after spending a few hours with Mr. Marr, I am very much looking forward to reading it….Mr. Marr is an exceedingly unique individual. I have never crossed paths with such a person. He is very serious, very dedicated, and very polished in his presentation…The care with which he his proceeded is commendable…his synthesis is formidable…."

Omni-Science and the Human Destiny

Paleontology, Professor **Carole S. Hickman**:
"(Mr. Marr's work) deserves the attention of serious scholars…an extraordinary intellectual undertaking…a unique framework…both intellectually and aesthetically stimulating…a bold and eclectic piece of scholarship that is, above all, refreshingly honest….His clarity of expression is exceptional. His logical consistency is a delight. The aesthetic quality of the model, in particular his attention to symmetry, provides a dimension that is appealing but sadly lacking in much of Western thought and tradition. The optimism, concern and compassion for humanity that are expressed in the application of the model to human behavior likewise commands attention…."

Zoology, Professor **Richard C. Strohman**:
"His views and thinking are quite original…a thoroughly logical system…might indeed fill a large gap in the way we think about evolutionary connections between ourselves and our world. I sincerely encourage you to listen to Mr. Marr. And I have one suggestion. His presentation is quite detailed and covers very large areas. My thought is that he and his listeners would all do much better in a small seminar setting so that there would be a symmetry between his own very wide knowledge and the ability for him to obtain meaningful feedback."

Botany, Professor **Herbert G. Baker**:
"…an extremely interesting experience…worthy of the attention of a wide variety of persons. If he writes as clearly and understandably as his oral communication, the book should be an important contribution towards understanding cosmology."

Paleontology, Professor **Donald E. Savage**:
"Professors and scientists at the universities of British Columbia, Washington, Oregon and California, to date, have each spent two hours or more listening to the powerful presentation of Anthony Marr of his erudite synthesis of scientific, philosophic and sociologic theory: OMNI-SCIENCE, A New Theory of Cosmology. I can add nothing to the praise that has been heaped upon Mr. Marr and his ideas by these men, and I endorse their statements with reservation. Now is the time for Mr. Marr's ideas to be published, for the scientific world and general public should become aware of his synthesis."

Institute of Human Origins, Berkeley

Dr. **William H. Kimbel**, President:
"I have recently had the great pleasure of listening to Anthony Marr describe the results of his thinking on cosmology.

"Owing to the large number of half-baked 'pop' theories on cosmology currently in circulation, I admit that I faced the prospect of my meeting with Mr. Marr with some trepidation.

"From the outset, however, it was clear that Mr. Marr is no amateur populariser. On the contrary, he is a dedicated scholar whose theories, I believe, make a profound contribution to the fundamental definition of humankind in relation to the broader universe.

"Although Mr. Marr has an uphill battle ahead of him, I firmly believe that his ideas deserve very serious consideration by a wide audience. Not only do they unify the fragmented Western scientific disciplines, but they have implications of great depth and breadth for the future course of human actions. In the current atmosphere of censorship and anti-intellectualism, Mr. Marr's concept of OMNI-SCIENCE is too important to ignore."

Stanford University

Sociology, Professor **Alex Inkeles**:
"Recently Mr. Anthony Marr persuaded me to give him an hour of my time, all I could spare in that cycle of my calendar, and at that it had to be at the end of a busy day. This obliged Mr. Marr, as he told me, to adopt a different style of presentation than the one he usually used, one much more compressed and involving a more top-down approach instead of his usual inductive procedure. Despite these handicaps, Mr. Marr managed to impress me not only with the quality of his presentation, but also the quality of his thinking. The range of his knowledge is broad, and for something so broad seems impressively authoritative. At the heart of his approach is a conception of all living and indeed nonliving matter as organized in systems, and this gave him a considerable edge with me since my own propensity is to think in system terms… exceptionally comprehensive…."

Philosophy, Professor **John Dupre**:
"A few days ago, I had a lengthy discussion with Mr. Anthony Marr about his philosophical ideas. I can certainly confirm the impressions gained by the various other scholars who have written on his behalf. Marr is a highly intelligent, thoughtful man who has evidently acquired a thorough knowledge of the impressively broad range of topics over which his ideas range. As we were talking, I asked him all the difficult questions that occurred to me as he was outlining his ideas. He was always very quick to get the point, and had intelligent and relevant responses. I was very impressed with his various intellectual accomplishments.

"Though his ideas are extremely intriguing and provocative, I must confess to having considerable skepticism about his project which he did not altogether dispel. However, I very much doubt whether anyone could dispel this skepticism, and certainly not in two hours. I am not convinced, that is to say, that a systematic view of the scope that Marr attempts is really an intelligible project. However, there is no doubt that such projects will be forthcoming, and such a system informed by Mr. Marr's deep and thorough understanding of the current state of scientific theory will undoubtedly be incomparably more edifying than the vast majority of such attempts, whether religiously based, or grounded on superficial impressions of science. Indeed, I am open to being convinced that such a project will address a pressing social need: if people insist on adopting comprehensive cosmological systems, then I would certainly encourage them to try his. I certainly share his concern about the dangers of many contemporary religious, especially fundamentalist, cosmologies.

"One thing, then I would say without any qualification is that I would strongly encourage any publisher to accept his book. I have not read the manuscript, but assuming, as I have no reason to doubt, that Marr is as articulate, clear and cogent on paper as he is in person, his system would make fascinating reading, and would, I suspect, attract a large audience…."

Omni-Science and the Human Destiny

Applied Physics and **Astrophysics**, Professor **Vahe Petrosian**:
"…elaborate…clearly well thought out and researched…I was fascinated by his novel ideas in this very ambitious task…a beautiful synthesis…what I heard was captivating and should be of interest not only to experts but to all thinking people of the world…will find a wide and interested audience…."

Anthropology, Professor **John W. Rick**:
"…very thought provoking…an integrative scheme capable of making sense out of a wide variety of natural science knowledge, which at the same time reaches out to philosophy and epistemology…clearly deserves extensive discussion…a serious, well-founded vision, not the product of trivial or eccentric thought. My feeling is that he deserves attention and his ideas should be published. I would recommend that those who have the time listen and argue over his presentation. One should not underestimate the time this may take, however, since his model covers a broad expanse of knowledge. I would think that his presentation would be an ideal forum in an academic department where a group of faculty and graduate students could take time to thoroughly examine his proposition…."

Physics, Professor **Leonard Susskind**:
"…the cosmic significance of life and evolution. Although this is not exactly my 'meat', I thoroughly enjoyed the two hours…I found myself stimulated, educated…His ideas are worth listening to, even for those of us who are not of the same philosophical bent…."

Philosophy, Professor **John Bogart**:
"I spent 3.5 hours with Mr. Anthony Marr…held my attention for the entire period…has plainly synthesized a great deal of information in a number of distinct disciplines…organized it into an interesting and coherent whole…compelling…intended to have moral import…can be cast into a form of interest to moral philosophy…would be of interest to a wide audience…."

Geology, Professor **W.R. Evitt**:
"I agree wholeheartedly…about his sincerity, imagination, intellectualism and scholarship. This afternoon was for me a unique and stimulating experience. In a highly logical series of simple steps, he developed a comprehensive concept of the interrelations and interdependence of all things…an immensely logical construct…should be accessible and acceptable to persons with a wide range of cultural, social, scientific and philosophical sophistications…meticulously thought out, with great care, to making his thesis externally consistent with the facts of science as currently perceived, and internally consistent in the interrelationships among its arguments…majestic in scope but intrinsically simple, satisfying and optimistic…should have a very broad appeal…These are important ideas with great potential for lessening the conflicts in a troubled world…."

Anthony Marr

University of Oregon

Geology, Professor **Greg Retallack**:
"Although initially skeptical, I found his whole system quite fascinating and thought provoking…I thought that his model was superior to those already available. His proposed books will be important advances in thinking on the origin and evolution of life and society…His presentation was made with the care and rigor of a serious and dedicated scholar. He has a good and up to date understanding of the natural sciences. I could not detect a trace of mysticism or journalistic pseudoscience in his presentation. Mr. Marr is a hard-headed thinker in the best scientific tradition. He deserves serious attention."

Biology, Professor **Stanton A. Cook**:
"Anthony Marr has explained to me his thoughts on physical hierarchies and evolution of organic hierarchies on earth. He elaborated a novel way of diagramming or organizing these thoughts that should be quite useful to an audience that has not thought much on these matters. I do believe that comprehension and appreciation of levels of organization has been hampered by a want of just such a methodical and visual approach…He left me with a clear impression that he has a well developed message…."

Biology, Professor **Dennis Todd**:
"Anthony Marr has developed a new theoretical framework that integrates a great deal of scientific information from diverse fields. His thesis deserves your careful attention.

"Mr. Marr impressed me with the breadth of his knowledge, the seriousness of his intellectual pursuit, and the keenness of his insight. He is a rare person: one who can understand the findings of specialized branches of various sciences, apply them to other branches, synthesize a meaningful and coherent overview, and present his conclusions in a masterly and cogent fashion.

"His philosophy unites the multiplicity of levels of organization, both biotic and abiotic, into a coherent system of analysis. The system that he proposes, with parallels between levels ranging from the atomic to the cosmic, provides a fresh perspective for those who wish to understand the workings of nature. Furthermore, his principles can function as a springboard for leaps into realms that, at least for the present, are purely philosophical - teleology, epistemology and ontology.

"Mr. Marr is a serious and dedicated scholar. I commend him and ask that you grant him an opportunity to present his ideas to you."

Ecology, John Burket:
"This letter is to urge the serious and positive consideration for the work done by Anthony Marr.

"I spent an afternoon talking with Anthony and learning the system of thought as set down in his manuscript. That short experience has instilled in me the kind of wondered awe that arises when previously nebulous thoughts, ideas and feelings suddenly crystallized into a

Omni-Science and the Human Destiny

framework of order.

"It is my opinion that Anthony Marr's system of Integrative Transcendence is the germ of a new worldview, and that the minds of people today are very fertile ground for this philosophy. The clarity and logical order of this system gives an immediate sense of recognition of ones place in the scheme of existence.

"Further, one can see from this philosophy how the future of our planet can be seen in terms of undeniable purpose and hope, a state of mind so lacking in these times.

"I urge you to listen to Anthony Marr and publish his work. His is an idea whose time has come."

University of Washington

Ecology, Ethology, Sociobiology, Environmental Studies, Professor **Gordon H. Orians**:
"During the past month I have had an opportunity to listen to a lengthy presentation by Anthony Marr of his comprehensive cosmological system. In addition, I have read most of his book-length manuscript titled OMNI-SCIENCE. These encounters have revealed to me that Anthony Marr is a deep thinking and widely read person. In those areas of biology where I am competent to judge, Mr. Marr is thorough and accurate in his presentation of fact. He has delved deeply into evolutionary, ecological and behavioral literature. He has also had extensive field experience, upon which he draws repeatedly in his book.

"Mr. Marr's mode of presentation of his ideas deviates strikingly from standard scientific ones, reflecting his philosophical ancestry and his goals. Primarily he is attempting to develop a philosophical scheme that can encompass both modern science and religion in a way that can be acceptable to both. His is also a futuristic perspective, offering hope at a time when so many of us feel a deep sense of despair. This is a daunting task but one which we avoid at considerable peril. Given the religious rejection of science that are so rampant in American culture today, thorough attempts to develop comprehensive cosmologies are badly needed and should receive our serious attention. Mr. Marr has provided one such system. I hope that it can be published and made available to a wide audience so that it can receive serious discussion by persons of many walks of life and varied persuasions."

Astronomy, Professor **Woodruff T. Sullivan III**:
"I am very impressed with his dedication, his abilities, and the synthesis he has produces. As an astronomer and historian of science who has long decried the compartmentalization of academia, I applaud all serious efforts such as this to cross disciplinary lines and to synthesize knowledge. We obviously do not know of Mr. Marr's picture is the 'correct' one, but it is well informed, does not appear to be in conflict with the state of knowledge in scientific fields with which I am familiar, and gives promise to lead to further insight…His ideas deserve to be published and, I think, will appeal to a wide audience of both lay-persons and scientists."

Medicine, Biomedical History, Professor **Keith R. Benson**:
"I found his presentation to be creative, highly synthetic, scientifically sound and eclectic, and extremely comprehensive. Obviously, Mr. Marr has read and studied extensively; moreover, his

Anthony Marr

new theory reveals his impressive ability to think carefully and critically.

"A an historian of biology, I am aware of the reluctance to construct cosmologies at the present time because they inevitably involve major speculative activity. However, I also think that it may be necessary for scientific literati like Mr. Marr to engage in this work. After all, we are bombarded constantly with cosmological schemes with the barest of scientific support. I find many aspects of Mr. Marr's system compelling. I urge additional support for his work."

Geology, Professor **Stephen C. Porter**:
"…an interesting and enlightening experience. It quickly became apparent to me that Mr. Marr is an extremely intelligent and knowledgeable person and his devoted a considerable amount of time and thought to the philosophical system he set forth in his manuscript. He is articulate and obviously is widely read in many fields of science. His knowledge, however, is not superficial, but demonstrates a keen sense of scholarship.

"He has undertaken a task, indeed a mission, that to many would appear overwhelming - the integration of many fields of knowledge, both scientific and cultural, in a hierarchical scheme that illustrates the place of human beings in the natural and temporal order of the universe.

"His thesis is thought provoking and, as far as I know, original in its approach. The subject is one that should interest both professionals and nonprofessionals, and could elicit considerable discussion. Assuming that the manuscript is engagingly written at the appropriate level, it could command a wide audience."

University of British Columbia

Biology, Professor **Ian McTaggart-Cowan**:
"This will introduce Mr. Anthony Marr…We met for a full afternoon during which he presented his objectives, his background preparation and led me through the development of his novel theory. We had an extended discussion in which I probed deeply in my area of expertise.

"I emerged highly impressed with his seriousness of purpose, his intellectual capacity, his ability to grasp and use unusually detailed information drawn from a broad range of scientific disciplines. He met my challenges forthrightly, thoughtfully and in detail.

"Subsequently, I read his book manuscript. In this he develops a philosophy that rests securely on basic scientific understanding. I followed with fascination the evolution of his theoretical concept of the progress of life on earth from inception to society…

"I am convinced that what he is striving to achieve is important.

"Mr. Marr is an unusually talented and discipline individual. He is one of the many millions of people who are deeply distressed by many of the directions and consequences he sees in the world today, but unlike so many, he has dedicated himself to struggling intellectually to develop and promote new attitudes.

"Mr. Marr is a serious scholar who both writes and speak with ease and confidence. I urge you to give his book the serious attention it deserves."

Omni-Science and the Human Destiny

Geology and **Oceanography**, Professor **R.L. Chase**:
"The work is a brave attempt to give us a new, science-based philosophy, with the aim of giving humankind a common purpose to unite the planet and seek societies beyond it. As a geologist I found his synthesis stimulating and refreshing. I have tried to work out for myself a philosophy based on paleontology and the physical sciences, but Mr. Marr has gone further to produce a more comprehensive worldview."

Evolutionary Biology, Professor **G.G.E. Scudder**:
"I spent a bout three hours with Anthony Marr…I found his approach to be logical and thorough. He has a good gasp of the basic principles and ideas in the natural sciences and is aware of the limitations of our current knowledge…I believe that his contribution is original and well founded. Mr. Mr. is clearly dedicated and talented…."

Astronomy and **Geophysics**, Professor **T.K. Menon**:
"I was highly impressed by his breadth of knowledge…There is no question in my mind about the seriousness f his pursuit and the need to have his ideas widely discussed. He deserves to have a wide audience to expose his ideas for scholarly appraisal, and I urge that such an opportunity be made available to him."

Biology, Profession **Lee Gass**:
"I am writing on behalf of Anthony Marr. My purpose is to document his seriousness of purpose, the strength of his commitment to understanding, his intellectual solidity and honesty, and his willingness and ability to consider an extremely broad range of issues in a way that can potentially clarify them for large numbers of people…

"He has responded to my most rigorous challenges extremely well, demonstrating a degree of intellectual discipline that is rare even among professional scholars…

"I have no doubt that he has dedicated his life to this project…."

Physical Anthropology, Professor **Braxton M. Alfred**:
"Mr. Marr's effort is in the tradition of 19th Century scholarship, but is based solidly on 20th Century science. There is simply no modern parallel for his accomplishment.

"His system is extraordinarily ambitious…It purports, and is successful in my opinion, to explain hierarchical structure in the phenomenal world…It is truly a grand scheme…

"He speaks with the power and confidence of one who totally commands the material. The presentation was scheduled for two hours. After four hours, mutually fatigued, we adjourned, and I was very reluctant to quit.

"It is a compelling indictment of the structure of contemporary academic departments that, undoubtedly, no graduate would be allowed to pursue such a project with any expectation of being awarded a degree. This is in spite of the fact that Mr. Marr's product is in every way superior to any of the Ph.D. degree this department has awarded in the twenty years of my appointment.

"It is characterized by careful, thoughtful attention and rigorous development. I recommend it, and him, without qualification."

Sinikka Crosland, President, **The Responsible Animal Care Society (TRACS)**
Omni-Science and the Human Destiny by Anthony Marr is a multi-tiered, dynamic masterpiece.

On one level, the reader is taken into the jungles of India, where poachers, corruption and politics collide darkly with tiger preservation efforts, and where issues of environmental devastation provide a haunting backdrop of human ignorance.

On another level, the author explores interpersonal relationships, including one that forms a primary thread throughout the story - the love between a small boy and a man who has become his dedicated friend, mentor and father figure, and forces that threaten a bond so strong that severance cannot terminate hope.

Finally, on yet a third level, Anthony Marr's presentation of an extraordinary concept holds startling implications: the possibility, and feasibility, of scientific logic co-existing with less tangible features of life on Earth, such as the depth of human emotion and spirituality. Through numerous transcendental encounters and communications with a "higher" presence, identified as Raminothna, a new science is revealed, thus taking the reader on an evolutionary journey into the world of *Omniscientific Cosmology*. The most striking features of this experience include a steadfast adherence to scientific principles, coupled with a recognition that the human psyche is capable of interacting with a universal being.

Omni-Science and the Human Destiny may well hold the key to many fundamental questions that have puzzled and plagued humankind, scientists and theologians alike, from the beginning of time. Its author, Anthony Marr, accepted the challenge, thereby helping to bridge the gap between science and spirituality.

And he has followed through, brilliantly.

Omni-Science
and the Human Destiny

Anthony Marr

Copyright 2003

Vegetarian Advocates Press, Cleveland, Ohio
0-9716676-2-4

Omni-Science and the Human Destiny. Copyright © 2003 by Anthony Marr. All rights reserved. Printed in the United States of America. No part of this book may be used or reproduced in any manner whatsoever without written permission except in the case of brief quotations embodied in critical articles and reviews. For information, address Vegetarian Advocates Press, P.O. Box 201791, Cleveland, Ohio 44120.

ISBN 0-9716676-2-4

For Christopher, with unconditional love.

"We shall not cease from exploration
 and the end of all our exploring
 will be to arrive where we started
 and know the place for the first time."

        — T. S. Eliot

Author's Notes and Acknowledgements

The events in the book are essentially reality-based and the journal in which they are recorded is itself real. So are the newspaper articles, reviews, letters and legal documents, most being presented verbatim. Some non-essential details, such as the timing of certain events or the names of certain persons, have been modified where appropriate for literary reasons involving synchronicity, clarification, legality, privacy or anonymity; nonetheless, the essential truth remains.

All the characters in the book, then, are real, human or otherwise, with but one big exception - Raminothna. This is not to say that Raminothna is unreal. On the contrary, in the context of this book, "she" could be super-real, since she is the intellectual guide and spiritual inspiration of the book itself. "She" could take many forms, and readers could make "her", or "him", or "it", whatever they wish, including an alien, an angel, ones "higher self", or perhaps even "God". Since the story unfolded in India, the author has written Raminothna as a Hindu Goddess of Compassion as a literary device, who in fact does not exist in Hindu religious literature. This does not necessarily imply that the author subscribes to that religion, or to any other religion, nor even to religion itself. This is the only major way in which the author exercised his poetic license, in favor of realism and with deference to truth.

Out of necessity, the author has created a number of new terms in the book, including "Organismization", "Ecosystemization", "Evolver", "Planetary Embryology", "Planetary Metamorphosis", Planetary Organism", "Universal Organism", "the O.S.E.S. Cycle", "Transcendent Integration", "Integrative Transcendence", and "Omniscientific Cosmology" itself. He has also made some deliberate "grammatical errors", such as placing commas and periods outside of quotations where his logic dictates, as he does in this paragraph.

The author wishes to thank the thousands of people who have supported and participated in his work in Omni-Science, wildlife preservation, animal advocacy, and/or otherwise simply enriched his life, especially since 1995 when his current career began, notably (in alphabetical order): Marge Adams, Dr. Braxton Alfred, John Alton, Lucienne Anchykowski, Gillian Andrews, Frank Arnold, Tammy Arnold, Joyce Arthur, Taroon and Dimple Bahti, Karen Beggs, Lindsay Bickford, Shawn

Omni-Science and the Human Destiny

Blore, Dallas Brodie, Chris Bruyere, Sandra Carlson, Adriane Carr, Peter Carter, Michael Chechik, Yvonne Chin, Carmen Crosland, Gale Cunningham, Guy Dauncey, Cecilie Davidson, Brenda Davis, Cory Davis, Paul Davis, Craig and Gloria Delahunt, A. Dionys de Leeuw, Fran Dietz, Darlene Dresser, Helen Evans, Fireweed, Don Fisk, Lori Fitzgerald, Roxy Flood-Pettifar, Joe Foy, Sue Fox, Gloria Fraser, Dr. Michael Futrell, Andrew Gardner, Paul George, Mary Lou Givens, Sylvia Grafton, Neil Gregory, Don Guild, Brenda Guild-Gillespie, Rico Habgood, Suzie Hamilton, Dian Hardy, Debbie Head, Cecile Helton, Susan Hudgens, Dale Hunter, Anne Jensen, Christiane Jensen, the Johnston-Okuyama family, Dr. Ray Kellosalmi, Faiyaz Khudsar, Frances Kirby, Evelyn Kirkaldy, Eleanor Kohnert, John and Rachele Kratky, Ashok Kumar, Christopher Lindstrom, Jocelyn Lovell, Matt Lowe, Jean McKenzie, Heather McMillan, Judy McMillan, Linda Ma, Matthew Ma, Melissa Ma, Rafe Mair, Kim Marchuk, Ruth Masters, Rick Maynard, Joan Miller, Laurie Moore, Tim Murphy, Noreen Nawrocki, Vicky Pewtress, Suzanne Philippe, Kim Poole, Nicholas Read, Joy Richardson, Evelyn Roth, Mel Rothenburger, Maureen Sager, Vicki Sawyer, Fred Schoenrock, Christine Schram, Vivek Sharma, Annelise Sorg, Barbara Stanton, Peter Strother, Neil Sumner, Annette Tanner, Scott Tanner, Linda Templeton, Irmela Topf, Carol Waddell, Dee Walmsley, Paul Watson, Judy Watson, Dave Way, Judy Williams, Rae Anne Williams, Anne Wittman, Belinda Wright and Tracy Zuber,

Thanks are also due to the many anthropologists, astronomers, biologists, chemists, ecologists, geologists, paleontologists, philosophers, physicists, psychologists, secular humanists, sociologists and theologians, who have provided valuable input into the Omniscientific Cosmology – too many to mention.

Where the book is concerned, Dr. Stephen Kaufman deserves special credit. His relentless and rigorous critiques of the manuscript contributed greatly to the quality and integrity of the book, though I remain solely responsible for the book's contents. His help has also made the CARE tour possible.

Special thanks are also due to Sinikka Crosland for the valuable time she has put in to proofread and critique the manuscript, and for her wonderful comradeship.

Fond memories for my deceased animal friends Bridlewood Poppy (horse), Massenet (horse), Beau Jest (dog), Sophie (cat), Tangerine (cat) and Jason (cat), and fond thoughts for my current animal friends Chopper (dog), Sandra (dog), Sparky (dog), Samantha (cat), Binky (cat), and Rafey (cat). And a mixture of the two for the tigers mentioned in this book, some deceased, other still living. All of these animals, each in her or his own fashion, have greatly enriched my life.

Last but not least, inestimable love and gratitude are due to my parents, who sacrificed their own careers for my education.

This book is dedicated to Christopher, who, as an infant, taught me the way of pure, selfless and unconditional love.

— Anthony Marr

Table of Contents

Prologue ❖ The Seven Cosmic Signs
1995
1996
1997
1998
1999-01-16
1999-01-19
1999-01-20
1999-01-23
1999-01-24
1999-01-25
1999-01-26
1999-01-27
1999-01-28
1999-01-29
1999-01-30
1999-01-31
1999-02-01
1999-02-02
1999-02-03
1999-02-04
1999-02-05
1999-02-06
1999-02-07
1999-02-08 ❖ The Miracle Worker

1999-02-09 ❖ The Heaviest Thing
1999-02-10 ❖ The Weight of a Million Worlds
1999-02-11 ❖ Passion in the Death Dance
1999-02-12 ❖ The Rich Poor Man
1999-02-13 ❖ Inner Light
1999-02-14 ❖ Risen Phoenix
1999-02-15 ❖ To Conceive the "Inconceivable"
1999-02-16 ❖ Long Way to Self-Understanding
1999-02-17 ❖ The Microcosmic Dream
1999-02-18 ❖ Four Ways to Visit a Planet
1999-02-19 ❖ The Truth Seeker
1999-02-20 ❖ Insect Society as Organism
1999-02-21 ❖ Extinction of the Superorganism
1999-02-22 ❖ Human Society as Organism
1999-02-23 ❖ Artificial Is Natural
1999-02-24 ❖ The Machines Are Alive
1999-02-25 ❖ Social Medicine
1999-02-26 ❖ Not a Bad Sign
1999-02-27 ❖ Delhi, Chichrunpur and Termite City
1999-02-28 ❖ INTEGRATIVE TRANSCENDENCE
1999-03-01 ❖ Interlevel Parallelism
1999-03-02 ❖ Organism-per-Species Ratio
1999-03-03 ❖ Organism as Ecosystem
1999-03-04 ❖ 20 Subsystems per Living System
1999-03-05 ❖ Multi-leveled Pentagon/Stars
1999-03-06 ❖ The T.I/I.T. Spiral and Its O.S.E.S. Cycle
1999-03-07 ❖ Planetary Egg Earth
1999-03-08 ❖ Planetary Embryology
1999-03-09 ❖ Planetary Metamorphosis

1999-03-10 ❖ Divine Providence
1999-03-11 ❖ The Savior Species
1999-03-12 ❖ Where Upward Is Outward
1999-03-13 ❖ Greatest Challenge on Earth
1999-03-14 ❖ Cosmic Chess
1999-03-15 ❖ Stairway to The Heavens
1999-03-16 ❖ The Psychosphere
1999-03-17 ❖ Neuronal Circuitry Is Memory
1999-03-18 ❖ Six Levels of Earth's Consciousness
1999-03-19 ❖ Freud and Jung in OMNI-SCIENCE
1999-03-20 ❖ The T.I/I.T. Twin Spiral
1999-03-21 ❖ Stellar Organism Sol
1999-03-22 ❖ Star Wars or Heavenly Peace
1999-03-23 ❖ 14 Levels of the Universe
1999-03-24 ❖ A New Planetary Classification System
1999-03-25 ❖ The Universal Organism
1999-03-26 ❖ A New Theology
1999-03-27 ❖ Transcendence Limit
1999-03-28 ❖ Gift of The Book
1999-03-29
1999-03-30
1999-03-31

Epilogue ❖ 2000-01-01 The Cosmic Hand of Destiny

Prologue

Dear Homo Sapiens,
whose footprints now roam the crater of the Moon:

    Heed the Seven Cosmic Signs of Earth.

    You may not perceive them as such while living on the surface of your planet, but they are obvious to any Earth observer from beyond, or to a set of extraterrestrial Earth-observation instruments established on the Moon for millennia.

    Collectively they portend an imminent, monumental and all-encompassing transformation to occur throughout your world, one leading to either planetary transcendence or global devastation.

    When one cosmic sign becomes manifest, the others would almost simultaneously arise. On the planet Earth, the Seven Cosmic Signs have all arisen.

    The First Cosmic Sign: For millions of years, Earth's night side has been invisibly dark, but now, suddenly, there is light, neon light.

    The Second Cosmic Sign: For millions of years, Earth's surface has been lush and green, but now, suddenly, there is massive deforestation and rapid desertification.

    The Third Cosmic Sign: For millions of years, Earth's atmosphere has been clean and its hydrosphere clear, but now, suddenly, there is pollution.

    The Fourth Cosmic Sign: Never in its 4.6-billion-year history has Earth generated a single thermal nuclear reaction, but now, suddenly, she is in danger of generating too many too soon.

    The Fifth Cosmic Sign: For millions of years, the ozone layer has shielded the Biosphere from harmful solar UV radiation, but now, suddenly, it is full of holes.

    The Sixth Cosmic Sign: For millions of years, as a radio source the Earth has been silent, but now, suddenly, it is inundating it's inter-planetary and interstellar neighbourhood with its newscasts, political speeches, documentaries, commentaries, movies, soap operas, sitcoms, sports, commercials... and let's not forget televangelical sermons which still preach that you are "the be all and end all of Creation".

Omni-Science and the Human Destiny

The Seventh Cosmic Sign: Earth was born of gravity, and by its own gravity its body parts have always been bound, but now, pieces of Earth – spacecraft, so called - are seen suddenly to fly away, some never to return.

Among Earth's spacecraft are the Apollos, from whose #8 was broadcast a prayer as follows: "Give us, o God, the vision which can see thy love in the world in spite of human failure. Give us the faith, the trust, the goodness in spite of our ignorance and weakness. Give us the knowledge that we may continue to pray with understanding hearts, and show us what each of us can do to set forth the coming of the day of universal peace. Amen."

And the Pioneers 10 & 11, each carrying an identity plaque showing the position of Earth and the image of Homo Sapiens (which some humans still consider "the image of God".)

And the Voyagers 1 & 2, each bearing an audio-visual recording of Earth sights and sounds, the latter including earthquake and thunder, bird and whale songs, human music and speech, the last being excerpted as follows:

From the President of the United States of America: "This is a present from a small distant world, a token of our sounds, our science, our image, our music, our thoughts and our feelings. We are attempting to survive our time so we can live into yours. We hope some day, having solved the problems we face, to join a community of galactic civilizations. This record represents our hope and our determination, and our good will in a vast and awesome Universe."

From the citizens of Earth: "We send all beings of the Universe an affectionate greeting of peace and happiness. May the future grant us the opportunity of meeting." (in Spanish) / "Greetings from our friends amongst the stars. If you can cross the barrier between Earth and sky then do it. It is our desire to meet you." (in Arabic) / "Welcome to our world." (in Polish) / "How are you? We are thinking about you. Come visit us some time." (in Chinese) / "We used to believe that the Universe was created for us humans on Earth alone, but we can no longer maintain this belief. We now think that you may exist to share this Universe with us, and have the power to help solve the many problems here in our world." (in Efic) / "Please contact." (in Gujurati)

From the Secretary General of the United Nations: "As the Secretary General of the United Nations, an organization of 147 member states who represent almost all of the human individuals of the planet Earth, I send greetings on behalf of the people of our planet. We step out of the Solar System seeking only peace and friendship, to teach if we are called upon, to be taught if we are fortunate. We know full well that our planet and all its inhabitants are but a small part of the immense

Anthony Marr

Universe, and it is with humility and hope that we take this step."

In short, three words: "Greeting", "Welcome" **and** "Help!" **And I, for one, hear them with joy and compassion. For the first, I salute you; for the second, I come to you; and for the third, I bear to you a gift of joy, of hope, of understanding and of peace.**

**I am Raminothna
the Fortunate and the Called Upon
at your service.**

❖   ❖   ❖   ❖   ❖

From the Journal of Anthony Marr

June 4, 1995

June 4, 1995 - the 6th anniversary of the 1989 Tienanmen Square massacre.

June 4, 1995, today, Christopher Mason is exactly one month old.

May 4, one month prior, was a doubly significant date in terms of birth. First, it is the anniversary of the birth of the pro-democracy movement in China almost a century ago. Second, my erstwhile girlfriend now platonic friend Christine gave birth to her first and perhaps only son, whom she has named Christopher, last name Mason, after herself.

Unfortunately, Christopher's grandmother, Joan, who passed away a few months too soon, didn't have a chance to see meet, except perhaps in spirit. Just as sad was the way she died, of what started as breast cancer, which eventually ravaged her entire body. Towards the end, it was pure unadulterated and undignified defeat and agony, for Joan of course, but also for all who loved her. Much as I dread hospitals, I went to see her every day or two, mostly to give Christine, who was there almost everyday, much needed emotional support. Most of the time Joan was so drugged she didn't even know I was there, and in those times when she knew I was there, she was embarrassed since she was incontinent, and in fact wetted her bed a few times in my presence. And this on top of the indignity of irrepressibly crying in pain. Many times, I've prayed that she would have a quick and painless exit, but in the end, it was Christine's brother Don who pleaded with

Omni-Science and the Human Destiny

the doctors to help her, and within two days, by divine or human intervention, Joan passed away. I've always leaned towards compassionate active euthanasia. Joan's death decided the issue for me. I will plan my own dignified exit when my time comes, and will support whomever making this wish for themselves.

❖   ❖   ❖   ❖   ❖

October 1995

Chinese versus Chinese over animals
By Linda Lee
Chinatown Times

    If a botanist and a zoologist were to stumble into where Anthony Marr now found himself, they would have a hard time identifying most of the items. In the glassed-in display shelves were trays upon trays and jars upon jars of dried this and that - all once alive, or parts of something once alive. Of dried mushrooms alone there were dozens of species, some as large as dinner plates. There were dried stems and roots and seeds and fruits of myriad medicinal plants, and shapeless bits and pieces of preserved animal parts. To Anthony's trained eyes, he saw dried sea cucumbers, dried sea horses, dried lizards, snakes in wine, deer musk glands, seal penises, shark fins, swallow's nests, thin slices of antlers still in velvet… And these were just what lay above the counter.

    It was a store called Wei Hai on Pender street near Main, the one with the big yellow awning in front - one of about two dozen traditional Chinese pharmacies amidst the restaurants and groceries and curio shops and book stores of Vancouver's historical and bustling Chinatown.

    Unsavory as some of the animal parts were up front, Anthony's quarry lay in the deeper recesses of the store. Here was a section where the so-called Patent Tradition Chinese Medicines were displayed. These were highly packaged items, usually pills in bottles, and bottles in glossy and brightly colored cardboard boxes.

    Anthony moved slowly, with stops here and there, towards the back of the store, using his peripheral vision to monitor the three store clerks behind the counters. There were two other customers in the store, which made him less uncomfortable. As he pretended interest in a bank of trays containing different kinds and grades of ginseng, he glanced out of the store and saw the large beta-cam on a tripod aimed straight at him from across the street, and the bearded Viking of a cameraman crouching behind it, and the blonde woman reporter standing beside it with a microphone in her hand, all standing out like sore thumbs amidst the smaller, dark-haired people milling around them, looking curiously at them, then following the camera's aim at Anthony. Fortunately, up to this point, the three store clerks have been too distracted by the customers to have noticed.

"If you can hear me, raise your hand," Anthony murmured into the conceal mike under his lapel, and saw the reporter do just that.

This would be the third time he showed his face on television, but the first time on national TV. This should be the one to make the difference on the federal government level. He glanced at the three store clerks to see if there was any sign of recognition or suspicion, but they seemed to just be going about their business, not that they had yet taken a close look at him, which they soon would.

Anthony moved deeper towards the back of the store and began scanning as nonchalantly as possible the hundreds of different multi-colored boxes lined up row upon row, all bearing Chinese writings and pictorial designs. There were bear bile pills, crocodile bile pills, seal penis pills, dog penis pills, deer musk pills, rhino skin pills, pangolin pills, but he had no need to look much further to find what he was looking for. On one of the higher shelves sat a large collection of boxes, about ten assortments in total, all bearing different renditions of the same majestic animal, and all sporting the beautiful Chinese character in various calligraphic styles, pronounced in Mandarin as "hu", and in Cantonese as "fu" - tiger.

He reached up and took down a few different boxes and began checking the ingredients lists printed on their backs. Most listed about a dozen ingredients each, all by their Latin and Chinese names, mostly medicinal plants which seemed to vary from brand to brand. But the one thing in common was the Latin name "Ossis Tigris" - tiger bone. Its listed concentrations ranged from 6% to 24% from brand to brand. Price - $8 for the box with 6%, and $22 for the one listing 24%.

He was looking at the boxes, mostly green or amber, but what he was seeing was red. Over the years, he'd been watching TV wildlife documentaries by the score, often in Caucasian company. Whenever the subject matter was the tiger or rhino or elephant or bear, especially the tiger, the concluding messages were usually one and the same, that these magnificent beasts were going down due largely to the Oriental, largely Chinese, use of their body parts for medicine. His sentiments at those times were disgust, outrage, embarrassment and shame. At those times, he could feel his Caucasian friends trying very hard not to look at him, not to say anything remotely anti-Chinese, when he knew that each and every one of them, like him, were about to explode. And the harder they tried, the worse it made him feel.

Finally, at the end of a National Geographic program about tigers in 1994, he said to those present, "Look at me. Am I not Chinese? Spit it out."

After still another few long seconds of uncomfortable silence, his friend Grant finally abided, "All right, no offence to you personally, Tony, but this Chinese tradition is obscene! It doesn't heal me of anything; it just makes me sick!" A significant pause. "Well? Does this make you feel better?"

"You racist pig!" mock-fumed Anthony. Then, seriously, "Yeah, man, that's better. Yes, it is obscene. So how do we stop it?"

"You answered your own question before you posed it," said Grant. "I'm a Whitey, see? I don't want to be branded a racist, which I know I will if I as much as lifted a finger, especially the middle one."

Then, almost inexorably, all eyes fell on Anthony, and stayed there. After looking at them one by one in turn, he returned his gaze to Grant and said, "Okay, Grant, you have a point there, but keep it in your pants. Serious, I do agree with you. It does take a Chinese person to do it, as it should, and you're looking at him."

One of the clerks moved towards him and said, in Cantonese, "Can I help you with something?"

It is a woman in her 30s, who now was looking point blank at his face, thin smile unwavering.

"Yes, maybe," he answered, in Cantonese as fluent as hers. "I'm from Hong Kong and am looking for some tiger bone medicine for my father, and a bear gall bladder for my mother. I see you have some tiger bone medicines here, but do you have any bear gall bladders?"

The woman looked at once nervous, her smile evaporated and her eyes shifted involuntarily to the back of the store before fixing themselves on his face again. "Just a moment," she said, then slipped through a door in the back wall.

Anthony returned to looking at the tiger bone medicines in his hands, but he sensed a sudden tenseness that had overtaken the two remaining clerks behind the counters. Now they were unabashedly scrutinizing him, and still, there was no sign of recognition.

Momentarily, the door squeaked open and a large man emerged, followed by the woman. He was of about the same height as Anthony's 5' 9" – medium tall for a Chinese - but twice in girth.

"I can outrun him for sure, and can probably kick faster, but I'd better not engage him in a wrestling match," Anthony thought.

Since the man was facing the front of the store, he was in line of sight of the TV beta-cam and the reporter across the street, but his attention was concentrated on Anthony, who took a quick step towards the back and took down another box of tiger bone medicine, thus effectively turning the man and the woman away from the front.

"So, you want to buy a bear gall bladder?" The man said while looking Anthony up and down.

To counteract the proverbial Oriental inscrutability of his opponent, Anthony invoked a poker face of his own. "Maybe more than one, depending on the price," he said steadily.

"What's your name?"

"Just call me Mr. Lee," he says without a blink.

"Where're you from, Mr. Lee?"

"Hong Kong."

"How long here for?"

"About three years."

"Where did you get your gall bladders from before?"

"I hunted."

"It's illegal to take the gall bladder in BC. Legal in Quebec, but not here."

"So it's illegal," said Anthony with a shrug. "It's also illegal to buy or sell them."

"So why do you stop hunting?"

"Who says I have? It's just too much work. Too messy. And lately, too much heat."

"What do you mean 'too much heat'?"

"Too much talk about gall bladders. People are getting upset." He shifted on his feet to a new stance. "Look. Are you doing business or are we just going to stand and talk all day?"

"Show me your driver's license."

"What are you? Some kind of traffic cop? No. I don't carry my driver's license around when I shop for bear gall bladders. I'm sure you understand."

The man frowned. "Where do you live? I'll deliver the bladders to you."

"Not so fast. How much are they?"

"One grand and up."

"Let's see them."

The man hesitates a moment, then brought out two fig shaped objects from his pocket, black, rock hard, one about the size of a thumb, the other that of a small pear. "One grand and five grand."

Anthony reached for the larger one, but the man closed his fingers around it. "Uh, uh, not so fast. Show your cash first."

"Where's it from?" Anthony tried another tack.

"A bear gall bladder is a bear gall bladder is a bear gall bladder."

"How do I know it's a bear gall bladder and not a cow gall bladder or pig gall bladder?"

"When I say it is, it is."

"How about selling me a small piece of it, so I could do a DNA test on it. If it proves real, I might buy a few."

"Don't know no DNA test. No go. The whole thing or nothing."

"Look, even if it is a real bear gall, it could be from a local Black bear, or a Grizzly bear, or an Asiatic Black bear, and prices vary accordingly."

"Four grand. Take it or leave it."

"I'll have to think about it."

"If you buy ten or more, I'll give you a good deal."

"How good?"

"Three grand each, same size."

"Not good enough."

"You name your price. I'll say yes or no."

"I'll buy this one for two thousand. Bottom line. After that, I'll talk volume."

"No. If you change your mind, come back. Meanwhile, excuse me. I'm busy."

"Fine. I don't have enough cash on me anyway. I'll just buy these tiger medicines for now."

"As you wish." And with that, the man disappeared again through the door.

Anthony sorted through the boxes in his hand, selected half a dozen different brands and put the rest back on the shelf. He paid for them at the counter, exited the store and j-walks across the busy street straight at the beta-cam. Pulling one of the boxes from the bag, he brought it right up to the lens.

"So, Anthony, tell me what you bought," asked the reporter, sticking her own mike in his face.

"Well, I bought, right off the shelf, six different kinds of Chinese patent medicines containing or purporting to contain tiger bone as an ingredient. This one I'm showing you," he said, while rotating the box in front of the camera so that the ingredients list now faced the lens, "lists 24% tiger bone by weight."

He noticed a few pedestrians stopping in their tracks to gawk at him and what he had in his hands, and tried to ignore them. "Did you get any shots of the bear gall bladder, by the way?" he asked.

"We sure did," boomed the beaming cameraman, "and your whole conversation with the store owner, every word of it. Of course, I haven't got the foggiest idea what you said."

"So, what did you talk about?" asked the reporter.

"Basically, they have bear gall bladders for sale under the counter, origin undisclosed. They want at least four thousand dollars for a big one, less by the dozen." Having been on TV before, he had learned to give sound bites, not long discourses.

"So, what is the legal status of bear gall bladders?"

"The legal status of bear gall bladders," he began, having also learned to repeat the question before answering it, "depends on the country or province you're in. All the Asiatic bear species are endangered and importation of their body-parts is internationally banned. In Canada, the law varies from province to province. In British Columbia and Manitoba, bear gall bladders, even those taken from Canadian bears, are illegal to possess and to sell. In Ontario, they are illegal to sell, but legal to possess. In Quebec, they are legal both to possess and to sell."

"Does this pose a problem?"

"It poses a big problem. Poached bear galls in BC, for example, can be laundered in Quebec. They'll even issue you a number and tag for each gall for selling and exporting purposes."

"What is the penalty for violations in BC?"

"The penalty for violations in BC is unreasonably light. Maximum $10,000, and/or 6 months in prison. The Korean man recently convicted of possessing 88 bear gall bladders and four times as many bear paws for sale-purposes was fined $3,500 and no jail time. This is less than the street value of the one single gall I showed you today, and he had 88. It is considered just the cost of doing business, and a very low risk business at that."

By now, a large crowd had gathered around the trio and their imposing machine. Anthony took a glance around and was shocked to see the store owner standing right behind the cameraman, glaring daggers at him. He felt a small but definite shove in the small of his back. He glances back at the reporter and sees no special alarm on her face about whoever was standing behind him.

"And what about these tiger bone medicines. Are they legal?"

"Tiger bone medicines are internationally illegal. Canada does not allow them to be imported, but currently allows them to be sold openly on Canadian store selves."

"This makes no sense."

"Exactly."

"Can you explain that?"

"The world organization called Convention on the International Trade of Endangered Species - CITES for short - classifies various species on their conservation status. CITES- I means endangered, CITES-II means threatened. Any time a species is classified CITES-I, they cannot be internationally traded, in whole or part, dead or alive. But then of course they can be and are smuggled, and the control of whatever smuggled into a certain country depends on the internal laws of that country. In Canada, case in point, there is no such internal law in effect. So, essentially, you cannot import these tiger bone medicines, but if you are smart enough to smuggle them in, you could openly sell them, which is what I'm in the process of demonstrating."

He stole another glance at the store-owner again. If looks could kill...

"What is your message to the government?"

"I have two messages to the government. One, that all provinces should make possessing and selling bear gall bladders illegal, and the fines of violation should at least be increased to match the street value of the goods seized. Two, that the selling of endangered species items should be banned throughout Canada, and the penalty for smuggling and selling violations should be high enough to be a deterrent."

"Can you think of anything to add?"

"Yes. Tigers and some Asian bears are within one decade of extinction, and our North American bears are not far behind. There is no time to wait. Immediate action is required."

"Well, that's great. Thank you, Mr. Marr." The reporter extended her hand and Anthony shook it.

Turning to the cameraman, the reporter says, "Let's go and interview the store owner."

"He's right here," said Anthony without hesitation, pointing at the man.

The cameraman needed no prompting and rotated the beta-cam towards the store-owner, and the reporter turned towards him without a break in her stride. "So, how many bear gall bladders do you sell a month, sir?" She pointed her mike at him like an accusing finger.

The man's inscrutability slipped. After a hesitation, he brought up his hand to block the camera lens, and, glaring at Anthony with renewed venom, he hissed a single line in Cantonese before dashing into a nearest alley, "You are a dead man."

❖ ❖ ❖ ❖ ❖

November 1995

Thanksgiving day, and I do have much to give thanks for. Let me ask: Would I let just anybody drive my car? Absolutely not. Have I let anyone drive my car? Yes, but only those very few whom I trust implicitly where driving my car is concerned – James and Jeanine. That's it. Now consider this. Here is this tiny little baby called Christopher, so much much much more delicate and vulnerable and precious than any Ferrari or Roll Royce in any showroom and yet, Christine lets me hold him, play with him, take him out by myself, whenever I wish. And there is an extra honor, considering that sometimes she does not grant the privilege to even Charles, Christopher's biological father.

Extra or not, the honor is earned. Christine herself observes how gentle and kind I always am to the baby. Sometimes, when I sit on the sofa, I would place Christopher on his back length-wise in my pressed-together thighs. This way, he could look up smiling at me and I could look at him and sing him his favourite songs. Christine finds this endearing. Charles is good with Christopher too – but only when he is sober, which unfortunately is few and far between - no more than two days in any given week. Christine told me that once she found Charles having left the baby carriage out in the street unattended while getting some booze. Not wanting to doubt Christine, I still find this unbelievable, but if true, it is absolutely unacceptable, and Charles indeed cannot be trusted in regards to Christopher.

Christopher, who won my heart the first time I set eyes upon him, was a 5-lb, premature, purple-colored little thing in an oxygen tent. Now, at age 6 months, he is a lively and pink though still tiny baby. In these few months of his gracing this world, he has won my eternal devotion. No mean feat, considering that I am still single and therefore demonstrably "unable to commit" myself "to anyone", as Christine once said about me. I'd say that he started life as a winner. And I will do all I can to help keep it that way.

Up to this point, I've been seeing him regularly about three times a week, three to four hours each time. At this rate, I will have seen him more than 500 times or 1500 to 2000 hours by his fourth birthday. Now that's a lot of time to give to someone, and time always seems to be my most precious commodity, even if I had a billion dollars. But for Christopher, I'm more than willing, especially in view of the fact that he wouldn't be getting a lot from his father.

I will do anything within my power and capacity to help give Christopher as good a head start in life as possible. Henceforth, everything I do will first and foremost be for his best interest. I will protect him from harm even if I have to stand in harm's way myself. I will help give him guidance and teach him all that I know. I will be his devoted and trustworthy "Uncle Tony." I will make all necessary sacrifices for him, up to and including my life.

James (my friend James Taft) is astonished at the intensity of my emotion for Christopher. For one thing, since Christopher was born, I have spent much less social time with James. Not just James, but other friends. I am myself astonished, not only by the intensity of my love for Christopher, but also its purity and selflessness. For all these years, decades, of falling in and out of love, I have never come anywhere close to this. Certainly not with Christine even in the best of times. Nor even with Jane, my first love and greatest love, whom I was more than ready to marry, until her parents broke us apart.

Just yesterday, James said to me, "Purity and selflessness? If I didn't know you so well, I'd think you rather self-aggrandizing." The context of the conversation was my not having spent much time in male-bonding activities of late, so he was sounding a little thorny. But that's the way James and I talk anyway. Blunt and to the point. No bullshit.

Still I was taken aback. "I wasn't referring to myself. How could that be self-aggrandizement?"

"If not, what *were* you referring to?" asked James, quite sincerely.

"I was referring to the love that I'm experiencing with Christopher, a love that I am myself amazed by. If God is love, then all I was saying was that God is great. If that is aggrandizement, it would not be on my part."

"Still, it seems somewhat overstated."

"You've never loved a child, have you?"

"Nope. Can't say that I have."

"Then how do you know that the love for a child is not pure and selfless?"

"Well, I love Stacy. Are you saying that my love for her is less pure and less selfless than your love for Christopher?"

"I don't know how you love Stacy. But I know how I loved Jane, and compared even to that, my love for Christopher still reigns supreme. It's not even in the same league. With Jane, it was an intense need, including sexual need, and certainly emotional need, intermixed with an intense caring. With Christopher, it is an intense and selfless caring, pure and simple. I don't have the same kind of need to be physically close to Christopher as I did with Jane. When I go on a tour, as long as I know he's healthy and happy, I'm happy. But if I still had Jane, I would miss her intensely, especially on the physical level. Still, my seeing Christopher I cannot deny is a great pleasure and reassurance, the pleasure of seeing him grow and learn, and the assurance and reassurance that I'm doing him good with every passing day. I don't know how else to put it."

"Let's use an extreme example," said James, who thrives on such heated discussions. "Say, Christopher's house is on fire and he is trapped upstairs in his bedroom. Would you go in there to save him?"

"Yes, I would." I said it before I even thought about it. This is partly because I have thought of similar scenarios a few times before.

"Even if you would get burnt?"

"Even so, as long as I see that there is a chance, I would take it."

"And if there is no chance?"

"That's an insufferable thought, James. But if you're asking me if I'm suicidal, I'm not. The thought of him burning to death all by himself is excruciating. Would I go in there just to die with him so his death would be less lonely? This is the only uncertainty. But at least I thought of it. I don't know. Only the moment of truth, should there be one, would tell. All I know is that if there is a chance of saving him, there is no way I would not take it, and this is a certainty."

"Words are cheap."

"I hope this would never be put to the test."

"And you consider this a selfless act?" Vintage James.

"Isn't it?"

"Yes and no." Still vintage James.

"What's no?"

"In a way, maybe even ultimately, you would have done it for yourself,"

"How's that?" But I knew the answer even as I asked the question. "Well, you have a point. I would never be able to live with myself if I didn't."

"But I'll grant you, that your love for Christopher is purer than mine for Stacy. Hold your fire. Yeah, of course there is the sex factor. But there is something else."

"What's that?"

"I had a moment of naked honesty with myself. I rank my score lower than yours in the burning house hypothetical test. For one thing, the thought of going into the house just so that she didn't have to die alone never crossed my mind. You win."

"All I know is - I have never said anything in greater seriousness and dedication than this."

"But still, why do you feel this way?" pursues bulldog James. "Sure, you find him cute. I find him cute myself, but obviously I don't feel the same way about him as you do. So, what makes the difference? The only difference I see is that you are a friend of Christine and I'm not."

Omni-Science and the Human Destiny

"No, I don't think that's it."

"But Christopher is not your own child. Why are you treating him as if he's your own son? It comes across as almost bizarre. I'm not saying there is anything wrong or pathological here, but it's so unusual."

"Do you have to own someone to love someone?" I said, a little testy myself. "As soon as I understand it, you will be the first to know."

"You do that."

"Well, one component of it could be the bonding process. There is no doubting the incredibly strong bond between Christopher and me. Now where did this bond come from? I remember seeing this guy on TV in his ultra light with a dozen or so Canada geese strung out behind him in a V formation. He got them to do that by being there when the goose eggs were hatching. The goslings bonded with him because he was the first thing they saw. Now, I was there on the day Christopher was born, and have been there religiously three times a week or more. I can explain that perhaps he became bonded to me rather than to his father. Maybe every child has the potential to be bonded with one man and one woman, who usually are the biological parents. But in the case of Christopher, it could be Christine and me, and may be on my end, I'm spiritually and emotionally responding to this bond."

"Maybe there is something to it. Maybe bonding is a two way street."

"There is also the factor of Christopher's father being an alcoholic. My mind tells me that Christopher is very vulnerable and deprived and needs a father figure and a male role model. But the love is a matter of the heart. My mind may be searching furiously for an explanation, but my heart is happy, content and at peace."

As I said so, I felt so.

❖ ❖ ❖ ❖ ❖

1995-11-22-3 *The Vancouver Courier* **by Kerry Gold**
[China-born environmentalist says many Chinese immigrants too urbanized to care about wildlife conservation]
"…While his current campaign focus is the illegal trade in bear and tiger parts, he says he'll get involved in any environmental issue…"

1995-12-02-6 *The Vancouver Sun* **by Nicholas Read**
[Animal parts for sale, and it's legal]

"…The Chinese awareness is really not there," Marr says. "Maybe the only person you saw in Chinatown today who knows or cares about the plight of the tiger was me…"

1995-12-06-3 *Ming Pao Daily* **(Chinese), Vancouver** by Eric Chan
[Ma Seeu Sung spreads environmentalism into Chinese community]
"'…If we don't change our ways and drive the tiger to extinction, our reputation will be forever mud,' says Ma Seeu Sung…"

1995-12 *Sing Tao Daily* **(Chinese), Vancouver** by H.N. Kwok
[Anthony Marr takes pay-cut to save environment]
"…When asked why he made this change, he said simply, "I just find my present work more meaningful…"

1995-12-18 *Chinatown News* by Wanda Chow
[Chinese environmentalist campaigning to change centuries-old tradition]
"…Perhaps because Marr is a Chinese person willing to speak out… he has had plenty of media attention. The public's reaction? One Maple Grove school teacher recently said, "For years I've been waiting for someone like him to step forward."

❖ ❖ ❖ ❖ ❖

January 1, 1996

I don't usually need to make new year's resolutions, but this year, I have to make one.

Having made my June 4 vow to Christopher in writing – to protect him from harm – I am now faced with my first test.

A big dilemma. What if I see what Christine is doing is harmful to him?

"Just tell her," said Diana. Yeah, right. But she doesn't know Christine the way I do.

I'm talking about her smoking, and Charles'. It is not that she doesn't know about the harmful effect of second-hand smoke, especially on the tiny lungs of an infant. And it is not for want of trying. She just can't quit. Days are stretching into weeks, and now into months. She's been talking about quitting since Day 1, but she

Omni-Science and the Human Destiny

is still puffing away. The thought doesn't even seem to have crossed Charles' mind. I'm afraid that I'm going have to do something on Christopher's behalf, and knowing Christine, it's going to be hell to pay, now or perhaps years down the road, but she will one way or another, one year or the next, exact it. But for Christopher, did I not also write that I would willingly stand in harm's way?

Second, Charles. He often shows up at Christine's door drunk. Christine's way of dealing with him is to send him away, with his van key in his hand. His van is near new, but it is already covered with dents. I'm also going to have to talk to Christine about this. It's a matter of public safety. What if he drives away and kills a child like Christopher? Again, Christine wouldn't like to hear it, not from me anyway. I can hope that her women friends would say it. She would take to their counsel much more kindly, but they haven't and wouldn't. It was in fact their collective view that Charles be sent away when drunk. One way or the other, it would be passing the buck on my part. I also don't feel right discussing Christine behind her back. So, again, it'll be up to me, and again, there will be unpleasant consequences.

But why should she feel so hostile towards me for asking her to quit smoking for her son's sake, especially when she can so self-righteously slap ultimatum upon ultimatum on Charles to quit drinking? At least Charles' drinking would not impact directly on Christopher's health the way their smoking would and does. But that's Christine. I've put up with her for more than two decades, but now I find myself at a cross roads regarding my behavior with Christine. I am going to have to stop putting up with certain things about her – those that I deem harmful to Christopher. I still believe that somewhere beneath her thorny exterior is a golden heart, but this heart must embrace the wellbeing of Christopher in its entirety, and not selectively according to habits and addictions.

❖   ❖   ❖   ❖   ❖

1996-01-08-1   *Times Colonist, Victoria*   **by Malcolm Curtis**
[Tiger, tiger, put it right]
…"If major endangered species of the world – bear, elephant, tiger, rhino – go extinct as a result of Chinese demand for their body parts, I would consider it a capital crime against nature, and the Chinese would be forever convicted," Marr said in an interview…"

Anthony Marr

1996-01-21   *The Vancouver Courier*   by Kerry Gold
[Chinese activist fearless]
… "My response is, I've got to be accountable first and foremost to myself, and I'm not going to compromise myself (by worrying) about offending certain people," said Anthony Marr…

1996-01-28   *The Vancouver Courier*   by Mrs. V. Kennedy
[Animal torture justifies anger]
To the editor: Your article on Anthony Marr was an eye-opener. Now I realize why those who struggle for the ethical treatment of animals are so vehemently angry…

1996-04-09   *Ming Pao Daily News* (Chinese, global)   by Eric Chan
[Federal wildlife trade law soon in force]
…Ma Seeu Sung hopes the new wildlife trade regulations will significantly empower Canadian law against the international illegal endangered species trade…

1996-04-10   *The Vancouver Echo*   by Mike Bell
[Asian community takes on animal parts trade]
It will take more than a little gall to stop the massive Chinese trade in animal parts, but Anthony Marr has a feeling deep in his heart that he's the one who can make a difference…

1996-04-10   Associated Press
[Poaching surges for bear parts]
… "Given a choice between a bottle of synthetic UDCA (Urso-Deoxycholic Acid) and a real bear gall bladder, an old-timer will choose the latter every time; it's half medicine and half mystique. It's hard to fight superstition with a test tube,' says Marr…

    … "If the Chinese really want to be modern, on par with the West, we have to do a lot of soul searching," he said…

1996-04-12   *Sing Tao Daily*, (Chinese, global)
[Grizzly-bear-poaching penalty increased to $25,000 max]
…Anthony Marr says that the new penalty, though raised, is still too lenient. For a criminal who trades in millions of dollars, a penalty of $25,000 is "less than GST"…

1996-04-14   *The Richmond News*   by Nevil Judd

Omni-Science and the Human Destiny

[Anti-poaching activist disappointed with response from local schools]
… "(Richmond is) the epicentre of Chinese activity," said Marr… "Certainly, the demand side of the equation rests squarely on the shoulders of Chinese, Japanese and Korean cultures…"…

1996-04   *Vancouver Magazine*   by Shawn Blore
[Loaded for bear]
… "Canada's laws could use an aphrodisiac," says Marr. "Where fighting endangered species trade is concerned, it is more or less impotent."…

❖ ❖ ❖ ❖ ❖

May 4, 1996

Christopher's first birthday. He has grown and developed beautifully. Many wonderful, memorable moments.

Once, when he was still crawling on his elbows and knees, he was near the front door when a Harley-Davidson went roaring by, frightening him. At once, he scrambled over to me and wrapped his arms around my leg. This simple act melted my very core. I picked him up and he held onto me tightly. I didn't know there was so much strength in him. Just writing about this slice of life that lasted all of one minute brought tears to my eyes.

Another time, when I was making ready to go home, I tip-toed into his bedroom to give him a loving look good night – I love to see him sleep, the epitome of heavenly peace. This time, however, he was still awake, and as soon as he saw me, he pulled himself on to his feet by the bars of his crib. Then he raised his arms up to me. Again, this simple act on the part of the child moved me to the core, or should I say from my core. I picked him up and held him and patted him gently on his back, and he laid his head on my shoulder. This was more of a religious experience than when I was baptized. At that moment, Christine came in and chided me for disturbing his sleep.

Charles' drinking went unabated, more heavily than before. His liquor of choice is vodka. His place, a basement suite five minute's drive from Christine's, is littered with empty bottles. Christine often finds empty vodka bottles under her sofa and other such places, at times several in different places. In any given week, his life would be a mixture of pain, abusiveness, self-pity and oblivion. And with every passing week, he emerges to see himself falling a little farther behind in his failing welding supply business, and in life in general. And upon seeing this landscape of waste and ruin, he drinks again into the temporary unawareness. It's become blatantly obvious to me that he cannot help himself. I want to help him, at least initially to get him out of his deep well and place him back on terra firma. But Christine is of another mind. She said that whatever need be done, Charles must do it himself. Perhaps she wants to see what he is ultimately made of, even if it means his self-destruction. At least then Charles' true nature would be revealed, in poor light of course. Quit alcohol or get lost, or drop dead for that matter. It's not that he doesn't know her terms, nor that he doesn't want to see Christine and Christopher, but to him, Christine's harshness is yet another load on his already overburdened back. Perhaps indeed he is too weak for her. But I can't see him drown in booze without throwing him a lifeline. And I need Christine's cooperation to pull him back to shore, which she has so far refused.

Christine sets an iron rule for herself that she will not take any abuse from anybody. But she seems to have no remorse for the abuse she periodically deals out to me. For peace I'll take it. For Christopher I won't, if at stake is his wellbeing.

❖ ❖ ❖ ❖ ❖

1996-05-07 *The Vancouver Sun* **by Nicholas Read**
[Help our Grizzlies; stop hunting them]
… Anthony Marr says…all sport hunting should be abolished…

1996-05-08 *Ming Pao Daily News*, **Vancouver** **by Eric Chan**
[Chinese Canadian launching province-wide anti-bear-hunting referendum]
… Marr considers killing of bears for entertainment or profit a "barbaric practice".

1996-05-15 *The Vancouver Sun* **by Brian Morton**
[Bear hunt wish not on list of foundation in Canada]
… The local chapter of Canada's Make-A-Wish Foundation has been swamped with calls protesting against a 17-year-old Minnesota boy's being granted a wish by Make-A-Wish-America to hunt a Kodiak bear… Anthony Marr, who is leading a WCWC campaign against bear hunting, said Make-A-Wish-Canada should try to

persuade international chapters to ban hunting requests.

1996-05-16   *The Province*, Vancouver   by Charlie Anderson
[Canvassers out to stop bear hunts]
…Anthony Marr said…, "It's going to require a massive effort, and we are counting on friends in other environmental groups to help out."…

1996-06-05   *The Westerly News*, Tofino, BC
[Referendum road tour aims to stop bear hunting]
… "We are convinced that if something is not done now, the bears in BC will go the same way as the elephant's and tiger's and rhino's paths towards extinction. It would be only a matter of time," said Marr. "The subject of this road tour is to halt this downward spiral."…

1996-06-07   *The Vancouver Sun*
[Laws to curb wildlife trade]
Ottawa - Environment Minister Sergio Marchi has brought in stiff new regulations to curb the illegal trade in wildlife and plants. The regulation provides fines of up to $300,000 and jail terms of up to five years…Under previous legislation, it was illegal to import tiger parts into Canada, but once smuggled into the country such parts could be sold openly.

1996-06-08   *Nanaimo Daily Free Press*   by Paul Walton
[Wildlife group campaigns for referendum to ban bear hunting]
… Marr believes that when poaching is included, about 10% of all bears in BC are killed annually… (he) said that the purpose of this wildlife road tour is to set up the infrastructure for a referendum vote on banning bear hunting in BC…

1996-06-12   *Alberni Valley Times*
[Wilderness group brings bear campaign to Port Alberni]
The Western Canada Wilderness Committee is on the road to protect bears. The Bear Referendum Road Tour 1996 will be in Port Alberni on Thursday, June 13… at the Friendship centre…

Anthony Marr

June 14, 1996, Friday, mostly sunny
[12:02 @ local activists and hosts Annette and Scott Tanner's residence in Qualicum Bay, Vancouver Island, BC]

Just ten days on the road, and I already miss Christopher badly, and vice versa I'm told. Another six weeks to go. When Christine told Christopher about this 8-week road tour, he cried. She said that my going away and not seeing him for two whole months would be traumatic for him. I reassured him that I will think about him and call him every day, and bring back a present to him upon my return. Finally, he hugged me, and smiled. Of course I make good my promise of calling him daily. This is an effortless endeavour, since it is impossible for me not to think about calling him at least ten times a day.

The night of the dreaded Big Confrontation in Port Alberni has come to pass, and it lived up to expectations and more. And it is only one day in the first week of the province-wide, 8-week, 12,000-km, 45-city Ban-Bear-Hunting-in-BC Referendum Initiative road tour. Just a few days ago, in the town hall meeting in Campbell River, a hunter pointed at my nose and said, "I saw you on TV this morning. The price on your head just went up $10,000."

Before leaving the Tanner's (my host the Qualicum Beach) to drive to Port Alberni yesterday afternoon, I asked Erica (my assistant) one last time if she would much rather stay behind than come with me. This is an "Option 3" situation – an overt meeting in hostile territory – the first two being an overt meeting in friendly territory and a covert meeting in hostile territory. The meeting is well pre-publicized in the Alberni Times, and heavy hunter turn-out is more than likely. Why the pre-publicizing? I think it might be just a self-dare from which I could not back down. And I do think that some heat will generate a high profile newspaper article. A statistical increase in danger is the price to pay. I don't know if I can be classified as an adrenaline junkie, but I sense more excitement than fear prior to the engagement. In lieu of fear, there was a degree of apprehension. There were the few hecklers in previous meeting, but they were in the minority. This time might be a whole new ball game. I had never faced a room full of hostile hunters before, and had no idea how I would perform. On top of this, I did not want to have to worry about Erica's safety as well as mine. But she said a firm "No" without hesitation, one even firmer than those before. I respect her for that.

What transpired in Port Alberni was a horrific free for all, the "all" being the 65 hunters in an audience of about 70, all crammed into a room meant for no more than 30, equipped with just that many chairs. Standing room only - wall-to-wall hunters,

Omni-Science and the Human Destiny

with both entrances blocked. It was 30°C outside, and ten degrees warmer in the room sweltering with body heat and smelling of sweat, beginning with mine. The red hot verbal exchange only added fuel to the fire inside the oven. We couldn't escape if we wanted to. Of the five or six supporters, at least two or three were so intimidated that they slipped away unnoticed, leaving my local host Maureen Sager and two or three other women and just one man to hold the bag.

The hunter group included two or three local hunting-guide-outfitters and a conservation officer who was openly chummy with the hunters. About two-thirds were men and one-third were women, the latter attired from T-shirts and jeans to business suits and high heels, but all with hints of blood lust in their eyes, especially as they unflinchingly stared in my direction. No doubt, however subconsciously, they were feeling that trembling excitement as they sighted their quarry through their rifle-scopes. Was there an extra-kick for them to have all sixty-five weapons trained on the same prey?

Their verbal barrage began right in the middle of the very first slide in the slideshow, and right in the middle of my first sentence. Thereafter, I estimate, of every ten sentences I attempted in my presentation, I could finish maybe two without interruption.

Maureen, an active woman in her 60s, did her best to keep order, but was totally ignored, and at times assaulted by such threats as, "This guy flies in and out, but you have to live here. So watch what you're doing, lady!"

Another jeered, "Not only is this guy from out of town, he is from out of the *country*, for God's sake, and he has the gall to barge in here and tell us what we can and can't do in our own backyard!"

An older man bellowed, "All Chinese immigrants should be charged $100,000 for the damage done to the Canadian culture, starting with this guy right here, right now!"

Yet another shouted above the din, "Us western hunters have been conserving wildlife since before you were born, in China!"

About a third through my slideshow, I found myself turning off the projector and saying, "Fine. If you want a debate, we'll have a debate." Strangely, this somehow pacified the proceedings a little bit, since the word "debate" invoked in ones mind the terms "order" and "rules of engagement", and if then they spoke out of turn, they'd be interrupting one another instead of me.

Basically, their message to us, obviously predetermined among themselves, was "Scrap your campaign, or else." The milder ones were thoughtful enough to say, "Change your campaign to strictly anti-poaching but pro-hunting, and we'll support you, or else."

If the men's assaults were bad, like punching in the gut, some of the women's were worse, like pinching your sensitive zones with needle-nose pliers. One woman in her thirties, seemingly having come to the meeting right after having dragged a dead bear into town, said with a killer glare, "What you're trying to do is to deprive my children of a great heritage that their forefathers created and God condoned, and their father and his mother now enjoy!"

Another, also in her thirties, deceptively genteel-looking, said with a sly smirk, "If you don't play the game, honey, you don't make the rules."

Through the first hour, Erica sat on the sideline. Finally, she couldn't contain herself any longer, and stood to make a point. Before she could finish her sentence, as was now the norm, another older man shouted, "Young lady, you are not old enough to teach me anything. Sit down!"

I pointed at the "honey" woman and said, "I've been listening to *this* young lady for the last hour. It's about time you listen to this young lady here for a change. Go ahead, Erica."

Strangely, the man acquiesced, and stranger still, the smirk of the "honey" woman changed into a sweet smile, if only for the moment.

In contrast to the physical heat that I felt hard to endure, I found myself handling them in a surprisingly relaxed state, with a steely coldness in my core, matching wits with them point by point without losing my cool, and in fact enjoying certain moments when I made a clean score.

Another hunter hollered, "Who gives you the authority to do what you're doing?"

"What do you think of the Chinese tradition of using bear gall bladders for medicine?" I asked him as if he hadn't spoken.

"I think that's obscene."

"Should it be banned?"

"Damn right, it should be banned! And it is banned, by the law, and by God, not by some freelance environmentalist."

"I agree with you on this, sir, but I think for a trophy hunter to kill the most magnificent creature he, or she could find," glancing meaningfully at the "honey" woman, "so that he or she could have a climactic moment and its head to hang on his or her wall afterwards is equally obscene, and it, too, should be banned, unless, like you, I have a double standard."

"Since you obviously don't understand this, darling," rejoined the "honey" woman, "I'll tell you that trophy hunting does not exist in this province. We pack out all the meat. We waste nothing."

Omni-Science and the Human Destiny

"You pack out the meat because you are required by law to do it. And this law, in case you're not aware, was due not to the hunters, but due to your despised Bear Watch, which dumped a skinned bear carcass they found in the bush on to the front steps of the legislature. Before this law, the bear head and hide are all most bear hunters pack out. Just yesterday, I heard a hunter complain about *having* to pack out grizzly bear meat, which he then just dumped."

"I eat the meat of everything I kill."

"Then may I suggest that you leave the head and hide, and the antlers, behind, since they are of no nutritional value."

The man next to her shouted, "How dare you insult our women, right here in our town?!"

"Only for as long as they keep on killing our wildlife, right here in our country."

At another point, when one of them was talking about "ethical hunters", I responded with, "If there are ethical hunters, there must be *unethical* hunters, then?" I couldn't resist exaggeratedly sweeping the room with my eyes. Some dropped theirs involuntarily.

After an awkward moment of silence on their part, I asked them point blank whether they had never deliberately broken any rule, never taken anything on the side, never left any kills unreported, never left any meat behind, never exceeded their bag limits, never wounded any animal that got away. "If you have never done any of these, raise your hand," I challenged them. Every hand came up without exception – eventually, involving unmistakable hesitations in many. Later, Maureen commented that I had very skillfully made the hunters obey my command. "It wasn't by design. It just worked out that way," I said truthfully. In retrospect, I can see that anything else I ask a show of hand for would be disrespectfully ignored.

At another point, another hunter repeated, "We are the original and true conservationists of wildlife. You guys are just long-haired, welfare-collecting social parasites, using us to raise funds with."

"If it is so easy to raise funds, even using you, the social parasites wouldn't need to be on welfare, would they? Back to your first question, I know that true conservationists conserve wildlife for its own sake and for the health of the planet, and false conservationists conserve only so that they will continue to have something beautiful to kill. Which kind of conservationist are you?"

I saw some fists clenching, and some blue veins bulging on red necks, but I've gone too far to back down.

"This guy's front is to attack the Grizzly bear hunt," said another hunter, except this time he is addressing his cohorts, "but in fact, it is an attack on the entire hunting tradition, establishment and fraternity, from the top down, and from the foundation up. His real agenda is to stop all hunting, of all species. Mark my word."

"For once, you might be right," I said. "Killing animals for entertainment is barbaric and morally bankrupt, no matter what you kill."

"Are you calling us 'barbarians'? You Chinese people are very good with that, I hear."

"My apologies on behalf of the Chinese people, historically speaking. But no, I did not call you a 'barbarian', although I do call your so called 'sport' 'barbaric', and I mean it."

A woman spoke up, "We don't kill for entertainment. Hunting is a noble sport. It is not killing. It is communing with nature."

"Hunting is not killing? Tell it to the bear, and the deer, and the moose. Well, they might consider you not a hunter, but a terrorist, if that makes you feel better. As for entertainment or not entertainment, maybe you should take a look at your hunting regs, ma'am. The term for your 'communing with nature' is 'Recreational Hunting'. So, fine, you don't kill for entertainment, but you kill for recreation. Big difference."

Take it easy, Anthony. Don't piss them off *too* much.

It has became clear to me that it would be futile for us to try to convert even one of them. Our job here is to rally the already converted into a coherent fighting force. But in terms of this evening's meeting being a work session, it was unproductive and even counter-productive. The few supporters who showed up either disappeared or were too intimidated to sign up, at least in the presence of the hunters.

But hardly all is lost. The important thing is that a reporter from the Alberni Times was present, and from the readers of her article may emerge a certain number of volunteers who did not attend the meeting, although I would think that those few who did attend would be the most gung-ho of them all. Partly because of the presence of the journalist, the hunters at least maintained a sense of restraint, but only in terms of physical violence, at least for as long as the reporter was around. They seemed determined to give her something dramatic to report about their nature without resorting to fists or, God forbid, guns, and I think they did an admirable job in that.

The meeting did not end until the hunters had spent their fury. Still, they left the room in a huff, with lethal parting-glares aplenty. Unexpectedly, the "honey woman" came to me and said quietly, "You have guts. I'll give you that much."

While packing and cleaning up with our hosts, one of the few women echoed "honey woman" unknowingly, except that her word was "brave". Maureen said in front of the others, "Anthony, now I have full confidence that you can talk your way out of hell itself."

Well, debating is one thing. Putting the pedal to the metal is another. While loading my car, I noticed a truck parked in the shadows on the same side of the street about half a block back, engine and lights off, but with two people inside. It was too dark to tell its color, maybe brown. I didn't lead Erica's attention to it. As I drove off, it did the same. I made one or two random turns and the truck followed suit, staying about half a block behind. I looked for a police car but couldn't find any. I looked for the police station and had no idea where it was. I reminded myself that when several Bear Watch women were surrounded and harassed by hunters in Campbell River a few weeks back, the police supposedly did not respond to their call for help. Finally, I took the plunge and got on to the highway due east towards the Tanners' at Qualicum Beach, as we had intended to. The truck did too. I could identify it because its right headlight was brighter than its left, and its right parking light was out. I stayed within 10 km/h of the speed limit, and the truck observed the two-second rule, for the time being. Still too close to town; give it ten k or so, I thought.

Erica and I talked for a bit, and she surprised me by saying that she could sympathize with the hunters' viewpoint, and that maybe we should re-examine our anti-hunting stance. I thought I heard bits and pieces of this talk yesterday at the Tanners' when she was talking to the reporter. She admitted that she had been thinking along those lines since almost Day 1. She said that if we dropped anti-hunting and just went for anti-poaching, namely to press for a ten-fold increase in penalties, we would get the support of environmentalists and hunters alike, and that we would have a resounding success. She even went as far as to say that she might start her own anti-poaching referendum if WCWC rejected her idea. She acquitted herself by saying that her first concern was the bears, and that if we won the anti-poaching referendum, lots of bears would be saved, whereas if we stayed our course against legal hunting as well as poaching, we would set up the hunters against us and would surely fail and end up with nothing, and that even if we could succeed, we would force many legal hunters to become poachers. So, she lost it, at least the original and central principle of the campaign. There suddenly seemed a wall between the driver's and passenger's seats.

I listened to her with one ear, and kept an eye on the rear view mirror. Erica reclined her seat and soon fell asleep. The lights in the rear-view mirror drew closer. I increased my speed. The truck did the same. I slowed down to see if it would pass. It drew even closer but did not pass. If it tried, I wouldn't have let it anyway, not wanting to be blocked; being able to see its license plate number probably wouldn't do much good under those circumstances. I sped up again, and the truck did likewise, and pulled closer to my bumper the farther we left the town behind. Before long, it didn't even bother to keep up a pretense and began tailgating. Was this just intimidation? Or was it a real attempt to push me off the highway? I was not about to put the latter to the test. I've been tailgated a thousand times by road rage loonies before, but never quite this tightly, and by a cold-blooded killer.

    I thought again about my options. I had already left the first one behind, not having used the cell phone while in town to call the police. I tried the cell phone now, but we were already outside any service area. I thought about doing a U-turn back to Port Alberni for the police, but the truck had come too close for me to do that safely. Only one thing left to do. I had to out-run it. My car is sporty, low-slung, aerodynamic, light and nimble, and quite powerful. Best of all, with its sport suspension and wide tires, it has a .86g lateral-g-force tolerance, whereas that of a truck's is less than .70g, which means that my car can take a corner much faster than the truck without losing traction or rolling over. The twisty highway, with narrow soft-looking shoulders and hemmed in by thick forest on both sides, and barely moon-lit, threw itself left and right, and up and down, constantly. This sounds forbidding, but I deemed it advantageous to my car over the truck. So I floored it and took the curves near the limit. The truck, probably with a big V8, could probably gain on the straights, but on this highway, its headlights receded, farther and farther until they finally disappeared behind a curve. Did I leave them in the dust? Or in the ditch? I smiled at the thought, but kept the speed up. I tried the cell phone again. Still no service, which strangely was comforting in that neither could the pursuers call somebody up ahead to intercept me. Unless some of their buddies called from Port Alberni, which seemed unlikely. Erica slept through the whole thing. When she woke up, she complained that I was driving too fast. By then, the glow of Qualicum was on the horizon. I kept the chase to myself, even from the Tanners. On the other hand, the hunter probably blasted it throughout his community that he ran me not only out of town, but right back where I came from, with my tail between my legs.

※ ※ ※ ※ ※

June 14, 1996, Fri.   *Alberni Valley Times*   **by Diane Morrison**
Bear hunters confront bare-faced petition to put them into permanent hiber-

Omni-Science and the Human Destiny

nation

Bears, whether Black, Brown, Grizzly or Polar, are not endangered species in North America. Anthony Marr wants to keep it that way.

The campaigner for Western Canada Wilderness Committee was in Port Alberni Thursday night with his effort to ban sport and trophy hunting of Grizzly and Black bears.

It was a very hard sell to the audience of about 70 dominated by hunters and hunting guides that packed into a into small, hot room at the Friendship Centre, made even hotter by the temper flaring up from wall to wall.

The hunters say they are the endangered species. They wanted the distinction between legal hunting and poaching to be clearly recognized. "Go ask the bears, to see if they can," said Marr. He also said that some hunters and guides make this impossible, because they are themselves poachers.

Marr believes that, with both legal hunting, poaching and conservation officer kills, about 8% of the Grizzly bear population and more than 10% of the Black bear population are being killed each year. He said the province's Grizzly Bear Conservation Strategy clearly states that the species can sustain no more than a 4% annual mortality before going into decline, and even this, according to Marr, is too high.

Members of the audience disputed Marr's numbers saying that, on Vancouver Island at least, the Black bear population has been increasing by 15% for the last 10 years. Marr countered that the Black bear populations on southern Vancouver Island, and some in Mid-Island, have been decimated in various locales, citing the Cowichan Lake area as an example, and challenged the hunters to produce written documentation to support their claim, which they did not.

A number of people asked why Marr's main thrust was to shut down legal hunting when the problem is poaching. Marr replied that both in combination is the problem, and that he has another sub-campaign targeting poachers and traffickers of bear parts. A Chinese Canadian, Marr has taken on both Canadian hunters and the Chinese demand for the body parts of these animals.

After about an hour of cross firing, WCWC campaign assistant Erica Denison finally stood up and said that until poaching can be brought under control, they want to buy time for the bears to recover. One of the hunters pointed at her and said, "Young lady, you are not old enough to teach us anything. Sit down!" Marr pointed at a middle-aged woman in the audience who had been quite outspoken in favour of hunting, saying, "I've been listening to *this* young lady for the last hour. Erica, please continue."

Marr needs to get hunters on his side, the woman said, not slam them, because hunters also want to stop poaching.

Some audience members said it is organizations such as WCWC, advertising the fact that bear parts are worth so much on the black market, that is increasing poaching. Marr scoffed at this as an "ostrich attitude".

They objected to being told that they can't legally hunt bears, but bears that get into garbage and smash bee hives can be killed for being a nuisance. Marr said, "The bears you kill are not nuisance bears, and that killing nuisance bears is not your job."

When shown a picture of a bear shut in a small cage with a tube leading out from its gall bladder to extract bile, one man said that countries that treat animals like that are not democratic and so they have no conscience. Marr countered that lots of capitalists have no conscience either.

Another man was convinced that if WCWC is successful in shutting down bear hunting, it will try to shut down all hunting. Marr said, "If another hunted species becomes threatened or endangered, I would champion its cause as well."

Back to poaching, Marr said that when an animal such as the tiger and the rhino is declared endangered, the demand and price, and so the poaching, skyrocket, hastening its slide into oblivion. "It is a very vicious cycle, and the purpose of this campaign is to try to keep our own bears out of it." . . .

※　　※　　※　　※　　※

1996-06-15   *The News*, Parksville/Qualicum   **by Chris Beacom**
[Bear Referendum meeting Friday]
… Anthony Marr and (campaign assistant) Erica Denison are visiting every town in the province to drum up support for a petition urging the government to hold a referendum on outlawing bear hunting… "We've had tremendous support on the island so far," Marr said, adding that 10% of all registered voters must sign the petition for a referendum to be held.

1996-06-18   *Nanaimo Times*   **by Kim Goldberg**
[Easy to bag – Let's vote on bear hunting]
… In the biggest and boldest campaign of its ecophilic history, the Western Canada Wilderness Committee has launched a referendum initiative which, if successful, could ban all sport and trophy hunting of bears in BC…

1996-06-18   *Times Colonist*, **Victoria, BC**   **by Malcolm Curtis**
[Crusader wants everyone to vote on the future of bear-hunting]
… "It's going to be difficult up north and in places like the Chilcotin, but in the urban areas we see no problem," Marr said Monday… An Angus Reid poll last year showed that 78% of British Columbians oppose sport and trophy hunting of bears… Marr will give a presentation at the University of Victoria on Thursday night at the Begbie Building, Room 159, starting at 7 p.m.. Admission is free.

1996-06-20   *Times Colonist*, **Victoria, BC**   **by Malcolm Curtis**
[Bear hunters shoot back]
Bear hunters are in a growlly mood over an environmental group's bid to force a public vote on their sport… "That's just garbage," Saanich hunter Terry Anderson said Wednesday, responding to a Times Colonist report about Marr's referendum drive. "Your newspaper did not do justice to the cause of ethical hunters."…Marr, meanwhile, is holding a meeting tonight at U.Vic.'s Begbie Building, Room 159, to promote his campaign.

1996-06-22   *The News*, **Parksville, BC**   **by Chris Beacom**
[Crusade to end bear hunting hits Qualicum Beach]
The system. Difficult to change and more frustrating even to try. Anthony Marr is finding out first-hand how far the provincial government needs to be pushed before change ensues… At the meeting the Chinese-born Marr was questioned by bear hunters for not cracking down on illegal Asian poaching instead of focusing on legal hunting… (Campaign assistant) Erica Dennis expects battles ahead, especially in towns like Williams Lake. "They already know we're coming. They have a front page headline saying 'Bear hunting isn't wrong", and a hunter there just got killed by a bear near town. It could be tough,' she said… Anyone interested in helping out with the cause can contact the WCWC at 1-800-661-WILD.

1996-07-03   *The Northern Sentinel*, **Prince Rupert, BC**   **by Mary Vallis**
[Bear hunt ban call]
… "It is perverted for people to kill for fun," Marr maintained, "particularly if adults take their kids and teach them to kill."…

1996-07-03   *The Daily News*, **Prince Rupert, BC**   **by Heather Colpitts**
[Bear petition circulated]
… "More than two decades ago, India banned tiger hunting and Kenya outlawed

lion hunting. We have a moral obligation to lead the world, not straggle behind other countries," said Marr…

1996-07-05 *The Prince George Citizen* **by Gordon Hoekstra**
[Fur flies at meeting to ban bear hunts]
It was barely civil and sometimes downright ugly. In the end, it took a representative of the Western Canada Wilderness Committee close to two hours to deliver a plea for help to ban bear hunting in BC. Anthony Marr was interrupted, shouted down, and generally abused by hunters in an audience of more than 100 that spilled out of the conference room at the Civic Centre Thursday evening…Marr had barely begun…before he was attacked…

1996-07-09 *The Daily News*, **Kamloops, BC** **by Michelle Young**
[Activist pleads for bear-hunt ban]
With calm and respect, Anthony Marr faced rapid-fire questioning from hunters and threw back a plea for them to stop hunting bears…

1996-07-09 *Echo/Pioneer*, **Chetwynd, BC** **by Rick Davison**
[WCWC wants bear hunting banned]
It will be a tough fight, particularly in these parts, but Anthony Marr of the WCWC is determined to stop the killing of bears in BC… His stand won him the admiration of some and the scorn of others…

1996-07-10 *Kamloops This Week* **by Michelle Daubney**
[Environmentalists and hunters lock horns]
… Marr likened letting hunters manage wildlife to "giving our babies to a known child abuser"…

1996-07-10 *The Daily News*, **Kamloops, BC by Robert Koopmans**
[Bear ban sets bad precedent]
The thought of dead bears in the bush, minus their gallbladders and paws, makes me cringe. But there's something in Anthony Marr's message that ripples my spine just as much… / It's not the specifics of Marr's anti-bear-hunting speech that are troubling, but what his campaign represents. Marr is the thin edge of a bigger wedge, an axe aimed at the heart of sport hunting in general…

1996-07-11 *The Daily News*, **Kamloops, BC by Mel Rothenburger**

[Culture greatest threat to wildlife]
Culture and the environment seem to be coming into conflict a lot lately… (Culture) can be a tremendous barrier to positive change… Earlier this week Anthony Marr spoke to a few dozen people in Kamloops… / The prime reason is culture… Marr, who grew up in Hong Kong, understands the culture behind the insatiable appetite for rare animal parts, but devotes his life to fighting it… Lest Canadians get a little pious about the atrocities against wildlife committed in the name of culture in other countries, they should pay close attention to what's happening in their own backyard…

1996-07-13   *The Daily News*, **Kamloops, BC by Mel Rothenburger**
[Impossible to get issue to a vote]
Nobody ever promised democracy would be easy. Anthony Marr is learning all about that in Canada… Aside from the cogency of his argument, what struck me most about his objective is the near-impossibility of success. The hurdles are staggering… Marr and WCWC simply won't be able to get it to a provincial vote…

1996-07-13   *The Globe and Mail*, **Ontario**
[Bid to end bear hunting to proceed]
The WCWC has cleared another hurdle in its bid to end sport and trophy hunting of bears in BC. Chief Electoral Officer Robert Patterson has announced… that approval in principle has been given to the group's initiative petition. The 90-day Initiative Petition period is set to begin September 9…

1996-07-16   *Elk Valley Miner*
[Group seeks to ban all BC bear hunting]
… "…Although BC's bears are not yet considered endangered, at today's rate of hunting, poaching and habitat loss, they soon will be. We must exercise some foresight and keep them from this terrible fate," says Marr…

1996-07-16   *The Times*, **Terrace, BC   by Jennifer Lang**
[A vote for the bears]
… Marr says BC's wildlife protection laws and policies haven't caught up with a new phenomenon… commercial poaching… He says there aren't enough conservation officers in BC to stop poaching, but he believes a hunting ban would make poachers easier to spot…

1996-07-18　　　　　　*The Vancouver Sun*
[Grin and bear it]
… Paul George, an executive director of the WCWC, in his role as private citizen, has launched an initiative for An Act to Prohibit the Hunting of Bears… Mr. George's worthy petition would have an uphill battle under the best of circumstances, especially in many rural areas. BC's absurd initiative legislation dooms it – and any other imaginable challenge to the legislature's monopoly.

1996-07-24　　　　　*Capital News*, Kelowna, BC　　　　by Jean Russell
[WCWC loaded for bear – Petition drive launched]
… about 15 prohunters turned out at the meeting in Kelowna on Friday. / Don Guild, secretary-treasurer of the Okanagan branch of WCWC, said Monday the hunting supporters made it difficult to make progress. "They tried to dispute (Marr's) figures before he even gave them…"

1996-07-24　　　　*The Morning Sun*, Parksville, BC　　　by Valerie Baker
[Taking aim at the trade in illegal bear parts]
… "During the next 60 days, we are scrambling to get as many official canvassers as we can," says Paul George, WCWC Founding Director… Anthony Marr is currently on an eight-week provincial tour garnering support… Since his presentation in Qualicum Beach on June 17, around 30 local people have volunteered to be canvassers…

1996-07-31　　　　*The Morning Sun*, Parksville, BC　　　by Valerie Baker
[Taking aim on the illegal trade in bear parts]
Editor's note: As many of you noticed – judging by your phone calls – our computer managed to muck up last week's story on the initiative… Here then is the way the story was supposed to read…

1996-07-31　　　　　*The Salmon Arm Observer*　　　by Gordon Priestman
[Seeks local support for bear referendum]
Anthony Marr brought his one-man crusade to Salmon Arm Thursday night… In what seems close to Mission Impossible, Marr has been touring the province since the beginning of June, hold at least one meeting a day and often more, seven days a week… Along the way he's run into a lot of opposition from organized hunter groups but that doesn't deter Marr… Marr believes in what he's doing…

1996-08 *Sing Tao Weekend Magazine* (Chinese), global
[When the bear hunt season opens, whose cry will be the loudest?]
… WCWC campaign director Anthony Marr spent June and July visiting over 40 cities and towns to publicize the initiative… He was interviewed by newspapers more than 150 times, and by TV and radio more than a dozen times. Along his route, he also signed up more than 1,500 volunteers…

1996-08 *EcoNews*, Victoria, BC by Guy Dauncy
[BC referendum to stop bear killing for trophy and sport]
This coming September, WCWC will be launching a 90 day campaign to collect signatures from 10% of the registered voters in every constituency in BC… WCWC is looking for 50 canvassers in each of BC's 75 electoral districts, to collect signatures. To be a canvasser, you must be a registered BC voter, have lived in BC for the last 6 months, and must witness each signature collected. If you want to be a canvasser, call…

1996-08-01week *The Daily News*, Kamloops, BC by Eleanor Kohnert
[Save the bears]
Editors: Anthony Marr from the WCWC is not alone… Organizations and an ever-growing number of individuals are supporting his endeavour. However, a huge hunting guiding and gun lobby will use all the firepower in their possession to defeat the proposal… Even if WCWC's efforts… fail… the issue will be moved into the political arena… The concession to First Nations of allowing Grizzly bears to be killed for ceremonial purposes (however) is ludicrous…

1996-08-01week *The Georgia Straight*, Vancouver, BC by Charlie Smith
[Hunters target Marr]
During a recent province-wide tour, WCWC wildlife campaigner Anthony Marr discovered how difficult it will be to achieve a ban on bear hunting… In public meetings to promote holding a vote on the issue, he was usually hounded by dozens of angry hunters who tried to intimidate him… Marr will speak about this issue on Thursday (August 8) at the H.R. MacMillan Planetarium at 7:30 p.m.- and he expects to see angry hunters in the audience. "I'm beginning to enjoy confronting them," he chuckled.

1996-08-02 *The Vancouver Sun* by Larry Pynn
[Activist angers hunters with campaign to outlaw bear hunt through refer-

endum]
Anthony Marr is on almost every hunter's hit list for his efforts to get bear hunting banned in BC... Marr has just completed a seven-week-tour of more than 50 BC communities... It hasn't been easy for Marr, who has been dogged by hunters equally determined to kill his campaign before it gets off the ground... 'I know some gung fu, but I can take on only one unarmed hunter at a time,' he says with a smile...

"Deep down inside, it's a moral issue," says Marr, who estimates that at least 90 per cent of hunters shoot bears for the trophy and that 65 per cent actually come from urban areas.

"It's immoral to kill for entertainment. And abominable that adult teach their children to kill for fun."...

The BC Wildlife Federation has set aside $40,000 so far to counter the environmentalists. The hunter lobby will place ads, and attempt to shadow petition canvassers as they make their way door to door...

Realizing that hunters would probably lose a referendum on bear hunting, the Federation knows it must stop the environmentalists now. The hunters will concentrate their efforts in pro-hunting interior communities and leave the urban areas alone.

"The hunters' message is that poaching is not out of control, that bear populations can support hunting and that hunting is a valid way for wildlife officials to manage populations.

"Even if all the logic is on our side, it is hard to counter emotion," Federation President John Holdstock) said.

Saying that hunters legally kill 4,000 Black bears and 350 Grizzlies a year in BC, Marr argues that the hunting ban will help protect BC bears from inevitable onslaught of poaching to meet the rising Asian herbal-medicine trade in gall bladders.

To that end, Marr is waging a simultaneous campaign to educate the Chinese community.

"We have a moral obligation to lead the world," he said. "I feel it will get much worse before, and if, it gets better."...

Marr... was born in China in 1944 and fled to Hong Kong with his family during the Communist revolution in 1949. He moved to Canada in 1965, first to Winnipeg and then to Vancouver, eventually receiving his bachelor of science degree from the University of BC.

He... worked as a geophysicist in the northern wilderness for mineral exploration companies - 'that's when I became bonded with nature' - before joining WCWC as a campaigner last year...

1996-08-08   *The Valley Voice*, **New Denver, BC**
[Bear Protection Act campaign gets under way]
Anthony Marr, lead campaigner for the WCWC, has received approval for $75,000 from the Canadian International Development Agency (CIDA) for his tiger conservation work…

1996-08-09   *Pique Newsmagazine*, **Whistler, BC**   **by David Gowman**
[Letter to the Editor]
… The extreme positions taken by environmentalists such as Anthony Marr are telling us all to wake up and smell the coffee before the pot boils over…

1996-08-17   *The Vancouver Sun*, **[Westcoast People]**   **by Mia Stainsby**
[Caught at cultural crossroads – Chinese-Canadian environmentalist upsets some Asians and Caucasians alike as he fights against the use of animal parts as Chinese medicines, among other traditions]
Anthony Marr, the man who's threatening to take all the fun out of bear hunting... is in a show down with hunters, who aren't taking too kindly to his quest... The winding path that brought him to this juncture appeared before him unexpectedly.

    In truth, Marr would rather be with his "baby", a book over 800 pages long, called [The Fortunate and Called Upon], which he began writing in 1978.

    "So, what is he doing in conflict over bear hunting, after spending decades writing about cosmic harmony? On a recent tour of 40 BC interior communities, he faced roomsful of angry hunters and has a fistful of press clippings about the dust-ups. On the other hand, he also found supporters in these communities.

    Being Chinese-Canadian has almost everything to do with Marr's environmental activism. The more he heard about the Chinese use of animal parts, especially parts from animals on the endangered species list, the more he felt compelled to speak up.

    "Something's got to be done about this," he said to his (mostly Caucasian) friends. "And I think a Chinese person should do it. And I think you're looking at him." That was three and a half years ago...

    "I was going to finish my book last year, but all of a sudden my time was usurped. Saving endangered species. It was more urgent, but the book, whenever it comes out, will remain the central core of my achievement."

    Love may have something to do with Marr's critical take on Chinese culture. "My first true love was a Chinese woman, but her family forced her to break up with me or suffer the pain of being disowned," he recalls. "That is a fate worse than death for a Chinese girl, and so she acquiesced. Her parents felt our two families' social positions didn't match. That was in 1967, and I became very disenchanted with the Chinese culture because of it. I've never dated a Chinese woman since," he said.

The Chinese reaction to Marr is mixed. At schools, where he gives talks on the Asian use of animals, he gets enthusiastic support from students (many of whom being of Chinese descent).

... "When I'm on Chinese radio talk shows, two of the most common questions are: "Why are you trying to blacken the Chinese reputation?" and "What is more important, humans or animals?"

"My answer is that, on the contrary, I'm trying to save the Chinese reputation from eternal damnation, because if we carry on the way we have and drive some of the species to extinction, then our reputation will be forever mud, and we can never regain respect in the eyes of the world. I tell them that I'm working for human beings too. What kind of world are we passing on to our kids?"...

1996-09-09　　　　*The Province*, **Vancouver, BC**　　**by John Bermingham**
[Bear-hunt opponents seek referendum]
... "The deadliest enemy is not the hunters, but the apathy of the 'silent majority'," said Marr...

1996-09-09　　　　*The Globe and Mail*, **national**　　**by Craig McInnes**
[All in favour of saving bear, vote yes – BC tests referendum law]
... the critics say the hurdles set by the law render hollow the promise that people will be able to take matters into their own hands if politicians refuse to act as citizens believe they should...

1996-09-10　　　　*The Province*, **Vancouver, BC**　　**by John Colbourn**
[Poaching won't be tolerated – Ramsey]
... "I respect the people who have brought this (petition) forwards," said (Environment Minister Paul) Ramsey. "Whether or not banning hunting is a part of preserving the bear population is something the public is going to have to decide."...

1996-09-10　　　*Sing Tao Daily* **(Chinese), international**
[Anti-bear hunt petition launched]
... Ma Seeu Sung urges the Chinese community to stand up and speak out...

1996-09-10　　　*Ming Pao* **(Chinese), international**
[Battle for the bear commences]

… Hunter Med Crotteau rebukes Ma's campaign as being insulting to the Chinese community…

1996-09-17   *The Daily News*, Kamloops, BC   by Michelle Young
[Bear crusader says pro-hunting side well organized]
An anti-bear-hunt crusader says he wasn't surprised by the response of callers to his appearance on a Kamloops radio talk-show Monday morning.

Anthony Marr of the WCWC said the show, hosted by Daily News editor Mel Rothenburger on JC-55, drew 19 callers in favour of the hunt, five against.

The pro-hunting side is well organized and plugged up phone lines, he said about his appearance against BC Wildlife Federation president John Holdstock… "The 5 versus 19 call-ins illustrates that the silent majority is still silent," he said…

1996-09-18   *The Daily News*, Kamloops, BC   by Michelle Young
[Bear-hunt ban campaign strains ties between wilderness allies]
… BC Wildlife Federation president… John Holdstock said the WCWC's effort …has already upset his group's members.

"I've never seen our membership so angry," he said. "An initiative like this goes to the core of what we do and what we believe in."… "Anthony Marr has been trying to sell it as an anti-poaching issue. It's a pro-poaching issue."…

1996-09-25   *The Vancouver Sun*   by Larry Pynn
[BC Wildlife Federation forced to apologize for accusing WCWC of terror tactics]
The BC Wildlife Federation … has pulled the fall issue of its magazine off newsstand shelves because it contains defamatory statements against the WCWC.

As well, in ads appearing in The Vancouver Sun and Province newspapers, the federation makes a public apology for describing the environmental group, which prides itself on adopting legal tactics, as terrorists… In his editorial, (BCWF executive director Doug) Walker likened the WCWC to 'terrorists groups who threaten human lives, burn houses, send razor blades in the mail or kill family pets to get attention…'…

Wilderness Committee director Paul George said in an interview the recall of the magazines and the apology in the Vancouver dailies is only a first step. The Federation must also apologize in smaller papers throughout the province and agree to pay all the Committee's legal costs in launching the BC Supreme Court libel suit against the Federation, Walker and president John Holdstock…

1996-09-26   *Terminal City*, **Vancouver, BC**   **by Paul Johnson**
[Ban bear hunting]
… One of BC's foremost environmental organizations has discovered just how difficult the process surrounding citizens' referendum can be. The WCWC is seeking to…

"The rules are just about unworkable," says WCWC's Anthony Marr. Their first problem is that referendum rules stipulate that there can be only one proponent for a referendum, but an unlimited number of opponents. In this case, Marr says, it's WCWC's Paul George against 107 parties: 69 organizations and 38 individuals… WCWC is also bogged down in the mechanics of the process… Marr points out that while referendums are common in many American states, "in BC things are so tough that no one has been successful in organizing a referendum."

1996-10-05   *Daily Free Press*, **Nanaimo, BC**   **by Mark Brett**
[Bear poaching on increase locally]
… Conservation officer Ron Heusen…said,… "We've had four kills in the last month right in the Nanaimo District area. In six years I've heard of maybe four carcasses poached for parts, and in one month, we've had four go down. There is no doubt it's increasing."… Meanwhile, Anthony Marr… is on his second road tour of BC…

1996-10-07   *Macleans Magazine*, **national**
[Hunted down by the law]
It was a case of ready, fire, aim for the BC Wildlife Federation, a group representing hunters in BC. With 25,000 copies of the September/October issue of its magazine, Outdoor Edge, already delivered to their BC members, the BC group had to abruptly cancel the remainder of its distribution, pull 60 copies from store shelves, and print a public apology in Vancouver newspapers last week. At issue were remarks that the cancelled edition contained about the WCWC…

1996-10-08   *The Northerner*, **Fort St. John, BC**   **by John Richards**
[Peace River Regional District takes a stand against ban on bear hunting]
… The BC Wildlife Federation is mounting its own campaign to counter WCWC's. Doug Walker, executive director of BCWF, rallied members in his column in Outdoor Edge magazine. The Federation is hoping to raise $500,000 for radio and TV air time and newspaper space in order to overshadow the petition. Walker is asking members to donate about $25 each to help with the cause. 'I think we can all give up one box of shells or a tank of gas to preserve our hunting heritage," he wrote…

Marr is stuck in a very hard place. If he only demands higher penalties and more protection for animals against poachers, he has hunters on his side, but as soon as he turns around and addresses the other side, he is met with complete opposition.

"Hunters go for the head and hide and poachers go for the gall and paws; they are all after bear parts…" Marr said...

1996-10-12-6 *The News*, Parksville, BC by Bruce Whitehead
[Bear Crusader takes man on the speaking tour from hell]
No matter how open-minded you are, you likely wouldn't pick mild-mannered Anthony Marr out to be an environmental activist - let alone one that some have called 'the most hated man in BC'. But the Chinese-Canadian physicist has almost single-handedly managed to fire up emotions in every corner of the province…

1996-10-12 *The Saturday Okanagan*, Kelowna, BC
[Anti-hunting campaign rolls into valley]
Anthony Marr is in the Okanagan this weekend organizing supporters to gather signatures against bear hunting… At least 20 local volunteers have applied with Elections BC to be registered canvassers. But so far, well into the petition period, the necessary paperwork still has not come through, Marr said…

1996-10-15 *Times Colonist*, Victoria, BC by Malcolm Curtis
[Anti-hunt activists face uphill battle for vote]
In areas where hunting is as common as walking the dog, canvassing for signatures is not for the weak-hearted… In a 12,000-km road trip to promote the referendum last summer, Marr often found himself confronting hallsful of angry hunters… The volunteers – 50 are already signed up in the Capital Region – have to be registered with the provincial government in a time-consuming process that involves 5 mailings…

1996-10 *Mainstreet*, Crawford Bay, BC by Susan Hulland
[The Ban Bear Hunting Initiative, an exercise in democracy]
… This initiative is part of a larger global process called the BET'R Campaign. Launched in 1995 and founded by an Asian named Anthony Marr…

The really interesting thing about this initiative is that there's more at stake here than first meets the eye. Some hunters believe this is the first step in the total ban on all hunting…

Understandably… the big guns will be coming out of the bushes representing all sides of the issue. Also, the gallery is filling up quickly with interested parties who stand to lose or gain in some way depending on the final result.

Hunters and hunting support groups such as guides, outfitters and taxidermists are lining up on one side with lots of ranchers and pro-gun lobbyists. Supporters of the hunting ban are being joined by numerous scientists concerned for species diversity, animal rights proponents, and pacifists of all kinds.

You can be darned sure the bad guys are watching, too. Irrespective of the final outcome... heightened public awareness about bear hunting issues will affect their way of doing business. This will reverberate throughout the community of those who prosper from both the legal and illegal killing of bears, from our local community poachers to the sophisticated international criminals who deal in the animals parts commodities market.

You can also be sure the politicians are watching this process. And... also lots of other public advocacy groups...

1996-10-16   *The Morning Sun*, Vernon, BC   by Richard Rolke
[Bear hunting ban under the gun]
... Marr said that... "the single proponent must work all 75 districts to ensure all succeed, whereas the 107 opponents need concentrate on just one district. If we fail in just one district, the whole project fails. The rules are stacked against us."

1996-10-16   *The Vancouver Sun*   by Larry Pynn
[Victim of bear attack back campaign to end hunting]
Chilliwack – Just two months after he was mauled while camping, Jackson Brown would seem an unlikely person to sign a petition against bear hunting.

But Brown says he holds no grudge against bears...

1996-10-16   *The Penticton Herald*
[Campaign to ban bear hunt seeks help]
... Anthony Marr said he has about 15 people in the Penticton area so far to collect 3,200 signatures... Marr said about two-thirds of some 2,000 volunteers have so far been approved...

1996-10-17   *The Sun*, Vernon, BC
[Bid to ban bear hunting spreading]
Despite the odds, Anthony Marr is bearing down... "Even though we may not succeed in the petition, we'll have launched one hell of an educational campaign," he said...

1996-10-18   *The Trail Times*   by Lana Rodlie
[Shooting to ban bear hunting]
Anthony Marr knows his chances of getting a provincial referendum on banning bear hunting is about as probable as a snowflake's chance on a hotplate, but he's trudging along getting signatures anyway… "Every observer says we can't do it," Marr said… While touring the province… he has been scorned, yelled at, intimidated, threatened and slandered.

    In Penticton, 50 hunters showed up to disrupt a meeting…

    … Marr doesn't care if he is up against insurmountable odds, he still hopes to get his message out… One of the most frequently asked questions by hunters is why they are being persecuted when the real culprits are poachers. Marr said that they are both culprits, and the difference between a hunter and a poacher is irrelevant if you're a bear.

    When told that hunters could help by watching for poachers, Marr said that was like "wolves keeping coyotes from sheep."…

1996-10-18   *Victoria News*   by Wendy Cook
[Anthony Marr targeted by angry hunters in the north]
… Marr says BC hunters seem to be short-sighted in their vision of the potential crisis. "They don't accept the global scene. They say 'This is BC, don't talk about Asia' but the world is getting pretty small. What happens over here has an effect over there and vice versa," he says.

    BC Wildlife Federation's Doug Walker does not agree. "To say expansion in China will increase the use of bear parts here is unfair…," he says…

1996-10-21   *Nelson Daily News*   by Bob Hall
[Hunting opponents struggle]
Anthony Marr admits it is a daunting task, but has vowed to go the distance in the effort to ban bear hunting in BC… "Pessimists say it is possible but very difficult and optimists say it is very difficult but possible," said Marr, who was in Nelson over the weekend to rally support of volunteers who are collecting signatures. "We're saying the latter and have to work on that premise to just keep going…"

1996-11-04   *The Trail Times*   by Lana Rodlie
[Petition booth axed after threats to mall]
… The problem stemmed from a visit to Trail several weeks ago by Anthony Marr… Although Marr was scorned, yelled at, intimidated, threatened and slandered in other

parts of the province, no one thought such tactics would be used here.

Unfortunately, for John and Rachel Kratky, intimidation raised its ugly head after Marr left.

The Kratkys volunteered to help Marr's cause by locally obtaining signatures. They approached Waneta Plaza and asked if they could set up a table in the mall.

The mall manager saw no problem and said it was alright. However, the decision was quickly reversed.

"We were told that we couldn't set up because the mall had received a bunch of phone calls from people threatening to picket," said Rachel Kratky… Waneta Plaza manager Linda MacDermid confirms… MacDermid said this is the first time anyone has ever called with threats over a proposed petition campaign or anything else.

"We've always had all sorts of groups with petitions. Even when we had Pro-Choice people, we've never had any calls. Yet…"…

1996-11-12 *The Citizen*, Prince George, BC by Gordon Hoekstra
[Bear hunt opponents bring the campaign here]

The WCWC is sending a swat team to Prince George in a last ditch effort… Expected to arrive this Friday for a three-day stay, the team is to roll into town with a caravan of two or three vehicles – at least one of them highly decorated with banners – and set up shop, said bear protection campaign manager Anthony Marr from Vancouver… This summer, prior to the launch of the 90-day petition campaign, Marr received a less than warm reception from hunters at an information session here.

Marr said he expects it will get even hotter this time. "We're in the home stretch, and we're fighting."…

The WCWC would be better off directing its attention to curtailing the Asian market that deal in bear parts, says groups like the BC Wildlife Federation…

1996-11-13 *The Citizen*, Prince George, BC by Gordon Hoekstra
[Malls turn away bear hunt opponents]

Unable to get permission to set up their ban-bear-hunting petition drive at any of the malls here, a Lower Mainland preservation group will try to gather signatures near the Civic Centre starting Friday.

In general, the malls told him that they didn't want to alienate anyone, Anthony Marr said Tuesday… Marr believes many more people would have become bear petition canvassers in rural areas, but they've been intimidated by a strong counter reaction to the ban-bear-hunting campaign, especially in the Central Interior…

But he added, "We've got a job to do, and we're giving it our best shot."…

1996-11-13 *The Globe and Mail* (national)
[Bear-hunt ban sought]
The WCWC is sending a team of environmentalists to Prince George in a last ditch effort to gather signatures to ban bear hunting in BC. The group will set up near polling stations during the civic elections on Saturday, said campaign direct Anthony Marr… Only 20,000 signatures have been turned in to the Committee (to date).

1996-11-14 *The Free Press*, Prince George, BC   by David Plug
[City won't block bear banners from polling stations]
… A mobile campaign by the WCWC sets up shop in downtown Prince George tonight, and organizer Anthony Marr says local polling stations will be key sites for their petition for a referendum on bear hunting.

While municipal campaigners won't be allowed within 100 meters of the polls, no such restriction applies to the WCWC canvassers.

"… There's nothing in the Municipal Act that prohibits it as long as they're not interfering with the election process or campaigning for a candidate," says Joni Heinrich, Prince George's deputy city clerk.

Of some concern is how heated encounters between canvassers and hunters will become… When asked if he expected some sort of fireworks when canvassers and hunters meet face-to-face, Marr replied, "No doubt, but we are willing to deal with it when it happens. We would like people to know that this is a totally legal process and totally democratic. We are playing by the book and hope the opponents do the same."…

Their mobile campaign will travel to the Peace River region next week and could return here again on their way to Prince Rupert… (Marr) has arranged radio interviews for tomorrow morning on CBC-AM and CIRX/CJCI but not with CKPG's Ben Meisner. "I've had two encounters with him and neither one was particularly enjoyable. I don't particularly want his air time," said Marr…

1996-11-14 *Island Tides*, Victoria, BC   by Serena van Bakel
[Bear Care on election day – first citizen initiative]
… Paul George, Founding Director of WCWC, is the first person (by law, a proponents must be a person, not an organization) to seriously attempt to use BC's new Recall and Initiative Act to bring forward citizen-generated legislation…

1996-11-15 *Victoria New*, Weekend Edition   by Brian Dryden
[Bear activists piggyback on polls]

… To hit the target in the Capital Region, (WCWC's Victoria campaign coordinator Liora Freedman says the blitz of municipal election polling stations will involve more than 80 canvassers who are registered to collect signatures.

John Marshall, deputy chief electoral officer for Victoria's municipal election, says…, "As long as they are not connected to any candidates then they can do that…"…

1996-11-16 *The Citizen*, **Prince George, BC by Gordon Hoekstra**
[Bear 'ban-wagon' gets cool reception]
… Battling the wind and –10ºC temperatures, WCWC canvassers from Vancouver set up tables Friday at the intersection of Victoria Street and 7th Avenue to gather signatures… Hunter Brad Davis stopped to protest the bear skin propped on top of the 24-foot, banner-decorated motor home, which he thought was in bad taste…

"It takes a lot of guts to be out here, and they need all the support they can get," said Chris Leischner, an avowed environmentalist who signs the petition…

The 11-person caravan came to the North because the petition has struggled here…

1996-11-16 *Times Colonist*, **Victoria, BC by Malcolm Curtis**
[Bear canvassers will go ahead]
… Greg McDade, lawyer for the Sierra Legal Defense Fund, said there is nothing wrong with people collecting signatures for a petition outside a polling place.

… Terry Kirk, chief electoral officers for Saanich, said his municipality will not be preventing bear referendum supporters from gathering signatures…

1996-11-16 *Times Colonist*, **Victoria, BC by Malcolm Curtis**
[Hunting foes target voters in bid to force referendum]
… Organizers of the Ban Bear Hunting Initiative say they will have canvassers outside 53 of 57 polling stations in Greater Victoria on voting day, in a bid to gather more than 20,000 signatures.

"We are quite shy of our goal," says Liora Freedman of WCWC… As of Tuesday, the group said it had collected fewer than 3,000 signatures from the 7 provincial ridings around Victoria.

"That's misleading," said Freedman, noting that many canvassers have collected more signatures, but have not yet mailed them in…

1996-11-19-2 *The Globe and Mail*, **national by Gordon Gibson**
[The bears and the ballot]

… On December 8 in BC, if the WCWC has its way, bears will have a date with democracy… Its gladiator in this fight is Anthony Marr, a Chinese-Canadian born in China… Mr. Marr feels a special ethnic responsibility and status in this crusade, which he has been pursuing with extraordinary intensity, barnstorming the province…

1996-11-19   *Alberni Valley Times*, Port Alberni, BC by Diane Morrison [Physician takes up cause of wild bears in valley]
Mike Barrett would rather see Black bears used as a natural resource to attract tourists than to see them used as an attraction for hunters to kill… Dr. Barrett is one of the volunteers collecting signatures…

"Eco-tourism, and soft adventure tourism, is the biggest growth area in the economy on the West Coast…," he said…

1996-11-20   *The Vancouver Sun*   Canadian Press [Bear-hunt foe threatens to sue]
Prince George - … Barney Kern of the WCWC was collecting signatures in the Civic Centre on Saturday while voting took place.

He said he was ordered to leave by chief electoral officer Allan Chabot and city manager George Paul. "We do not need permission to collect signatures in a public place," said Kern…

1996-11-20   *The Mirror*, Sooke, BC   by Mitch Moore [Bear hunting protestors cry foul]
… Kerry Fedosenko, the returning officer at the Saseenos school polling station, said she was instructed by the chief electoral officer Thomas Moore to ask a lone canvasser to move from the school… The canvasser, Jefferson Bray, complied.

Later, however, Bray and two other supporters moved back closer to the entrance and Moore contacted the Sooke RCMP.

Bray said he reluctantly complied until he was told by other 'Bear Day' volunteers that Fedosenko had no authority to ask him to move.

"I was told that I was well within my rights to be there. I wasn't blocking people's access and I was not representing any of the candidates… He refused to move when asked by RCMP officers. They eventually let him stay…

1996-11-21   *The Tribune*, Williams Lake, BC   by Jonathan Desbarats [Bear campaign confrontation]
A group campaigning to ban bear hunting in BC was turfed out of Boltanio Mall

yesterday after a confrontation with the president of the Williams Lake Sportsman's Association...

1996-11-21 *The Daily News*, Kamloops, BC
[Bear Care-A-Van parked for petition]
... while (Marr) was in Prince George, one man threatened to punch him in the face and another deliberately bumped his shoulder while walking past... hard enough to spin Marr around.
But in two days, 1,700 signatures were gathered in Prince George...

1996-11-22 *Kamloops This Week* by Jennifer Muir
[Hunting protest in homestretch]
WCWC volunteers Barney Kern and Jon French do their best to stay warm while collecting signatures on the ban the bear hunt petition at the corner of Third and Victoria Thursday... WCWC spokesman Anthony Marr says at present the organization has up to 40,000 signatures...

1996-11-22 *The Daily News*, Kamloops, BC
[Bear-ban campaign passes through city, collects 450 more signatures on petition]
... You couldn't miss Gloria Fraser, decked out in a hot pink snowsuit as she asked passersby if they wanted to put their names to a petition to stop bear hunting in the province.
"I have watched the demise of our wildlife for over 50 years," she said....

1996-11-24 *Ming Pao*, global (Chinese) by Eric Chan
[Ma Shiu-Sang incites Chinese Canadians to sign anti-bear-hunt petition]
... Ma Shiu-Sang and his volunteers gathered several hundred signatures at the Aberdeen Centre in Richmond yesterday...

1996-11-25 *The Trail Times* by David Wilford
[Shoot surplus bears and cougars]
To the Editor: ... The next enemy we have is a guy called Marr...

1996-11-26 *The Penticton Herald*
[Sights set on saving bears]
... Barney Kern... At his own expense, he took time off work and rented a motor

home to collect signatures for the Ban Bear Hunting Initiative…

1996-11-29 *The Free Press*, Prince George, BC by B. Elliott
[Bear hunting ban signers should be proud]
I was not surprised by the intimidating, dirty behavior of some wildlife killers during Western Canada Wilderness Committee's visit… Some wildlife killers and their supporters carried over their violent actions from defenseless animals to non-violent animal supporters, going so far as to tear up petition sheets filled with signatures…

1996-11-30 *The Vancouver Sun* by Ian Graysom
[Who cares about bears?]
… Marr… says while Kenya and India had outlawed lion and tiger hunting respectively, "Canada is still quagmired in the 'Great White Hunter' tradition."…

1996-12-02 *Salmon Arm Shoppers' Guide*
[Bear Caravan stops in Salmon Arm]
…according to (WCWC volunteer) Jon French… a small percentage of people exhibited very childish behaviour, swearing, and even shouting racial epithets as they passed by. These racial slurs were directed at Anthony Marr, who is Chinese Canadian. He has led the drive to prevent bear hunting…

1996-12-04 *The Courier Islander*, Campbell River by Dan MacLennan
[Anti-bear hunt backers get cool local reception]
Supporters of a total ban on bear hunting collected signatures in Campbell River Monday despite some less than friendly responses.
 "We got kicked out of the Tyee Plaza around 11:30 even though we had permission," (WCWC Bear-Care-a-Van member) Steve Quattrocchi said…

1996-12-04 *The Mirror*, Campbell River, BC by Matthew Plumtree
[Protesters, hunters clash]
Chilly temperatures and a posse of hunters… made life difficult for those seeking signatures… "I was trying to be a dink, but after all these years, it sure feels good," said (local hunting guide David) Fyfe…

1996-12-04 *The Times*, Maple Ridge, BC by Corinne Jackson
[Bear petition on the hunt for names]
…There are about 20 people gathering names locally… Mike Gildersleeve said he's

collected about 400 himself… The response has been "really positive", he added. "People that have seen me come marching up and ask 'Where can I sign?'"…

1996-12-07 *The Vancouver Sun* **by Herb Gilbert**
[Who cares about bears? Quite a few readers.]
… I hope more people will come to see the big picture of what is happening to planet Earth. And when the light goes on in their minds, they will turn green, like the Paul Georges and Anthony Marrs of this world.

1996-12-07 *The Vancouver Sun* **by Larry Pynn**
[Bear-hunting petition falls short]
… (WCWC founder Paul) George said efforts to collect signatures were hampered on a number of fronts - canvassers were frequently denied permission to operate in rural shopping malls, hunters shadowed canvassers and intimidated citizens who might have otherwise signed…

1996-12-07 *Times Colonist*, **Victoria, BC** **by Malcolm Curtis**
[Anti-hunting effort falls short]
BC's referendum law needs to be rewritten, otherwise the public will never have a chance to vote on any initiative… Anthony Marr acknowledges Friday the group's bid to force a referendum on the hunting issue will fall short… In Washington state, where voters last month approved an initiative to ban hunting of bears using dogs and bait… The Washington referendum system has more relaxed rules…

1996-12-10 *The Province*, **Vancouver, BC** **by Charlie Anderson**
[Drive for bear-hunting referendum falls short]
Supporters of a ballot on bear hunting are bloody but unbowed… "The law itself is an ass," said (WCWC founder Paul) George, who favors referendums based on the U.S. model. "No issue, no group could ever get that amount of signatures all sorted by electoral district."…

1996-12-10 *The Province*, **Vancouver, BC** **by Michael Smyth**
[Law "designed to fail"]
… Critics then and now have attacked the Recall and Initiative Act as unworkable, phony legislation.

And now we have proof… The group had an emotional issue, apparently broad public support, hundreds of volunteers and one of the environmental movement's

best-organized, well-financed public relations machine at its disposal.
    Despite these resources, the group's BC-wide petition drive fell far short…

1996-12-17   *Positive Action News*, **Victoria, BC**   by Nicholas Ford
[The fight to help bears through the tool of law]
… Anthony Marr is October's hero… He has bravely faced up to repeated intimidation from hunters and debates them on lecture tours. He is a man with a vision… (His) activism in BC on bears is based on excellent foresight…

1996-12-18   *News Leader*, **Burnaby, BC**   by Rob Gerein
[Bear hunters come under fire]
… The majority of the population doesn't like guns, doesn't like trophy hunting and, increasingly, they don't like hunters…

1996-12   *Sing Tao Daily News* **(Chinese), global**
[Three Chinese-Canadian eco-warriors]
… Anthony Marr's prime motive is to ensure a healthy and beautiful world for our children… He plans to go straight into the tigers' homelands - India, China… to save them where they live…

1996-12-28   *The Vancouver Sun*, **West Coast People**
[1996's Top 10 - The leaders who made a difference]
… Anthony Marr…has been in a showdown with bear hunters, who aren't taking kindly to his quest…

    ❖   ❖   ❖   ❖   ❖

1996-12-31

    New Year's Eve. Time to summarize a very good year.
    First and foremost and be all and end all of course is Christopher. I am his "godfather", but I love him as I would my own son, and in the near constant absence of "Dada", he all but considers me as any child would his own father. Christine wants me to go through some kind of church Godfatherhood ceremony, but I declined. There is nothing any ceremony in any church that can add to the promise I

have made directly to Christopher and to myself, and to God if you must. On the contrary, I feel that it would distract from the purity of my promise and further, perhaps even cheapen it by imposing some institutional covenant over it. I am here because I want to be here, not because some institution tells me to be here. I have always been pro-essence and anti-ritual, and after all these years, Christine should know it if not respect it.

Almost every weekend, I would take Christopher out by myself to give Christine a break. He loves the outdoors – forests, beaches, rivers, lakes… He loves animals – my cats, horses in the field, birds on the wing, fish beneath the waves… And like any child, he loves playgrounds. And with his enjoyment of them, his vocabulary of them grows accordingly.

Often times, during the week, Christine would also ask me to baby-sit Christopher when she goes with her friends on their "ladies' night out".

Again I must acknowledge Christine's inestimable trust in me. On my part, I'm always very safety conscious. I never ever let Christopher out of my sight. I'm always kind and gentle with him. I never ever use coercion on him, but always use reason with him. I interact with him closely and as an equal. He looks to me for protection, for safety, for security, for guidance, but most of all for friendship. I'm always there for him whenever he needs me. We are physically and emotionally very close, always holding hands, hugging, piggy-backing, talking, laughing… At home, we play our "castle" games, I give him "airplane rides", I help him brush his teeth, give him baths, read him bed time stories, tuck him in… In the car, while on the way out or in, he usually sleeps. I take care to shield him from the sun, keep him dry in the rain and warm in the snow. I am the only dedicated man in his life. I love him more than any other person in mine - past, present and, I have little doubt, future. I cannot understand why some fathers are so neglectful, let alone abusive, to their own biological offspring. Christopher can't say much yet, but he can fill volumes with the pure love of a child.

❖   ❖   ❖   ❖   ❖

1997-01   *Wildlife News and Views*   **by Andrea Stevens, North West Wildlife Preservation Society**

[Seeking an end to Bear hunting in BC]
… Motivation for attempting the huge petition came from a 1995 Angus Reid poll

Omni-Science and the Human Destiny

which showed that 78% of those polled support banning trophy hunting of black bears in BC…

1997-01-11-6   *The Review*, Richmond, BC   by David DaSilva
[Hunting presentation called off in latest enviro-hunting clash]
… Students in an environmental club at Palmer Secondary School arranged to have Anthony Marr… speak… But when Doug Walker of the BC Wildlife Federation heard about it, and (told the school to either cancel out on Marr or give them equal time), the event was (suspended)…

1997-01-17   *Daily News*, Nanaimo, BC   by Anthony Marr
[Vanderhorst misled with numbers]
… WCWC's stand on the anti-hunting campaign is to start and end with the bear, but for once, Vanderhorst is right about me. I am against recreational and trophy hunting… of any species… Ultimately, everything has to do with one species - our own, regarding how civilized we truly are.

1997-02-13-4   *The Vancouver Sun*   by Anthony Marr
[Tiger, tiger, burning…out?]
… If we commit to Gaia our heart and soul, our children may just see a new world emerge, one more compassionate than ever before, perhaps one destined for the stars.

1997-03   *New Internationalist* magazine   by Ross Crockford
[Bad Medicine – Ross Crockford tells the story of a man who has stepped on toes from Campbell River to Hong Kong to stop a pernicious trade…]
Anthony Marr knows what it feels like to be endangered. Last summer the Vancouver environmentalist was touring small towns in British Columbia… Often the reception he got was downright hostile. Many people in the countryside claimed he was trying to destroy their livelihood and their heritage...

   Now, Marr is taking his campaign around the world… He knows there will be some risk; organized crime is directly involved in the endangered species trade... But after tangling with British Columbia's hunters, he should be ready.

1997-03-19   *The Hindu*, Delhi, India
[In aid of the vanishing Bengal Tiger]
Finally, the BET'R Campaign of Western Canada Wilderness Committee to save

bears, elephants, tigers and rhinos has entered India as well…

1997-04-24 *The Georgia Straight* **magazine, BC by Shawn Blore [Old Superstition and New Cosmology: Anthony Marr wants to stop the medicinal use of tiger products before it destroys a magnificent species]**
Pessimist give the world's tigers 5 years. Realists, 10.

They're the kind of numbers that make you want to quietly despair, to give up, to flip the channel and think about something more pleasant. Melrose Place maybe, or Roseanne. Marr, however, whether from a sense of conceit, ignorance, or a staggering sense of confidence, saw nothing impossible in the task of bringing the tiger back from the brink...

... To highlight the extent of Vancouver's tiger trade, Marr kicked off a media blitz in January 1996. Local journalists were invited on an endangered species tour through Chinatown's apothecaries. The tour began in the low-ceilinged warren that serves as WCWC's headquarters. Marr upended his leather briefcase, spilling out 15-20 boxes of Chinese patent medicines: tiger plasters, tiger pills, tiger-based medicaments for rheumatism, tired blood, soft bones, and sexual impotence, all of them purchased in shops in Vancouver's Chinatown. Pointing to the ingredients lists on the diverse packages, Marr picked out the symbols, words, and phrases that in Latin, English and Chinese spelled out "tiger bone".

The next part of the tour was a trip along Pender, Main and Keefer Streets, with Marr indicating here and there the shops and apothecaries dealing in tiger medicinals and inviting journalists to go in and check the shelves for themselves. Six shops out of 10 stocked a variety of boxes, cartons and bottles labeled with some variation of the word Os Tigris - tiger bone.

The media loved it. Marr made it on to TV news both locally and nationally, and stories appeared in city magazines and community papers. He used his pulpit to heap scorn upon Canadian wildlife regulations. "Canada's wildlife laws could use an aphrodisiac,' Marr said, "because right now, they're totally impotent." He was equally hard-hitting in his presentations to Chinese community groups and at Eastside Vancouver high schools. Traditional Chinese medicine's use of parts of animals like tigers and rhinos, Marr said, and the cutting of many urban trees for that matter, were based on nothing but pure superstition. That superstition was destroying a magnificent species. The fact that the practice was tolerated by the Chinese-Canadian community only blackened their reputation in mainstream Canadian society.

Environmentalists heaved a sigh of relief. Here was someone tackling a problem they had long known about but dared not touch. "It's great that it's a Chinese person doing the work he's doing." said Nathalie Chalifour, World Wildlife Fund Canada's tiger expert, "because when it's a person like me doing it, well, I'm white; I'm more likely to be accused to being racist, which is really unfortunate, but it does happen."

Vancouver's Chinese media were as quick to jump on the story as their English counterparts. Marr's campaign was covered by both the Ming Pao and the Sing Tao newspapers, and he appeared on several Chinese language radio programs. According to Ming Pao columnist and CJVB radio host Gabriel Yiu, the Chinese community's reaction to Marr's campaign was mixed. His straight talk on superstition did offend some, but there was also those who took pride in the fact that a Chinese Canadian was working on environmental concerns. "For a long period of time when people are talking about monster homes, tree cutting, killing wild animals for some of their body parts," Yiu said, "people do have the impression that the Chinese community is the cause of that. I think the work Anthony did set a very good example that we do have people in the Chinese community who are concerned about these issues."...

According to Vancouver city councilor Don Lee, Marr's effectiveness was limited... "I don't know Anthony Marr that well. The Chinese Community doesn't know him well at all," Lee said. "We don't know where he comes from. We don't know why he's doing all this." As it turns out, those are two of the most interesting questions that could be asked about Anthony Marr.

Born in February 1944, in southern China, Anthony Seeu-Sung Marr fled to Hong Kong along with the rest of his family shortly after the Communist revolution. Family legend has Marr's father burning the deeds of the family's extensive land-holdings for a moment's warmth during the first refugee winter...

(In 1965), Marr came to Canada to study science at the University of Manitoba... At the same time, his relationship with a Hong Kong girl fell to bits when she dropped him on orders from her parents. Marr has never forgiven Chinese culture for the snub. "As a result of that incident, I have never dated a Chinese girl again," Marr said. It's a decision that isolated him somewhat from the Chinese community, but, according to Marr, it also allowed him to integrate more fully into Canadian society than other Chinese immigrants of his generation.

In 1966, Marr switched over to the physics department of the University of British Columbia. His summers he spent in the bush in northern Manitoba and British Columbia, working as a geologist's assistant. It was work that can only be idealized by someone who has never done it. Marr said, "The student is the geologist's personal servant - more like slave, considering the pay, which was only $280 per month. I made and carried his lunch, and every few feet, the geologist would pick up a rock sample about twice the size of my fist and drop it into my knapsack. I had to carry that ever-heavier thing all day, wading into swamps that would sometimes come up to my chest or higher. Your shirt would be black with flies and mosquitoes. There could be a bear behind every tree. It was brutal, but also absolutely beautiful. And this was how I bonded with nature."

After he graduated with a B.Sc. in 1970, Marr took a job as a live-in housefather for emotionally disturbed kids, then a career in real estate. He said he had a heavy student loan to pay off. One senses he also had a need to gain acceptance among the Vancouver business community. "I made rookie of the year, then Gold Club, Diamond Club, all that," Marr said. "I bought a couple of horses - hunters-jumpers - and got involved with the high social elite you see down in Southlands." Snap shots from the time show a short-haired Marr in boots and riding breeches, sitting atop a bay Thoroughbred gelding.

The real estate phased continued for several years. Marr bought a small acreage in the suburbs. He dated but never married. "The work first became routine, then boring, then irksome, then unbearable. I was still good at it, but the initial challenge was gone," he said.

About this time, things took a strange turn. Whether from boredom, a need to be alone, or perhaps simple a desire to see the sights, he left his job and set off on a solo journey in East Africa, primarily in the Kilimanjaro, Serengeti, Ngorongoro Crater and Olduvai Gorge region of Tanzani. At some point during that three month sojourn, something happened that changed the whole focus of Marr's life…

Whether his confidence came stems from, when the "'19th-century scholar' decided to prove himself as an environmental saviour, he displayed a thoroughly 19th century sense of ambition...

… Although some conservationists predict the tiger will be extinct in five years, Anthony Marr is convinced he can reverse the prophecy…

… China imported the equivalent of 400 grown tigers and exported 27 million tiger derivative products from 1990 to 1993… About 39,000 individual tiger containing products were seized in BC in 1996, including everything from medicinals to tiger claws…

A Vancouver branch of Asian Conservation Awareness Program is planning to begin an ad blitz this June, timed to coincide with the dragon-boat festival. Ironically, Marr will likely not be invited to participate. According to ACAP's Vancouver organizer Ling Zheng, Marr's confrontational style doesn't fit in with ACAP's approach, which hinges on establishing partnerships with the Chinese community groups and obtaining sponsorship from prominent corporations. "We're trying to reach out to the Chinese community, so we try not to use his name," Zheng said. "If we mention Anthony Marr, I will probably not get any help from organizations like SUCCESS or the Chinese Cultural Centre. He can be quite harsh towards certain Chinese people, and I've even heard that in the Chinese community he's considered like a traitor."

Whether that's true or not, Marr has shifted his efforts from reducing consumption into preserving tiger habitat. With the aid of a $75,000 grant from the Canadian International Development Agency, Marr has gone to India to work towards protecting two Indian tiger reserves from encroachment and poaching by local villagers. The plan is to take a traveling multi-media show to villages around the tiger reserves and convince the villagers that the tiger is worth more to them alive than dead.

"Do you think these women enjoy walking five miles every day into the bush to collect a bunch of twigs and carry it back to the village on top of their heads? They do it because they have no choice," Marr said. "If we give them a choice and say, Look, we're going to develop ecotourism, we're going to organize tourist groups to come to your village, and maybe you can develop some native products to sell to them… Wouldn't you rather stay at home and weave baskets with your kids than walk five miles to haul water?" Other conservationists from other groups have made these arguments before, often with little success, but with characteristic confidence, Marr is convinced he will succeed….

1997-05-08   *The Georgia Straight*, Vancouver   by Roland Goetz
[Save tigers rather than saving feelings]

… According to the article ([Bloody Superstition] - April 14), Garry Grigg of the Canadian Wildlife Service says, "We don't want to be too heavy. We have got too many new Canadians here, and it takes a while to assimilate. We're dealing with something that is thousands of years old."

My question is, would we allow other cultural practices, such as incest, clitoral mutilation, bestiality, or polygamy, to be imported into Canada?…

… to save some feelings, we (may be allowing) a magnificent species to be destroyed.

1997-05-15
[Korea Leads Illegal Trade in Bear Parts]

LONDON — (ENS) - In a report released this week, an international coalition of wildlife organizations, including the London-based World Society for the Protection of Animals (WSPA), expose South Korea92s leading role in the illegal trade in bear parts. The report, "Killed for Korea" concludes that "South Korea and Korean people abroad represent the bears' worst enemy after habitat loss."

Undercover film recently taken by animal campaigners shows Korean-sponsored bear poaching and gallbladder smuggling on an international scale as well as the killing of endangered bears for South Korean restaurant-goers.

The bears are desired for bear paw soup, a highly prized delicacy in South Korea. Diners will pay in excess of US$1,000 for a bowl of bear paw soup.

WSPA, together with the Korean Federation for the Environment Movement (KFEM), Humane Society of the US/Humane Society International (HSUS/HSI) and the Global Survival Network (GSN), is lobbying the US government to sanction South Korea over the illegal trade in bear parts. The organizations, with a total membership of over four million people worldwide, are considering an international boycott campaign of Korean goods, if their current approaches to Korean authorities are unsuccessful.

Andrew Dickson, WSPA chief executive, said, "Consumption of bear parts is a national disgrace for South Korea. We are trying to persuade the Korean authorities to stop this illegal trade which is pushing Asian bears towards extinction."

WSPA's campaign is being backed by the Korean Federation for the Environment Movement (KFEM). Kwon Heanyol, spokesperson for KFEM said, "This outdated practice is a slur on our national reputation. It makes us look cruel and barbaric. Herbal, synthetic and Western alternatives exist for bear gallbladder. Why can't all Koreans use these instead of continuing to torture and slaughter bears?"

Anthony Marr, organizer of Bears, Elephants, Tigers, Rhinos (BETR), a conservation campaign based in Vancouver, British Columbia, confirms that South Korea is the world's leading consumer of bear parts. Marr says, "South Koreans sometimes import black bears on the pretext of using them for zoo exhibits, then they have them killed in front of restaurant customers to prove authenticity and freshness."

Marr says he has read reports of caged bears lowered live onto hot coals to have their paws cooked. This procedure is supposed to guarantee freshness, authenticity and entertainment for the customer.

Marr has a video showing a 1989 restaurant menu from the posh Hilton hotel in Seoul offering "bear palm soup. Price - current."

Bear paws are considered a delicacy, not a medicinal, but bear gall bladders are prized for their medicinal effect.

The powdered bile taken from the bear galls has a whole range of uses, primarily for digestive healing and intestinal illnesses including parasites and bacterial infections. The powdered bile is used as an anti-spasmodic, a pain-killer, tranquillizer, an anti-allergenic, and a cough remedy. It is also considered to be a general purpose body tuning tonic. Bear bile is even said to restore a liver damaged by overdrinking.

Unlike tiger bones and rhino horns which have no real medicinal value, bear galls do contain ursodeoxycolic acid which does have a medicinal effect. This acid was patented as a synthetic in Japan in the 1930s. Today, 150 tons are used annually worldwide.

There are seven species of bears in the world, excluding the panda and koala, which are not considered to be true bears. Three bear species are endangered, particularly the Asiatic black bear, which used to be the main source of galls. The Asiatic black bear is now almost completely wiped out in China and Korea.

To meet the demand from Korea and other Asian countries, poachers have been taking bears from Russia and North America. Marr says poaching is "huge" in North America. Poachers have been caught in British Columbia recently, but provincial laws have no teeth, as the indigenous bears are not yet listed as endangered.

The penalty is very light when poachers are caught in B.C. Marr says, "Someone recently caught with 90 galls, which would easily sell for US$250,000 thousand in Korea, was fined $3,500 bucks, not even the price of one gall in Korea. For every batch of poached bear parts discovered by law enforcement officers, 49 get away. Customs officials estimate they can check only 2-3% of what goes out of Canada."

Marr estimates that between 20,000 and 40,000 bears are poached in Canada yearly. Legal trophy hunting kills 22,000 more.

In London, the WSPA is offering broadcast quality undercover footage showing the killing of endangered bears for South Korean diners and the farming of bears in China, some of which are destined for the Korean market

From the Environment News Service: http://www.envirolink.org/environews/ens/.

1997-05-18-3 *The Free Press*, **Prince George, BC   by David Plug [Poaching for gall-bladders – Asian demand pushes up numbers, says conservationists]**
Animal advocates and wildlife officials agree that most poachers of bear parts are never caught, but differ wildly on the scale of the problem in the north,

To Anthony Marr… last week's laying of 67 charges for unlawful possession of bear parts against a Prince George resident is just the tip of the iceberg…

1997-05-25-1 *The Vancouver Sun* **by Anthony Marr [Unbearable bear facts]**

Anthony Marr

Recent radio ads (by the BC Wildlife Federation) portray deliberate misrepresentations of truth… that "96% of BC's residents rejected" last year's Bear Referendum objective, citing that only 4% of BC's residents signed the petition…

… the ad itself is a demonstration of the usual illogic and dishonesty of the trophy hunters, and shows that the BC Wildlife Federation is worried. If they really believe that 96% of BC's residents support trophy hunting, what do they have to worry about?

1997-07   Discovery Channel, cable TV - *Forbidden Places* series
[Killer instincts]

Forbidden Places' examines Canada's thriving poaching trade - … Only small victories can be claimed. For a bigger victory, there must be a public outrage - which may begin with programs like this. – Anthony Marr featured.

1997-07-08   *The Ottawa Citizen*, Ottawa, Ontario   by Finbar O'Reilly
[Animal activist targets Chinatown]

… One Ottawa professor of traditional Chinese medicine, who asked not to be identified, said she abides by Canada's laws banning the sale of tiger and bear parts, but that doesn't mean she agrees with them.

"How come you have to protect the tiger, but not the cow?" she asked. "I am a doctor. I want to treat people. If you care more about human than animal (sic), then why not use animal parts for safety?"…

Mr. Marr, who plans a visit to the Chinatowns of both Toronto and Ottawa (to demonstrate that the new law) is not being properly enforced…

1997-07-11   *The Toronto Sun*   by Tom Godfrey
[Tiger goods on shelf]

"… Toronto has become a hotbed for the sale of animal parts, including penises…," said Anthony Marr…

… within an hour he was able to buy processed medicines containing or claiming to contain tiger bone, seal penis, deer penis…

1997-07-15   *The Globe and Mail*, national   by Michael Valpy
[The trade in seal and tiger parts]

This is a Canadian story. Anthony Marr, a Chinese Canadian who lives in Vancouver, is sitting in a Toronto hotel restaurant waiting for a television crew.

When the crew arrives, he will take its members to Toronto's Chinese community's downtown commercial district on Spadina Avenue. Here they will wire him with a microphone and film him buying illegal tiger bone pills and legal, regrettably, seal penis pills…

Mr. Marr, an intense man, says he (as a Chinese Canadian) has been embarrassed by all these practices…

1997-09   **Video production**   **by Terry Brooks**
[Unbearable] – on Anthony Marr's BET'R Campaign
Winner of: Global Vision Award / 1997 Cascadia Festival of Moving Images, Award of Excellence (3rd) / 20th Annual International Wildlife Film Festival (2nd) / International Film & Video Festival, Silver Seal Award, Merit Award for Conservation Message

❖   ❖   ❖   ❖   ❖

September 25, 1997

Christopher is on the point of verbal blossoming. For the last few weeks, he's been expanding in vocabulary daily. Now, he can name numerous kinds of animals and plants and inanimate objects, and can begin to form four-word sentences like "I love you mommy", even five-word sentences like "I love you Uncle Dodo." Music to my ears. Everything he says and does is so indescribably delightful. Everything about him is so infinitely lovable. (Have I already said this, and if so, how many times?) And he is such a loving child. I feel so honoured to be his beloved "Uncle Dodo".

And he loves his mommy. When I take him out by myself, maybe to Coquitlam River or Pacific Spirit Park, he would find something to bring back home to mama, be it a leaf or a twig or a stone or a berry. When Christine says she's tired or not well, he would go and hug her.

❖   ❖   ❖   ❖   ❖

October 1, 1997

Just on TV: "Alcoholism and the Gene". Is alcoholism genetically based? Is it hereditary? And my personal question: Has Christopher inherited a genetic predisposition to alcoholism from Charles? I hope and pray not, but if he has, then all I can hope for is that we can build for him a strong enough emotional foundation and a high enough self-esteem for him to overcome his genetic weakness. In this context I view myself as a highly beneficial source of strength for him, seeing that I have a reasonably solid emotional base and a reasonably high self-esteem, plus the guarantee that I do not drink – since I have a genetic predisposition to get an immediate hangover upon ingesting any alcohol, so why bother? I have never experienced being drunk in my life, but however nice it might feel, I'm glad I would have not occasion to subject myself to the undignified drunken behavior I have observed on skid road, and, at closer quarters, in Charles.

Also, according to the TV program, and to my own experience with emotionally disturbed children, he must be protected from traumatic experiences at all cost, especially when he is very young, since very young children with such experiences are much more prone to depressions and other psychological problems later in life, which could act as triggers to drinking. At Browndale I've experienced first hand the intensity and causes of the agonies of emotionally disturbed children. I must safeguard Christopher's emotional wellbeing to the best of my ability.

❖ ❖ ❖ ❖ ❖

1997-10-01-3 *News Leader*, **Burnaby, BC**
[Gilmore students join efforts to "Save-the-Tiger"]
… "Unless a huge conservation effort ignites now, the tiger will be extinct in the wild within a decade…" said Anthony Marr… who gives the slideshows to the schools. "Some adults say, 'How many tiger are there in Canada? Why should we be bothered?' Go ask the kids.…"

1997-10-04-6 *The Peace Arch News*, **Surrey, BC** by Tracy Holmes
[Care for the cats]
Save the tiger.

That was the message students of Peace Arch Elementary received at a presentation by… Anthony Marr…

Under the watchful eyes of a 50-foot inflatable tiger, the kids learned that only 4,000 tigers remain in the wild, and that some subspecies totaled less than the number of students in the gym.

But, "I do not believe the tiger is doomed," Anthony Marr told the kids. "The reason I believe this is because nobody has ever asked kids like you to help out. If we can get kids around the world to say, 'I want to save the tiger', I believe the tiger will be saved."…

He also asked them to come to WCWC's Save-the-Tiger Walk at Stanley Park Oct. 18.

1997-10-08-3 *The Vancouver Courier* by Gudrun Will
[Students take tiger by the tail]
High school environmental club rallies behind animal activist.

An auditorium full of Kitsilano high school students roared in appreciation…

Inspiring youth, Marr believes, is the only hope to save the rapidly diminished species in the long run…

1997-10-10-5 *The Toronto Star* by Joseph Hall
[Seals killed to fill demand for sex potions, group charges]
… Group brings together prominent Canadians…

Canadian taxpayers are subsidizing an international trade in seal penises to create dubious Chinese sex potions, a new anti-sealing group - Canadians Against the Commercial Seal Hunt - has charged…

Vancouver environmentalist Anthony Marr says seals are shot or clubbed at random and then turned over to see whether they're males.

He says that most of the seal penises harvested in this way went into Chinese aphrodisiacs that have no scientifically proven value (just like tiger penis medicines)…

1997-10-16 *The Westender*, Vancouver
[Halloween fun, Tiger Walk set]
… The WCWC has organized Save-the-Tiger Walk '97…

1997-10-19-7 *The Province*, Vancouver
[Walking for wildlife]
Hundreds of concerned people took part in the 'Save-the-Tiger Walk' in Vancouver's Stanley Park yesterday. They were walking to raise money to protect the dwindling number of tigers left in the wild.

1997-10-19-7 *Ming Pao Daily News* **(Chinese), global**

[1,000 people walk to save 4,000 tigers]
WCWC's Save-the-Tiger Walk attracted over 1,000 children and their teachers and parents, and raised $20,000…

1997-10-29-3 *The Comox Valley Echo* **by Diane Radmore**
[Service to remember animals]
Animal lovers of all kinds are invited to come hear guest speakers and attend an outdoor gathering called In Remembrance of the Animals at noon Saturday, November 1, at the Sid Williams Foundation in downtown Courtenay…

… Anthony Marr, initiator of the worldwide BET'R Campaign… will also be in attendance…

1997-10-31-5 *The Comox Valley Record* **by Diane Radmore**
[Vigil for lost wildlife]
Local activists to speak at downtown rally tomorrow…

… Since last year's referendum on bear hunting in BC campaign, Marr has been to India on behalf of the dwindling tiger population and was a guest speaker at last week's International Fund for Animal Welfare Conference concerning the East Coast seal hunt…

1997-11-08-6 *The Vancouver Sun* **by Alex Strachan**
[Mason Lee can be bright, witty and hugely irritating]
On the Edge (Global TV), with Robert Mason Lee…

… A recent debate between Vancouver Aquarium director John Nightingale, UBC animal welfare professor Dan Weary, Western Canada Wilderness Committee scientist Anthony Marr and the Humane Society's Ingrid Pollack about the moral and ethical implications of keeping whales in captivity was informative and captivating.

Another recent discussion about smokers' rights… was pointless and irritating…

❖ ❖ ❖ ❖ ❖

1998-01-21 *The Vancouver Sun* **by Stephen Hume**
[Bear hunting foe attacked in city]
BC environmentalist Anthony Marr is recovering after being beaten by a burly man who said, "Let this be a lesson to you."

[Photo] Caption: Beaten but unbowed – Anthony Marr says he is undeterred in his campaign despite beating.

An environmentalist known for his opposition to bear hunting and the black market for animal parts was recovering Tuesday after being attacked in Vancouver's West End.

Anthony Marr said he was waylaid about 7:30 p.m. Monday in the 1600 block of Haro Street as he made his way to his car after a dinner with his parents at their home.

Environmental groups have been complaining about a sharp increase in threats of physical violence directed at their members…

"I was parked in the lane", Marr said. "There was this guy waiting for me by my car. He advanced a few steps and said, 'Are you Anthony Marr?' I said yes and he immediately launched his attack."

Marr… said his assailant was "over six feet and around 200 pounds" and rained blows upon his head and face, fracturing facial bones and damaging his eye socket.

"Then he said, 'Let this be a lesson to you,' and walked off," Marr said.

The University of British Columbia Hospital confirmed that Marr was admitted and treated in the emergency ward shortly after 7:30 p.m. Vancouver city police confirmed receiving his report of the attack about 8:40 p.m.

Marr recently led a controversial and widely publicized Western Canada Wilderness Committee campaign to have bear hunting banned in BC.

He has also been active in successfully pressuring government for controls in the black market on endangered species parts in the Asian community…

Marr's silver 1993 Mazda sports car and its license plate became well known during the anti-hunting campaign, he says.

Marr drove 12,000 kilometers and visited almost every significant community in BC during the summer of 1996, holding public and private meetings that laid the groundwork for a province-wide initiative petition towards driving a referendum vote on banning bear hunting.

Campaigners obtained 93,000 signatures in a 90-day blitz that mobilized 1,800 volunteers, but fell well short of the 250,000 or 10 percent of the electorate - needed to force government action under recall and initiative legislation.

The petition campaign, however, gave Marr a high media profile.

He said he was constantly harassed by pro-hunting (forces). Pickup trucks tailgated his car and he received anonymous threats of violence by phone.

"My reaction is that it merely strengthens my resolve to continue with this campaign…"

Paul George, a director of the Western Canada Wilderness Committee, described the attack on Marr as "deplorable" and said it was time for police and government to take seriously the "threats of violence and all the rhetoric that our people are subjected to."

"I think this [violent rhetoric] unleashes hate against environmentalists just as much as it does against Jews or people of a different sexual persuasion or anything like that," George said.

1998-01-21 *Ming Pao Daily News* (Chinese), global
[Ma Seeu-Sung assaulted]
… Around 7:30 yesterday evening, when Ma was returning to his car after a dinner with his parents, a man approached him and asked if he was Anthony Marr. When Marr said 'Yes', the man launched his fist attack…

"It was so fast and sudden I didn't even have time to turn the other cheek," Ma added with a wry grin…

1998-01-22 *The WestEnder*, Vancouver
[Protector of bears mauled by attacker]
… Anthony Marr received a flurry of blows to the face and head, resulting in a fractured cheekbone and damaged eye socket…

1998-01-26 *Canadian Firearms Digest*
From: H. Roy Stephens
Subject: Anthony Marr
… As it was reported here, he suffered broken facial bones including damage to the orbit of one of his eyes. That is hardly a "bloody nose". Furthermore, in light of the fact he WAS the target of verbal threats regarding bodily harm from some of the more brain dead and irresponsible alleged members of the hunting fraternity, it becomes quite obviously newsworthy.

Emotional issue + verbal threats + serious assault = the news. Simple.

Not so simple I'm afraid. His injuries when reported in medical terminology sound impressive indeed. However, they weren't. Moreover he makes it his business to command attention by whatever means to promote his cause. Further more, regardless of who made the threats, (assuming they were in fact made - I'm more of a skeptic each day) there is not a shred of evidence to connect anyone or any group with his misfortune. To convict the hunting fraternity in absentia & by implication is only newsworthy if you don't have a critical bone in your body, and I stand by my assessment of the CBC Afternoon Show interviewer in that regard.

Now that he has been beaten up - whether by a hunter or by somebody involved in the illicit animal parts trade - the yapping of the idiots will come back to haunt hunters. A very tiny minority threatened to physically harm him, and now he has indeed been seriously beaten. How does this make us look as hunters to the non-committed citizen out there - most of whom get their view of the world from the mainstream media? Whoever is responsible did hunters a major disservice.

Just to put it in perspective he was not seriously beaten. As he stated he was punched in the face a couple times and was fine from the neck down. He walked away after the incident. I agree that the yapping will come back to haunt hunters. If you were in his shoes that is exactly what you would want! Again, we do not know if a hunter or poacher was involved. Don't fall into their trap. For all we know he has other enemies. He says he has none, but are you willing to take his word for it?...

That the CBC unwittingly has been aiding Mr. Marr is very much to its discredit. Where is the balanced coverage?

I don't think covering a serious criminal assault after the man was publically (sic) threatened is exactly unbalanced coverage. He claims the assailant said it was for his stand on bear hunting - should CBC feel obligated to not report what a victim says his assailants said?

I listened to the CBC interview and Marr clearly stated that the only thing his assailant said was, "Are you Anthony Marr?" Serious criminal assault? I guess it's all relative. I don't see it that way…

1998-01-29   *cdn-firearms-digest@broadway.sfn.saskatoon.sk.ca*
From: Rick Lowe
Subject: **Anthony Marr**
Re.: "I have watched this thread develop and I am a cynic. I do not think it is beyond the realm of possibility that this was a staged beating to garner sympathy from the public."

Well, perhaps the doubters are right and I am wrong. Perhaps Marr did arrange to have himself beaten to the point where he suffered facial fractures which had the potential to damage his eyesight, threaten his life, or even kill him.

Maybe there is something for us to learn here - we have much in common. Marr has been fighting a losing battle to have legislation allowing bear hunting thrown out. We have been fighting a losing battle to have legislation which bans and prohibits firearms thrown out. I guess the only question that remains is if we can meet the dedication that Marr has apparently demonstrated in arranging the beating he took.

So... we need a few volunteers willing to undergo a beating severe enough to inflict some skull fractures in hopes of getting a sound byte on the news some night. Hands up please, volunteers... line forms to the right.

Come, come, surely some of us can meet the same level of dedication as that shown by a contemptible, lying anti hunter like Marr. If he can "take the bullet" to the extent he did to further his cause, then it seems that hunters and shooters as dedicated as we are would be willing to just as eagerly step forward for a similar beating. The chances are reasonably good that these injuries will heal with no permanent effects - Marr apparently lucked out, and our volunteers probably will as well...

For myself, I reluctantly admit that I'll stick to letter writing, informing others, legally monkey-wrenching the system, and bugging my MP. I don't have the courage that Marr and our volunteers have, to willingly submit to those kind (sic) of injuries in hopes of getting a one day sound byte in the news.

1998-01-31 *Sing Tao Daily* **(Chinese), global**
[The next Year of the Tiger may see no more wild tigers]
… Anthony Marr calls upon all Chinese, Japanese and Korean people around the world to stop using tiger bone, bear gall and rhino horn medicines…

1998-01-31 *Ming Pao Daily* **(Chinese), global**
[Tigers may be extinct within one decade]
… Anthony Marr speaks out from the Year of the Tiger booth at Aberdeen Centre…

1998-02-24 *The News, Parksville* **- Qualicum Beach, BC**
[WCWC's Bear Man returns to QB]
Anthony Marr will be in Qualicum Beach next Tuesday, presenting slides of his two recent trips to India…

Marr has stirred up a media storm…

Marr will be "Champions of the Tiger" in Omni-Film's Champions of the Wild series on Discovery Channel this fall…

1998-02-24 *Comox Valley Echo* **Fireweed**
[Saving the Tiger theme for slideshow]
… Please come out to witness the beauty of these magnificent animals and celebrate the ray of hope that Anthony brings us.

1998-02- *The Free Press*, **Nanaimo, BC**

["Champion of the Tiger" visits]
The "Champion of the Tiger" will share his story with Nanaimo…
    The slideshow starts at 7:30 p.m. at the Maffeo-Sutton auditorium… on March 5…"

❖ ❖ ❖ ❖ ❖

1998-02-25

I'm enjoying my birthday present to myself. The present is in the form of a low-keyed tiger conservation educational and media outreach road tour that would take me throughout Vancouver Island in a week. Finally a low risk road tour. I invited Christine and Christopher to come with me, and to the glee of all three of us, she accepted.

During the drive down the Island Highway, while Christopher was asleep in the baby seat which is permanent fixture in my car, Christine said, "With this in your car, you can never pick up any women."

"I don't care," I said, quite automatically.

Christine said something to me that moved me to tears. "Tony, I want you to know how much I value your friendship. You have been wonderful to Christopher and a loyal friend to me. I know that when I need you for anything, you would always be there. When mom was dying, you are the one to come to the hospital almost daily to give me support – I know how you dread hospitals! We've known each other for more than two decades and have been through many things together, good and bad. I hope that we will always keep the good things in mind and if possible forget the bad ones. I know that I've been mean to you once every so often. Please forgive me. I love you and I hope you love me. I know that you love Christopher as you would your own child, and I know he loves you as he would his own father. And, by the way, thank you for this trip."

All I could do was to take hold of her left hand with my right, steer the car with my left, and let my tears stream unintercepted down my face.

❖ ❖ ❖ ❖ ❖

1998-02-27   *The Comox Valley Record*

[Tigers in danger]
WCWC hopes all to celebrate the Chinese Year of the Tiger with Anthony Marr...

1998-03   *Technocracy Digest*   **by Bette Hiebert**
[The Year of the Tiger - so, why are they killing them?]
For money, of course...

    Anthony Marr... is on his way to challenge the East Asian destroyers in their lairs, to confront these people who are making millions killing these beautiful cats...

    Mr. Marr believes that if we commit to the Earth our heart and soul, our children may see a new world more compassionate than ever before. We hope he is right, but as long as there is the almighty dollar, there will be no compassion, and our children will see nothing but barren earth...

1998-03-21   *Times Colonist*, Victoria, BC   **by Judith Lavoie**
[Seal hunt protested with blood]
... Anthony Marr... said he does not usually advocate breaking the law. But he is considering withholding his income taxes this year because tax money is being used to subsidize the commercial seal hunt...

    [*Note: This reflects my personal view only, not that of WCWC, whose policy is to campaign strictly within the limits of the law* – Anthony Marr]

1998-04-29   *Ottawa Citizen*, Ottawa, ON   **by Michael Den Tandt**
[RCMP cracks down on trade in endangered animal parts]
Toronto - The RCMP and the Ontario Ministry of Natural Resources have taken a bite out of this city's lucrative trade in endangered animal parts, a move conservationists say is long overdue...

    Asked whether (Viagra) may take some pressure off endangered species, Mr. Marr said... "If it doesn't harm the environment, or any species, and it helps someone's quality of life, then it's a private matter."

    He added, "I've seen one or two people on TV - and they really vouch for it. Including their wives."

1998-05-13   *The Vancouver Courier*   **by Gudrun Will**
[Beating no bar to bear pal - Marr back on the road in defense of grizzlies]
Animal conservationist Anthony Marr is anything but intimidated after getting a fist in the face in a West End alley, delivered with the not-so-cryptic message: "Let this be a lesson to you."

The January attack by an unknown assailant broke his nose, cracked his cheekbone and damaged his right eye socket. Rather than shutting him up, it inspired him to undertake another road trip to stop the grizzly bear hunt in BC…

1998-05-22   *Capital News*, Kelowna, BC   by John McDonald
[Grizzly hunting under fire]
Hunters and anti-hunting activists came face-to-face last night at a forum to discuss a campaign to ban the harvest of grizzly bears…

Veteran anti-bear hunt campaigner Anthony Marr was in Kelowna hosting a multi-media presentation…

1998-05-25   *The Daily Courier*, Kelowna, BC   by Chuck Poulsen
[Protecting the Grizzlies - Project aimed at ending hunt]
Environmentalist Anthony Marr… was in the Okanagan recently as part of a six-week campaign that will take him throughout BC handing out cards that he hopes hunting foes will mail to Premier Glen Clark…

"…Estimates of the number of Grizzlies in BC vary. Marr says independent biologists put the figure at 4,000-7,000, which on the high side was the government's estimate in 1979.

"In 1980, the government was charged with over-hunting, (but instead of lowering the limit, the government) raised the population estimate to 10,000-13,000," he said. "The government and the hunters have been playing up the population and playing down the amount of poaching (to justify continued over-hunting)…"…

1998-05-27   *The Trail Times*   by Lana Rodlie
[Anti-bear-hunting campaigner struggles on]
After failure to get enough signatures in 1996 to force a referendum on the hunting of bears in the province, and after having his face seriously rearranged by someone who doesn't like his politics, Anthony Marr is back on the road, more determined than ever, to put an end to the trophy hunting of the grizzly bear in BC…

"The BC Wildlife Federation and the government have worked close together since the 1940s to… maintain hunting. It is hunting policy for hunters, by hunters," Marr said…

1998-05-29   *Capital News*, Kelowna, BC   by Judie Steeves
[Grisly details reveal the awful truth about bear attacks]
… In October 1995, this community was shocked by the deaths of a well-liked

Gorman Brothers' Lumber employee and his buddy who were both killed by a grizzly bear near Radium Hot Spring while they were hunting.

Yet, Anthony Marr… was in town last week calling for a ban on grizzly bear hunting…

1998-05-30   *The Daily Courier*, Kelowna, BC   by C.W. Holford
[Hunt controls poaching]
To the editor:
It is apparent that Anthony Marr has embarked on another pilgrimage to ensure an ample supply of grizzly bear parts for his countrymen's medicinal chest…

Though it does generate a great wealth for the few that Marr and his associates seem to be cohesive with, poaching bears generates little if any tax revenue…

1998-06-05   *West Kootenay Weekender*, Nelson, BC   by Darren Davidson
[Profile: Conservationist Anthony Marr bares his stripes]
Being beaten for what you believe in is nothing exceptionally shocking for animal conservationist Anthony Marr…

When asked if he saw being beaten up as a personal sacrifice, Mar said, "No. It's a professional risk. It just comes with the job."…

… In 1996, Marr and WCWC launched one of the most high profile animal conservation crusades Canada has ever seen…

DD: "Your story is certainly one of personal conviction."

AM: "Well, I have a lot of respect for children. When young children, in elementary school, tell me they think killing animals for fun is wrong, I feel an obligation to champion their cause, because they cannot yet speak for themselves. That is a very powerful motivation for me… I also have my own personal feelings, of course… I do love these animals that they kill."

1998-06-07   *The Vancouver Courier*   by Gudrun Will
[Tiger volunteers paint mural to save species]
On a scalding Wednesday afternoon, underwear clad painters dab tropical sunset colours on the front wall of downtown Davie Street hangout DV8. The artists are creating a tiger mural in preparation for a silent art auction to help save the species.

… Organizer Tracy Zuber, a tiny 29-year-old in black sports bra and plaid shorts, is a self-professed tiger fanatic. Images of the wild animal cover her apartment walls. "They're the personification of beauty, power and grace. They're a figurehead of primal life power," said Zuber.

Her preferred felines, however, are also a rapidly dwindling species; little more than 4,000 are left in the wild, and two are killed per day. Zuber was inspired to raise funds to slow down the tiger's beeline to extinction while participating in the Save-the-Tiger Walk last fall with her daughter Fija. The Year of the Tiger seemed an appropriate time to make an effort, she says...

… conservationist Anthony Marr will present a slideshow that night…

1998-06-14   *Capital News Weekend Close-Up*   by Judie Steeves
[Loaded for bear - Bear hunting under fire]
… Anthony Marr… says that bear-watching eco-tourism can create more jobs and revenue than bear hunting…

1998-06-19   *Kamloops Daily News*
[Group asks public to support ban on grizzly bear hunts in BC]
Environmentalists will try again to get a ban on grizzly bear hunting in BC, this time by going straight to the people.

Anthony Marr said that the latest campaign weapon is a "do it yourself postcard open poll".

The WCWC will distribute thousands of postcards across BC and Canada, allowing people to say what they think about grizzly bear hunting. The cards allow both hunters and environmentalists to express their opinions.

The "3-part-post-cards" - picturing a live grizzly bear on one part, and a dead one with a grinning hunter on another - are addressed to Premier Glen Clark and the BC legislature…

❖   ❖   ❖   ❖   ❖

1998-06-22

Went hiking up Lynn Headwaters Park along the river with Christine's friends Tasha and Wilhelmina, and their friends Deborah, Ruth and Miriam – at their invitation. It was a beautiful hike, but I didn't feel comfortable with it, still don't. The reason for my discomfort is that Christine was not invited. Christine had already complained that she had been excluded a few times before, due to her needing to bring Christopher, which hampered their progress. I was also slightly put off by their excluding Christine on account of Christopher, but they all but insisted that I went, so I did.

I didn't mention the hike to Christine afterwards, not wanting her to again feel left out. Also, if she found out about her exclusion, it should be from Tasha and Wilhelmina, not from me. Further, if I told her and she went to them about it, it would make me look as if I was telling on them. All in all, I was put in a very awkward position.

The worst thing is that I know that she will find out about it sooner or later, and she would then feel that I "lied" to her. With Christine, sometimes there is just no winning.

Already, something traumatic has happened to me, which will impact on Christopher, though he does not yet know it. Things have not been going well with Christine over the last few months. Mostly, it had to do with our different ways of relating to Christopher, and inevitably, when our ways crossed, there was conflict. Just little things, but Christine is one who holds grudges for ages, which are therefore cumulative.

Once, for example, after Christopher had gone to bed and Christine and I were having tea in the kitchen, Christopher came running down and cried that there was a ghost in his closet. Both of us brought him back to his bed and tucked him back in. But our ways then diverged. Christine went to the closet and shouted into it. "Go away, you nasty ghost! Don't you dare scare my little boy!" On my part, I held his hands and stroked his hair and said softly to him, "Christopher, there is no ghost. It is only a little mouse. It is more scared of you than you are of it." Christine heard what I said and shot me daggers.

Another time, when I went out to Christine's car to fetch something for her, I noticed that she had wrapped the lap belt around the outside front of Christopher's car seat near the bottom instead of through the frame of the seat near the back. I tested it by pulling the top of the car seat forward, and of course the whole seat came tumbling out of the restraint. I could have just reset the lap belt through the frame of the seat the way it is supposed to be, but I wanted to show Christine how it should be done so she does it properly next time. It's a matter of life and death and I could not just shrug it off as I often do with trivial matters, but I did not relish correcting her. Still I went back into her house and asked her to come out and showed her the whole thing, starting with the tumbling test. She took everything in, and reset the belt herself. But then, the last thing that happened indicated that another hell-to-pay is in the offing. She turned to Christopher who was there watching and said cuttingly, "Well, don't you know that Uncle Tony is always right?!"

Another time, I went visiting and did not see Christopher. So I asked Christine where he was. Christine said that he had been confined to his room for something that he had done. I asked what he had done and she told me. Hearing my voice, Christopher called my name. I was about to answer when Christine hushed me. Christopher called me again, and again. My heart went to him. Without further hesitation, I went upstairs, opened his bedroom door and went in. He was crying. I held his shoulder and soft talked to him, telling him that what he did was wrong and asked him if he was sorry for what he had done. He said he was. I asked him if he was willing to apologize to mommy. He said yes. So I took him in my arms and carried him downstairs. I took him to Christine and he very sincerely apologized, saying that he was wrong for what he had done, and that he would never do it again. But Christine wasn't listening. She ordered him back upstairs, and ordered me to leave. It was only after I had begun driving back home that I realized the magnitude of my error. But again, it was too late.

Yet another time, as soon as I entered their house, I heard Christopher screaming from the top of the stairs, "NO, MOMMY! DON'T HIT ME WITH THE WOODEN SPOON ANY MORE! I WON'T DO IT AGAIN!" Christine was standing at the bottom of the stairs, with the wooden spoon in her hand, held in a threatening manner. I saw red and without thinking, grab the spoon and took it from her hand. She did not say anything for the moment, but again, I knew that irreparable damage had been done. Except this time I was not in the least sorry for what I did.

And then, several days ago, an interim verdict did come down. Without preamble or explanation, Christine unilaterally cut down my visiting frequency from four days a week to twice a week. There was and is nothing I could and can do about it. Worse, knowing Christine, the verdict is irreversible. It is a huge loss to both Christopher and me.

When I told Jeanine about this devastating development, she shook her head and said, "She's a power monger and a control freak. Other single moms would just love to have a man like you for their sons, not a wimpy yes-man, and take some pain to work out these minor differences. How sad, especially for Christopher."

"I don't remember if I've already told you, but once, when I said that I would do all I could to 'help her raise Christopher', she almost tore my head off. That was not long after she watched that infamous episode of Murphy Brown on TV, you know, the one where she deliberately got herself pregnant, kicked out the man, to raise the child by herself."

"Just because she could."

"Or her belief that women should."

"Now I understand," sighed Jeanine, who is not one to mince words. "How doubly sad. A woman of low self-esteem using her own child to boost for her big but sagging ego."

※ ※ ※ ※ ※

June 29, 1998

I took Christopher out by myself today. Christine decided to stay home for a break. First, we went "playground cruising", that is, we just drove around a certain neighbourhood looking for playgrounds, and whenever we came across a half decent one, we'd stop and play there for awhile, then move on.

It is always a great joy to see him at play. Sometimes, one of the slides would be a little too high and intimidating for him, but he would come down it anyway, as long as I promise to catch him at the bottom. His trust for me is total. As long as I'm there with him, he'd feel that nothing bad could happen to him. His laughter of glee is music to my ears.

After an hour or so of that, we went for a walk at Coquitlam River. The huckleberries and blackberries were ripe for the picking. Christopher and I stuffed ourselves with them. After some time, I said to him, "Now Christopher, you've had lots of berries. Why don't you take some home for mommy? She'd really like that."

He said with a slight child's grimace, "I don't want to, Uncle Tony. I like you more than mommy. She is mean to me."

I was stunned. After a moment, I said to him, "Christopher, mommy loves you very much. It's just that she has to make sure you don't do wrong things, and when you do, she has to make sure you don't do them again."

"I don't do wrong things with you, do I, Uncle Tony?" he said, plaintively.

"No, you don't Christopher, but you don't live with me either."

He thought about it for a bit, then said, "Okay, Uncle Tony." Then, he began picking berries and putting them into the plastic bag I gave him.

When we got home, he ran out of my car and dashed excitedly into the house and shouted, "Mommy, mommy, I picked some berries for you!" Christine was delighted.

At dinner time, as is almost always the case, I took them out to our favourite Chinese restaurant, for a scrumptuous dinner. I always pay, since Christine is currently a welfare mom, and she does sometimes "feed" me. And though Christine seldom verbally thanks me, her obvious enjoyment of the dishes is thanks enough for me. Plus, there are two large saltwater tropical fish tanks there with some very exotic looking fish. Christopher always looks forward to going there and saying hi to his favourite "Mr. Eel."

After Christopher had gone to bed, I made another big mistake. I told Christine about the conversation between Christopher and me, thinking that she ought to know what Christopher felt about the way she dealt with him, so that she might adjust her behavior accordingly to prevent damaging Christopher's love for her. But even before I had finished, I saw her face visibly darken. At once, I knew what that meant. I know her well enough I should have known the way she would process the information. Worse, I felt I had betrayed Christopher's confidence. But again, it was too late.

I'll be away again for a whole month or more. I must do some fence mending before I leave.

❖   ❖   ❖   ❖   ❖

1998-07-03 *The Globe and Mail* **(national)**
[Man set on saving grizzlies]
Vancouver - Anthony Marr is renewing his effort to ban grizzly bear hunting in BC despite a gruesome beating by an alleged critic that left him with a broken nose and eye socket.

The campaigner… hit the road yesterday to visit 30 BC communities to fire up support for a bear-hunt ban campaign that has been criticized by hunters…

1998-07-09-4 *The Sun*, Vernon, BC
[Activist wants bear hunting banned]
The Canadian grizzly bear population should be glad they have a person like Anthony Marr on their side…

During his 30 city tour… Marr is urging people to sign postcards with an unnerving photo of a dead grizzly bear on its cover…

Marr said over 25,000 of the cards have already been sent out and plans to circulate more than 200,000 by the time he is done his trip…

Canada is seen as a very forward thinking country internationally, but Marr said this country is lagging behind many Third World countries in terms of trophy hunting… The country really does not deserve its pro-environmental reputation, and it's not a great country of spiritual development until we've got rid of trophy hunting."

1998-07-14-2 *Penticton Herald* **by Donna Henningson**
[Committee targeting grizzly hunt]
Ask Anthony Marr where the light at the end of the tunnel is in his fight to stop the grizzly bear hunt in BC.

"The end of the tunnel is when the grizzly hunt is banned," said the wildlife campaigner…

1998-07-15-3 *The Daily News*, **Kamloops, BC** **by Robert Koopmans**
[Bleak future seen for grizzly]
Poaching, habitat loss and trophy hunting will be the downfall of BC's grizzly bears, environmentalist Anthony Marr told a small group of people Tuesday night…

He frequently compared the grizzly to tigers in India. In the space of a few decades, tiger populations have plummeted from more than 50,000 to virtual extinction. Marr said BC needs to look at the tigers and take steps to prevent a similar catastrophe with the grizzlies.

One man in the audience challenged Marr on his statements about hunters' ethics. Marr asked the man why he would want to kill a grizzly anyway…

1998-07-17-5 *Comox Valley Record*
[Grizzly defender speaks]
Anthony Marr… is returning to the Comox Valley on Thursday July 23 at 7 p.m. at the Lower Native Sons Hall…

This man has endured the threats and harassment of hunters across BC, and survived a back alley attack in January of this year, all on account of his opposition to recreational hunting of bears…

1998-07-18-6 *The Daily News*, **Kamloops, BC** **by Mel Rothenburger**
[Saving BC's grizzly bears a daunting task]
Anthony Marr has one of the toughest challenges on earth. In a world that values the preservation of cultural traditions, he is trying to erase one of the most powerful. In the process, he hopes to save several major animal species from extinction.

An ambitious goal to say the least. Despite devoting himself to it full time for the past several years, he has obtained only limited success. But that hasn't discouraged him.

Marr became a fairly well known media figure two years ago (and a despised one among recreational hunters) when he championed an attempt to ban all bear hunting in BC. He and WCWC failed... but he's back at it with a brand new strategy...

I doubt that any policy will be changed this time either, but I admire Marr's determination...

He has a plan to pose as a wealthy Chinese businessman and secretly video-tape the killing of a captive bear at a Korean "bear banquet", "where they sometimes lower a bear in a cage on to a bed of hot coal until their paws are cooked, for maximum freshness and perhaps extreme entertainment," said Marr.

It's a long way from China or Taiwan or Korea to the backwoods of BC where trophy hunting takes place, but Marr is convinced that all of the atrocities against bears must be dealt with together...

That of course is where domestic opposition comes in...

A meeting here during the referendum campaign brought out some serious heckling. Almost disappointingly, there was little of that this time around. A debate with hunters is always fun, and often productive, and Marr enjoys it...

Anthony Marr has a huge job ahead of him, and I hope he will one day succeed.

It is strange to me that those who kill animals for entertainment control wildlife policy in this province, rather than those who want to keep them alive. If you doubt that, allow me to point out that the BC Wildlife Federation, which is an organization of hunters, proposed to Environment Minister Cathy McGregor earlier this year that non-hunters should have to buy a license to use the woods.

She said she will seriously look into it.

1998-07-21-2 *Comox Valley Echo*
[Bear activist speaks here Thursday]
... Local organizer Ruth Masters finds any killing of bears "atrocious" and reminds that one bear is poached for every one legally killed. "And the bears don't know if the guy pulling the trigger had a license or not. They are still dead."...

1998-07-24-5 *Campbell River Mirror* **by Sharon Bennett**
[Bear activist hits the road again]
... The attack only stoked Marr's fiery passion to save the grizzly, and for the month of July he's touring the province to warn the public of the grizzly's imminent demise.

... He recounts the story of a South Korean man who was caught in possession of 88 bear gall bladders and four times as many paws - a street value of about

$500,000 US… He was fined CDN$3,500, roughly the same worth as one gall bladder.

Marr says he questioned the judge about why the fine was so low, and admitted the judge's argument makes sense… The trophy hunt is driven by European cultural tradition, the judge said, and the medicinal hunt is driven by Asian cultural tradition. Therefore, Marr says, the judge decided it would be wrong to punish one culture's tradition while the other culture's tradition is still legal…

1998-07-24-5 *The News Weekender*, **Parksville** **by Jeff Vircoe**
[Bearing the controversial issue to QB]
He's been beaten up for his opinions. He's been called a turncoat by his own people. And he may be the Grizzly bear's best friend… A one-man wrecking crew for those who believe hunting Grizzlies is okay, Marr's controversial stance… has irritated countless hunting enthusiasts…

When hunters say that (bears will turn aggressive if not hunted), Marr says studies in Glacier and Yellowstone National Parks show that bears do not get more aggressive merely because they are protected…

1998-07-29-3 *Comox Valley Record* **by Karen Kwan**
[Speaker brings shocking story]
The images are disturbing.

On the parched ground, many elephants lie crumpled, their tusks removed, their trunks just bloody stumps where they have been sawed off.

A live tiger is strung upside down in a cage, hanging by his spread-eagled limbs, while people peered between the bars, gawking.

Deep in the woods, a bear cub, who had scrambled up a tree to get away from poachers, was shot four times with arrows…

These scenes weren't made-in-Hollywood horror stories, but are all too real - some of it happening right here in BC, according to animal conservationist Anthony Marr… who was in Courtenay Thursday evening…

1998-07-30-4 *Nanaimo Daily News*
[Bear essentials aired at debate]
When environmentalist Anthony Marr brought his campaign to ban grizzly bear hunting to Nanaimo, his audience listened. Not everyone in the Beban Park meeting room Tuesday night agreed with him, but they all paid attention.

Bob Morris, past-president of the BC Wildlife Federation, and Bill Derby, vice-president of the Nanaimo Fish and Game Protection Association, were two of a party of hunters who came to hear what Marr had to say about bear hunting. And to challenge his conclusions.

Morris didn't trust Marr's motives, or those of WCWC. "Basically their goal is to try and ban hunting altogether, using the grizzly bear as an icon."

Marr replied that that would be a glorious quest, but one too distant for his remaining life span.

Derby said the grizzly bear hunt is "very tightly controlled", taking fewer bears than die as road kill. Morris said there was no need to ban the hunt, as the grizzly population is rising. Marr replied that grizzly bear hunt victims number about 300, higher than the road kill number, and that even according to the BC government, the grizzly bear population is decreasing in the long run.

Derby said banning hunting might lead to more bears getting killed, because as they got more accustomed to being around people, they would get bolder.

Marr answered that he's heard all these arguments before. There was no evidence that stopping the hunt would make the bears more dangerous, such as in the Yellowstone and Glacier National Park, where grizzly hunting is not allowed…

Marr's campaign has won him a variety of enemies…

1998-07-31-5 *Times Colonist*, **Victoria, BC   by Cindy E. Harnett**
[Crusade against grizzly hunt reaches Victoria]
Anthony Marr's renewed campaign to ban grizzly bear hunting will take the high, rocky road to Victoria for a slideshow tonight at 7:30 p.m. in University of Victoria's law building and a rally at the legislature on Saturday… This stop is one of the last in a month-long, province-wide tour…

Marr's visits are known to spark fiery debates between hunters and non-hunters…

On a moral standpoint, Marr said this week, "… The moral reason alone… is big enough to ban hunting for entertainment and ego."

But BC Wildlife Federation immediate past-president John Holdstock said morality has nothing to do with hunting…

1998-07-31-5 *The Victoria News* **by Stephanie Coombs**
[Rally against bear hunt targets legislature]
… "The grizzly population is decreasing over the long term - slowly over the last 200 years - but we can't say by how much at present," says Nancy Bircher, the director of the wildlife branch at the ministry…

Bircher says about 300 Grizzlies are legally killed each year by people with licenses, another 50 are termed "nuisance kills" - due to conflict with humans - and about 90 die as unreported kills or from poachers.

"The poaching figure is absolutely unfounded and hugely at odds with what international authorities report," says Marr. "They estimate a continental average of one bear poached for every bear legally hunted. They also estimate that BC is among the most poached amongst all the North American states and provinces. According to this, the poached/hunted ratio should be one or two to one, not one to three or four."

He says the province is intentionally skewing the facts to favour hunters.

"They project as high a population number and as low a poaching number as possible to give the general public the impression there are so many grizzlies that not only can they be hunted, but that they should be hunted…"

1998-08-02-7   *Times Colonist*, Victoria, BC   by Cindy E. Harnett
[Grizzlies attract 150 supporters at rally]

… Main speakers included WCWC founder Paul George and wildlife campaigner Anthony Marr. Many in the audience had helped to gather signatures for WCWC's 1996 campaign in which about 90,000 signatures were obtained to save BC's bears.

At that time, Environment Minister Cathy McGregor did not act on any of the organization's three requests: to stop bear hunting, to further protect bear habitat or to increase fines for poachers. The minister re-stated her commitment to hunters last week.

"Trophy hunting is a concern to some British Columbians, but there are real economic benefits to hunting around the province. In the interior, hunting is very much a way of life and the way in which some areas of our province gain economic opportunity," she said…

Marr says there are (possibly as few as) 4,000 to 7,000 grizzlies left. He expects in 20-30 years, they will be extirpated from almost all of southern and central BC if no action is taken.

1998-08-17-1   *Times Colonist*, Victoria, BC   by Anthony Marr
[Grizzly situation]

… In spite of our hard work and publicity, and all the polls showing that a vast majority of British Columbians feel likewise about our cause, only about 150 people came to our demonstration against grizzly bear hunting in BC, but same evening, same place, there was a fireworks display, and over 40,000 people showed up. I've said it before and I'll say it again. Apathy is our worst enemy…

❖   ❖   ❖   ❖   ❖

August 22, 1992

I'm on another 3-week road tour, but this time a nonconfrontational one – to merely network with local environmentalists over coffee. I brought Christine and Christopher for the first week of the trip as a treat. We met up with my friends Diana and Alex, and their children Crystal and Dylan who were then touring eastern BC, and spent the weekend with them at Banff and Lake Louise in the Albertan Rockies. We all had a whale of a time, including a good splashing in a large hot spring. After that, we went our separate ways. Christine, Christopher and I spent the night at Hinton, Alberta, where, the following morning, they took a "choo choo train" back to Vancouver.

Christopher, by now a seasoned road tourer, took to car traveling very well. The only glitch was shortly before we arrived at Hinton. We were about 20 km from Hinton when he woke up and began getting restless in the car seat. It was well past his bedtime. Christine tried to get him to go to sleep, but he just wouldn't, or couldn't. Seeing that 20 km at highway speed would take only 10 minutes, and that if he stayed awake, he'd be fatigued enough to fall asleep right away as soon as we hit the beds, so I said, "Okay, Christopher, you can just stay awake." But again, as soon as I said it, I knew I had made another mistake, for which I would again have to pay in some way some time in the future.

And yet another mishap with consequences occurred in Banff, which would not be for another woman than Christine. I came across a beautifully made model of a brontosaurus in a toy store. So I bought it for Christopher. He loved it and brought out his other three small dinosaurs Christine gave him a few weeks ago that Christopher had brought with him. He arranged them on the motel table. "Look Uncle Tony, mommy dinosaur and baby dinosaurs." Christine should be pleased, but she was obviously not. She did not show the big dinosaur one smidgeon of appreciation or affection. Her dark look said, "You have again shown me up," referring to the big dinosaur's being more expensive than the three little dinosaurs combined.

How do I deal with all these – syndromes?

❖ ❖ ❖ ❖ ❖

1998-09-02-3 *The Japan Times* **by Françoise Giovannangeli**
[An unbearable prospect - a Canadian icon faces new and growing threats]
… "Most countries have banned trophy hunting of grizzlies - all except Canada, Russia and the US state of Alaska," said Anthony Marr. "That is why so many foreign hunters are coming to Canada - because they can't do it in their own countries where the brown bear has become endangered or been wiped out. It's the Canadian grizzly that is soaking up and absorbing the pressure of trophy hunting lust from around the world as well as the profit lust of guide-outfitters and poachers," he said….

If the pace keeps up, Marr says, the future does not bode well for North American bears. "Asiatic bears were not endangered a few decades ago. Today, they have been hunted to the verge of extinction by the demands of Japan, Korea, Taiwan, China and Singapore. The Chinese economy is improving fast, and pretty soon, there will be a huge middle class. I believe that at that point, there will be a jump in demand for bear galls far in excess of the current already high level. It may have already started. And the target will be the North American bears this time around."…

1998-09 *The Vancouver Sun*
[Champions return to Discovery]
"It took the tiger 10 million years to evolve to its present state of magnificence," says Anthony Marr, "but less than one century to fall to the brink of extinction. This, sadly, is the way of humans."

The Chinese-born Canadian is featured in the Bengal Tiger of India episode of the award-winning TV documentary series Champions of the Wild, now in its second season on Discovery Channel…

Each episode highlights the efforts of a particular conservationist, from Clark Lungren's work in the Nazinga Game Reserve, airing October 5, to Marr's multi-faceted campaign to protect the tiger on October 12…

Champions of the Wild was produced by Omni Film Productions, in association with the National Film Board, BC Film, and the Discovery Channel, with the participation of Telefilm and the Cable Production Fund.

1998-09-14-1 *Times Colonist*, **Victoria, BC** **by Cindy E. Harnett**
[Seaborne protest in native whaling controversy]

... "I respect native rights, but we human beings are past the point where we need to kill these beings to survive…," Marr said… "Tradition to me, which is so sacred to so many people, is actually a dirty word, because it stands in the way of the evolution of the human spirit."

The World Council of Whalers, a 20 country group, was put together two years ago to ready people for hunts all over the world. The Makah have accused animal-rights activists of trying to "put their culture into a museum."

Marr said the reverse is true. "A living culture evolves with the times and is not stuck in the past. If they want to go into the past and maintain the past status quo, they are putting themselves into a museum."

1998-09-18-5 *The Globe and Mail*, **national   by Celia Sankar**
[BC won't end annual grizzly hunt; minister says no harm done to bear population]

The BC government is not about to stop the province's annual grizzly-bear hunt, despite criticism from environmentalists and dissent from one of its own biologists…

A senior habitat biologist with the BC Ministry of Environment said hunting as administered by the province "has the potential to drive grizzly bear populations dangerously close to extinct. There is no ecological, biological or social justification for continuing to hunt grizzly bears," Dionys de Leeuw wrote in a private paper widely distributed to wildlife officials within the ministry April.

Mr. De Leeuw argued that the system for issuing licenses for bear hunting "is based on unconfirmed population estimates for grizzly bears" that "substantially overestimate bear abundance."

Mr. De Leeuw's paper, copies of which were (confiscated) by ministry officials, was leaked yesterday by the WCWC.

"The Canadian authorities list the grizzly as a vulnerable species and we should not allow it to cross the line and become endangered. We think it is quite close right now," Anthony Marr said.

Mr. De Leeuw described as "an injustice in the extreme" the situation where the interest of "an infinitesimally small" number of trophy hunters continue to be protected by the government while those who oppose the activity are ignored…

1998-10
Bengal Tigers. (Champions of the Wild Series, 18).
Andrew Gardner (Director), Christian Bruyere (Producer), Michael Chechik (Executive Producer). National Film Board of Canada, 1998. 25 min., 30 sec.

Grades 4 and up / Ages 9 and up. *Review by Susan Fonseca.*

This video opens with a carefully edited scene of a Bengal Tiger patiently stalking and then attacking its prey. The plight of the tiger in India is very serious. At the turn of the century, there were over 100,000 tigers. This number quickly diminished to 30,000 by the 1940's due to the trophy hunting which was a national sport. Conservationist Anthony Marr has championed the cause of the tiger for two reasons. He believes that "if the tiger is gone from this land, the land will have lost its soul." He also understands that one of the greatest threats to the tiger's survival today is the huge Chinese market for tiger parts. A dead tiger is worth $100,000 in China where it is believed that, next to the mythical dragon, the tiger is the most powerful animal. Through Chinese medicines, healers use tiger parts to transfer that power to humans. Being Chinese himself, Marr believes that he may have a greater impact.

The video contains brilliant camera work which captures the power and beauty of the tiger. The sound track echoes the India countryside by using instruments native to the land. The narration is clear and easily understood. Many of the scenes are very graphic, showing tigers tearing apart gazelles or revealing hunters and poachers destroying the tiger for its pelt or bones. These scenes are balanced, however, by the joy of a playful young kitten or a delightful scene that allows the viewer to watch as a very hot tiger gingerly and slowly sinks into a cool pond of water.

Marr has targeted children as one of the avenues of support for these endangered creatures. This goal will probably be most effective with the children in India, but the biggest obstacle will be the poor Indian villagers who have been displaced without compensation so that the government can create sanctuaries for the tiger. Incentives are now being created that will offer these people a better life if they will help to save these endangered animals.

Bengal Tigers has aired on **Discovery Channel** and **Animal Planet**. The video also includes previewing questions and post-viewing questions in addition to several web sites. The video would support a study of endangered animals and also could offer many opportunities for the students to problem solve and to create their own solutions.

Highly Recommended.

Susan Fonseca is a teacher-librarian at Glenwood School in St. Vital School Division in Winnipeg, MB.

1998-10-02   *Victoria News*   by Bev Wake
[Grizzly population overestimated]

… In Victoria again last week, Marr looked intent, yet weary, as he held up the leaked document (by Dionys de Leeuw - see 1998-09-1805 Global and Mail article)...

The document backs Marr's belief that the ministry has overestimated BC's grizzly bear population...

"We must begin to protect our bears today," Marr says. "Our objective is to prevent them from becoming endangered... It's a vicious spiral... It is a double-edged sword for a species to be declared endangered, because it drives up the black market value, thus encouraging more poaching. We can see that cloud on the horizon," he says...

Part of the problem, he says, is that BC's hunting policy is set by three bodies - the provincial Environment Ministry, the BC Wildlife Federation and the BC Guide-Outfitters' Association, all of which, Marr charges, has vested interests in hunting.

Again, de Leeuw's report backs Marr up, saying "BC's decision regarding grizzly bear allocation have almost exclusively accommodated the interests of trophy hunters, who make up less than one tenth of one percent of the people."

1998-10-05 *Monday* **magazine** **by Ross Crockford**
[Splendor Sine Occasu]

...Saturday morning, I went down to the legislature grounds to hear a speech by Anthony Marr...

I asked Marr whether it wouldn't be better to allow limited trophy hunting, as they've done with elephants in South Africa, and put thousands of dollars in taxes on the licenses and then plow them into regional projects... Marr replied that grizzly viewing was a better option. He knows of a lodge in Knight Inlet that takes foreign tourists to watch bears feeding on salmon, and charges them $700 a day, and employs 22 people. The only problem is that hunters gun down the bears the moment they step out of the tiny protected area around the salmon stream, and the tourists get very upset. The old economy and the new one aren't mixing very well...

1998-10-05-1 *Times Colonist*, **Victoria, BC** **by Richard Watts**
[Greenpeace neutral on whaling]

Greenpeace - which made its name battling to save whales from being hunted to extinction - is now sitting firmly on the fence over the Makah hunt...

John Vanderhoeven, director of field operations for the provincial SPCA, said the group is opposed to the inhumane killing of any creature... "I'm not sure how a person could bring about the humane death of a whale," said Vanderhoeven.

Anthony Marr... said, "We oppose killing whales, whether for cultural or economic reasons, if only on account of the inevitable cruelty."

And he says his group is appalled by the Canadian government's decision to allow the Makah to pursue a wounded whale into Canadian waters to finish it off.

Marr says the Canadian position was like a wounded man coming to your door for help, "and you invite the assailant in to finish the job."

Meanwhile the Nuu-Cha-Nulth Indians of southwest Vancouver Island, who include the Washington Makah among their members, say the hunt is justified and are supporting the Makah hunters…

1998-10-06-2 *Penticton Harold* **by Anthony Marr**
[Whale's rights come first]
I respect aboriginal rights, but I respect even more the right of whales to live, and live in peace and harmony with humans…

The Pacific Grey whales annually migrate up and down the North American coast… have been living in peace and harmony with humans for more than 70 years. They've come to enjoy human company and allow us the privilege of touching them.

If now a few humans begin to kill them, for any reason, I would consider our species as a whole to be betraying the sacred trust established with another sentient species. A few whales will lose their lives, but Homo sapiens will lose its humanity…

1998-10-09-5 *The Vancouver Sun* **by Anthony Marr**
[Whales shouldn't be on the sushi menu]
… The Japanese and Norwegians are strong backers of the Makah's "right" to kill whales. They have given at least US$10,000 for the Makah's whaling campaign.

These pirate whaling nations are not acting out of interest in the Makah as a people or respect for aboriginal rights. They are using them as a can opener to restart whaling for "cultural need". Once the Makah succeed in taking their first whale, the Japanese and Norwegians can then claim the right to whale for "cultural needs" of their own.

Tom Happynook, a Nuu-Cha-Nulth relative of the Makah and head of the World Council of whalers, say the Japanese are justified in continuing to kill whales and dolphins for so-called "scientific" reasons in the face of a global whaling ban by IWC. Maybe he can tell me how much science is involved in consuming a plate of whale sushi…

1998-10-11-7 *The Province*, **Vancouver** **by Jonathan McDonald**
[Species run for their lives]
Premier - Champions of the Wild - Mondays at 6 and 10 p.m. on Discovery Channel.

... this 13-part series is only partly about the animals who are running for their lives. It's mainly about the people - Canadians by and large - who are doing whatever they can to reverse increasingly hopeless situations.

"It's vital," says Anthony Marr, a Vancouverite who heads the Tigers Forever campaign and is the subject of "Bengal Tigers of India", which premiers Monday night on Discovery Channel. "The tiger is an icon of wildlife conservation. It is one of the world's most admired and also most endangered animals. If it falls extinct, the whole global conservation effort will lose steam, and the world will lose an immeasurable amount of beauty."

Marr is not kidding. Seeing the Bengal tiger sleep, prowl and hunt is wondrous. Seeing the work of poachers - tiger skins and medicines - is no less than horrifying and offensive. And seeing Marr sit down in an Indian village to tell the children about the beauty of the tiger - an animal, he urges, that deserves to be on Earth - is the perfect reflection of Canadians' work around the globe.

"They're extremely dedicated," says Chris Bruyere, Champion's producer... "Often, these are people who don't believe there's such a thing as fighting a losing battle."...

1998-10-11-7 *Ming Pao Daily News* **(Chinese), global**
[Chinese campaigner saving 4,000 remaining wild tigers]
The WCWC set up booth at the Vancouver Public Library Saturday to publicize tiger conservation, and will lead the Save-the-Tiger Walk at Stanley Park next Saturday...

Anthony Marr says that of the original 8 subspecies of tigers, only 5 remain, totaling no more than 4 or 5 thousand, of which two die daily to poaching and other causes. At this rate, there will be no tigers left to celebrate the next Year of the Tiger...

1998-10-18-7 *Ming Pao Daily News* **(Chinese), global**
[100 walk to save 4,000 tigers]
... Last year's Save-the-Tiger Walk brought out 2,000 people and raised almost $20,000 for tiger conservation. Unfortunately, this year's Walk picked the worse possible time weatherwise. Only 100 people showed up to brave the heavy rain and high winds...

1998-10-22-4 *Nelson Daily News* **by Anthony Marr**
[Rights of whales must supersede aboriginal rights]
... I have no doubt that whales are not only sentient but intelligent. Even small

cetaceans like dolphins have brains larger and more convoluted than ours. They have sophisticated social and behavioral patterns. They have complex languages and different Orca pods have different dialects. The songs of the humpback changes from year to year… We may freely give each other the right to kill these highly advanced beings, but in the high scheme of things, we have no right to give such rights to anyone…

… I urge all to examine their own traditions and voluntarily shed those elements within them that are no longer consistent with today's environmental and humane principles. I ask those within the aboriginal communities to follow the lead of the Makah's Alberta Thompson to voluntarily forego the whale-killing element of their tradition.

Finally, I must make one thing clear. I am against killing whales, period, for any reason, by anyone, be they Japanese, Norwegian, Russian or Makah.

1998-11-07   *Toronto Sun*   by Michael Clement
[Animal Parts illegally sold here: activist]

A west-coast wildlife activist alleges he purchased three bottles containing parts of endangered species, being sold illegally in a store in Toronto's Chinatown yesterday…

Marr asked reporters to accompany him to the Po Chi Tong Chinese pharmacy on Dundas St. W. yesterday where he purchased the three bottles. The bottles of pills purportedly contained bear gall bladder secretion, possibly from the endangered Asiatic Black bear, secretions from the musk gland of the endangered Musk Deer, and tiger bone, possibly from the endangered Bengal or Siberian Tiger, Marr said.

"Internationally, endangered species are totally forbidden to be traded, alive or dead, in whole or part," he said, adding that in June 1996 Ottawa enacted laws "forbidding the sale of anything containing endangered species parts."

"The point of this exercise is to prove that the law is not being effectively enforced."…

1998-11-26-4   *Nelson Daily News*   by Bob Hall
[Kids in the tiger's grasp]

Anthony Marr… is touring area schools this week promoting the Save-the-Tiger campaign. With the help of the Nelson Youth Environmental Group who put on a play of Dr. Seuss's The Lorax followed by Marr's slideshow… Wednesday morning, Marr talked to Hume Elementary School students in front of a 12 foot high, 50 feet long inflatable tiger prop. To bring further attention to the issue there will be a Save-the-Tiger Walk-a-thon this Saturday at Lakeside Park starting at 11 a.m. For more information contact the Nelson Eco-Centre.

1998-12-02-3   *Trail Daily News*   **by Lana Rodlie**
[WCWC shares extinction fears with area students]

… Bring the message about diminishing tigers to area schools, Anthony Marr is hoping to save the tiger, one child at a time…

Pointing out how every living thing affect the life of something else, he asked the children, "How many cows do you think live in India? Would you believe 350-600 *million*? That is more than the American and Canadian human populations combined.

"Cows eat grass. Deer eat grass. Tigers eat deer. If the cows eat up all the grass, what do you think will happen to the deer, and the tiger?…

"Still, if you go into an Indian national park, you're not allowed to touch anything, take anything, not even pick a blade of grass. But would you believe that in a BC park, you are allowed to kill grizzly bears?"

❖   ❖   ❖   ❖   ❖

1998-12-25

Christmas Day, 1998. Christopher's third. Christine invited me to stay overnight to be there when Christopher opens his presents first thing in the morning. A very family affair, just the three of us. Of course there would be visits by friends and relatives, but those would come later. In the morning, there would be just Christopher, Mommy and Uncle Tony. The three of us hugged together.

I wonder what his daddy is doing today. There is nothing from him among the presents. Is he still alive? If so, what is he doing? What is he living for?

One thing has been bothering me lately. Since more than a month ago, the Christmas hype has disturbed Christopher's daily order and routine so much that he has become somewhat unruly. As a result, most of the time when I was visiting (only twice a week since Christine's June verdict) or while on the phone with Christine, I've often been pained to hear Christine yelling at him to stop doing whatever he was doing, and at times screaming at him about how bad he was. I know that living with a three-year-old around the clock, 24/7, must be taxing, so I haven't said anything, but I've been thinking:

One, that you can't teach a child not to scream by screaming at him, and

Two, that telling me I'm a bad man would not hurt me since I know I'm not, but telling a three-year-old that he's bad, especially repeatedly, will convince him that he indeed is. This would then impact negatively on his self-image and self-esteem. And I have noticed another thing. Christine has a way to talking condescendingly to and even screaming abusively at her cat, such as "Get out of there, you stupid cat!" Christopher observes this and translates it into physical language which is the language of a three year old, such as hitting it, and Christine would then scream at him.

Last week, I took Christopher to visit my friend and ballet buddy Catherine. He was very excited about it, because Catherine not only has a cat, but two dogs! We had a wonderful visit, just Christopher, Catherine and I, and of course Tangerine the cat, and Lyon and Tigger, the miniature poodles. At one point, I came back into the house to help Catherine with kitchen chores, and Christopher was left momentarily in the fenced yard with just the two little dogs. Both Catherine and I could see him through the kitchen window, but he couldn't see us. He played with the dogs for awhile, and then began looking for me, and called out "Uncle Tony!" I went out and he ran to me, hugging me tightly. Catherine later said to me, "He adores you."

"And I him", I said.

A few days ago, I took Christopher, also by myself, to meet Diane, Alex, Crystal and Dylan at the toy complex on Granville Island to visit "Santa Claus". The three children were totally engrossed in the white bearded man, and we adults were totally engrossed in the children.

❖ ❖ ❖ ❖ ❖

1998-12-31

So, this is New Year's Eve, and the shit did hit the fan. I came home not long ago from visiting Christopher and Christine, perturbed. Once again, Christine was verbally badgering Christopher and telling him now bad he was, and he was cowering. At one point, I had to stand up for him, just defensively, but if anyone else did the same to Christopher, I might have offensively told him to just shove off.

After I had come home, I decided that things had gone far enough, and in spite of a severe foreboding, I picked up the phone to call Christine to talk about it.

As soon as she answered the phone and heard my voice, she knew what I was calling for. Her hostility was spontaneous and intense. Before I could say anything, she said in a voice that I could only describe as threatening, "Don't you dare interfere!"

I was committed, so I said my piece.

But before I could finish, she shouted, "HOW DARE YOU!!" and hung up on me.

This was nothing new. She'd done it many times over the years. And I knew her pattern. She would either not answer the phone after that, or else take it off the hook, so I didn't bother calling back. I also know that she would not call me for days, or forever, which means that I wouldn't be able to see Christopher for just as long, and I know she knows that sooner or later, I would come crawling to her, if only for Christopher.

And I know something else much deeper, and much more long term destructive. Whenever we disagree, Christine would never interpret my actions as for Christopher, but against Christine.

So much for the way 1998 ended, and 1999 began, since it is already past midnight.

Happy New Year, Christopher.

❖   ❖   ❖   ❖   ❖

January 16, 1999, Saturday

Yesterday, I had an enjoyable "date" with Christine's cousin Donna. Around Christmas time, for the first time in the twenty-plus years I've known her, she issued me an invitation – to her six year old son Colin's birthday party, which took place at her house last week. There were lots of children there, Christopher of course included. So Donna and I didn't get to talk much, nor did other adults among themselves for that matter. When I was making ready to leave, Donna said to me, "Now that you know where I live, don't be a stranger. Come and visit me some Friday evening. We could watch a video or something after Colin has gone to bed."

"I would love to, but hasn't Christine told you about my oncoming trip?"

"You go on so many trips. Which one do you mean?"

"The one I'll be leaving on Wednesday next. To India. My third trip there."

"Wow! How long do you plan to be away for?"

"About 10 weeks."

"So you wouldn't be back till…?"

"April 1. Thereabouts."

"Well, what are you doing this Friday?"

I arrived at 7 p.m., Friday, as arranged. We went to a video store and picked Grand Canyon – a very mediocre film as we later judged it. After that, we just talked over tea – quite a few pots of it. We were uninhibited verbally and covered every topic under the sun, including relationships and even sex, which is often a sign or signal of mutual romantic interest. At one point, she asked about my relationship with Christine, implying sexual content. I said "Platonic", and wondered why she asked, and more so, why she had to ask. Doesn't she already know? And if not, why not? I mean, I've been platonic with Christine for well over a decade, and have had other romantic interests since.

At one point, I noticed that she had been massaging her own shoulder off and on for about an hour. "Would you like me to do it for you?" I offered.

"Better not," she said. "I can't let a man touch me."

"Why not?"

"I haven't been with a man for over three years. I don't trust myself."

I didn't know her well enough to interpret this, so I just let it rest. But I couldn't resist saying, "If and when you change your mind, just let me know."

She gave me a hug in appreciation, which lasted all of five seconds.

At about 1 a.m., I said, "It's getting late. Time to go."

"You don't have to leave on my account. We can have another pot of tea if you want."

Finally, at 3 a.m., we did hug good night, this time lasting at most ten seconds. I would call this a decent date, in both senses of the word.

I've always admired Donna's Latina good looks and sexuality that she seemed to exude without trying. But what made me first take notice of Donna as more than just "Christine's cousin" had nothing to do with sex. It was her genuinely loving smile for Christopher when he was a new baby. "This woman has heart," I remember thinking. But over the years, we've hardly said boo to each other. Now, I've come to like her as a person as well. There might be a second date yet, but not till earliest April.

Did I tell Christine about Donna's invitation before accepting it? Did I tell her about the date before going on it? No and no. It would seem too much like asking for her permission, no matter how I put it. Donna and I are adults, and whether or not we consent, it is our own business, not Christine's.

This is the first warm and sunny weekend for a month. I took Christopher out by myself, with Christine electing to stay home for a break. Originally I had in mind to take him to Minnekhada Park in Maple Ridge, since bears would still be hibernating (last year, there were reports of bear encounters in the park). But seeing that he fell asleep in my car almost instantly and Minnekhada is not that far away, I decided to drive out to Campbell Valley Park in Langley, which is one of our favourites. Christopher slept like a baby the whole way, and when I woke him up, he opened his eyes, saw me and the trees, and broke into a smile. What a sweet angelic child. So we did the 4 km circuit, took sitting and snacking breaks on benches and board walks over marsh waters, with me giving him shoulder rides part way when his little legs got tired, saying hellos to people and petting dogs passing by, checking out the "ant castles" (tree stumps inhabited by colonies of ants on the Scenic Meadow), marveling at the flitting swallows and the darting humming birds, and in general basking in our love that fills earth and sky. What a perfect afternoon.

When we got back, the three of us went to Skillcourt for our usual "family dinner", to winding up a picture-perfect day.

A more heart-warming few fare-thee-well days simply cannot be had.

❖　❖　❖　❖　❖

1999-01-19

The eve of my 10 week India trip. I took out extra insurance, beneficiary: Christopher.

The last few persons I see before leaving are my parents, my special friend Jeanine, the Buckingham family and of course Christine and Christopher. This will be the longest I'll be away from him for. It will be our toughest separation yet. Other than the total length, there will be long stretches when I will be out of telephone contact, not to mention internet access, with the rest of the world. And even in the center of New Delhi, a 10 minute overseas phone call could cost more than what an average Indian would make in a month. I tried to explain this to Christopher.

"Even if I cannot call you, I will still be thinking of you," I said to him. "Even if you don't hear from me, I will still be loving you. Do you understand this, Christopher?"

"Yes, Uncle Tony. But I will miss you." With this he broke out in tears, soaking my shoulder.

"I know, Christopher, I will miss you too," I paced the carpet back and forth, patting him softly on his back. "But remember, I'll be back. What would you like me to bring back to you?"

"You, Uncle Tony."

"I'll come back to you, Christopher. I promise."

My tears joined his on my shoulder.

In fact, I said good-bye to them twice. The second time, I drove back after about 15 minutes to give Christine a little care package that she appreciated very much, plus my debit card complete with access code in case she needed emergency funds while I was away, the entire amount being the limit. All she said was, "You're crazy."

No matter how many times I hugged Christopher goodbye, I'd always want to hug him just one more time.

January 20, 1999, Wednesday, 100% humidity, 25C

Hi Christopher:

[04:05 @ Rm. 450, Pan Pacific Airport Hotel, Kuala Lumpur, Malaysia]

It is a relentless 26 hour flight from Vancouver to New Delhi, with but two hour-long stops in Los Angeles and Tokyo, and an overnighter in Kuala Lumpur where I am now.

This is my third tiger conservation expedition to India in as many years. The first time, in early '97, I traveled alone; the second, in late '97, with the Omni-Film crew; and this time in the company of volunteers Jane Kirkpatrick and Kim Poole.

In the plane I read Mark & Delia Owens' Survivor's Song. When my eyes got tired, I turned off the overhead light, reclined the seat, closed my eyes, and thought of a thousand things, which of course began and ended with Christopher. But in between, reminded by the presence of Jane and Kim, I thought of the people who have volunteered so much of their time and support over the years, who always rise to the challenge when called for, many of whom being activists in their own right – Frank Arnold, Joyce Arthur, Sandra Carlson, Yvonne Chin, Gay Cunningham, Cecilie Davidson (herself the President of the International Year of the Tiger Foundation), Fran Dietz, Rico "Spoorman" Habgood, Dale Hunter, Cecile Helten, Jane Jensen, Christiane Jensen, "Bearwoman" Evelyn Kirkaldy, Frances Kirby, Tanya Lebar, Kim Marchuk, Ruth Masters, Joan Miller, John Mullen, Diane "Fireweed"

Omni-Science and the Human Destiny

Radmore, Phyllis Reahil, Evelyn Roth, Neil Sumner, Carol Waddell, Dave Way, Rae Jane Williams, "Tigerwoman" Tracy Zuber...

"So many," you may say, but I think, "So few." So much to do, so few people to do it, with so little money, in so little time.

We arrived at Malaysia's international airport at Kuala Lumpur almost right on the equator about 01:00 local time (09:00 Vancouver time). It is a super-modern palace of an airport that outshines all others I've seen, even Vancouver's prize-winning YVR. Like the weather-sealed and climate-regulated "Biosphere" in Arizona, the interior of the airport-hotel complex is an environment apart, totally insulated from the steamy, dripping heat outside which we could experience any time by just walking out onto the tropical vegetation festooned terrace several floors under my window. The hotel is attached to the airport's main building by an air-conditioned walkway and my hotel window looks back at the terminal. Across the road from the terminal is what looks like a plantation where the trees look too geometric and monocultural to be a natural forest. Still, in the dawning light, the countryside looks green and lush, with the city slowly awakening on the horizon. We have no time to sample Kuala Lumpur's charms, though I cannot help but wonder what contrast may exist between this almost surreally palatial airport and the not-too-distant slums.

At 10:00 local time, I'll meet with Jane and Kim for breakfast. We'll then take the 12:30 flight to New Delhi, due to arrive at 15:30 Delhi time. I'll be looking down upon whatever tropical rainforest still remains on the Malaysian peninsula while the plane flies lengthwise over it en route to India.

I should say a few words about Jane and Kim. Kim, a blonde, pretty, petite and gregarious woman of about 40 who works in the travel industry, has been a volunteer for the bear and tiger campaigns since 1996. On this trip, she signed up as a volunteer for Avtar Grewal's tiger-oriented ecotourism business – Magnificent Tours - which in turn provides all her room and board during her stay of minimum 3 months, maximum six. Jane, brunette, fair skinned, tall, with dark yet bright and intelligent eyes, is a corporate lawyer in her late twenties, whose unbound spirit is expressed in her abandoning her lawyer's job and coming as my volunteer for 10 weeks, then for Avtar the rest of her 3-6 month stay. I like both women very much as people, and I find them both attractive as women.

Avtar Grewal is the son of the late great Ravinder Grewal, upon whose awesome reputation I have chosen his organization Tiger Fund as WCWC's CIDA grant "Southern Partner". Ravinder Grewal was among the first conservationists who raised a voice in favor of protecting the tiger as early as the 1950s. He spearheaded the crusade and succeeded in helping rescue the species from the brink of extinction in an age when tiger hunting was all the rage in high society – both British and Indian. In his effort to have tiger hunting banned, he faced death threats. He studied tigers in a time before tiger reserves, in a blind that could be destroyed by a single tiger paw swipe. His research results alarmed him, particularly the alarming rate at which the tiger population is shrinking. He was a distinguished naturalist and a forest officer, who played a key role in establishing various national parks in India. He has written over half a dozen books on the subject. He also has authored books on National Parks and Indian wildlife, and has written a number of scientific and popular science articles. He was the founder of Tiger Fund. Ravinder Grewal was an inspiration to many. "Was" because he passed away several years ago – a great loss to the world.

According to granting parameters, the Southern Partner receives 60% of the grant money to perform tiger conservation work within its country, and WCWC uses its 40% to conduct mostly educational and publication activities in Canada. So, of this year's C$100,000 budget, WCWC retains C$40,000 and Tiger Fund gets C$60,000, in four quarterly installments.

Avtar Grewal, who inherited Tiger Fund from his father Ravinder, has proven a congenial and efficient host in India. He took care of all my personal needs while I was on my first trip in the winter/spring of 1997. He facilitated almost unlimited opportunities for me to visit the tiger reserves, view tigers and photograph both animals and habitat. He provided royal treatment at his ecotourism Tiger Lodge at Kanha and Bandhavgarh tiger reserves. He arranged all lodging and transportation for me in urban areas. All in all, Avtar Grewal proved himself first class in the tiger-oriented ecotourism business. I had only one dissatisfaction. I was treated more like a tourist than a campaigner. I was factored almost no work to do in India, so I just created my own work as the opportunities arose.

Back in 1997, the first task I set for myself was to create a tiger conservation slideshow. That was less of a task than a hobby, since I have delighted in wildlife photography for decades. Since I was going into the tiger reserve on a daily basis with at least one camera in my bag, what more natural than to take pictures of the place and its inhabitants? The only problem was that most of the time, I was given to sharing the same vehicles with tourists. And most tourists want to see only one thing, tigers. They have little patience with anything else – jackals, deer, birds, let alone trees. I felt constantly rushed around, looking for tigers, but missing out on everything else. So many beautiful park scenes with exactly the right lighting were forever lost because I did not want to ask the driver to stop again on my account.

Omni-Science and the Human Destiny

Finally, I did get my own Gypsy (Indian-made, gasoline-burning, 800 cc motor, 4WD). Then I spent whole days in the park, taking my time, making every frame count. Thus, the Tigers Forever slideshow was born. Having shown it to thousands of children in Canada in the last two years, I've now brought it back to India to show it to Indian educators, students and villagers.

In November and December 1997, I went to India for the second time, this time with the crew of Omni Film Productions, there to make the Bengal Tiger episode of the TV wildlife documentary series Champions of the Wild. Again, Avtar played host. But somehow, the Omni Film crew had a fall out with him, and they moved out of Avtar's Bandhavgarh Tiger Lodge in mid-stay. They were originally going to include Avtar in the documentary, but after that incident, they excluded him. That rang some alarm bells. I myself had a first hand experience that gave me pause. The film crew left India four days before I did, and left enough money for Avtar to cover my hotel expenses. On the last day, I asked Avtar how much the hotel room cost. He said $40 per day, totaling $160 over the four days. But, he said, Omni gave him $80 per day, and he had claimed it. "Let's just keep this to ourselves." I did not give my consent and I did tell Omni Film about this after my return to Vancouver.

This year, of course I'll revisit these most enchanting of places, and revitalize and enrich the slideshow, but I'll have to do something more proactive, to do what I as a campaigner has come here for, to perform what I'm best at, to get most bang for the CIDA buck. What will it be? I'll keep my eyes and mind open, learn as I go, act as I learn, and let opportunities be my guide.

The first thing to be done in India, while in New Delhi, is for me to give a series of tiger conservation slideshows at urban schools. Shortly before Christmas, I sent out media packages to two dozen of India's most prominent media outlets. The packages included newspaper articles about WCWC, my work and contact information of both WCWC and Tiger Fund. Indian media would surely contact Tiger Fund rather than WCWC, so Tiger Fund would organize media coverage of the school events.

While in Delhi, I'll also visit a few of the most prominent tiger conservationists in India, including Ashok Kumar, Belinda Wright and Valmik Thapar.

After the school talks have all been done, which may take about 10 days, I'll again take the 24-hour train into deep rural India for the rest of my stay. At least, that's my plan, and if not Avtar's plan, it is nonetheless the most logical thing to do. I'll find out what Avtar has arranged soon enough.

Have a good day, Christopher. I'm thinking of you. This "goodnight" is the proof. Goodnight, Christopher.

Uncle Tony

❖ ❖ ❖ ❖ ❖

January 23, 1999, Saturday, "sunny" (actually, smoggy) 6-18C

Hi Christopher:

[09:56, in train from Delhi to Kanha]

After three almost intolerably smoggy days in Delhi, but only three as determined by Avtar, instead of the ten in the logical plan in my mind, I'm now in a train with Jane and Kim on the way south to Kanha National Park, which is situated approximately at the geographical center of the Indian subcontinent.

I'll be staying at Kanha until Feb. 2, then go back to Delhi for two weeks of school presentations and the Valentine's Day Save the Tiger Walk. A week of heaven in tiger country before plunging back into the eye-stinging, nose offending, lung-burning atmospheric cesspool of the over-polluted city where every breath one takes seems to contain enough smoke from ten cigarettes.

Mind you, the above is the complaint of only those who can feed themselves. For those who cannot, their next meal would be their only concern; the hydrocarbon fumes in the air would not be a factor, at least until they begin to develop cancer, to which the majority of New Delhi residents are said to eventually succumb. In Indian cities, the sub-poor are everywhere evident – oil-stained card-board curb-side domiciles that have a well used, permanent look, tent cities so firmly entrenched that whatever surviving vegetation conformed itself to the boxes and benches that seemed rooted to the ground, street children fighting over worthless spoils, grotesquely deformed beggars who are said to be the victims of deliberate crippling as children to engender sympathy in potential donors, and the mothers of crying babies with eyes pleading and hands plaintively out-held. This last I find the most irresistible. This is my third trip in India and I should know better, but I still find my hand dipping into my pocket and reaching out to fill those hands, in spite of the chidings I have received from my Indian colleagues whenever they catch me doing it. These women are professionals, they tell me. The babies may not even be theirs, but rented on a day-to-day basis for the purpose. Babies have been found to have flies inserted under their eye lids to make them cry, etc, etc. All in all, Delhi is a huge emotional torture chamber for anyone with empathy and sensitivity. The only thing in North America I can think of that could bring out a similar level of empathic pain is a factory farm, be it for debeaked hens crammed into battery cages, veal calves in standing stalls, pregnant sows in "gestation crates" and pregnant mares in "pee lines." I cannot wait to get out of Indian cities.

On the other hand, though "on a train" and "go back" may conjure an effortless, even enjoyable image, going from the average street of misery into a train station crammed full of suffering humanity is like leaping from a cauldron into a frying pan, and boarding a train at a Delhi train station is like jumping from the frying pan into the fire. Speaking of fire, if one broke out in a train carriage, the passengers would be toast, since all the windows are barred with iron grating.

Just to talk about something apparently trivial like orderliness, while the Delhi streets are at best chaotic vehicular-traffic-wise – especially in the eyes of a drive-between-the-lines and signal-your-intention-half-a block-ahead Canadian driver, the train station resembles a war zone, with people jostling one another to get at the ticket booth, then jostling one another to squeeze into the train – crowds everywhere, people sleeping on most benches and on the floor along most walls. But not a single queue in sight. Had the windows not been barred, people would swarm into the carriages through them. Luggage loss seems a matter of momentarily distractions. Chaining ones suitcases and bags to fixtures at once is a must, so much so that most of what the hawkers sell at train stations are locks and chains. One cannot relent ones vigilance for even a moment. Sleeping comes in fit and starts, and only from fatigue.

The journey itself involves a joint-aching 20-hour train ride plus a bone-jarring and take-your-life-in-your-own-hands 4-hour car trip, one way, totaling 26 strenuous hours not including waiting time. As I recall from my previous trips, and experience now once again, the train would first pull out from the centre of Delhi, through the heavily urban areas, then the "suburbs", the tertiary-urbs, then quaternary-urbs, etc., until it finally leaves the city complex behind. A measuring rod of distance from city center is the density of garbage strewn on the ground, mostly unidentifiable piles of oily brown and black substances inter-mixed with countless bits of white and blue from disintegrating and disintegrated plastic bags and other non-bio-degradable plastic ex-items, plus the opacity of the air, the intensity of the smell, the frequency of ghettos and tent cities, and the density of the people, male and female, children and adults alike, standing and/or squatting beside the train track relieving themselves, "small convenience" and/or "big convenience" (in Chinese lingo), facing in whichever direction (over 25% of the time therefore facing the passing train), in plain view of the passengers, who pay one another not the least attention. Even right in busy street corners in New Delhi, there are open urinals (for men only) visible to every passerby or passengers in every passing car or bus. Then, the tightly crammed row buildings and narrow alleyways of the city imperceptibly thinned into the houses of more open and less festering townships, then the widely spaced mud huts of villages. Then, the train would begin chugging through intermittently lush and desiccated countryside comprising mostly paddy fields, wheat fields, irrigated fields, dried out fields, mango groves, papaya plantations… - across rivers and belts of semi-desert. After sundown and at night, we'd clattered through miles of pitch darkness punctuated by clusters of dim dots of orange light, each a small cooking fire or a kerosene lamp. Then suddenly, the glare of yet another train station with people sleeping on the dusty ground and hawkers pushing their ware and trays of local delicacies, some raising the merchandise up to the train's windows – not recommended fare for tender-gutted foreigners. And some bring their steaming jugs of chai right on board. When they walk by, and I catch a whiff of the aromatic tea, my automatic response would be to call out, "Roco! Roco!" The few minutes of pleasure would return us inevitably to another hour or two of tedium. Hard as we might try, we'd lose count of the number of stops, which seem never-ending.

And the same thing all over again in reverse from Kanha back to Delhi, and from Delhi back to Kanha within the next three weeks. Discomfort aside, it is a waste of four working days in my limited time in India, in which every minute is precious. Bloody poor planning if you ask me.

This is why I'm dissatisfied by the schedule Avtar has set for me. At best, I could take a six hour car ride from Kanha to Nagpur, then fly for two hours from Nagpur to Delhi, but it is much more expensive, and would still consume two otherwise productive working days, without the payback of even pleasure. So, setting a schedule that involves an extra back and forth trip, as the one Avtar has arranged, does not show good judgment and organizational skill, especially given all these past weeks, no, months, of preparatory time.

Or - the dark thought emerges - does this involve some kind of perfidy or caprice or treachery as well?

By this arrangement, considering extra traveling expenses, Jane and Kim will have to stay on at Kanha and/or Bandhavgarh instead of coming back to Delhi with me for the Tiger Walk and school slideshows.

One dark thought is that Avtar wants Jane and Kim to be at the tourist lodge as soon as possible to serve his customers instead of being my assistants in New Delhi for educational outreach.

While in Delhi, the two people I work most closely with, other than Avtar, are Magnificent Tours manager Raman Johal and Tiger Fund employee Sarita Pannu, who used to work for WWF – World Wildlife Fund - at the Ranthambhore tiger reserve.

There are lighter moments. One day, at a MacDonald's joint (! - Raman's idea) having a "maharaja veggie burger ", Jane said that most of her friends wouldn't consider marrying a man who can't cook.

I took the bait and said, "That explains why I'm still single."

Kim, in her usual somewhat sarcastic way, said, "That's one of the reasons."

Sarita, a darkly yet girlishly beautiful woman in her twenties, came to my rescue. "He's married to the tigers," she said.

"So are you, but *you* are married." I said self-deprecatorily.

"I'm married to a real live tiger, but don't tell him," she said with a wink.

Back to Jane, I said, "May those women who use cooking ability as a vital criterion end up marrying some wife-beating gourmet chefs."

I brought Jane and Kim to visit Ashok ("a-SHOOK") Kumar – world known tiger conservationist specializing in urban undercover sting operations, having uncovered stashes of tiger skin and sacks of tiger bone in Delhi and Calcutta in yesteryears. He is also an executive director of Wildlife Preservation Society of India (WPSI). In spite of his exploits, he is a gentle and mild mannered man, with a good sense of humor. On his desk is a plague with a quote from the lawyer of one of his enemies: "Next to God, Ashok Kumar is everywhere." And yet, in spite of his high international profile, he is not well known in his own country, at least by appearance, and he wants to keep it that way to prevent blowing his cover. Ashok invited us to his place for dinner some time before we return to Canada. He said he would invite Belinda Wright as well.

Belinda, a regally beautiful British woman who has lived her whole life in India, is also a WPSI executive director and a world renowned tiger conservationist in her own right, who was the first to investigate tiger-poaching in the 1980s and among the first to bring the tiger-poaching and tiger-parts-trade issues to world attention. Her TV documentary Land of the Tiger is both poignant and magnificent, and her book Through the Tiger's Eyes is exquisite and deeply touching. When I first met Belinda, it was at the Tigers 2000 conference in London, England, in 1997, as part of my first trip to India. Before my departure from Vancouver, I had written Ashok and Belinda about the trip. In the conference, we sought each other out. At first sight, she took an intense look at my face. Then a smile began to beam on hers. "Perfect," she said.

"Thank you," I said, a little taken aback. "I've never had that word used on me before."

"I've been looking for an Oriental man to participate in a sting operation in Calcutta with us. You look perfect for the part."

"Oh, I see. You want somebody looking perfectly like a tiger-bone-trading criminal and a tiger-penis-ingesting weakling. Thank you very much."

Of course I said yes.

Avtar was not present at the conference. When I told Ashok and Belinda that Avtar was chosen as our project partner, they exchanged an open glance and said, also in sync, "Why *him*?"

"What's wrong with him?"

"He's not even active."

Belinda invited me to stay at her place after we re-met in New Delhi, which, like her, was beautiful in a regal fashion. After being driven by Belinda herself in her unidentifiable car (some Indian make) through the chaos of Delhi traffic, a few more turns of her steering wheel brought us into a quiet and miraculously garbage-free suburban road. Soon, we turned into a walled estate with manned gate, and, voila, a piece of earthly paradise filled all my senses. What a treat after several days in grey and brown metro Delhi; just the colors alone are intoxicating. I will not attempt to describe its beauty, since words would do it no justice. Suffice to say that her home was a miniature palace, and her garden, replete with exotic flowers, a miniature Eden. She had two dogs – a cocker spaniel and a street dog. The spaniel had the run of the house, and the street dog's domain was the expansive garden. Notable was that after seeing the thousands upon thousands of scrawny, unkempt and flea-infested street dogs everywhere in Delhi, I found this one a specimen of its breed at its best – medium small, but exceptionally handsome, well proportioned, athletic and muscular, even compared to most domestic dogs on North America, albeit somewhat detached and aloof – definitely not a couch-cuddler. And there were a few Indian persons in attendance, which treated Belinda like a benevolent queen, and me, by osmosis, like a – duke? Belinda Wright is one extraordinary woman.

Of course, all this pampering had a price to pay. Back then, in early 1997, after two weeks in Belinda's residence, I was flown over to Calcutta to be fed to the wolves. In Calcutta, we met up with Ashok and had a couple of strategizing sessions. At the second one Ashok had dyed his silver hair black. Not a good job in my opinion, looking more like shoe polish than hair dye. Unfortunately the sting had to be aborted mid-operation due to Ashok's being recognized in the wrong place at the wrong time. He considered himself lucky to have escaped alive. Later, I heard that another undercover agent whose shoes I earlier attempted to fill, was killed in a subsequent operation. These people are dedicated and gutsy. Belinda herself, being a white woman, stands out like a dove among crows, and yet, she is as much on the front line as Ashok and other Indian operatives. Both are of course well known to the criminals, especially one Sansar Chand, the most notorious illegal wildlife trader in India. Belinda and Ashok brought about Chand's arrest. "If looks could kill," said Belinda. But within days, Chand was set free, and went right back to his dirty deeds.

The following month, Ashok also invited me to stay at his house in New Delhi and I did so for about ten days, this time treated like a prince, during which period I also befriended his daughter Malina.

Yesterday, I stayed at Avtar's Magnificent Tours office to check and write and send e-mail while Raman, Sarita, Kim and Jane went ahead to the Dilli Haat fair-grounds around 14:00, where a craft fair featuring exclusively Gujurati folk products was taking place, to set up the "Gigantic Tiger Cub" ("Big Cub") which we brought from Canada with us. It is a 45 feet long, 12 feet high nylon tiger inflated with a fan, with a zipper in the rear where people could go in and out. It is big enough to accommodate over 100 children side.

Delhi is a city of dust besides smog. Smog-wise you can't see two blocks. Dust-wise, it covers everything, indoor and out. While I was typing away on my laptop, a servant girl came into the room and began sweeping the floor with a broom. Wherever the broom went would rise a cloud of dust, and the dust would then settle on the shelves and the books and the furniture and my clothes and the computer key board and screen and on my sweaty face and inside my straining lungs. Then she would begin to dust the shelves and books and the furniture with a feathered duster, and the dust would fly again. Come to think of it, I have never seen a single vacuum cleaner anywhere in India that I can recall. This office is a microcosm of most Third World cities I've seen. Many African places are the same.

I arrived at the Dilli Haat around 18:00 and found that, right off the bat, Raman burnt up one of the two heavy voltage-converters we took pains to bring from Canada. He applied the 500 watt one on the blower used to keep the Big Cub inflated instead of the 750 watt one I specified. So now, we have only the 750 watt one left and can't run the blower and the slide projector at the same time. I cursed beneath my breath.

It began to get dark. The evening was supposed to be when the majority of the people would come. I went through the fairgrounds with Sarita and bought a handcrafted 100 watt lamp. We put it inside the Big Cub with the shade removed, plugged it in and lit up the Big Cub from within like a lantern. The reporter from Asian Age did come and gave me an hour-long interview inside the Tiger Cub, with the lamp casting the shadows of our talking heads on its butt. Jane loves the lamp. She bought it from us after the fair to send home to her parents.

Email-wise, I received several from WCWC, and several from friends, but none from Christine. I've sent several to her and Christopher. I checked one last time just before leaving and still nothing. This does not justify an expensive phone call, but it does leave a lingering disappointment after I had left the Magnificent Tours office to go to the train station with Jane and Kim.

Right now, as the train clatters along, Jane is reading by the window, and Kim is writing in her journal, each sitting in our respective bunks.

This time we've taken packed meals with us, prepared at the Bajaj Indian Home Stay where we stayed the last couple of nights without health problems, to forestall eating train food which did make me sick in my first train trip in 1997. I remember having to go to the toilet to throw up, which was basically a hole in the floor through which one could see the gravel underneath rushing by. The floor of the washroom is awash with urine. I bent down to vomit, and my favourite pen fell out of my breast-pocket right through the hole out of sight. When I staggered my way back, I was treading urine all the way to the foot of my bunk which means that there were urine-tracks leading from the washroom to every bunk, already dried or still wet. Enough to make me want to go back to throw up again!

Having conversed in English with Jane and Kim for some time along the lines of the last paragraph, except instead of "urine" we were saying "piss", I felt obliged to be neighbourly to the lone older Indian woman in a sari sitting in a meditative position in the bunk diagonally opposite mine, and gave her a palms-together, head-bowed greeting of "Namaste". She returned the greeting, smiled and said, "Nice to meet you. I'm from Detroit, here to visit my daughter in Agra." Shit! I mean, oops!

Something with what happened or did not happen over the last three days bothered me, significantly enough to cause me to share my concerns with both women, first with Kim on an impromptu basis while Jane was sleeping, and then with Jane after she had awakened with Kim participating.

First, the total lack of media at the Ahlcon School presentation. It was more photogenic than any presentation to any Canadian school, with an exotic setting and a huge audience. It was a glaringly missed golden opportunity. Back in December, when Avtar came in to WCWC for a meeting with me and the WCWC executive directorship, we agreed that I would send off media packages to the Delhi media ASAP, which I did before Christmas, with a cover letter and some 20 pieces of highly persuasive newspaper articles including the Georgia Straight, the New Internationalist, the Hindu, the Global & Mail, the Vancouver Sun, the Toronto Sun, the Vancouver Province, etc. All Tiger Fund would have to do was to make one follow-up phone call each to the 25 or so Delhi media outlets I mailed the packages to, or, even easier, fax them a media release with my speaking schedule as Avtar has arranged it. Evidently, they did none of these. And then, the significant question: What did Tiger Fund do with all the incoming inquiries resulting from my mailing? The Asian Age interview was due to the in-coming call from the AA reporter to Tiger Fund's office *while I was there*. It was Sarita who answered the phone. When I asked to speak to the reporter on the phone, Sarita either did not hear me, or refused to hand me the phone. Goodness knows how many other phone inquiries came in when I was not there. So what happened to them?

Second, when I expressed that most logically, all the school presentations in Delhi should occur within the first week or ten days I was there and all the media in Delhi done before I go to Kanha and there to stay for the next two months, Sarita said that it was difficult or impossible at this time for one reason or another.

Third, they pretty well herded me out of town, but not before having me leave my slides and the Big Cub in Delhi for their own presentations. At one point, while reading her draft for the bilingual pamphlet for distribution to the students, I thought that it would serve very well as the opening of the tiger portion of the WCWC 98/99 members' report. So, with Sarita's permission, I copied and pasted the draft into my members' report draft file. But when I read down to the bottom of the piece I found this:

The program Schedule for the visit of Mr. Anthony Marr and team:

Date	*Venue*	*Time*
1999/01/21	Ahlcon Public School	9.00 a.m.- 11.00a.m.
1999/01/22-23	Dilli Haat	all day
1999/01/25	Sri Ram Public School	10.30 a.m.-1.00p.m.
1999-01-28	The Frank Anthony School	11.30 a.m.-1.30 p.m.
1999-02-14	Save the Tiger Walk	10.00a.m.- 2.00 p.m.

The question is: Why did they cut me and WCWC out of the Sri Ram and Frank Anthony schools? They did not even tell me about these engagements. When I asked them about the timing of the train trip, they just curtly stated that the train tickets had already been booked. What's the big deal about canceling a train ticket and booking a new one? Did they ship me out to Kanha just to get me out of the way? Kim and Jane arrived at similar conclusions independently.

Anyway, the train is rolling; it cannot be turned back. Time to look forward. We'll arrive at Gondia shortly before 05:00 tomorrow, eighteen hours from now. Another several hours by jeep to Kanha. So, hello tigers, here I come!

I would wish that you were here with me Christopher, but this choo choo train ride might be a bit hard for you to take. Anyway, Christopher, kisses and hugs, and good night.

Your ever-devoted
Uncle Tony

January 24, 1999, sunny, 5-16C

Hi Christopher:

[17:36 @ Tiger Lodge, Mukki near Kanha National Park, Madhya Pradesh, India]

Finally, again, I'm back in the embrace of Kanha National Park and tiger reserve ("KAA-na" – why is there an "h" where it is not pronounced?). After the excruciating 21 hour Delhi-Nagpur-Gondia train ride, which started around 08:30 yesterday, plus the bumpy and dangerous 4 hour jeep ride from Gondia to Mukki in a vehicle whose shocks were shot and tires were bald, we finally arrived at Magnificent Tour's Tiger Lodge at Kanha by about 10:30 today – over 26 hours in total.

Between the 26 hour plane trip from Vancouver to Delhi and the 26 hour train trip from Delhi to Kanha, which do I prefer? The plane trip, believe it or not. Still, through these two long rides, , Kim and I had lots of times to get to know each other better.

The four hour highway ride was a nasty follow-up to the train ride, not as uncomfortable and filthy as unnerving and dangerous, with the dare-devil driver *almost* hitting pedestrians or street dogs or cows or oncoming traffic about five hundred times, often with but inches to spare. This combined with his total inability

Omni-Science and the Human Destiny

to take his thumbs off the horn, whether or not there was anybody other than ourselves to hear it, delivered us at the Kanha Tiger Lodge more or less dazed.

But, Kanha, sublime Kanha, to see you again – a few days sooner - makes even the two unnecessary train trips combined far more than worth it. My mind aside, which is still grumbling about poor organization and lost opportunities, my heart is singing, right now, that I'm here in Kanha and not in Delhi. I cannot deny, lovely Kanha, nor describe, how happy I am to be back in your embrace – the place, the flora and fauna, the villagers I recognize from previous visits, the good smell, the clean heat, the wooded loveliness and rustic familiarity of the Tiger Lodge and the lodge workers who welcome me back with pomp and circumstance and ceremony. Ecotourism-wise, I can't deny that Avtar runs a fine ship.

Of Kanha, it is written:

"This is without a doubt one of India's most spectacular and exciting parks. The dense sal forests, bamboo thickets and Mekal river provided the inspiration for Rudyard Kipling's 'Jungle Book'. The park is situated in the Mandla district of Madhya Pradesh, its interesting mix of river valleys and steep rocky escarpments provide a diverse habitat for all manner of indigenous wildlife.

"The park was created in 1955 and one of its first ambitious projects was to protect and preserve the local population of Barasingha (a unique type of swamp deer). This involved the relocation of several villages, a process that has been replicated in several parks with considerable success. The park came under the Project Tiger umbrella in 1974, and despite some setbacks has grown into one of the largest national parks in India.

"At nearly 2000 sq km Kanha is one of India's largest parks, and after Sunderbans, home to the second largest population of tigers. The mixed forests of sal and bamboo provide good breeding grounds for approximately 200 different species of birds, as well as 22 mammal species. The large open meadows are the true trademark of this park, with numerous waterholes attracting a variety of birds and mammals, and providing excellent photographic backdrops. As well as the barasingha, herbivores include chital, sambar, barking deer, nilgai (Blue Bull) and the magnificent but shy gaur (Indian Bison), sadly there is just one solitary male Blackbuck remaining inside the park. Feeding off these prey species are jackal, leopard, wild dog (Dhole), hyena and of course the tiger.

"Over the years Kanha has received a fair amount of international attention, having featured in numerous newspaper and magazine articles. It is one of the best places to see tigers in the world and many argue that it is one of India's best run

National Parks.

"There are visitor and interpretation centers located both inside and around the park, which are both informative and entertaining. Jeep safaris enable you to view larger areas of this vast park, and offer the mobility to track tigers by following fresh pugmarks and alarm calls. As in Bandhavgarh, elephants are also employed to find tigers off road.

"Kanha lies in the heart of India and can claim to be its most prestigious National Park, the land painted so vividly by Kipling does not disappoint. The park is open from 1st November till 30th June.

Yes, Kanha, my beloved Kanha, I am here not just to bask in your splendor and swoon in your embrace, but to fight for your beauty and in your honour, don't you know?

My mind again edged my heart aside. Too bad I have the tiger's future to worry about, and the best use of my time this week would be to give tiger conservation presentations twice daily to urban schools in Delhi. I *love* to be in the midst of tigers in tiger reserves. Those precious moments are monuments in time and experience, but if by wading back into the quagmires of urban enclaves to spread the word and to turn up criminals I could do more good for the tigers than by just sitting here ooing and ahhing at their beauty, I am willing.

But now that I'm here, I reacquainted myself with lodge manager Manohar Dhami, his lovely wife Deepfee and the other workers, most of whom I have met in previous visits, including Faiyaz Khudsar ("fai-YAZ KOOD-sar"), a lean and forthright man in his late twenties, with an open, honest and earnest face. Faiyaz has a Master's degree in environmental studies, and is the Tiger Fund field-officer I'll be working with over the coming weeks. I also met American volunteer CJ, a boyishly handsome and very likeable young man with a great sense of humor expressed with a sunny smile. He served as a Peace Corp volunteer in Mali, West Africa for almost 3 years before finding himself wandering into deep rural India and somehow stumbling into the Tiger Lodge.

Had a highly constructive informal meeting with Faiyaz, CJ, Manohar and Deepfee regarding slideshows to tourists and fund raising for Tiger Fund from tourists. We also discussed the concept of raising Kanha's gate charge and have the revenue split between park services and villagers, a la Chitwan National Park, Nepal. They also took to the idea of solar-cooking with great enthusiasm. Tomorrow, we will do a field test of the portable solar oven that we have brought from Canada.

Omni-Science and the Human Destiny

Now, the group has taken the [Champions of the Wild – Bengal Tiger] video to show the free-school children, some of whom I befriended back in 1997. Love to see them again. But I'll wait till tomorrow.

And perhaps tomorrow, in Kanha National Park, I'll meet a tiger I've met before.

Wish you were here, Christopher, good night.

❖   ❖   ❖   ❖   ❖

January 25, 1999, sunny, 6-20C

Hi Christopher:

[19:21 @ Rm. 117, Tiger Lodge, Mukki (mook-KEE), Kanha National Park]
I had a full day. How about you?

I rose before dawn, about 05:30. Into the park by 06:30, with Jane, CJ, a lodge guide and a park guide, Manohar at the wheel of the green Tiger Lodge Gypsy.

Kim and another Magnificent Tours volunteer named Janice, from Nova Scotia, came down sick in the stomach and stayed in the lodge. They are the only two among us who had the mango pickle last night. I also got sick from mango pickle back in 1997, in a Delhi hotel, and since then the smell of mango pickle has been unpleasant, in fact mildly nauseating, to my nose.

Highlights of the safari – two massive Gaur bison (the largest bovine species in the world, bigger than the American bison and even African Cape buffalo, but less dangerous) and a gorgeous Indian Roller (a robin-like bird with florescent multi-hued blue plumage, the most exquisite of which being under the wings, so that it flashes brilliant blue with every wing beat as it flies, and since it sits more than flies, it is very difficult to capture its maximum beauty photographically, which so far I have not succeeded). I did expose a full roll of 36 on the animals and plants we saw today, and well worth it. In regards to plants, we have to bear in mind that in a Canadian forest we may count 20 tree species, but here at Kanha, there are some 300 species of trees, and a comparable number of bird species. The biodiversity here is phenomenal.

In mid-morning, we stopped for brunch on the bank of a small lake, or large pond. With water fowls feeding, and swamp deer belly deep in water munching on aquatic plants, and herds of chital (spotted deer) grazing serenely on the meadow, and birds calling here and there, and bright red dragonflies flitting about, I have reached my nirvana, even with no tiger visible today. Still, moment to moment, I wish that Christopher were here with me, though I would not wish the plane flight and train trip on him.

When I saw the glow on the enchanted faces of CJ and especially Jane in her first sight of Kanha, I saw myself as I was the first time I entered a tiger reserve two years ago. Perhaps from Manohar's point of view, my face is glowing with enchantment still.

Upon arrival back in camp, we found a Caucasian couple in their 50s - Albert and Andrea Loughran, from Bristol, England - having tea in the vaulted-roofed but wide-open-unwalled dining pavilion. The husband, whose uncle still lives here, was born in India. We chatted a little about how London used to be like Delhi, pollution-wise, and Delhi is "out of control". A few days ago, while our plane was approaching Delhi from Kuala Lumpur, we identified the city by first identifying its smog. As soon as the plane's door opened, our noses were assaulted by a thick fume-cocktail. In traffic downtown, visibility is down to about one or two blocks. Thick bluish-brown smoke pouring from the exhausts of the ubiquitous 3-wheeled auto-rickshaws, whose 2-stroke gasoline-engines are being fed a diet or dirty burning kerosene. Delhi is now a massive laboratory. Its air has never been as bad as this, even twenty years ago, even ten. It is not that they aren't aware of the problem. They just can't do anything about it. They can't just install a Canadian style Air Care system and refuse insurance to those vehicles that don't pass the emission test. First, they don't give a hoot about insurance. Second, just about every vehicle would fail, so what's the point? And if government clamps down and bans the auto-rickshaw, transportation would be semi-paralyzed, and millions of people would be out of a job, and there would be a mass uprising. So what do you do?

Street garbage-wise, about the same. Twenty or thirty years ago, it would be by and largely bio-degradable. But not the plastic-filled garbage of today.

During lunch, the gentleman looked at me intensely and finally said, "Are you in a television wildlife documentary about tigers?"

"Uh, yes, a few. The one you're talking about is probably called Champions of the Wild."

"Yes, that's the one. You know, Mr. Marr, it is because of that documentary that we've decided to come to Bandhavgarh and Kanha."

Omni-Science and the Human Destiny

Jane said that at the Vancouver airport, an airport employee asked her, "Is he Anthony Marr? I read about him in some newspaper article some time back."

As for me, I've learned to just shrug it off. This kind of thing happens about once a week in Vancouver. Dimitri, the owner of Sunshine Diner on Broadway and McDonald, even asked, several times, to have a picture of me to hang on the wall, along side Elvis Presley, Marilyn Monroe and the Beatles; I gracefully declined. Back in February or March last year, Vicki and I saw on the front window of the Hemp Shop on 4th & McDonald a copy of the Vancouver Sun article about me being beaten up, with photo. When I went to visit the Sea Shepherd, Lisa Distephano was heard to tell the crew, "That's Anthony Marr over there. He's awesome." While having a coffee with Vicki and Rico in Victoria, a man passed near our table and just said, "Keep up the good work, Mr. Marr." When I turned to thank him, he had already turned the corner. Well, keep up the good work, Mr. Marr, but don't let this go to your head, Anthony.

In the afternoon, around 13:30, Faiyaz and a lodge employee from Lahkma village named Sarup (19), took me behind the lodge for a 4 k hike along a very scenic rocky river – the Mekal - to visit a village of about 150 Baiga tribal people. Since the sun would set shortly after 17:00, we had to walk fast if we wanted to spend any time in the village at all. Walking along the river after sundown is not recommended due to the presence of Nauxalite tribal rebel terrorist activities in the area.

When we got there, the villagers were digging a well. Their present water supply takes the form of village girls packing water in cans or urns on their heads up from the river, which lay a good distance away. Their village used to be inside the current Core Area of the park. When the park was designated a Tiger Reserve of Project Tiger in the early 70s, there were some 20 villages in the designated Core Area. They relocated all of them into the surrounding Buffer Zone which today encompasses 178 villages with a total human population of about 100,000 and about as big a cattle population. This particular village we visited today is among the 20 that were relocated. The river we hiked along forms the Core-Area/Buffer-Zone boundary in this park sector, so this village we visited is situated on the edge of the park. When the village was being relocated, the government made promises as to what services would be provided. It seems that at least where a well is concerned, the government still hasn't delivered. And the villagers are tired of waiting and are taking things in their own hands. The name of the village is Chichrunpur ("chich-run-POOR"), meaning, incredibly, God-forsaken Place.

When the well-digging villagers saw us approaching, they paused and stared. When we crossed a certain invisible line, they closed in upon us. We hadn't made an appointment, since there was no phone at the village to make an appointment with. While approaching the village, Faiyaz advised me to keep the cameras in my knapsack. He introduced me as the "chief" of my troop, and asked for the village chief, who happened to be out of village. So we just chatted with the villagers a little, including the teacher of the village school, with Faiyaz acting as my translator.

Soon, Faiyaz gave me the nod. I pulled out the Polaroid camera first and took a few group shots, inciting glee and excitement when they saw themselves in the photos we gave to them on the spot. Then I took some shots of the village with my main camera. We chatted a little more. They trusted me to hold the babies and looked at me with undisguised curiosity and jabbered unrestrainedly behind my back.

One woman said something to me and Faiyaz translated that she was asking me for money. I replied that I am here to help them help themselves, and I will see what I can do for their village as a whole. First, I want to understand their culture and way of life, and only after that will I devise a plan. Meanwhile, I gave them a number of Tiger Walk buttons, and made an arrangement to come back to visit them with Kim, Jane, CJ and Faiyaz on Wednesday early afternoon, when the chieftain will be in.

I observed one thing, confirmed later by Faiyaz – when I talked about WCWC and Tiger Fund, they listened neutrally, but when Tiger Fund was linked to the tourist business, the villagers seemed wary.

Yesterday, Faiyaz asked me, very seriously, "Anthony, do you think that non-profit environmentalism and for-profit business should mix?" He didn't say much, but I can tell that he is very disappointed and frustrated about something. By conversation's end, I had gathered enough to know that in short, Avtar keeps Magnificent Tours on the front burner and Tiger Fund on the back burner more or less as a rule. Through the course of his employment under Avtar, Faiyaz has made several proposals, none of which Avtar seriously entertained, let alone accepted, much less implemented. I asked him to provide me with a summary of his ideas, so I could make my own judgment. He is an exceptionally knowledgeable, sincere, passionate and dignified man, genuinely keen, almost obsessed, on saving wilderness and wildlife. If there is one thing I am happy about regarding what Avtar has done for me on this trip so far, it is to put Faiyaz to work with me.

Within 5 minutes of our arrival back in camp, the afternoon safari group, comprising Jane, Kim, CJ, the British couple and Manohar, came back in. Around 18:00, I went to sit in the free school class, with CJ, Kim, Jane and the British couple entering at various times. The class is held at the Ravinder Grewal Conservation Centre.

When you enter the Tiger Lodge grounds, you first go through the entrance gate guarded by two beautifully painted tiger-striped gateposts made of plastered brick. You then proceed along a long and unpaved driveway curving to the left, with vegetation on both sides. After about 100 meters, you arrive at a sandy parking lot. The driveway leads on to the left past the parking lot another hundred yards to the service area of the lodge. From the parking lot lead two footpaths: the one to the left enters a sal forest, which ends in a large glade where the lodge-proper is situated, and the one to the right leads to the conservation centre. The conservation centre is basically two plaster-over-brick huts, one big enough to seat about 50 people, equipped with a TV/VCR, a black board, a small collection of wildlife oriented books, a few pictures and charts and posters on the walls, including the 1998 WCWC tiger paper, a blank white wall serving as a projection screen, and the slide projector that we have brought from Canada.

Under Deepfee's guidance, the students continued with their regular activities for awhile, then they turned to me and began asking questions directed at me, whom they have seen in the Champions of the Wild video shown to them yesterday. Faiyaz served as my translator, and he is very sharp and fast with it, sentence for sentence, both from Hindi to English and from English to Hindi, without a moment's pause. The first few questions were all from boys, and I encouraged the girls to ask theirs. Most of the boys' questions had to do with numbers of various animals, including the Canadian bears, but one very young girl asked about me why we "white" people were white. (White? Who? Me?) I struggled for an answer. How do I explain to them in a few sentences the theory of evolution and the origins of the human races? So I gave an off the cuff part-truth, "The white chapatti dough turns brown when you put them into an oven. Your country is hot, so we 'white' people will turn brown soon enough." I didn't think it was all that funny, but the kids laughed hysterically. The kids then sang some songs for us. On the spur of the moment, I offered to sing them the Save the Tiger song, with Jane, Kim, the British couple, Deepfee and Faiyaz singing the chorus.

Tiger Song is the creation of Tim Murphy, my assistant over the last two years.

lead (me)	_chorus_	_melody_
SAVE THE TIGER	Save the tiger	(doe ray mee doe)
THEY'RE OUR FRIENDS	They're our friends	(mee fa so)
THE TIGERS ARE IN TROUBLE	The tigers are in trouble	(so-la-so-fa mee doe)
LET'S HELP THEM	Let's help them	(doe _so_ doe)

136

A good time was had by all, and again, wishing Christopher were here.

[00:21]

Around 20:00, an official of the Forest Department came to visit, as invited by Faiyaz. He and I talked one-to-one for awhile, then, around 21:00 (9 p.m., India's standard dinner time) all of us sat down and ate together. After that, they (including the British couple, Manohar, Deepfee, Faiyaz, CJ and the official) watched the Champions of the Wild video.

It was an easy sell. The British couple wants a copy of the video to take home. Manohar wants a copy for the lodge. The official talks to me with obvious respect. The topic of conversation turned to the solar oven. We discussed its socio-economic benefit, benefit to women, benefit to the tigers, to the environment, the village, the entire buffer zone, the entire province, the entire India, the entire planet. But the natural resistance to change, the T-word - "Tradition" - will need energy and patience to overcome.

We came up with new ideas for the solar oven concept. Now this is really exciting. Communal solar cookers can be made of brick, an excellent insulator, with double paned glass on top, and metallic reflectors around. Manohar estimated the cost at no more than Rs 4,000 or US$100. It can practically last forever. The official played devil's advocate for awhile, then began to participate in the planning process. Faiyaz said he could build one within ten days. Meanwhile, the portable model will be tested tomorrow. After that, Deepfee will give a demo to the kids that come to the free school, and village elders will be invited for lunch cooked with the cooker. Everyone was, is, excited with the prospect.

Faiyaz is the person I talked to the most today. We discussed how to reach all 178 villages during my stay at Kanha. I certainly cannot go and visit each and every one of them. So we formed a plan. I will give daily slideshows for village elders at the conservation centre. Faiyaz will go out in a Gypsy daily to invite them and make appointments, and also pick up the village elders of the day. We would also take the opportunity to take the village elders for a short safari in the park, for though they live in the park's Buffer Zone, most of them have never been inside the park's Core Area where the tigers live, and therefore no sense of pride for the park and their national symbol the tiger.

"National?" Do the names India and Canada mean anything to them? Can they tell Canada from Mars or Venus? As far as they're concerned, Manohar, who is from Rajasthan state, or Faiyaz, from New Delhi, could be as much of an outsider as me, though our illiteracy in their language would make us farther-outsiders.

At the end of the slideshow, we would drive them back to their villages. Not a short spin for lodge driver Surinder.

Originally I said I would go with Faiyaz to visit the villages, but he thought it less intrusive if only he went on the first visits, my being yet again definitely a visual minority (a common term in cosmopolitan Vancouver, referring to people not of the Caucasian majority). So I gave him my thick media folder which contains many newspaper articles with my photos in them, to take to the villages as my calling card and to pique their interest, as well as for the eyes of Faiyaz himself.

Wishing you were here, Christopher, repeatedly. Good night.

❖   ❖   ❖   ❖   ❖

January 26, 1999, Tuesday, sunny, 6-20C

Hi Christopher:

[12:56 @ Tiger Lodge, Kanha National Park]

A day the equal of ten good days, and it's barely noon.

This morning, there were two options. One was to go to a local school to see a Gantantra Diwas (Independence Day) celebration and the other was to go into the park. I opted for the latter – with Manohar, Kim and the British couple. Jane elected to go to the parade with Faiyaz and CJ.

While paying our park fee at the park gate, we encountered a troop of children chanting some slogan parading past. When they saw me, they spontaneously suspended their chanting and started shouting excitedly something sounding like "Bagh Cha Cha". "Bagh", if that's the right word, means tiger. "Cha Cha" I have no idea, except for a 1960s dance in which I used to be fluent – 1, 2, 1-2, 1-2-3. I waved at them and they waved back. I took a couple of shots at them with my camera, and they waved some more.

As soon as I entered the park gates, I had second thoughts. I could go into the park any day of the week, and this festival is a one-time thing. Plus, going to the festival would present P.R. opportunities galore. But as soon as we turned the first corner and the buildings disappeared behind us, all thoughts of civilization vanished.

As it worked out, from a wildlife photographer's viewpoint, I made the better choice of the two. What I had was one of the best tiger sightings at Kanha I've had. We were sitting in the shade of a tree, with engine off, just listening. What we were listening for was not the roar of a tiger, since tigers hardly ever roar, that I've heard. What we did hear after what seemed like a long wait were the honking alarm calls of deer and monkeys. At once, Manohar started the engine and took off in the direction of the sound. We arrived just in time to see the tiger disappearing into a forest. Manohar took another road and stopped in a glade on the far side of the grove. There he turned off the engine and we waited. Sure enough, within minutes, the same tiger emerged. It was a tigress in prime condition, whose pug marks we saw earlier identified her as Pipal, the mother of three young cubs. When we saw her, she was alone, meaning that she was out hunting, having hidden her cubs in some thicket nearby. It so happened that on the far side of the glade was a small herd of wild boar. She stalked them stealthily for some interminable minutes, but before she had reached charging distance, the wild boars, already tense, alerted by the earlier alarm calls, spotted her and dashed away. One of her twenty or so failures before her next success, statistically speaking. She would never be so discouraged to stop trying – a lesson for us humans to learn.

In the Gypsy I had a happy chat with the ecstatic Loughrans - ecstatic, of course, because of their very first tiger sighting, of which up to this point they had been deprived. As per their request I promised to send them a Champions-of-the-Wild tape, a tiger T-shirt for their 10 year-old nephew and a few duped slides of today's tiger sighting, since they considered my camera, with its 28-200 mm zoom lens, the best of the four on board.

When we got back to the lodge at noon, Jane said to me, "You have a very good reputation with the kids."

"What do you mean?"

"They call you 'Bagh Cha Cha'."

"Yes, that's what I thought I heard this morning at the park gate. What's it mean?"

"You are their 'Tiger Uncle'," said Jane, very pleased.

The Lougrans left Kanha after lunch.

[17:19]

This afternoon, Jane said to me, "It seems that your concern about Avtar as discussed on the train has some truth to it. I've been speaking with Faiyaz. He was hired as Tiger Fund field officer to do conservation work, but instead is placed under the control of Manohar, of Magnificent Tours, to serve Avtar's commercial interest.

Omni-Science and the Human Destiny

This is not what he accepted the job for. His heart is in working with the villagers and park personnel and government officials towards saving the tiger and other wildlife, not in entertaining tourists to profit Avtar's Magnificent Tours. It is only because there is currently no tourist at the lodge that he has the time to work with you. He says he's been seriously considering resigning. He's being paid only 4,000 rupees (C$150) a month and has received job offers with much better pay from other employers, but he's sticking with Tiger Fund for now because he still hasn't given up all hope that things will improve, especially with you being here."

I produced the CIDA project expenditure list I promised while on the train, and went through it item by item with Jane. In WCWC's boardroom in Canada, with the executive-team bring accustomed to dealing with high Canadian labor costs, Avtar's budgeting for his program might have looked reasonable, but once on Indian soil and become aware of the cheapness of Indian labor, I had arrived at the inevitable conclusion that Avtar's half of the bargain is grossly underpowered and overpriced, and devoid of inspiration and drive or even sincerity. Given a budget of C$60,000, a much greater result should be expected, with a full time field team, perhaps by a factor of five or more. Conversely, the cost should be much less with things as they are.

The so-called medicinal plant garden, for example, which comprises only a small 20' x 20' plot with no more than 20 plants, claims a cost of $8,000 in the budget, which should not cost more than a couple of hundred dollars as is, even factoring in maintenance by Faiyaz. Avtar simply had not spent any money on developing it in the past. The two items "survey of visitors" and "project monitoring" claim a combined cost of $27,000 out of the budget, a huge amount when used in India, and a big chunk out of the grant. The worst thing about it is that they serve no proactive purpose. Even if they do serve a proactive purpose, they should not cost a small fraction of the amount. What the "survey of visitors" serves best is Magnificent Tours, whose name is projected to the tourists staying at other lodges showing them that Magnificent Tours' Tiger Lodge has a conservation program that other lodges have not. And project monitoring? What project is there to monitor? Of whom, by whom? The monitoring is almost more expensive than project itself.

The "Conservation Centre" – little more than a mud-brick hut with a few chairs, a TV/VCR and posters on the wall albeit excellent ones hand-made by Faiyaz - yet another several thousand dollars. There is also a big claim for producing educational material. In 1997, Tiger Fund was supposed to produce a tiger conservation comic book in Hindi. It did not materialize, and the unused grant money was not returned, nor carried over to 1998, as far as I know.

Jane was further incensed that given Avtar's now living in Vancouver – he bought a palatial house there in 1997, the same year Tiger Fund began working with WCWC under the CIDA grant - CIDA covers his expenses to travel between India and Canada, which is semi-personal, but does not cover mine, which is completely business.

Finally, for what would be really effective – Buffer Zone outreach - there is zero budget. I have a theory to this. One of the selling points of Magnificent Tours is that it has a conservation component to it in the form of Tiger Fund of the late great Ravinder Grewal, versus other lodges being purely profit making enterprises. My take on the lack of an outreach component in Avtar's plan is that such a component would take Tiger Fund activities into the field, away from the "Conservation Centre", rendering the work invisible to tourists.

Back in 1997, it was Avtar who proposed the idea of the "mobile educational centre / medical clinic", which I thought to be an excellent and truly magnificent idea (pun intended). But later he killed it, and more than once refused to resurrect it at my urging, nor at Faiyaz's suggestion. No reason ever was given. Probable reason – once again this would take Tiger Fund activities from tourist view.

So, if he wouldn't do it, I'll have to do it unilaterally. But I'll try it with Avtar one more time.

I'm not the only person excited about the all-Buffer-Zone-outreach plan. It's clearly the way to maximizing the bang-for-the-CIDA-buck. Faiyaz, Manohar, Jane, CJ and I piled into the Gypsy and drove to Baihar, the nearest town about 10 km distant, to call Avtar to discuss the plan. Avtar is Faiyaz's boss after all, and of course should be consulted, but when after numerous tries our phone call finally got through to the Magnificent Tours office in Delhi, Avtar was not available, nor was there any message left for us.

Slightly dowsed, our spirits nonetheless flew into the night sky on our way back to the lodge in the open deck of the Gypsy.

Good night, Christopher.

January 27, 1999, Wednesday, 6-20C

Omni-Science and the Human Destiny

Hi Christopher:

[09:36 @ Tiger Lodge, Kanha National Park, MP, India]
    The Gypsy has developed a starter problem, so no safari today. Instead, I will hold a meeting with Faiyaz at 10:00. What I have in mind to do is to draw up a jobs list similar to that in Avtar's budget, which I haven't shown Faiyaz, and ask Faiyaz to do a cost estimate on it, and further to do one on the alternative plan we have designed, including a whole-Buffer-Zone outreach. It is nearly 10:00 now. More later.

[18:25]
    Just returned from a most successful visit to the Baiga village Chichrunpur about an hour ago.
    But first, the 10:00 meeting. It was also attended by Jane and CJ, whom I totally trust. It was understood to be a strictly confidential meeting. In general, several items were deemed way overpriced. All deemed the "survey of visitors" and "project monitoring" to be way too passive to be able to answer the urgent call of the tigers - basically a waste of money, money that can be better used elsewhere by far. Most of all, all agreed that the absence of an outreach program, which limits the contact to only 3-4 villages out of the 178 in the Buffer Zone, to be the fatal flaw of Avtar's program, rendering it impotent.
    Tiger Fund as an organization doesn't even have its own dedicated vehicle in a place where, in the absence of phones, not to mention fax and email, the lack of a vehicle means total paralysis. As it is, Tiger Fund depends on Magnificent Tours for vehicular use, but only when MT's Gypsy could be spared. A good used Gypsy costs about C$5,000 (about US$3,000). Spread out over three years, the cost is only C$1,750 per year, although it would have to be cash up front. Fuel cost would be in the region of about C$1,000 per year. We would also need two full time outreach staff, one of whom being Faiyaz, at C$2,000 per annum each, to reach and maintain contact with all 178 villages in the buffer zone. All told, even with cash up front for the vehicle, it would cost only C$10,000 for the first year and C$5,000 each for the second and third years, fuel included. If it is two Gypsies and a full time staff of four, the outreach cost would be only C$20,000 for the first year including vehicle purchase and C$10,000 for subsequent years, compared to the $27,000 in Avtar's budget for the "visitor survey" and "project monitoring", which is stated to employ only one person for 8 months, with no vehicle. How Avtar managed to stretch out the cost to $27,000 was totally beyond us. Faiyaz also mentioned that

not one brown rupee has been released towards building the 4-acre full scale "medicinal plant nursery", which Avtar priced for $20,000 in the budget. The budget for the "medicinal plant garden", referring to just the tiny 20'x20' plot, which contains about 20 species, one plant each, which could be tended by a lodge employee at near-zero cost, was $8,000 in Avtar's budget. If we were to scratch the "visitor survey" and "project monitoring" and spend the $27,000 + $8,000 = $35,000 on the outreach program and the nursery, the results would be monumental, and still with rupees to spare.

And what of the other $25,000 in Avtar's budget?

Avtar is of course pro-tiger, but first and foremost because his Magnificent Tours capitalizes on tiger viewing as its main profit draw. It's almost, though not quite, on the level of a Canadian guide-outfitter protecting grizzly bears so that they would continue to have grizzlies for their clients to hunt, which in Avtar's case is tigers for his clients to view. This is perfectly fine, as long as it does not undercut real conservation work, which in Avtar's case it does.

I have also observed how Avtar and Faiyaz deal with villagers. Faiyaz relates to them on their level; Avtar does so from above. The only thing about Avtar I can trust is that he would not betray his father totally, but this does not mean he would bust his guts for Tiger Fund either.

I reiterate that the total annual budget of CIDA – Canadian International Development Agency - is C$2 billion, of which only C$1.2 million is for conservation (versus development) – less than 0.7% of the total - of which C$100,000 goes to the WCWC/TF program. I'll be damned to let this precious grant be misspent, misused and/or misappropriated, to put it politely.

I asked Faiyaz if it was true that he was thinking about leaving Tiger Fund. He simply nodded. CJ said to me on the side later, "Faiyaz doesn't give a damn about money. To him it is 100% the cause." WCWC's kind of guy.

Speaking of dealing with Buffer Zone outreach, we - Jane, CJ, Faiyaz, Janice, Kim, Sarup and I - had a most successful visit to Chichrunpur. In our morning meeting, we predetermined that we would not preach, would not condescend, would not patronize, would not insult, would not impose, would not fault, would not trick. Around 12:30 Manohar arranged a picnic lunch for us on the bank of the Kanha river behind the Tiger Lodge grounds, involving 4 helpers. After the lunch, we started the hike to the village and got there around 14:30.

On the way along the river, we came across a tree that had been illegally cut down since our previous visit, which was only day before yesterday. It had already been cut into 5'-long sections, and imbedded in one of the sections, splitting it length-wsie, was a wedge made of extremely hard hardwood. I took the wedge and continued walking. (Is it theft on my part?) Soon, we came upon the villagers of another village performing a 15-days-after post-funeral ceremony. We introduced ourselves and paid our respects, and were of course regarded with undiluted curiosity. As we carried on, closer and closer to Chichrunpur, more and more we saw tree stumps and grazed out pastureland littered with cow-pies, and of course the cows themselves.

At Chichrunpur, we were given the royal treatment. The village chief insisted that I sit in the best chair the village had to offer, a heavy bench seat with back and arms hauled down to the site of the new well from another part of the village up the hill. Regarding me as the "chief" of my "tribe", the village chief shook my hand with both hands and bowed to me deeply. I returned the salute in kind. I did the talking and Faiyaz did the interpreting. I thanked the chief for letting us visit their village. I said that I represent Canada in general and about 25,000 Canadians in particular – the membership of WCWC – as well as the thousands of Canadian children I have given my tiger conservation slideshow to - that I was there mainly to learn about them so as to find out how to help them help themselves.

Indeed they are capable of helping themselves. The proto-well is the evidence. In my last visit, it was just started – 10' in diameter but only 1' deep. Today, it's easily six feet deep.

At one point, to break whatever ice still remained, I asked Faiyaz whether the villagers held the flat-Earth or round-Earth worldview. Faiyaz asked the village teacher, a young man of about 20, who answered that the Earth was round. I then said to those around the well, "If you dig your well deep enough, you may come out in my backyard." This incited uproarious laughter in the villagers. After that, I felt totally at ease. I told the teacher, via Faiyaz, that I aim at linking their school with a sister primary school in Canada, and the Canadian kids can help them directly. He in turn told the chief, and both seemed very pleased.

The chief asked me what I had in mind when I said to help them help themselves, although in his mind, it's probably still, "What can you do for me?"

I asked Faiyaz to ask him how he would feel if we showed them how to cook rice and other foods without burning wood, in fact, without burning anything at all, including kerosene and even biogas. He seemed to think that it was a joke. I said further that we could come another day to give them a demonstration with a device that could do just that, and if they became convinced, we could teach them how to build a large permanent unit capable of cooking rice and other foods for several families at once. The families could do communal cooking to save effort, plus the effort saved from wood cutting and gathering. This would free up their time for developing other activities and enterprises. The teacher responded with something surprising. "If such a machine does work and we know how to build it, we could make them in numbers and sell them to other villages." Smart man, even though his own education is probably no more than the Canadian equivalent of Grade 3.

We arranged to visit them again on January 30, Saturday, around 11:00, with our portable demo solar oven, and that we'll bring rice and other foods and cook a lunch with the oven for all to share.

We left the village at around 16:00 to make the lodge by sundown. On the way back, Faiyaz said to me that he was surprised at how I raised the solar cooker concept so quickly and smoothly and pressed it home, that he had thought we would have to go by a much more tangential approach to get to that center. I told him that one thing which made it possible was in fact what he did. Some time during the visit, he grabbed a hoe and jumped into the then 6' deep proto-well, and started digging away with the other two villagers. CJ followed suit, and then I did too. Between us three, we deepened the dig by another foot. Tough work. All three of us ended up with blisters on our hands before the layer was done. Then Jane came down and filled one of the baskets with the dirt, put it on her head, struggled out of the pit, and staggered the 20' feet as if on a high wire to dump the content on to the dirt pile where children were playing king of the mountain. The villagers had a good laugh at our clumsiness. This is something that Avtar would never do. We were given a warm farewell. The chief said, "Please bring your camera again when you come."

All in all, even though the day began on a note of discontent, it is ending on a note of satisfaction.

Good night, Christopher.

January 28, 1999, Thursday, 4-19C

Hi Christopher,

[11:57 @ Tiger Lodge, Kanha National Park, MP, India]
This morning's park visit was one of the best to date. We - Jane, CJ, Faiyaz,

Omni-Science and the Human Destiny

Janice, Kim, Manohar, the obligatory park guide (whose job in fact is to make sure that the tourists and tour operators don't violate park rules, including leaving their vehicles and going on foot) and I - saw the tigress Pipal - mother of four new cubs according to Manohar - lots of birds, swamp deer, a large herd of wild boar and a very rare pack of six wild dogs. Photographically the only tiger sighting better was the elephant-back sighting of the Sita family in Bandhavgarh on Omni Film's first day out back in late 1997 with writer-director Andrew Gardner and executive producer Michael Chechik.

Mid-morning, we stopped in the shade of a large banyan tree on the edge of the forest, overlooking an expansive meadow. Manohar laid out the packed brunch on a few stainless-steel trays – vegetarian samosas, "pop-corn omelet", hard-boiled eggs, mandarin oranges, chai.

At first sight, the meadow would strike uninitiated eyes to be peculiar in two ways. First was that underlying the grass was a vague rectangular grid pattern. I had found out in previous expeditions that the meadow used to be the paddy fields of one of the 20 villages that had been relocated out of the park Core Area to the surrounding Buffer Zone. In the ensuing years, the paddy field had reverted to a sparsely treed grassland. Maybe I was looking at the relics of old Chichrunpur itself.

The second peculiarity was what might appear to be a strange geological formation, which comprised buttressed reddish rock spires up to 10 feet high. The densities of the trees and the spires were about the same; evenly spaced in the meadow were about a dozen trees of good stature and about a dozen tall rock spires, plus a number of saplings and "budding" spires of various heights and girths. These "spires" are of course termite mounds, and the largest ones, since the old village was moved away about 60 years ago, is about 60 years old. Grazing among the trees and spires was a herd of Chital, and soaring the thermal above were three or four vultures, waiting for earth-bound tragedy to happen.

We all sat in the shape of the Banyan tree, eating in companionable silence. "Ah! This is the life," sighs my heart. And again, I wished that Christopher were there with me. This would beat all the other trips I've taken him on combined.

[18:17]

We tested the portable solar oven and to everyone's delight, not only did it cook the rice, it overcooked it. Faiyaz confessed that there was a little doubt in his mind before, about whether the solar oven actually worked. Now, his uncertainty has been allayed.

This afternoon, everyone stayed in camp except Manohar and Faiyaz, who went to Baihar to try to contact Avtar again. On Manohar's part, he needed money from Delhi to run the lodge. Faiyaz would also check for the availability of a metal tub for making the communal solar oven with. We decided on building a large portable communal oven rather than a stationary brick one.

Late yesterday evening, Faiyaz, CJ and I had another pow wow, and came up with an even better idea for the communal cooker in terms of its costing next to nothing. Recalling the well-digging at Chichrunpur, I suddenly had a idea of an underground solar cooker. Instead of building a brick chamber, which is cheap enough, why not just dig a cubical pit, place the glass plates on top flush with the ground, and a few adjustable reflectors. The earth itself is an excellent insulator, though perhaps a vapor barrier of sorts might be required. At most, we could line the inside of the pit with brick or cement. No metal box required. All three of us are excited.

Faiyaz and Manohar came back from town and told me that Avtar will arrive on the 31st, who will then fly back with me to Delhi on the 2nd for my first presentation on the 4th. Wish I could stay here forever.

[18:58]

I visited the free school, took photos of the kids, then invited some villagers over to show them the Champions of the Wild video. Two village elders (of the nearby Lahkma and Manjitola villages), Sarup and a forest guard were also present. What followed was a three hour post-video discussion between me and the four gentlemen, with Faiyaz interpreting and speaking out for himself. Jane, Kim and Janice, Sarup, Manohar present, and CJ capturing the entire meeting with WCWC's Hi-8 cam. They all had ideas of their own.

"Wild boar and chital come to our village and eat more than half of our crop," said the chief of Manjitola, one of the nearest villages to the Tiger Lodge of the 178 Buffer Zone villages. "What can you do for us?"

"We have little financial resource to directly help you," I said as evenly as I could, "but with your cooperation we may be able to facilitate changes in the system which could be beneficial to you, such as raising the park fee for foreign tourists and have part of the increased revenue come to you in the form of a compensation, and maybe for some fencing."

"What good is a tiger? Why protect it?" And this is after Avtar has spoken with them on this before. The chief is one of the four people Avtar talked with back in 1997 when Omni Film was here. So why is he still asking the same question? Is this just a test question? Or truly reflective of the Buffer Zone's state of mind?

With a Canadian student, I could talk about ecological balance and the tiger

Omni-Science and the Human Destiny

being endangered, but to the chief I said, "The tourists come to see primarily the tiger. If we can raise the park fee, the tiger will be your financial benefactor."

"Eco-tourism has not benefited us, so far," which is his way of saying, "Yeah, right. I'll believe it when I see it."

I explained, "This is not just a theory. It's in practice elsewhere. Kruger National Park in South Africa, for example, charges around US$25 entrance fee, and Mountain Gorilla viewing in another African country costs about US$200 per *hour*."

His eyes were like saucers as he converted the amounts into rupees.

I pressed on, "And Chitwan National Park in your neighbouring country of Nepal also charges about US$25 per visit, with the revenue split 50/50 between the park and the villagers. But as you know, Kanha National Park here charges a ridiculous US$2.50 per full day, with the villagers seeing just a lot of red dust as tourist jeeps go roaring past their villages."

I didn't mention that the only people who profit from the current Kanha system are the handful of hoteliers and tour operators, such as Avtar. Not in so many words, but I explained my proposal to reform India's park system along the lines of Nepal's, to which the chief reacted with enthusiastic nods. I haven't talked to Avtar about this idea, mainly because he has not been available by phone. I wonder what he would think of it.

Back to the village chief I said, "The tiger is beneficial to you in another way. It eats chital. Together with the leopard and the wild dog and the hyena and the jackal, the tiger keeps the chital population down."

Faiyaz flashed me a bright smile. "He understands what you're saying."

"What is your motive to come here?" said the chief of Lahkma. This was not a hostile challenge, but a genuine and reasonable question.

I replied that I was here to help in whatever way I could - in such a way where the tigers and the villagers would mutually benefit.

"But what is in it for you?" Spoken like a North American.

"I personally love Kanha and Kanha's tigers," I said. "I also love Kanha's children. I want the best for them both. I'm also speaking for about 30,000 Canadians who wishes us success. I also have a beloved godson called Christopher. I want to help save Kanha and the tigers for him to enjoy when he grows up.""

I will have to systematically rally the support of the chiefs of all 178 villages around Kanha, and eventually also those around other Indian tiger reserves, perhaps in the form of a petition to start the park reform ball rolling, which we will present to Project Tiger on the federal level. The chiefs seemed to know what I was talking about, and further to agree with it in principle. We'll see when the time comes for him to put his signature on the petition.

To begin winding up, I invited them to lunch at noon tomorrow, rice cooked with the solar oven.

The Manjitola chief looked openly skeptical about the solar oven. Faiyaz assured them that it would work as claimed. I said, "We promised to not overcook the rice this time."

Good night. Christopher.

❖ ❖ ❖ ❖ ❖

January 29, 1999, Friday, sunny, 6-20C

Hi Christopher:

[11:11 @ Kanha Tiger Lodge]
Today is medical clinic day, when the conservation centre becomes the waiting room.

The clinic will open its doors shortly after lunch. Faiyaz told me that the average number of people coming to the clinic is now only about 25 per clinic day, versus the 65 or so back in 1997. Why the steep decline? Surely their state of health has not so drastically improved in this short time.

We're now sitting around the unlit fire pit. A doctor from Malanjkahn, the nearby copper mining town about 40 minutes by Gypsy via a dirt road, just arrived and joined us. He was fetched with one of the two lodge Gypsies on 30 km's worth of rutted road by lodge employee Surinder, and will be driven back, which means 120 km's worth of gasoline. He came on a half-volunteer, half-professional basis, since the mine has a "pro bono" arrangement with Tiger Fund's conservation program. He is a man of about 50, bald, heavy set, and has a superficially pompous bearing. But deeper, he proved very personable, to me as well as to the lowest lodge employees. His way with the children, which I will shortly observe, will tell the definitive story.

The medical clinic is in session, so I'll go and observe and video/photo-document the proceedings.

Omni-Science and the Human Destiny

[12:31]

I video-documented the medical clinic, which about 30 villagers attended, with Faiyaz serving as dispenser and Jane as secretary. The village chief is here again, sitting outside the clinic on the dried-mud ledge built around the trunk of a tree. When he saw me, he respectfully stood up, took my hand in both of his, and gave me a reverential bow. I returned his respects in kind, which has become second nature. I brought him over to the solar oven set up on the sunny side of the parking lot. Faiyaz had already loaded it with a pot of raw rice ready to cook. So I lined up the oven to the sun, set the reflectors and started the cooking process, while the chief watched with noncommittal interest.

[22:37]

I discussed with Faiyaz, Jane and CJ this evening about equipping the medical clinic with a microscope as a medical as well as educational tool. The villagers could then see the micro-organisms for themselves. We could set up a display booth on the side showing the role micro-organisms play in diseases, including the parasitic malarial amoeba. We could also set up a micro-biology display for the children at the free school.

Meanwhile, CJ entered his new tiger poem into my computer, which he wrote last night:

Tiger's Song
by CJ

Dedicated to Anthony Marr and all others on his mission

Today I jumped into the jungle with a group of friends,
Whose desire I share, to guard all forest lands.
A misty magic morning warmed up by the sun,
Green and blue, bright life images reflected in the ponds.
A call across the meadow beckoned us that way,
A sharp eye discovered something I live for everyday.

Today I saw a tigress in all her majesty,
Marching through the jungle without an eye on me.
Powerful cat of the forest strolling through the trees,
Crossed the road to grassy plains drifting away like a silent breeze.
Stunned, bewildered, we shivered, without a care as she went,

Out of our sight disappearing, a powerful message had been sent.

Today I lived a dream, I think of others that'll come like me,
To India's great jungle where tigers still roam free.
This illusion made me happy but I know that it's not true,
For this great cat lies in danger everyday being killed two by two.
There are people who want their bodies and parts for easy gain,
A quick dollar they're looking for in this evil black market game.

This symbol of a country and a rich forest land,
Will disappear overnight without some special plan.
So give them a place to live with people who understand,
That all life in the forest is sacred in Mother Nature's plan.
For our ancestors there were many, today only a few,
Their finite numbers dwindling, so much for us to do…

If tomorrow we'll see a tigress in all her majesty,
Think of all the others that'll come to live this dream.
For in the future lies one question,
What will there be to see, in India's great forests
Where the great cat still roams free.

We'll the save the tiger for you, Christopher. Good night.

❖   ❖   ❖   ❖   ❖

January 30, 1999, Saturday, sunny, 7-20C

Hi Christopher,

[18:46 @ Kanha Tiger Lodge]
  In another three days I'll be back in Delhi. I want to stay out here and work with the villagers, but there are two reasons I look forward to going back there. I'll be speaking to Indian children by the thousands and reaching Indian citizens by the millions via media. And there is one more reason. I'll be hearing something from you. Praise be to email.

Omni-Science and the Human Destiny

    A full and exciting day, despite an inactive morning.

    We had lunch at 12:00 and began the hike to Chichrunpur at 12:30. Faiyaz and I, with lodge employee Rahesh who had the portable solar oven slung over one shoulder, charged ahead, leaving the slow pokes (Jane, CJ, Janice and Kim) way behind, who also got lost along the way, necessitating Rahesh to go back to look for them. We arrived at Chichrunpur by 13:00. Because the villagers had to go to the river to fetch cooking water, we didn't start the solar cooker until around 13:30. Given the semi-success back at the conservation centre with the Manjitola chief yesterday (too short a cooking time), we kept the cooker on till 16:15 before opening it. The rice was cooked perfectly.

    While waiting, we did all sorts of things to keep the villagers entertained. Polaroid snap shots are always big hits. At one point, I challenged Faiyaz to a foot race between two trees over uneven terrain about a hundred meters apart. CJ yelled, "Count me in!" Faiyaz, with his cheetah-like build, came in first; I blame it on my age for losing by less than half an elephant's nose. CJ, due mostly to his sandals, brought up the rear by about a cow's length.

    Faiyaz, the honorable victor, dispensed aspirins and quinine pills. CJ orchestrated an impromptu eco-skit with the village children who played different animals. Most of the activities were photographed (mostly by me) and video-taped (mostly by CJ). The response of the village chief and teacher to the solar oven demonstration was to talk quietly in front of it, then pick up a stick from the ground and take crude measurements of the oven box with it, and make hand gestures meaning "enlarge". Too bad I didn't have the camera at hand when they were doing the measuring. It would make a distinctive picture in the annals of tiger conservation.

    Upon returning to the lodge, we found Janice, a Magnificent Tours volunteer from Nova Scotia, Canada, normally stationed at the Tiger Lodge at neighbouring Bandhavgarh tiger reserve. She heard about our program and took it upon herself to come to Kanha to join us, seeing as there are no tourists booked at the Bandhavgarh Tiger Lodge over the next week or so. She was also more than obviously bored out of her tree and consumed with this great desire to escape. If she asked Avtar for permission, he would probably have refused. It took some courage for a single white woman to take a public bus, let alone a relayed of three public busses from Bandhavgarh to Kanha, when driving non-stop by car would take seven hours. She said that she had heard about our work even when back in Canada, and to be a part of it is her dream come true.

    Faiyaz just knocked on my door to inform me that Assim Srivastava, director of Kanha's Buffer Zone, has just arrived and would like to meet me. More later.

[22:46]
The meeting with the Buffer Zone Director was successful to the extent that I think I made him see that increasing the gate charge for foreign tourists is beneficial to tigers, park and villagers alike, which needed no lead-in, since one of his opening questions was "What do you tell a villager who asks you why we should protect the tiger?" We worked out that if we charge the 4,000 foreign tourists each Rs1,000 (US$25) instead of the present Rs100 (US$2.50), the revenue would be Rs4,000,000 (US$100,000) which, though not a huge sum in Canadian terms, is a large sum in Indian terms, and is in any case ten times better than the Rs400,000 (US$10,000) per annum. He suggested asking the tourists to see if they're willing to pay more for the tiger. Now, here, finally, is a worthy question for the survey, but one I doubt is on Avtar's list for the survey he has in mind, and it certainly wouldn't cost $27,000. Jane happily volunteered to do it, and I have no doubt of the outcome. We also showed him the Champions of the Wild video. He estimated the number of people who have seen it and will see it worldwide probably number in the millions. He thought it would have a good effect on Bandhavgarh, Kanha, and tiger conservation in general. I think something good will come out of this meeting.

Good night, Christopher.

January 31, 1999, Sunday, sunny, 5-18C

Hi Christopher:

[17:09 @ Kanha Tiger Lodge]
Just two more days to hear something about you. How exciting!
The most dramatic photo of a tiger I have ever taken was taken today.
This morning's safari, with Kim, Jane, CJ, Janice, Deepfee, Manohar at the wheel, was yet another one of beauty and wonder, and of warm and happy bonding. The creatures that presented themselves were mostly of the avian kind, and in our path, lots of confusing tiger pug marks. We got off road into the sal and bamboo thickets on two elephants, and found the tigress Pipal sleeping on her side amidst dense foliage, with the half eaten carcass of a wild boar within tail-flicking distance

behind her. She'd be sleeping her lunch off and finish the wild boar for supper. She will stay right here and safeguard it till then. Perhaps her four suckling cubs were hidden nearby. She was not going anywhere. My mahout kept urging our elephant closer and closer to the tigress. I told him to cool it after we had attained spitting distance. When the second elephant approached from the right, with CJ aboard manning the video camera, the elephant began loudly snapping branches and saplings, which aroused the tigress, who, now crouching, showed her displeasure first with low growls, then an explosive fang-baring hissing roar, which I captured on my still camera. It's going to be a good one, since the roar was delivered straight up at me.

But not so good for Pipal. If this happens to her several times a day, she wouldn't have a moment's peace, nor needed rest.

Today marks the arrival of Avtar at the lodge. No one seems to particularly look forward to it, myself included, even though he holds no power over me. Manohar has been cramming his paper work over the past couple of evenings. Especially given the influx of tourists in short order, CJ considers Avtar's arrival as the beginning of the end of tranquility at Kanha. The whole camp seems bracing for a siege.

Faiyaz has also lost some of his exuberance. How could he not, knowing that his freedom of action to his heart's content for what he loves most will likely be curtailed?

[22:34]

Well, Avtar is in camp, and short-notice changes have already come down.

During dinner, Kim who was sitting to my right, whispered to me, "I need to communicate."

"With me?"

"Yes. Come to my room at 10 and we'll talk."

I didn't know what it was about at that point, but after she had left the dining pavilion, Avtar made a few announcements. For one thing, Janice was chastised for leaving Bandhavgarh without permission and ordered back, departure at 09:30 tomorrow, and Kim with her. Kim will stay at Bandhavgarh for the whole month of February, and will switch with Jane for the month of March. My opinion was not sought about this switch even though whom I have to work with is of relevance to me.

While he was at it, Avtar gave me, too, an order. "Anthony, you will come with Greg and I into the park tomorrow." A friendly invitation, but again stated in command form, and again without asking me first if I had had anything planned.

To cap it off he said aloud, "Anthony, Sarita told me that you will do only one presentation a day. I thought you're here to work." How the hell dare he?! And

Anthony Marr

it's not event true. Two a day is always my optimum, in Canada, in India, wherever. I have 10 days in Delhi and they booked only 4 schools, so what's the gripe? He may have said that as a joke, but first there is nothing funny about it, and second, his jokes, even if funny, are usually at the expense of someone-else's dignity as in this case. I like to joke too, but I appreciate the Woody Allen self-deprecating kind better. All I said was, "You have been sadly misinformed."

Greg Johnson is a ruggedly handsome man cast in the Viking mold, who came in camp with Avtar. He is a biologist by education, a long time conservationist in Africa who has personally worked with Dian Fossey at her mountain compound in the capacity of a graduate student, and is now an ecotourism operator, owner of an outfit called Global Expeditions. He has come to India to develop a wildlife tour package for his largely American clientele. He is right now on a cross-country tour to check out the itinerary Avtar has designed for him, with Avtar serving personally as his guide. Ecotourism-wise he is experienced with Africa (esp. Uganda, esp. the mountain gorilla) and South America (esp. Amazonia).

Unfortunately, his comments about Dian Fossey, who is one of my heroes, were largely negative. He said that she behaved as if she owned the mountain and the gorillas, and that her hard-line approach did more harm than good. I happen to have a copy of Virunga on me, by Farley Mowat, about Fossey, which I haven't yet read, and which Johnson also criticized as bad journalism. I did a quick search in the index of the book while back in my room, and did find a few mentions of Greg Johnson. The comments aren't all that complimentary either. Still, he is extremely intelligent and articulate, and makes a good casual-conversation companion.

On February 2, I will go back to Delhi with Avtar and Greg. On the 9th or 10th, I'll go to Jaipur ("Jai-POOR"), Rajasthan, where two more presentations have been arranged. Then back to Delhi for the "Love-the-Tiger Walk" on St. Valentine's Day. After that, back to Kanha, and there I'll stay till the end of this tour.

I just returned from Kim's room. She said that one of the things she intends to do at Bandhavgarh is to get to the bottom of Sita's death. Yes. Sita, the world's most famous tigress (National Geographic, December 1997, cover article) is dead, killed by a poacher just a few weeks ago. May you get right to the bottom of it, Kim. And may you fall in love with Bandhavgarh as I did. And I will miss you.

Good night, Christopher.

Omni-Science and the Human Destiny

February 1, 1999, Monday, sunny, 7-20C

Hi Christopher,

[07:12 @ Kanha Tiger Lodge]

Just one more day, and I will be reading email. I hope there will be a few from you and mom. I will send these diary entries to you, so mom could read them out for you.

I did get up early enough to go with Avtar and Greg into the park, but I declined just before they left, partly due to Avtar's imperious manner, and partly because of my real preference to spend my time with Jane, Faiyaz, CJ, Janice and Kim instead, before Kim and Janice leaves for Bandhavgarh later in the morning and before I leave for Delhi tomorrow. And perhaps also, I simply didn't want to go.

Faiyaz made his morning's appearance in a state of dejection. Last night, he made two requests of Avtar: one, for Tiger Fund to go outreach with me to the 178 Buffer Zone villages, and two, that he be put on outreach duty as Tiger Fund operative, not under Magnificent Tours. Avtar rejected both flatly.

Well, he has no power to order me, and I will do it myself if I have to.

[22:14]

At about 07:40, I knocked on Kim's door to wake her for a last coffee before she leaves for Bandhavgarh. She rose at once, but took about 45 minutes to do her morning chores and to pack for her relocation to Bandhavgarh later in the morning. When she did knock on my door, she was fresh, with hair damp. She sat on my bed and I on my computer chair. We've known each other since Bear Referendum '96, and it's only in these last few days I've got to know her personally. But now, too soon, she is being whisked away. But it's her choice. Were it Jane that Avtar had named to move to Bandhavgarh, I would have put a stop to that. Kim and I both know that Kim would rather work with tourists than villagers. Her own profession in Vancouver is tourism, so I can understand it. It just means that if and when I have to choose between Jane and Kim as my assistant, I would choose Jane. This means that come March, when it comes to switching them between Kanha and Bandhavgarh according to Avtar's plan, I may have to take action to retain Jane with me unless I go to Bandhavgarh as well on March 1 which, given our outreach plan at Kanha, is highly unlikely. These are just my thoughts. I didn't voice them with Kim. But I think she already knows. Still, we have a personal rapport that underlies everything, and my choice of Jane over Kim is purely professional, although I like

Jane very much too. I will miss Kim, that is for sure.

And then, the Tata Sumo (Indian-made diesel jeep used on highways, but not in tiger reserves, which do not allow diesel vehicles) arrived, and she and Janice were whisked away.

In the meeting with Faiyaz, Jane and CJ, I told Faiyaz that I will talk to Avtar about the outreach program myself. His face wore a big question mark of uncertainty in my success. I also talked about the possibility of having them in Delhi for the St. Valentine's Day Love-the-Tiger Walk. The stumbling block is of course time and money. The plane fare one way is US$135, US$270 return, plus overland Rs10 per km, return 650 km, or Rs6500, or US$160. All told US$430 or CDN$600+. Too expensive for too little. Also, seeing in my mind the dangerous highway and reckless driving especially in Maharashtra state where Nagjur is situated, it's not worth it. The alternative is a 50-hour return trip by rail for two. Nah, forget it.

Avtar spent the rest of the day mostly with Greg and Manohar. In the afternoon Faiyaz, Jane, CJ and I went for a walk through the sal forest to the river less than a kilometer behind the Tiger Lodge grounds. It is a picturesque river about 30' wide which flows serenely through a jumble of exposed rocks.

We walked downstream for a change. After only about 100 meters, Faiyaz pointed to a tree stump on the other side of the river. "Look over there. More deforestation of the park at work. If you sit here for long enough, you'll see cows."

"Is that the park over there?" Jane looked at the forested bank across the river where the tree stump stood like a sore thumb.

"Yes," answered Faiyaz. "Core Area over there, Buffer Zone here. Tiger and deer over there, people and cattle here. Wilderness over there, so-called civilization here. But civilization is over there too. You'll see."

At that moment, as if on cue, a white cow emerged from the forest on the other side of the river, and then another, and another…

Good night, Christopher,

※　　※　　※　　※　　※

February 2, 1999, Tuesday, sunny, 6-20C

Omni-Science and the Human Destiny

Hi Christopher,

[01:07 (1999-02-03) @ the F18 Inn in Delhi, next door to Avtar's Delhi residence]

Arrived in Delhi about an hour ago, after a six hour jeep ride from Kanha to Nagpur (about 12:00-18:00), more than two hours' waiting and a 1.5 hour plane ride from Nagpur to Delhi (22:30-00:00). This hotel has no internet connection. I'll have to wait till tomorrow morning to check email at Avtar's home next door to the hotel or office. It usually takes long minutes and numerous tries before getting online, and the connection is tenuous at best. Don't want to trouble his family in the middle of the night. Damn!

The drive from Kanha to Nagpur, with our jeep constantly passing lumbering trucks against heavy oncoming traffic on a narrow and bumpy highway, was not exactly relaxing. This combined with the road condition, vehicle condition, and the total lack of road-line and signage on a road with many unexpected hazards, is downright bloody dangerous. On the other hand, if you don't drive like that, you'd be sandwiched between diesel trucks, sucking fume and eating dust all day instead of for half a day.

Reminders of this danger lie along the highway every so often, mostly in the form of smashed cars or overturned trucks along the highway. In a previous highway trip, we came across a two-vehicle accident, where one of the drivers and his passenger were dragged out of their vehicle, by their hair, and roughed up, more like lynched, by the other driver and some of the spectators. Still, Greg Johnson made a good travel companion.

But Avtar is really getting on my nerve. He can be very charming and likable, but right now, I'm finding him more and more insufferable, and am having a tough time trying to contain my feelings about him in his presence. Other than to preserve harmony, I'm trying to see how far he would go. But there is a limit, and he is getting pretty damn close to it.

While Avtar was gassing up at a town, again seeing cows all over the place, Greg, asked me, "In your tiger conservationist's point of view, what is the toughest obstacle to overcome?"

"Cattle overpopulation," I said, with nary a hesitation. "It's a tougher problem to solve than even deforestation and poaching. One of the differences being: the cattle owners have religion on their side"

"And what is your solution?"

"Frankly, I have none."

"I have one."

"Oh really? Pray tell. Unless it's professional secret."

"The Kalashnikov."

I laughed politely. "The AK-47? Yeah right. There is only one problem."

"And what's that?"

"I don't know about you, Greg, but I can't afford 500 million bullets," I said.

Half way in the trip, we had to stop at a town to fix a flat tire. As usual in a town, the jeep was instantly surrounded by dozens of people, young and old, with their faces stuck to the car windows and wind shield. Makes you feel like caged animals in a zoo. Probably not recommended entertainment, but I pushed opened the car door and got out. The people parted like the Red Sea. I extricated myself and went for a walk down the street, drawing half the crowd with me, and not a moment too soon. About a block away, I found two boys in the process of stoning a white puppy to death, and no one was intervening in the least. A couple of stones that missed the puppy struck the concrete, sending chips flying. A couple that hit the pup sent it tumbling and yelping. I violated Star Fleet Command's code of non-interference with the natives. I reached out my hands to the boys, palms up. The boys looked at me, then looked around. Everyone was just watching to see what would happen next. Then they looked sheepishly at me again, and dropped the stones into my hands.

"Thank you, and don't do it again," I admonished them in English, hoping that the tone was the message.

The pup had one leg broken and was backed against a corner, quivering, whining pitiably.

"Is there a vet in town?" I asked the crowd at large.

Blank stares in return.

"Veterinarian. Animal doctor," I shouted.

A man walked up, looked me in the eye, then moved towards the puppy. He reached down, petted its head once. Then snapped its neck.

At that moment, the car pulled up and blew its horn at me. I took one more look at the tragic puppy, then got back into the car.

Nagpur is another Indian city looking ten times worse than Vancouver's Downtown Eastside at the tail end of a month-long garbage strike. It's hard to imagine it. You've got to see it to appreciate what I'm saying. On the streets people dress neatly, and the wealthier women look like well-preened peacocks, but their dainty feet had to pick their way through piles of garbage everywhere. There seems a glaring lack of social conscience, or is it just a very bad garbage collection system?

While waiting in Nagpur to board the 22:30 plane, Avtar took us into a lavish

Omni-Science and the Human Destiny

hotel for an array of appetizers, during which someone came behind me and said, in a British accent, "Are you Anthony Marr by any chance?"

"Yes." I turned around and saw a middle-aged Indian Man.

"I am Arun Patel, of Essex, UK. I saw you on a tiger program on TV awhile back. It was that program that got me interested in coming to Bandavgarh National Park, where we just spent the last week." The second time this very thing was said in a week.

About half an hour later, I was at the hotel's counter cashing a traveler's cheque, when Arun again approached me from behind. "Anthony," he said, "this is my cousin Shirish Patel. He is a doctor living in New York. He would like to know how he can help you save the tiger."

I asked for their addresses and numbers, and said that I would be in touch after I return to Vancouver.

The bill for the snack was, by Indian standards, exorbitant. Avtar footed it without blinking an eye. The amount was about half of the monthly salary he pays Faiyaz.

I woke up in the middle of the night last night and had a brainstorm re. a communal parabolic mirror fryer that costs less than $10 to build. All I need is one of those 8'x4' thin and flexible polished steel sheets, three large sheets of plywood to cut into parabolic templates, an 8"X6" dark metal plate to serve as hot plate, and two supports for the hot plate on either end. All we have to do is to press the metal sheet into the parabolic templates which are placed on the ground, line up the long axes of the mirror and the hot plate to the sun, and cook away – chapatti frying, rice cooking, sauces, soup, you name it. When the cooking is done, all we have to do is to take the mirror out from the templates and roll it up, tie the three templates together and off we go.

The driver of the jeep, after dropping us off in Nagpur, went to purchase three 8'X4' steel sheets, two to be cut into the four 4'X4' reflectors for the communal solar oven, and one to be the parabolic reflector for the fryer. Can't wait for the trial demo.

CJ left me 6 e-mails to send out, and Jane, one, plus a request to have Raman take care of booking a hotel room for her in June in Shimla.

I'm going to be fairly busy in Delhi, though only about half as busy as I would have liked to be. I have to attend to my share of WCWC's 98/99 members' report, the letter to WCWC to update progress, and of course the nearly daily presentations:

99/02/03	Motibagh School	Delhi
99/02/04	Colonel Satsanghi Kiran Memorial School	Delhi

99/02/05	Sri Ram Public School	Delhi
99/02/06	Rotary Club at Taj Mann Singh	Delhi
99/02/07-09	Off and Jaipur	
99/02/10	Springdales	Delhi
99/02/11	College of Vocational Studies	Delhi
99/02/14	Save-The-Tiger Walk	Delhi

Note. Sri Ram School is in this list, but Frank Anthony school is not.

Being back in Delhi brought back an old resentment, which is exacerbated by something Avtar said in the car from the airport. He told me that tomorrow's slideshow presentation will be given by Sarita, because the school booked is not an English speaking school. He said that English speaking schools receive such presentations all the time and its no big deal to them, but Hindi speaking schools will give us much more meaningful receptions. Again, I have to question their motive and action. First off, he wasn't at the Ahlcon Public School presentation, which gave us a HUGE reception. Second, the short few days I'm here, it should be English-speaking schools. Even if it's a Hindi-speaking school, Sarita could translate for me as Faiyaz does. I don't know how many schools in total (at least two) Sarita gave presentations while I was in Kanha, and how much media have attended these presentations, featuring Tiger Fund but not WCWC.

Made a phone call after midnight (about 11:00 a.m. Vancouver time) to my parents. Mother was thrilled to hear from me, but said that father had the flu. I'll wait to check email tomorrow before calling Christopher and Christine, if I have reason to.

Being again submerged in the polluted, chaotic and noisy Delhi street traffic, one cannot possibly ignore the cacophony of Delhi's transportation system. A large part of Delhi's traffic noise is from most drivers' seeming inability to remove their hands from their horns. Avtar explained, "In Vancouver, honking your horn is usually an auditory one-finger-salute, but here in Delhi, it just means 'I'm here.'" In the unregulated street traffic, maybe horn blasting is not only helpful to prevent accidents but necessary. Not having developed my "road ears" in the orderly Vancouver traffic, I have no doubt that I would be more accident prone than those brought up in Delhi traffic. I love to drive, but in Delhi, no thanks. On the other hand, riding in those three-wheeled, flimsy, smoke-spewing auto-rickshaws isn't much safer either. You just cross your fingers and hope for the best.

I'm also crossing my fingers about email tomorrow.

Omni-Science and the Human Destiny

Good night, Christopher.

❖   ❖   ❖   ❖   ❖

February 3, 1999

[22:38 @ F18 Inn in Delhi, next door to Avtar's Delhi residence]   God damn you, Christine! How can you do this hideous things to your own son?!!! And to your long time, loyal friend?!!! And poor, dear, dearest Christopher. How could your own mother have done such a hideous thing to you, to us???!!! Oh God, *why*???!!!

You have studied one year in psychology, Christine. Shouldn't you at least know what serious and irreversible harm has been and is being done to his tender psyche by your bull-in-china-shop actions? Please, stop your destructive course, I beg of you, before anything serious and irreversible is done. Stop, in the name of love!

Let me cool myself first before writing on.

I have heard the term "impotent rage" many times. Now I know exactly what it feels like and what it means. Here I am, shut up in a small hotel room above an ill-lit street in the innards of New Delhi, when my nearest friend is 12 time-zones away. Where Christopher is half a world away. The damage is done, and I cannot even hold him to comfort him.

What happened? Here is what happened. I check email first thing and no email from Christine. *None*. After two *weeks*.

So I used what little time I had to answer other emails, before logging off to get ready for the Motibagh school presentation. I also emailed my last diary entries to Christine to read to Christopher like bedtime stories. The adventures of Uncle Tony in Tigerland.

This morning and early afternoon, 10:30-13:00, we (Avtar, Sarita and I) had an excellent presentation in the auditorium of the Motibagh School to about 300 girls and about 5 boys from the neighbouring school, with Sarita doing the introduction, I the main slideshow and Avtar some kind of epilogue. Both theirs were done in Hindi, but I did catch one or two key words such as "China", "1949" (the year my family escaped from China right before the Communist take-over), "mining" (my previous field work) and "physics" (my university education). Avtar later told me that what he said was, "Anthony here is a Chinese Canadian who is rebelling against an old obsolete tradition, and I urge you as Indians to do the same." – something like that. Not bad.

After the slideshow, we set up the Big Cub in the football field, where another 2,000 kids formed a long and serpentine queue to go inside. At one point, Sarita counted over 150 kids in the Cub, which is a record, the previous, set in Canada, being about 120. You really *can* stuff more people into the same space in India.

In spite of this morning's presentation's being again another huge and highly photogenic success, there was still the same short-coming – no media. I have requested both Avtar and Sarita to please call those media I have sent packages to. A big fat ZERO up to this point.

When I finally confronted Avtar on the total absence of media, he said that he would invited all the media to the Tiger Walk. I replied that we can and should get media to cover both the schools and the Tiger Walk. I have no idea if media was present at Frank Anthony School while I was at Kanha.

Greg, who will be flying back to Washington DC tonight after three weeks with Avtar, took umpteen photos of the event, and groaned when he heard what Avtar said, saying to me in private, "This is one of the biggest missed media opportunities I've ever seen." He, however, will put our Gigantic Tiger Cub and the hoards of bright-eyed Indian school kids into his new brochure to show how his new Wild India Expeditions would benefit the tiger – a good move on Greg's part, which should also suit Avtar just fine in terms of using Tiger Trust to promote Dynamic Tours. But I think he has other ideas, some of which being somewhat transparent.

All day long I looked at the clock. Every time was the wrong time to call. Vancouver still deep in sleep. I checked email again in the early evening. Still nothing from Christine. Finally Christopher's morning came, and my evening. So I called - at about $5/min, which by the end of the conversation suddenly seemed unimportant even if the call cost a thousand dollars.

When the call was finished, I was immobilized by shock. When the shock had worn off sufficiently, I opened my laptop computer and typed down every word that transpired in that conversation. It had been replayed in my mind about a couple of hundred times since I dropped the phone. I vouch for high fidelity in the following transcription:

"Hello?" Christine's pleasant voice.
"Hi, Christine, good morning."
Silence.
"I'm calling from…"

"What do you want?!" A sudden and drastic change of tone. The usual hostile line.

"What did I do this time?"

"Christopher, come and talk to Tony."

"Hi Uncle Tony!" He sounded excited, but unhappy, an unusual combination..

"NOT UNCLE TONY, JUST TONY!" came Christine's voice in the background.

"Hi, Christopher, what's the matter?" I asked him.

"Uncle Tony, you are a very bad man. You hurt me and hurt mommy. You can't come and see me any more. And I don't want your toy." He was sobbing between almost every word.

"What? Christopher, what are you saying?!"

Suddenly, he heaved a sigh seldom heard in a child, and said, "Now, I said it. Can I tell you what I did today?" And he began to tell me what he did, though still sniffling due to the tearful bout.

My mind seemed still not having registered what I had just heard. I heard him out, then as I said, "Christopher, you know where I am? I'm in India. I'm so far away that when it is morning where you are, it is evening where I am. You can ask mommy to explain how this can be. So, have you had breakfast yet…"

Christine's voice came back on. "See how upset Christopher is?"

Christopher began sobbing in the background.

"Yes, but…"

"See how you've hurt him? Are you happy now?"

"Me? Hurt Christopher? What are you talking about?!" Because this was a public phone, I had to keep my voice down, which was a good thing.

She began screaming into the phone. "YOU ARE NOT FIT TO BE CHRISTOPHER'S GODFATHER! YOU ARE A DISGUSTING MAN! YOU'VE HIT ON EVERY ONE OF MY FRIENDS, AND NOW YOU'RE HITTING ON MY COUSIN DONNA!! I HAVE TALKED TO ANNA, TASHA AND WILHELMINA AND EACH AND EVERY ONE TOLD ME THAT YOU TRIED TO GET INTO THEIR BEDROOMS! NOW, YOU'RE TELLING DONNA THAT YOU'RE AVAILBLE FOR SEX WITH HER! YOU'RE A SEXUAL PREDATOR! SO, WHO'S GOING TO BE NEXT?! DONNA'S SISTER?! OR HOW ABOUT LAURA OR MAYBE CLAUDIA?! YOU DO FIND CLAUDIA QUITE ATTRACTIVE, DON'T YOU?! YOU HAVE THE MORAL OF A PIG!! STAY AWAY FROM MY SON FROM MY NOW ON, YOU SLUT!!!"

She was screaming so loud that the concierge walking past the wall phone gave me a strange look. I must have looked totally dumbfounded, though perhaps not yet distraught.

Finally, I managed to stammer, "I can't believe what you're saying, and doing, especially to Christopher. What have I done against you? What you said about your friends is not true. I've never made a pass at Wilhelmina, or Anna…"

Click.

I called back. The phone lines were busy. I called again and again. When finally the connection was again made, the call was not answered. This was consistent with Christine's pattern. I would be surprised that she would answer the phone. I made the calls out of sheer desperation. Just something better than nothing. I don't know if the call, especially if answered, would be worse than nothing, but at that moment, and now, nothing is exactly where the worst is.

[03:43 February 4, 1999 @ B57 Inn in Delhi]

Cannot sleep. I just tried calling again. Still the same.

I am not too overly distressed about Christine's tantrum. This is her regular pattern, once every month or two for as long as I can remember, with or without reason. But I *am extremely* distressed over what Christopher said. What is this woman doing to the tender psyche of this innocent child? What is it I can do that can make things right for him again? What can be done at all, by anyone, Christine included, to make things just like before again?

Somehow, Christine has forced the idea into Christopher that I am a "very bad man". She is trying to destroy his respect for me, over something, even if true, does not warrant such a verdict, and that Christopher is too young to comprehend. This should never be put upon him. I can't believe that Christine can be so evil, especially when I have never spoken a single unkind word about her to Christopher, ever, even when he said to me that he didn't like her because she was "mean" to him. Nor to anyone for that matter, in her presence or behind her back, except to Jeanine, and what I told her were facts, not opinions.

Again, I've been forced to ask this often-asked question: What have I done to deserve this? Have I not given my heart and soul to your family, your son? Have I not been the one you would call upon whenever you needed immediate help? Over the last three and a half years since Christopher was born, I've been too busy to even date. So I dated Donna, but it was at her invitation. I don't frequent bars and haven't gone to nightclubs for years. I don't date the women at work. I don't date the women at home, except once in the 18 years I've been in this shared house. I have visited with Wilhelmina, but was always there to play chess and drink tea. I have never made anything vaguely similar to a pass to her, not that there is anything wrong with it, my being a single in a singles city. The reason is simple. I was just not interested. I've visited Anna a few times while going out with Christine, but that was way back in the 70s, and our visits were always platonic and above board. I have visited with Tasha a few times and gone to a movie, once. When I went to visit any of them, I was almost always the one invited, though sometimes I would call just to say hi. I seldom, if ever, invited myself, or invited them, to anything, or to do anything, except once, to be exact, about a shoulder rub with Tasha, and nothing happened. Some sexual predator. Some slut.

The treatment she gave me today would suit a child molester or a serial rapist. The periodic abuse I have taken from her before and since Christopher was born I can tolerate. But this time, she has outdone even herself. This time she has gone off the deep end. She is definitely sick and needs help. I should feel compassion for her, but right now, all I can think of is Christopher, poor, dear, beloved, traumatized Christopher. How could she do something like THAT to you???!!!

[05:27]

I cannot sleep. I thought and thought and thought, agonized and agonized and agonized, in tighter and tighter spirals. I called upon God, time and time again. I received no reply, or discernable reply. Where is "He" when I need help most? Has "He", too, forsaken me? Perhaps "He" wants to test my nettles. Perhaps "He" wants to see me push my envelope? Come *on*! Wake up! Don't flatter yourself! Has it occurred to you that "He", if "He" exists, may not even care? I can rationalize all sorts of excuses for God to let this happen to me. Or should I say for God to do this to me? But how could any god allow something so horrendous to happen to tender and innocent Christopher, not to mention do it to him?

And the last tightening of the spiral – my last two emails to Christine were bounced back, blocked.

Morning has broken for me, Christopher, and your darkest night is falling.

Have a peaceful night, Christopher, if possible. If not, then in the throes of your sleeplessness, remember that I love you deeply, as deeply as I am capable of loving anyone, always.

February 4, 1999, Thursday, sunny, 6-20C

Christopher,

[09:19 @ F18 Inn, New Delhi]

I am thinking about you. I thought about you through the night. I did not, could not, sleep a wink. The street sounds kept me company. I got out of bed many times to gaze out the window, just to seek comforting empathy in the pain of a Delhi street by night.

I'm a stranger in a strange land, here to meet my most tragic of fates. I've called Avtar to beg off today's engagements, except the school presentation, pleading not feeling well, which is not untrue.

Christopher, this is the first day of our new tragic era. The new silence sounds even worse than the hurtful things that were said. Perhaps between you and me, I'm the luckier one. At least I'm now out of your mother's life, and she from mine. At least I'm now freed from her abusiveness. But how about you? Other than the wooden spoon, I have never doubted your security at home, but now, what am I to think? If your prime care-giver would do what she did to you yesterday, what would she not do tomorrow? How can I now fulfill my mission as your godfather, your father figure, your male role model, your protector and your guardian?

I feel tired, exhausted, but still cannot sleep. I cannot get out of the loop of tragic thoughts, nor escape the maelstrom of tragic emotions. I'm trapped in the tragic moment, which stretches into a dark eternity.

How are you feeling now, Christopher? It is your bedtime. I would be telling you a bedtime story. Tucking you in. You would smile at me and hug me good night. But now? How are you feeling now? I can't imagine. I dread to imagine. Since yesterday I've been filled with an unrelenting anger, no, rage, and sadness, no, despondency, and pain, no, agony. The dagger, no, axe, of betrayal has lodged itself inextricably in my back. This murder of love and respect is premeditated, perhaps has been for months. It's a first degree. And the pain that Christopher now suffers at her hand, she would blame all on me, and would tell him so in the years to come, without me there to defend myself, nor to defend him.

And for what, Christine? To be a good disciple of Murphy Brown? To finally achieve something "all by yourself", using Christopher as your stepping stone? To get rid of his loving and beloved Uncle Tony, so that you could own his love and eternal gratitude? To remove all his Uncle Tony's influence so she could claim all credit? Up to now, there is nothing that I could not forgive; as of now, forgiveness seems an impossibility.

[22:36]
I did get through today's presentation to Colonel Satsanghi Kiran Memorial School, with a standing ovation. I knew I would not be at my best, but I actually surprised myself at how well I did, considering. Nobody cast a concerned look my way. So maybe I have the oriental inscrutability in my genes. How I've been feeling is quite another picture. It seems just the opposite to the way I felt the day after getting assaulted last year. Then, I looked worse than I felt. Now, I feel infinitely worse than I look.

This evening, Avtar succeeded to dragged me out for a meeting with Piara, a charming and vivacious middle-aged woman with far-reaching media connections. It was a good thing, getting my mind off the subject if only for the moment. Her apartment is high-ceilinged and well appointed, with exquisite Oriental furniture. She paid me keen attention, as if checking me out for a certain role in her plan, whatever it be. She asked me what I've done in the past and what I plan to do in the future. I did my best to exert some feel of optimism and passion, but the overwhelming sadness ensues, which I'm sure she could read. Perhaps she mistook it for my feeling about the dwindling tigers. All I could tell was that she found what I was saying favorable. When we were leaving, she said, "See you tomorrow."

Tomorrow? Avtar didn't tell me anything about tomorrow, and I didn't ask him. Asking Avtar questions sometimes risks the don't-speak-unless-spoken-to responce. With him I've learned to just prethink all options, let things happen, and react to them when they happen to the best of my ability.

Due to this feeling of weakness, the strongest thing I could do today is to refrain from calling Christine. If she answered, she would kick me to a pulp while I'm down.

Down I certainly am. Out, I don't know. I hope not.

I emailed what I wrote yesterday to Diana, Jeanine and James seeking their advice on what to do next. They have all responded. Their advice in common is to call Christine again, if only to let Christopher know that I'm still there. Only if they knew Christine the way I do.

I am exhausted. Feel exhausted. Sleep should come now. Still, your wailing, sobbing, crying keep echoing in my head. I tried embracing you, comforting you, but your sounds of distress just keep rolling on and on, undiminishing, like a broken record or a falsely triggered car alarm. Your innocence and your happiness has been suddenly stolen, no, robbed, as has your dedicated male role model whose place the thief, the robber, can never fill. And there is nothing I can do to protect you from this catastrophic onslaught. I have failed in my vow to keep you from harm. And there is nothing I can do to cure you of it. I'm so sorry, Christopher, so very sorry.

Good night, Christopher.

❖ ❖ ❖ ❖ ❖

February 5, 1999, Friday, sunny, 6-20C

My dearest Christopher:

[21:45 @ F18 Inn, New Delhi]
    At long last, the saddest day in the life your Uncle Tony is near its end, a day sadder than even day before yesterday. Why is this day sadder than even that day? It is because on that day, the hope still lingered. Today, it died.
    But let us give it a happy, if dreamy, funeral. As of today, the memory of you shall be my inspiration to finish my life's work. And I will dedicate it to you. This shall be the present I promised to bring back to you.
    Now, it is five hours after our last conversation, our *last* conversation. Here it is, word for word, to be preserved for posterity, but who will read it?
    After hours of hesitation, after wading through the morass of trepidation, after dialing your phone number many times to the second last digit, having steeled myself to the hilt, I finally pushed it through. I must make just one more try. I must bid a proper good bye. I must say what I need to say. And I must hear Christopher's voice just one more time. I wish I had a tape recorder, but all I have now is my computer keyboard.

    "Hello?"
    "Hi, Christine, it's me. How are you?"
    "None of your concern. Haven't I told you not to call?"
    "May I speak to Christopher please?"
    "What for?"
    Your excited voice in the background, "Uncle Tony! Uncle Tony!"
    "I would like to say good night to him."

"Fine, but just this last once. And it is not good night. It is good-bye. From now on, don't call again, EVER! Here Christopher!"

"Uncle Tony! Uncle Tony! You are a very bad man. You hurt mommy and you hurt me. I don't want your present. And I can't see you any more." Same thing, word for word. And again, tears in your voice. How did it happen? How many times did she make you repeat this horrible quatrain?

Being slightly more prepared this time, I seized this our last moment together and said my bottom line. "Christopher, listen to me very carefully. You know that Uncle Tony loves you very very much. Don't you?"

"I know, Uncle Tony." It was wailed, not spoken.

"Christopher, I love you more than anything in the world. I would never do anything to hurt you. I would do anything for you. You know that, don't you, Christopher?" I could hardly speak myself.

"Yes, I know that, Uncle Tony."

"Christopher, remember, wherever I'll be, I will always love you."

"I love you too, Uncle Tony."

"Tell me, Christopher, has your Uncle Tony ever done anything to hurt you?"

"No, Uncle Tony, but mommy says that you are a very bad man. You hurt her and you hurt me."

"Christopher, your Uncle Tony is not a bad man. He is a very good man. And you know that too."

"Yes, Uncle Tony. I know that too."

Christine's voice in the background, loud, cutting. "What is Tony telling you?"

"Uncle Tony says he is a good man."

"HE IS LYING! HE IS A VERY BAD MAN, AND DON'T YOU FORGET IT!! DON'T BELIEVE IN ANYTHING HE SAYS TO YOU EVER AGAIN!!!"

I heard you cry, as the phone was taken from you for the last time.

"You will send back my suit case, and I will send back your debit card, and that'll be it. Do you understand?!"

"Please, Christine, I beg of you, for the sake of Christopher, please don't do this. He is only three years old. He has nothing to do with this and doesn't understand any of this, and neither do I. He and I love each other with all our hearts. If you break us up like this, he may become an emotionally disturbed child when he grows up. You know I have worked with emotionally disturbed children. I know what I'm talking about. He is your own child for God's sake. As for Donna, it was she who invited me. The same applies to Wilhelmina and Tasha…"

"Look! My friends are out of bounds to you, just like your friends are out of bounds to me!"

"That's not right."

"Look. You remember when your friend John took up with your friend Debbie, how upset you were."

"That was different. I was a little in love with Debbie and John knew it. Are you in love with me? Am I your boyfriend? Are you my girlfriend? We're just friends, Christine."

"Were."

"You don't own your friends, Christine, nor your cousin."

"You have no morals or ethics. You are disgusting. Good bye."

At that point, I knew, finally, that all was lost, forever. "This is a hideous thing you're doing to Christopher…"

Click.

I didn't even get to say a proper good-bye to you.

Am I really free from Christine's power sphere? Don't kid yourself. In fact, I've been drawn deeper towards its centre than ever. Hence forth, the way she will seek to exert her power over me will be through Christopher. I have no doubt that she would use him for this purpose with impunity. And the way I will respond to her will always involve upholding Christopher's emotional safety and integrity as top priority, and she knows it. She knows I now know that she is capable of doing anything to Christopher to achieve the objective of removing me from his life. Already, she is using him as her weapon to sever his own love and respect for me. What she has done gives "character assassination" a brand new meaning. In your mind I may already have begun to die.

Christopher, child of my spirit. So what happens now?

Over the last four days, it's been one school slideshow presentation per day, and in spite of the tragedy in my life, all have been excellent in various ways and to various extents. But today's presentation, given at Shri Ram Elementary School, tops every other one so far - in terms of connectedness with the students, their discipline and attentiveness. And this is when I am at my most exhausted, not having slept for two nights.

Though once it was done, I fell into a deep sleep in the car. I think it was the children who gave me the energy, for me to give my slideshow back to them.

Sri Ram is one of the two "hidden" schools. Apparently Avtar changed his mind about this being a non-English speaking school and therefore it should be Sarita who would give the slideshow. This morning, he changed his mind and wanted me to give it instead. Fine by me. But in the beginning, seeing the age of the students (about 9 or 10), and the audience size (over 300) I gave an inner groan. One thing I didn't want was to shout in English while the kids chat among themselves in Hindi. I thought about asking Sarita to give the slideshow in Hindi as originally planned. But after hearing the teachers pre-talk to them in English, I decided to give them a try, and was astounded by the result. The children were glued to my every word and gave me all sorts of great feedback. The school was impressed enough to invite me back to talk to a more senior group in late March when I get back to Delhi in late March or early April.

I have experienced Indian students enough to be able to say this. They relate to me as if I were a star or even a minor god. They gaze at me, they touch my hair, they look entranced when I lay my hand on their heads, they crowd around me, they clamor for my autograph, they come in respectful groups to talk to me after my presentations. Maybe my having come from a faraway place put a bit of a halo around my head. Maybe my being on TV makes me in their eyes a little larger than life. But one thing, through them I learned about myself, about being human, about the inexhaustible energy in love. Most people would think that the more one is looked up to, the more proud one would become, but according to my own experience, right now, it is a humbling experience. Why? Because I know I'm not as high and mighty as they think I am.

But let's get back down to earth here. There is still zero media. Come on, Avtar! Speaking to the hundreds is a privilege; speaking to the millions is a must.

Over the last two days, I've been concentrating on putting all the field journal entries to date, purged of all emotional and personal content, into a single file for e-mail transmission to WCWC. Finally, got it off this morning around 10:00 (Vancouver time 20:30) from Avtar's office. Later I called WCWC at Raven's Call (home of Paul and Adriane in Sechelt, a ferry ride away - when they were doing their annual retreat. Talked to Andy, Andrea, Alice, Tim, Paul and Joe. When Andrea was on, she said that Sue wanted to come on, but for some reason, she didn't. After Joe, he incited everyone to give me a roaring verbal high-five. Very heart warming indeed. Made my day somewhat. I needed it.

This evening, we (Avtar, Sarita and I) went to meet Avtar's friend Reshem, whom I've met in a previous visit, with Piara and another middle-aged woman, a lawyer named Sultana, who is also a director of Tiger Fund, whom I also have met, also present. The meeting was a semi-work session to prep for the "Love-the-Tiger Walk", re-named from "Save-the-Tiger Walk" by Avtar, on St. Valentine's day.

Piara said she would put me on the Times of India profile column, and arrange some TV interviews. To facilitate that, she took about a dozen newspaper articles from my media folder. She commented that she liked my "long, black, flowing mane", saying that it is a "favorable element from a media view point". I joked that I was just thinking about having a crew cut. Avtar laughed. Piara, who has short hair herself, looked at my short-haired photos in my media folder and reasserted her preference of long hair on my head. I've always detested the crew cut, especially on myself, which was forced on me by my elementary school and my father, whose orders in this department I began to defy as of the time Elvis Presley and the Beatles came on the scene. It never ceases to amaze me how some crew-cut "Christians" would have paintings and prints of a long-haired Christ hanging on their walls, but treat live long-haired people with blanket contempt. But though I've heard slurs, I have never felt systematically discriminated against on account of my hair length or my race, in any country I've ever been to, except in the ex-British-crown-colony of Hong Kong where being Chinese, versus being British, makes one automatically a second class citizen. And now, amazingly, as a foreigner, I'm being treated like a celebrity in yet another ex-British-crown colony.

Always a light and funny side to life, although for the life of me I cannot see any light and funny side to what is happening to us. Still, you must admit, I put up a strong front today, even in this diary entry. Good night, Christopher.

February 6, 1999, Saturday, sunny, 7-21C

Dearest Christopher:

[17:21 @ F-18 Inn in New Delhi]
    Thinking of you constantly. Watching over you as always. Loving you forever.
    For now, things look bad, and promise to look worse, without ever getting better.
    I called Tasha, Wilhelmina and Donna, begging them to please, please, please, intervene, if only for your sake. All three ladies had sympathetic responses and promised to do what they could, but all concluded independently with their own versions of hopelessness.

"How is Christopher?" is my ubiquitous question.

"Christine says he's devastated," Donna answered. I couldn't quite read the tone.

"And she is pressing the course."

"Yes, she is pressing the course."

"So she is intentionally devastating him, isn't she?" I said bitterly.

Donna gave no audible reply.

"Okay, in other words, she is subjecting her own three year old child to intentional and calculated emotional abuse."

"Aren't you afraid I might tell her you said this?"

"Oh, would you? Then you may as well tell her this too. She is using Christopher as stepping stone for her self-esteem, and as hostage in her war to grab exclusivity to his love."

"She is his mother."

"Does this make her deed more evil or less?"

Donna again gave no reply.

I ranted on, "She has taken psychology at university. She should know what havoc this kind of trauma would cause in a child's whole future life. I've worked with emotionally disturbed children for a year. I know what agonies they live through. And what would this do to his faith in love, that someone so devoted to him would all of a sudden abandon him? And what would happen to his belief system, when all of a sudden, someone he had looked up to all his life as the icon of goodness and kindness has suddenly become a "very bad man"? You've got to stop Christine pushing this any further, before it is too late. Please, for Christopher's sake."

"I'm very sorry, Tony, but it is too late."

And I knew it was.

"By the way," Donna added, "In case you are blaming me for this, Christine said she has been thinking about this for quite some time. It's just that your long trip to India is her opportunity to give you 'the heave ho', in her words."

In another phone call, Wilhelmina said, "I've never told Christine that there was anything between us. We just play chess and drink tea. And I can tell her that you have not made any sexual overture towards me. But her mind is made up. She has already moved on. There is no turning back."

Tasha said to me intensely, "Tony, one thing I have to tell you. If push gets to shove, I will be on Christine's side. She and I grew up together. I will support her come what may."

"Now I know why you call your boat the Cumquat May. So, it is loyalty above all, is that it? Above even principle?"

"I'm afraid so, Tony."

"Even over the emotional integrity of an innocent child, is that it?"

"Yes, that is it."

"Would you rather not mediate to prevent the pushing turning to shoving in the first place?"

"There is nothing to mediate. Her mind is set. The wheels are rolling. The ball is in your court, but she has left. I'm just telling you that if you make pushing into shoving, I will be on her side."

"I get it loud and clear. Thank you for your candor, Tasha, and good bye."

"Good luck, Tony, and I mean it."

Wonder of wonders. Just one tiny chat with Avtar, and the whole situation turned 180 degrees. Has he been thinking about doing this all along? Or have the contents of our confidential meetings back at Kanha been leaked to him yesterday or day before? Or was he moved by my speeches (which he has never seen before – he did comment to Piara, this time from personal observation, of my being a good speaker, so much so that she at once booked me into her Habitat House public program for late March sight unseen)? Or have I somehow changed him with just a few days' close contact? Or has he somehow read my e-mail-to-WCWC? Or has Adriane e-mailed him one hell of an arm-twisting letter? These I don't know, and may never get to know. What I do know is that as late as February 1, when Faiyaz talked to him again about going outreach with me to the villages in the Buffer Zone instead of serving tourists in the lodge, Avtar gave him a flat "no", citing again "dilution" of Tiger Fund's in-lodge work. A huge though not unexpected blow to Faiyaz. CJ even commented that Faiyaz "aged 10 years in one day". Now, with this new development, Faiyaz will be rejuvenated 20 years overnight. Anyway, here is the deal.

- Avtar is buying a brand new Gypsy for Tiger Fund and not for Magnificent Tours, *for outreach purposes only*.
- Faiyaz can go outreach with it all he wants
- It is also placed at my disposal, and if I want to, I could drive the vehicle myself (since Faiyaz doesn't drive).
- Avtar is honoring our agreement that Jane will serve as my volunteer during my stay in India, and therefore she can go outreach with us (in spite of Feb. being the peak tourist month).

Omni-Science and the Human Destiny

Can't be more made-to-measure than this.

Avtar also surprised me slightly with how hard he is pushing for the Love-the-Tiger Walk. All his activities these last few days have been towards promoting it to the max. He's been working on sponsors and succeeded in getting two plane tickets from Delhi to Kajuraho as a draw prize. He himself put in two free stays at the Bandhavgarh Tiger Lodge as additional prizes. Other things include printing raffle tickets, printing a brand new glossy brochure for Tiger Fund (*not* Magnificent Tours, with WCWC getting honorable mention) and other literature, getting head-bands, arm bands and banners made for the Walk, arranging media coverage. And today, he gave two speeches both in 5-star hotels, one at the IATO (Indian Association of Tour Operators) convention where he talked about the Tiger Walk only, and the other at the Rotarian Convention where he spoke on pure conservation, with his Magnificent Tours and Tiger Lodges not even mentioned. The Big Cub was set up on the front lawn of the Taj Palace Hotel where the huge Rotarian Convention took place; in fact, it is still there, attended as we speak by the Sarita – resplendent in her royal blue sari. At the end of his Rotarian speech, Avtar even got the highly conservative audience to repeat after him the four lines of Tim's Tiger Song, albeit in spoken words only. He took to it immediately when, as Sarita suggested, I led Piara, Reshem, the lawyer lady Sultana and him to sing it yesterday, whole-heartedly embracing it as the Tiger Club Song for all schools. He and Sarita are always present at the school presentations, except for the presentation yesterday, when he had to arrange media for the Walk. Today, he had me interviewed by the Trav Talk magazine at the Taj Palace. Next Wednesday, I'll be interviewed by another travel magazine. In a couple of days we'll be in Jaipur, where more media and schools await. Back to Delhi next Tuesday for three more school presentations and media and then the Tiger Walk. I have never seen him pour so much of himself into something that may not directly benefit his tourism business but purely for tiger conservation. Well, those travel magazine articles will benefit Magnificent Tours as well as Tiger Fund, but what the hell. The Gigantic Tiger Cub has never been busier and more seen. So, finally, things are happening. Just one lingering question. Where is media for the schools?

During the Rotarian Convention, while waiting for Avtar's speech, I was privileged to witness, and video-tape, two speeches by two prominent speakers – the excellent Dr. Karan Singh, and the transcendent, long-haired, full-bearded but young (40?) spiritual leader Shri Shradhalu Ranate of the Sri Aurobindo Ashram who is about the most mesmerizing speaker I have ever seen, whose speech title was "India's Destiny And Your Part In It."

During lunch, I asked Avtar whether Indian custom has it that gifts are not to be accepted. I was referring to Deepfee, who is an avid bird watcher whose own pair of binoculars wasn't quite up to the task. I brought to India a pair of pre-set binoculars that she loved at first use. I gave it to her on the spot, but she has steadfastly declined. He said that Deepfee actually talked to him about it when he was there, saying that I was already doing so much for them, how could she go further to take my binoculars from me. Avtar told her that I offered them to her out of love and appreciation for her hobby, and that it was okay for her to accept them. So, she did. And I'm glad.

Avtar said that I had the option to go back to Kanha after the Tiger Walk or go to Bandhavgarh via Kajuraho. The overlanders from Kajuraho to Bandhavgarh and from Nagpur to Kanha are both 6 hours. Both are tempting, but of course I will go back to Kanha to get right back into the thick of things. I'll bring the two unassembled solar ovens with me, which are currently in Delhi, to be assembled at Kanha, and maybe send one over to Bandhavgarh.

This morning I was given the phone bill by the F-18 Inn, and about had a heart attack. The 15-minute phone call I placed to my parents cost Rs2660 or CDN$105. The call to WCWC cost likewise. My personal calls, charged against my Vancouver personal account, cost another $500.

I chatted with the taxi driver who drove me from the Taj Palace to the Asian Age office then back to the F-18. He does not own the rat car he drives. So first, he pays Rs500 (C$20) to the owner daily. He has the car for 24 hours. He drives as many of the 24 hours as he could, up to 16 hours, 7 days a week. He has a wife and 3 children in a town 400 miles distant. His wife works in the rice fields. There is no work for him back there. He nets Rs400-500 a day, and sends to his family about Rs2,000 per month. He lives in a single room and pays Rs1,500/mo. for it. He has no time for anything except work, sleep, eat, work, sleep, eat, and work some more, which reminds me of my father when I was a child. The cab driver goes home by bus to see his wife and children twice a year, several days per time, 6 months apart. He struck me to be an honest man. I left my camera bag in the taxi and went upstairs to the Asian Age to get a copy of the article for almost 15 minutes, and he could have driven away with it and I would never find him. The fare by the meter was Rs210. I paid him Rs300. I know in my gut he did not take the long route. Many Indian people are like this. Faiyaz is like this. I should not let the rotten apples taint the whole barrel.

Back to Avtar. He's now 43. He seems to have a genuine love for the tiger, but not the passion of his father. When he is not in his superior mode, when he shows due respect, he is very likeable, and I like him as I write. He is hard working and his people respect him at least as a boss, though also fear him, which is not my way. He has a certain sense of fairness and justice that cannot be denied. The other volunteer at Bandhavgarh other than Janice, Julian, violated Avtar's code by going AWOL and was fired. In fact, Avtar seems to have fired both Julian and Janice, the latter for her going over to Kanha without his permission. Yesterday and today, they came into Avtar's office together, and have now been reinstated.

So, is it all sweetness and light with Avtar now? No. There is still the corruption factor to address, which may overshadow everything else. With Avtar, at this point, my attitude should be that of the recovering alcoholic - "one day at a time". I seldom say it, and hardly ever live it. I always live with some goal ahead, which I seldom lose sight of. But today must be special, since I'll be using the expression twice, since "one day at a time" is exactly the way I have to live where Christopher is concerned.

Christopher, now and forever, I will be your Uncle Tony.

❖   ❖   ❖   ❖   ❖

February 7, 1999, Sunday, overcast and rain, 7-21C

Dearest Christopher:

[00:43 on train to Sawai Madhopur]
I thought getting out of Delhi, where we had our heart-breaking phone calls, would distance me from the pain, but since I cannot leave you behind, the pain follows. Would I rather leave you behind so the pain would stay behind? Not a chance. I will never leave you behind, Christopher. I will carry you, love and pain, in the centre of my heart, wherever I go, from now to eternity.

Some hours ago I paid internationally renowned tiger conservationist Valmik Thapar a courtesy visit. In his usual gruff fashion, he made me welcome. He reminds me of being the Indian version of Paul George, both bears of men, both seemingly always on edge, but both having a hearty laugh as the situation warrants. Unfortunately, today, my situation did not warrant Valmik laughing, so he did not. Instead, he showed me a very detailed and masterfully executed charcoal drawing of a charging elephant. He asked me to guess who the artist was.

"Robert Bateman?"

"Close."

"I don't know."

"You wouldn't. He is just a teenager. An Indian kid whose name you cannot even pronounce. He won an art competition at school a couple of years ago. Fateh Singh Rathore's wife recognized his talent and, seeing his poverty, gave him free art training in her art school at Ranthambhore. He finished this drawing last month. I paid him handsomely for it. Now his family is not so poor, and he is pursuing his dream."

With this, Valmik led me to a large well-lit room where a collection of wildlife drawings and paintings were displayed, among them many oil paintings of tigers, some in the setting of the ancient ruins in Ranthambhore tiger reserve. In my unprofessional judgment, all of the paintings are works of art if not masterpieces. I took photos of some of them in sunlight. An art program would be an excellent addition to our rural educational outreach effort.

To make a long conversation short, I decided to take a night train to Ranthambhore. Given this alternative, the thought of spending another sleepless night in that hotel room seemed insufferable. So, here I am. It is a much more modern train, with coach-type seating. Much more comfortable.

It has magazine racks featuring brochures about Ranthambhore.

One piece says:

"Many regard this park situated in southern Rajasthan as the jewel in the crown of India's tiger parks. The reserve derives its name from the hill top fortress, which dominates the approach to the park. The mixture of ancient temples and summer palaces, alongside abundant Indian wildlife, provide magical photographic opportunities unique to Ranthambhore.

"The ancient mountain ranges of the Aravali and Vindhya meet here, producing a mixture of flat tablelands and steep cliffs criss-crossing the park. This varied topography provides a diversity of habitats for animals like the jackal, mongoose, sloth bear, leopard, and of course the tiger.

"Most years, even during the hottest months, water is provided by the park's three man made lakes, Padam Talao, Rajbagh and Malik Talao. Jogi Mahal, the lakeside lodge used by the late Rajiv Ghandi to view wildlife, is set in an idyllic spot on the edge of Padam Talao. The lakes, especially in the evenings, are like giant magnets, attracting all of the surrounding wildlife to their life sustaining waters.

Omni-Science and the Human Destiny

"Ranthambhore was declared a wildlife sanctuary in 1957, and in 1974 under Indira Ghandi's Project Tiger initiative became one of the protected sites. There are 200km of tracks in Ranthambhore divided into pre-determined routes which allow large areas to remain undisturbed, since everyone requires some solitude. For visitors to the park access is provided by either jeeps, which hold up to four persons comfortably, or the larger canters (trucks) which carry approximately twenty persons.

"The park is regarded by many professional photographers as the best place in India to both see and photograph tigers. This is mainly due to the diurnal behavior exhibited by the tiger population which adapted to the changes brought about by an inspired park director, Fateh Singh Rathore. Mr. Rathore and his loyal staff were involved in an ambitious project to relocate nine villages from the core area to new land outside the park boundaries. This initiative proved to be a resounding success, especially for the wildlife in the core area, and in particular the tiger. With far less human encroachment in the park, the tigers shed their nocturnal cloaks and tiger encounters rose dramatically during the eighties.

"The sheer diversity of the fauna and flora in Ranthambhore is remarkable. With over 300 types of trees, 272 species of birds and approximately 30 different types of mammals, Ranthambhore is packed full of life and a safari here will suit the general wildlife enthusiast as well as the serious ornithologist. We can also take you outside of the park for the chance to see Black Buck Antelope in nearby tribal villages, river dolphins and crocodiles, leopards by night and vast numbers of migratory birds around tranquil lakes.

"Ranthambhore is well connected by rail, approximately 350km from Delhi; it is also situated close to Jaipur and Bharatpur. The park is open from 1st October to 1st July. The number of jeeps allowed inside the park is strictly limited to just fourteen, bookings should be made at least sixty days in advance. We can offer you a wide choice of accommodation, including the 1930's former hunting lodge of Maharaja Sawai Man Singh and 'Sher Bagh', the soon to be opened camp close to the park managed by relatives of Fateh Singh Rathore and Valmik Thapar. A portion of profits from 'Sher Bagh' are donated to the Ranthambhore Foundation and other local organizations working to improve the quality of life in the surrounding villages."

Sounds nice and upbeat. Another piece says:

"The Ranthambhore forests were the former hunting grounds of the Maharajas of Jaipur and it was only in 1955 for the first time that this area was declared as the

Sawai Madhopur Wildlife Sanctuary. In 1973 it was included as a potential area under `Project Tiger' and was the smallest of the nine areas selected. It was felt that this 392 sq.kms of dry deciduous habitat could viably sustain healthy tiger populations. In 1980 it was notified as a National Park. Today Project Tiger Ranthambhore is responsible for the management of 627.13 sq.kms and included in 1992 is also the Keladevi Sanctuary under this same umbrella of management, taking the total area to 1174 sq.kms with 392 sq.kms as the core.

"20 years ago in the first ever census of tigers the population in Ranthambhore was estimated at 14. In 1991 tiger numbers were estimated at 45. Today estimates reveal that there is a decline. The original 392 sq.kms is surrounded by 62 villages with an estimated population of 225,000 people, 150,000 livestock and the never ending pressures of migratory livestock. The population of both people and livestock are directly dependent on this forest area for pasture-land, timber and firewood for fuel, and any other vital minor forest produce that they require.

"In nearly 20 years since the inception of Project Tiger only one scientific survey has been conducted in Ranthambhore National Park. This was done in 1987-88.

"This research was undertaken by the Wildlife Institute of India and published in a paper entitled "Grazing and cutting pressures on Ranthambhore National Park in Rajasthan India".

"Suffice enough to say that the last line of this scientific report states: "Meanwhile it should be emphasized with alarm that only about one quarter of the declared core-zone area remains as effective core."

"Between 1976-1979 12 villages that existed within Ranthambhore National Park were resettled outside. These people made the biggest sacrifice for Ranthambhore National Park, its tigers and bio-diversity, by agreeing to resettle so that the Park could enrichen. The statistics of the above report reveal that without human settlements there are problems and further in depth analysis is necessary to determine if such sacrifices by people are worthwhile, in the interest of the bio-diversity of an area. This resettlement, like that of Kanha was one of the milestones in the history of Project Tiger Reserves.

"Recently a land use and Forest Map of Ranthambhore National Park reveals the wide ranging problems due to biotic pressures that exist on the buffer and fringe areas of this forest.

"This dry deciduous habitat has a rich diversity of flora and fauna, with over two hundred species of birds, a wide array of mammals and reptiles and of course the tiger. During the 1980's the tigers of Ranthambhore were the most visible compared to anywhere in the world. They performed much to the pleasure of those that

Omni-Science and the Human Destiny

observed. The tiger and its behavior patterns revealed many new dimensions to its life and in a way it was rewriting its own natural history. But by the late eighties and into the 1990's a gradual decline started in tiger sightings and the process culminated in 1992 with the seizure of a tiger and a leopard skin from a gang of poachers.

"Ranthambhore has many problems. They don't just concern the tiger. They concern growing biotic pressures, the threat of poaching, the lack of serious research, problems with motivation and dedication of the staff, problems of tourism management and control, and so on. A public litigation case which encompasses all these problems is under hearing in the Supreme Court.

"In the instance of the late Prime Minister Shri Rajiv Gandhi the first eco-development project was launched in the Ranthambhore Tiger Reserve in 1989. Today a special eco-development plan is under formation that would attempt to reduce biotic pressures through the participation of people in effective land-use. In the last year extra vigilance against poachers and a series of training programmes for the staff are being conducted. Several NGO's are extremely active outside the Park to try and develop collective strategies for the future. Such activities signal a sign of hope for the future.

"According to Valmik Thapar, member of the Steering Committee of Project Tiger who has been associated for 17 years with this area, "Ranthambhore is one of the most remarkable dry deciduous habitats of the tiger that I have ever encountered. Today this tiger reserve has serious problems with increasing biotic pressures, poaching and a general systemic failure that afflicts this entire country. But a collective resolve and concern by people, and especially the local communities who live around the Park can resolve some of the problems so as to ensure the survival of this very fragile wilderness area into the future. Genuine problems that are faced by the field staff require quick and early solutions and when this happens an effective collective approach to the future might usher in a period of hope and optimism to ensure the health of this incredible tiger reserve"

[19:26 @ the Ranthambhore Bagh tourist lodge, Ranthambhore tiger reserve, Rajasthan, India]

Nature has a wicked sense of humor. Rajasthan is a desert state, and this is the dry season, and no rain has fallen on Ranthambhore for weeks. Today, a huge dark cloud followed me from Delhi to Ranthambhore, and dumped on it till the dust turned to mud.

Something Valmik Thapar is quoted as saying rings a bell. "…a general systemic failure that afflicts this entire country…" When I reread some of my diary entries, it seems that whenever I talk about India, all I do is to criticize its pollution and garbage, but of course it runs much deeper. Where tiger conservation is concerned, we need to, first of all, make the Indian government see it as a high priority, then allocate some serious rupees to the endeavour. And I maintain that the way to achieve this is not through writing a nice letter to the Indian government, though it certainly could do no harm. If someone thinks that by just writing a letter to the government ones job is done, one is sadly mistaken. The three key words to getting government attention are: media, media and media. But what do I read in the Times of India? While India has "no money" for tiger protection, it is slating U.S.$1.8 *billion* to develop a new star wars system against Pakistan. And in ten or twenty years' time, that star wars system would be obsolete, and the tiger would be gone.

What India prides itself on – that it is the world's largest democracy – is also its major weakness. By the "largest democracy", it also means the largest number of political parties – over 70 on the federal level. These parties form ever-changing opportunistic alliances to topple existing regimes, resulting in a rapid succession of recent prime ministers. Usually, when a new P.M. comes in power, he would know very little about tiger conservation. But by the time he finally learns enough to want to do something effective, he is overthrown. The current Indian P.M. is Mr. Vajpayee. I hope he lasts long enough to do some good.

Anyway, here I am. In room 13 of the Ranthambhore Bagh (Ranthambhore Tiger) safari lodge. And it is raining outside for the first time this year. Since I'm their only new guest today, the proprietor called me their "rain-maker". I wish I could call upon the rain to rain on our smoldering ruins, Christopher.

Outside, the last thing I saw before nightfall was a camel cart carrying vegetable produce slowly passing by. Just two weeks ago, could I have predicted that today I would be a broken-hearted man seeing a camel cart out a bedroom window? What a ludicrous combination. I told you. Someone up there has a wicked sense of humor and of the absurd.

Still, I'm not smiling.

And still I cannot sleep.

Now, it is dusk for me and dawn for you. Good morning, Christopher.

Omni-Science and the Human Destiny

February 8, 1999, Mon, sunny, 7-21C

Dearest Christopher:

[20:11 @ Ranthambhore Bagh lodge, Ranthambhore tiger reserve, Rajasthan, India]

    When I look back from the end of my life, today might stand out amongst its peers as being pivotal. When I looked into the mirror this morning, I saw despair. When I look into the mirror now, I see hope. No, the situation hasn't changed, and the pain and anger are still in full force, but something happened to me that has given me reason to believe that I will be able to deal with the anger, the pain, and the situation itself, as best one could.

    I woke up to bright sunshine this morning, but the dark cloud over my head did not dissipate. How could it when every wakeful moment I am so keenly and painfully aware of your despondency, over even my own, and the further psychological damage you would sustain with each passing day? Each passing hour. Each passing minute. What are you doing now, this very second? It is about nine in the morning your time. You have probably had your breakfast. What then? How are you yourself dealing with this awful situation? Have you been crying? Acting out? Throwing tantrum? Who could blame you if you have? Who but Christine. How would she be dealing with you now? Seeing her opening salvo, how she could so recklessly devastate your emotion, I dread to imagine what her ensuing barrages would be. I cannot bear the image of the wooden spoon in her hand, and the psychological equivalent of the wooden spoon. And what else besides the wooden spoon? I cannot bear to continue with this line of thought. For the protection of my own sanity I have every time cut it short. I have never once completed a single scenario in my mind about what happens behind the closed doors of your home. But every time when I discontinue the thought, I feel cowardly, knowing that you would be unable to discontinue the act, for even a moment's respite. I have my distractions, namely my work, but what distraction do you have? If your reality becomes unbearable, where can you escape to? Who can you turn to? Christopher, you know that if by bearing your pain I could make you whole again, I gladly would.

    But while it's raining in my heart, my eyes cannot deny the sunlit beauty of this most exquisite place on Earth. After tomorrow, I may not be here again to see it. Not long after morrow, God forbid, it may no longer be here again to be seen. SO, Christopher, my promise to you today is this: I will do my best to help save these beautiful place for you. If I cannot benefit you directly, I will benefit you indirectly. Christopher, I will dedicate all my work to you.

After a vegetarian Rajasthani breakfast, I called Fateh Singh Rathore by phone from the hotel. He invited me to just go on over. The hotel manager offered to drive me there, which was just a few miles down the road towards the park from the hotel. So I wiped as much pain and anger off my face as possible, and knocked on his garden gate. It is an earthy house, replete with objects of art, many from Madame Rathore's art school, with an atrium replete with what to me are exotic plants. The garden is not huge – perhaps an acre in size - but it is full of botanical wonders. And it shines a radiant green in the beige background of the Rajasthani semi-man-cow-goat-made semi-desert.

I was treated to chai and sweet cakes served by Madame Rathore herself. I could not see the art school, since it is not in the immediate vicinity, but I did get have a nice communion with the good lady and the great man. Even though youth have passed, Fateh Singh's shining passion remains undimmed. I have seen an older picture of him as a younger man. He was standing in a Gypsy, beaming up at two tigers on the ramparts of the Ranthambhore ruins. They could have just jumped on to him, but they looked very relaxed in his company. They were two of the original 45 or so tigers in Ranthambhore. Think of it. Just 45. But today, perhaps 15 remain. He still exercises his special privilege to go into the park at will, which works out to be about twice a month. Just as Belinda Wright once said to me, she doesn't visit tiger reserves any more. She just works for them from beyond, where she is most effective, even if it is a place of smoke and dust and heat like New Delhi.

Among other things, Fateh Singh is training a team of young anti-poachers, who are reformed poachers whom Fateh Singh himself caught. Fighting fire with fire on the poaching front. He is no stranger to fighting for the tiger and taking the occasional set back. He had been beaten "to near death (from my previous reading" by villagers opposed to having their village relocated when the park was formed. Today, there is a shrine in that relocated village in his honor.

He asked me what I was doing in India, and I explained. He had a word in Hindi with a young man present, named Ram, who then gave me a four hour guided tour by jeep, first into the park, then out of the park on the other side to visit a transplanted village – the Ranthambhore equivalent of Kanha's Chichrunpur. The magnificence of the park goes without saying – a delicate and feminine kind of exquisiteness compared to the rugged splendor of the Rocky Mountains of British Columbia, or even the raw lushness of Kanha. After yesterday's rain, it looks vibrant and fresh. On the other hand, the rain had washed away all the pug marks, and new ones are few and far between. No tiger graced my visit, but my beholder's eyes are overflowing with beauty.

Omni-Science and the Human Destiny

The backside of the park is a different story. Signs of infiltration by poachers and wood-cutters are everywhere evident. Tree stumps. Severed limbs. Cattle trails. Paucity of wildlife. Not long after we had exited the park, the forest thinned out to nothing. We encountered several women walking along the side of the rutted road, packing heavy bundles of tree branches on their heads. They were two young girls and an old woman. The old woman's spine is curved. She weighs no more than 90 lb. The bundle of wood on her head probably about the same. While passing the women, the young man at the wheel, named Ram, informed me that he was resetting the trip-meter to zero. I looked forward to seeing a village, but had long to wait as the jeep toed its way over the ruts on the road. Finally, when we did arrive, the trip meter read 5.2 miles. And the women had already left the trees behind them by a mile or two when we came across them. So they walk seven miles out every morning to reach the trees, cut a bundle of branches, and walk the same distance back with the wood on they heads. And the distance increases every day, as more and more wood is cut.

"Ripe for solar cooking technology, I'd say," I observed aloud.

"Yes. That's why I'm driving you here. To see for yourself. And to see what could happen to Kanha too," said the eager young man.

Behind the village was a wasteland of a valley. The landscape looked surreal - more like a moonscape than an Earthscape, except for some widely dispersed, thin and naked tree trunks pointing straight up at the sky, with all branches torn away. Such is the law, I was told. You cannot cut down a tree, but you can rip all its branches off. The ground was bare rock and sand, without a blade of grass in view.

"Between deforestation and overgrazing, especially by goats, which nibble down to the roots, killing the plant, the land doesn't stand much of a chance," said Ram. "Not long ago, this used to be a forested Eden. Now... Now, India is losing about 60,000 supertanker-loads of fertile soil washed irretrievably into the Indian Ocean."

He parked down the jeep near a small dam on the bottom of the valley near the village. The dam was initially a beneficial project. It was a small piece of desert turned into a large watering hole for humans, cattle and wildlife alike. In the first few years, wildlife actually increased, but deforestation and overgrazing here and up-stream has silted it up, leaving just a lifeless, muddy pond, surrounded by lifeless, irresurrectable desert.

Ram went into the village to talk to the chieftain. "It'll take a while. Maybe an hour. I hope you don't mind."

"No problem. I can just walk around. Take your time."

"If you're up to it, there is a shrine to the goddess Raminothna up on top of that hill. Raminothna is the goddess of compassion. If you have a question to ask her, you might be rewarded."

"Sure. Thanks," I said perfunctorily.

It was not stiflingly hot, but there was no shade except in the lee of the jeep. So I sat down there and tried to read. Once action ceased, however, thoughts began to contend for dominance. And the dominant thought, by far, is Christopher, and all thoughts of Christopher have become inseparable from agony.

So, even solitude, one of the most valued aspects of my life, has been ruined. Instead of peace and tranquility, solitude has now become my emotional torture chamber. And if it has this effect on me, what effect would it have on Christopher? The destruction knows no bounds.

Action, then, is my only escape. So, I undertook the most physically challenging activity at hand, and did climb the conical hill on the other side of the dam, and there, I did meet my destiny with Raminothna.

It was initially a little disappointing. The shrine was just a weathered stone plaque bearing carvings in Hindi, looking centuries old. I touched it, and it felt smooth and polished by centuries of rubbing, but nothing unusual. It stood at the foot of a tree in the bottom of a crater-like depression at the peak of the hill – the only tree left unmolested in a treeless landscape. The tree was about twenty feet tall and looks gnarled and ancient, but it offered to all interested a rich crop of small berries ranging from green to yellow to red to a deep purple – the purple ones looking ready to burst. My mouth was dry after the climb. I picked a purple one and tried it gingerly. It tasted sweet yet unfamiliar. It was very thirst quenching. I picked few more that were right at hand, and one led and next into my mouth. While doing so, I was again involuntarily reminded of Christopher, how we went berry-picking along the Coquitlam River in our happy days. And yet, strangely, there was no pain, no anger, just the happiness in its purest form, that which would be preserved in my heart till the end of time.

Did I say green and yellow and red and purple? It now looked as if the words life and youth and passion and compassion would be more appropriate, descriptive and true. The leaves and fruits, even the trunk and branches had somehow taken on a certain shimmering vibrancy. The whole tree seemed to be aglow with a certain inner light, a living radiance that transcended even the fierce sunlight imposed upon it. I was sure that at night, it would glow like a Christmas tree. Perish the thought – as soon as it was formed, it had struck me to be somehow a little insulting. If it were a Christmas tree, first, it would need no ornaments, and second, it would need no gifts at its foot, and third, it is already plugged into the Earth, which is a part of the

Universe, and fourth, it would have not dozens but billions of miniscule light bulbs, each the size of one of its billions of cells.

Before long, I felt drowsy. So I lay down in the shade of the tree. I looked up at the underside of its canopy, and was amazed by yet another of its self-revelations. In physical terms, the underside of the canopy should be no more than ten feet above my eyes, and yet, it seemed somehow hundreds, no, thousands, no, tens of thousands, of feet high. No, it was downright stratospheric. Were I Alice in Wonderland, I would have shrunken in size to that of an amoeba. But there is one last strange thing. When I raised up my hand to look at it, to compare it to the arm of the Statue of Liberty would be an understatement. I felt that if I really reached up, I could touch a star. And my feet - they seemed miles distant, more so, as if they were resting on the other side of the horizon.

I thought I closed my eyes for only a moment, but when they opened again, the sun had shifted enough to shine straight into them. And yet, something dazzled me even more – the vivid memory of a dream. I have recorded it as follows, in the first person, but in the name of Raminothna. The man, I think, is supposed to be me.

❖   ❖   ❖   ❖   ❖

Dear Homo Sapiens of Earth:

Your legend has it that in the snows of Kilimanjaro, the carcass of a plains leopard was found. No one knew what it had gone up there to seek. But when this human climbed the mountain, he knew, for he was there to seek the very same thing, which the leopard evidently succeeded in finding.

Days before he boarded his one-way flight two weeks ago from Vancouver to Dar Es Salaam, he had gracelessly quit his job, and ruthlessly gave away the physical remnants of his life – his real estate holdings, his car, his money, his credit, even his beloved horse. He had not bid farewell to a single soul, nor had he once looked back.

At pain of extra weight, he carried a gun, not that there was much to hunt up on the altitudes, nor to fear, but the gun itself. In five daily segments, he had made the snow line, where he dismissed his porter without explanation. Another half-day's solitary ascent brought him further up to this ice-cave into the depths of which he had withdrawn, from the world and from himself.

Not an hour ago, as the sun was declining in the western sky, transforming the cave into a glowing, rosy tomb, he was sitting exactly here, with the gun aimed at the temple of the temple of his soul.

Some say that when one is about to die, ones past life would flash before ones eyes. While he was sitting there, shivering in the descending cold, in the meditative position that seemed fitting for his final contemplation, his past life did not exactly flash by, but was instead painstakingly replayed, episode by episode, scene by scene, which were then drained into the sump in the dungeon of his mind already brimming with pain, anger, guilt, disenchantment, purposelessness and despair.

Failing to pull the trigger after some eons-long minutes, he had set the deadline for the fatal moment, that by the time the last glow of day had faded, either his head would have been blown apart, or he would deem himself a terminal coward. He would slink back to the meaningless existence he had climbed up here to escape, but thereafter it would be just his body undergoing the physical processes of survival, for his soul would have since irretrievably departed.

It was when he could no longer discern the fingers of his free hand held out before his eyes, and his gun hand had started trembling from the cold and his trigger finger had become numb from the strain, that I finally addressed him for the first time.

"Forgive me for intruding at this final moment of your privacy. So I will be brief, if you will allow me."

It was to him not exactly a voice that he had heard, for all his ears could discern was the whistling of the wind at the mouth of the cave, but rather, a clear and unmistakable thought that seemed to have come from far beyond. Or was it from deep within?

For at least a hundred of his remaining heartbeats he did not respond, and I spoke again, "I'm seeking a miracle worker, to work a miracle upon this Earth, for her sake and on my behalf. Since you appear to have no further use for this amazing instrument of yours which you call your body, and which obviously is in excellent working condition, will you donate it to me such that the purpose of this my sojourn on Earth be fulfilled?"

This notion was clearly so alien to him that he could hardly claim it as his own. So the first question that leapt to his mind was, "Who are you?"

So I told him truthfully, "I am Raminothna, the Fortunate and Called Upon, at your service." Again, of course, no sound was involved.

"Say again?" **He just wanted to "hear" my "voice" again.**

"I am Raminothna, the Fortunate and Called Upon, at your service."

"Ra-mi-noth-na? Be it as it may, that's just a name. What are you, then?"

"What am I? Yes, one of the deepest of all universal philosophical questions. I can only say this: Once you have come to know what you are, you will know what I am."

"Look, I have no inclination, nor the time, for a philosophical discussion right now."

"If not now, when?"

"Maybe never. Who cares?"

"I do."

"Alright, fine. Let's get this over and done with. What do you want?"

"As I said, I'm seeking a miracle worker, to work a miracle upon this Earth, for her sake and on my behalf."

"So, we're back from the universal philosophical question to the big fat joke, are we?"

"No joke."

"For me to perform a miracle? I can't even if I wanted to."

"Is this a yes?"

"No."

"Is it a no then?"

"Yes. No. I don't know."

"What exactly is it?"

"I mean, look at me. Do I look like a miracle worker to you? I can't even exert five ounces on the trigger, let alone perform a miracle."

"What does a miracle worker look like?"

"The last one I know looked like Jesus Christ."

"And what does Jesus Christ look like?"

Da Vinci's Last Supper materialized in his mind.

"What are these creatures?"

"What creatures?"

"The thirteen creatures depicted in this painting."

"They are human beings, for Christ's sake!"

"Which among these human beings is Jesus Christ?"

"The one in the middle."

"What makes him different from the rest? They all look essentially the same to me - all human, that is, as human as you."

"He had God in him."

"Where is God?"
"God is omni-present – anywhere and everywhere."
"Including the space currently occupied by your body?"
"Well, yes."
"Then you have God in you as well."
"Look. Just like the other twelve in the painting, in fact, like the other five billion, nine hundred and ninety nine million, nine hundred and ninety nine thousand, nine hundred and ninety-nine human beings on Earth today, I'm no miracle worker. Can't you just accept that? Let me give you a piece of advice. You are wasting your time to seek a miracle worker amongst us human beings, whatever you are."
"Define 'miracle'."
"No! *You* are the one who want to talk about miracles. You define it!"
"Very well. Let's say: A miracle is an impossible physical feat with a profound spiritual significance."
"So you're saying I can perform not only an impossible physical feat, but one with a profound spiritual significance?"
"Exactly."
"I'm glad we finally got this point straight. So now I can say, definitively, no ifs and buts, and for the last time, I cannot do the impossible, and for those possible things that I've done, none was of any significance whatsoever, which means, therefore, that I am not a miracle worker, at all, period…"
"If I prove to you that you can, will you?"
"… And even if I were, I would not lift one finger to glorify this selfish, heartless, cruel and destructive species which I am ashamed to admit to be my own..."
"If I prove to you that you can, will you?"
"… In fact, the more power we have, the worse we get… Pardon. What did you say?"
"If I prove to you that you can, will you?"
"What kind of proof?"
"Let me give you a basic one. I tell you that you can raise ten gallons of water from the plain 18,000 feet below up to here, in liquid form from beginning to end, all in the matter of five days, without artificial aid of any kind."
"Ten gallons of water? Without artificial aid of any kind? No buckets, no hoses, no boilers, no condensers . . .?"
"None, except the clothes you are now wearing, and the boots on your feet."
"Impossible, even with buckets."

"Thus, according to our definition, miraculous, considering its profound spiritual significance."

"What spiritual significance?"

"First and foremost, that you are a miracle worker."

"Circular reasoning."

"Indeed. With no beginning and no end."

"I can't produce this proof for you, I'm sorry."

"You already have."

"I what?"

"You have already raised the water."

"What water?"

"The water you've already raised up, of course."

"All ten gallons of it, I suppose."

"And all in liquid form, as stipulated, minus your sweat, to be exact."

"And where is this water I have raised up without artificial aid of any kind?"

"Right where you are."

He cast a glance around. "I see lots of ice, but it's been here for eons, and certainly not due to me. Besides, it is in solid form. Liquid water? There is not a drop in sight, except the couple of pints still in my flask, and the flask is an artificial aid."

"It's here."

"Well then, you'll just have to show it to me."

"Before I do, you must promise me one thing."

"O Lord! What now?"

"The power of miracle is never to be abused."

"Sure, no problem. If I do have this power, I will never abuse it. Alright?"

"Nor to be neglected."

"Nor will I neglect it."

"Then, look inward, inside your skin, where you will find, flowing through your arteries and veins, and tissues and organs including your heart and your brain, ten gallons of warm, living water. You can baptize the world's lost souls with it, and quench the world's thirst for understanding with it. Even, you can fertilize the deserts of humanity with it, extinguish the fires in your nuclear weapons with it, and dissolve in it the despair of humankind. With this sacred water, you can change your world, even save your Earth."

Without his knowing, as the moonlight filtered through the ice onto his gun, it had settled itself into his lap, on which glistened a drop of his liquid tears.

So, softly I said unto him, "Henceforth, I shall see through your eyes, hear through your ears, feel through your heart, think through your brain, and work through your hands, until your greater miracle is accomplished. May the Tao be with you, Homo Sapiens of Earth."

I am Raminothna
the Fortunate and the Called Upon
at your service

❖ ❖ ❖ ❖ ❖

I returned to the jeep and Ram was waiting.

"Sorry to be late," I said. "I fell asleep under the tree next to the shrine."

"The shrine? What shrine?"

"The stone tablet."

"Oh. That's not the shrine. That is just a label."

"Oh? Really? Then I didn't see any shrine."

"Oh yes, you did."

"Tell me."

"The Raminothna Tree."

"You mean, the tree is the shrine?"

"That is correct."

"So what does the plaque say?"

"Oh. Something like, 'Eat one berry and I will stay with you a year. Eat two, a decade. Eat three, a lifetime. Eat four, and you may never be able to get rid of me at all. Yours Divinely, Raminothna.' Something like that."

"How old is that tablet?"

"No one knows."

"Who carved it?"

"No one knows."

"What is the name of that tree species?"

Oh, something something Raminothnansis. It is supposed to be slightly toxic, highly psychedelic, and has long lasting effects – in terms of months or years. You didn't eat the berries, did you?"

"Uh, yes, I did."

"How many?"

"About a dozen."

"Oh my God! I forgot that you couldn't read Hindi. You're probably the first non-Hindu who has ever gone up that hill. I'm very sorry. Are you alright?"

Yes and no.

Good night, Christopher.
Good night, Christopher.

❖   ❖   ❖   ❖   ❖

February 9, 1999, Mon, sunny, 7-21C

Dearest Christopher:

[07:11 @ Ranthambhore Bagh lodge, Ranthambhore tiger reserve, Rajasthan, India]
Another day is opening for me and closing on you. How did it go? What did you do? How did you feel? Do you know that every moment of every day and night, whether or not I happen to be thinking of you or dreaming about you, you are always on my mind? You are on my mind now.

[10:17, @ Ranthambhore Bagh lodge, Ranthambhore tiger reserve, Rajasthan, India]
Like a drowning man grasping for a lifeline, or a man suddenly in love, I hired a cab right after breakfast to drive me back to the dam. I paid him to wait there for me. He grinned broadly. "No trouble, sir. I'll sleep till you come back. I need it." He drives 16 hours a day, seven days a week. His kind of day.

"Welcome back," she smiled at me as soon as I entered the crater. **"Though you need not have come back at all, since you have taken me deep inside of you and I'll be with you for many lifetimes."**

The "smile" was metaphorical, as are her words, as is Raminothna herself, of course, I think. But I'm back here, am I not? In this a refuge for the desperate? I looked at the berries. I reached for a purple one, hesitantly.

"Have more of me if you must, but you already have all of me."

I withdrew my hand.

"Rest under my shelter."

I settled into a meditative position in the shade of the tree. The silence is golden, except for the call of a solitary cicada, which makes it platinum. I am alone, but am not lonely. I have company, but have regained my solitude. Pain would have again filled earth and sky, hatred would have again taken hold like a strangling fig, outrage would have again risen like magma..., but they did not. I don't exactly feel optimistic, confident or at peace, let alone happy, but I feel in control and reasonably calm.

"You may ask your question."

"The same old one throughout human history: What then must I do?"

"Depends on what you want to achieve."

"Christopher's happiness."

"What are you prepared to pay?"

"Anything I can, up to and including my life."

"It should include yours then?"

"My what?"

"Happiness."

"I'm unhappy now. So, what the hell. Though I'm not sure I know what you mean."

"Suppose the only way Christopher can be happy is to feel bad about you."

"What are you *talking* about?!"

"He already calls you 'a very bad man', doesn't he?"

"He recited that! He was made to say it!! He didn't know what he was saying!!!"

"One day he might, knowingly."

"That's an insufferable thought."

"He might have to hate you for his psychological survival, and despise you for his sanity."

"Oh, stop. I can't stand it. I dread to think what would have to happen to him to make him feel that way about me."

"Would you still love him?"

"Yes, I will."

"No matter what he may become?"

"No matter what he may become."

"Easier said than done."

"Count on it."

"I will."

"But still, what are you talking about?"

"Just be forewarned."

"Do you know something I don't?"

"Everybody knows something everybody else doesn't."

"So tell me."

"Certain things are best left unsaid and unknown, at least for the time being, or until it happens."

"I already know that I will die some day. Although indeed I would not want to know when, or how for that matter. I'm a bit if a coward, aren't I?"

"At least you're one step ahead of the cicada, who has no idea that it's remaining time span is only thirteen days. Suppose I tell you that your remaining time span is…"

"DON'T!!! I don't want to know!"

"I said 'suppose'."

"But still."

"Fine. I won't tell. And I wouldn't fault you for lacking in courage either."

"Why not? I *am* scared to know."

"You do know that one day you will die. Somehow. Somewhere. Somewhen. Aren't you scared of that?"

"To death."

"See what I mean?"

"See what?"

"That in spite of your fear, you still have not lost your sense of humor. That's a sign of courage.

"So, what does this leave me? Back to my original question. What do I do now?"

"What *can* you do?"

"Nothing. Nothing I can do can do Christopher a smidgeon of good, that I can think of."

"Is doing nothing is an option?"

"No, because every passing day I do not contact Christopher, will be one day closer to his total despair."

"It is not a viable option, I tend to agree."

"So, again, what then must I do?"

"Your options do all seem to be indirect at best, at least for now."

"You mean working for the greater good so that he, too, will benefit?"

"I mean working for the greatest good."

"What is the greatest good?"

"Tell me. What is the heaviest precious object in your world whose full weight you can take on the palm of your hands?"

"Precious object? Heaviest? How about a hundred-pound diamond?"

"Not precious enough."

"A hundred and fifty pound diamond then. That's stretching it."

"Still not precious enough."

"Oh! How right you are! How could I be so bloody materialistic?! It is Christopher. He is what you mean, isn't he?"

"Indeed he is, unless, as soon as you have his full weight on the palm of your hands, your feet would rise six feet off the ground, bearing no weight at all."

"You've lost me."

"You heard me."

"Are you saying that this 'heaviest precious object' is such that once I've taken its full weight on the palms of my hands, my feet would simultaneously rise six feet off the ground, bearing no weight at all?"

"Word for word."

"Impossible."

"The 'I' word again?"

"Even if that is possible, what am I supposed to do with it?"

"Take care of it, for the sake of Christopher."

"I still don't understand."

"You will, before you leave."

"Now what?"

"Ask me another question."

"Okay. Raminothna, What exactly are you? Are you really a Hindu goddess? Or are you a Christian angel? Or are you a fallen angel in disguise? Or are you in fact an alien? And if you were, are you benevolent or malevolent? Or are you more like E.T. the extraterrestrial? Or could you even be God? Or could you be nothing more than a figment of my imagination?"

"Which would you prefer?"

"It is not I prefer. It is what you are."

"I am what you imagine me to be, beginning with this tree."

"So you're saying you're nothing but a figment of my imagination?"

"You are at liberty to imagine that I am real."

"Real what?"

"**As I said, I am what you imagine me to be.**"

"If I imagine you to be the Devil in disguise?"

"**Do you? Really?**"

"No."

"**Thank you. Alright, very well, let me give you a hint. Let me say this: 'Dear Homo Sapiens of Earth, whose foot prints now roam the crater of the Moon, heed the Seven Cosmic Signs…***… I am Raminothna, the Fortunate and Called Upon, at your service.**" (*** See the Prologue – "The Seven Cosmic Signs".)

"This is nice, but it still doesn't tell me what you are. You could still be a goddess, or an angel, or the Devil in disguise, or an alien, or God."

"**Yes, I could be.**"

"Well?"

"**Well maybe you should change your line of questioning.**"

"I see. Alright, I'll let you off the hook for now."

"**Was I on the hook?**"

"Okay, I do have a question."

"**Shoot.**"

"These Seven Cosmic Signs. What do they signify?"

"**Good question. I'm glad you ask. Let me start to answer by telling you this: These Seven Cosmic Signs have another name.**"

"Which is?"

"**The Seven Critical Symptoms.**"

"Sound more ominous by the hour. So what are these 'critical symptoms' symptomatic of?"

"**The Six Planetary Diseases.**"

"Sounds even more ominous still."

"**Some prefer to use the word 'ailments' rather than 'diseases'. It is up to you.**"

"Tell me what they are first."

"**Are you sure you really want to know?**"

"I don't want to, but I think I should."

"**Alright. Here they are then: The First Planetary Disease - Planetary Fever.**"

I thought for a moment. "Are you talking about global warming?"

"**Which could become global roasting if you're not careful.**"

"The 'runaway greenhouse effect'. Sure. If we are that stupid, we *should* roast in Hell. Next." **"The Second Planetary Disease - Planetary Auto-Immune Deficiency Syndrome – PAIDS for short."**

"What is the planetary auto-immune system?"

"What is Earth's natural defense system that protects life on Earth from a certain natural external threat?"

"What is this threat? Asteroids?"

"That too."

"Solar UV radiation?"

"Exactly."

"So, this planetary auto immune system is the ozone shield?"

"The very same."

"And this PAIDS - it is the totality of all the damage done to the biosphere by solar UV radiation due to the damage done to the ozone shield?"

"Well put."

"And the Third Planetary Disease?"

"Planetary Cancer."

"What is this cancer?"

"Guess."

"Cancer is ones own body cells multiplying unchecked."

"Right. So what are the 'body cells' of Earth's biosphere multiplying unchecked?"

"My species?"

"Good guess."

"Dare I add – our cattle? I don't mean to offend you, you being a Hindu goddess and cows being sacred in your religion. But both humans and cattle do multiplying unchecked, uncontrolled, and even out of control. And they *are* born of the biosphere, which now they are feeding upon unsustainably. So, indeed, we are the scum of the Earth."

"Except for one thing."

"What now?"

"Cancers cells don't have a choice. You do."

"True. But then, it could be even worse. At least, cancer cells do not intentionally become cancer cells. We human beings, at least for now, are cancer of the Earth by choice."

"You could also deliberately stop doing what is harmful that you used to do, and begin deliberately to live a non-cancerous way of life."

Omni-Science and the Human Destiny

"Could you give me an example of a non-cancerous way of life?"

"The key word is 'sustainable'. You yourself used it just now. A sustainable way of life is not cancerous."

"Such as a vegetarian diet? It is said that if everybody on Earth eat like the average American or Canadian, we would need three planet Earths to feed us all."

"Global dietary change is undoubtedly a central factor of planetary evolution."

"And the Fourth Planetary Disease?"

"Planetary Wasting Disease."

"Involving weight loss?"

"Involving a global biomass loss."

"Deforestation."

"For one thing."

"Over-fishing."

"For another. And let's not forget another major bio-loss."

"Loss of bio – diversity? Biodiversity?"

"Exactly."

"Via over-hunting and habitat destruction, as usual."

"This valley being a prime example."

"Must be painful for you."

"The devastation to this whole planet, to me, is about as hurtful as the devastation of Christopher is to you."

"Oh, Raminothna. I'm so sorry to hear this. Must be unbearable for you."

"Was being nailed to the cross bearable? Yet he bore it."

"He died from it. And why, as a Hindu goddess, do you speak in Christian terms."

"If you, a mortal, can do it, why can't I?"

"You have a point. More on the loss of biodiversity. I hear that we are losing about one known species an hour, and an unknown number of unknown species per minute. Our quest for efficiency has resulted in monoculture of crops and unification of strains within species. Furthermore, there is a push to eliminate predators of species we want to consume, and even eliminate those who compete for the food that our "preferred" species consume. Diversity of species and variation within species reduces short-term efficiency, but remains a natural hedge against long-term ecological change. Yet, ecological change is happening incredibly fast, increasing greatly the need for diversity to avert ecological crisis."

"The first order of business in terms of preservation of biodiversity is to

safeguard the integrity of the natural ecosystems that still remain on your Earth."

"Yes. I'll vouch for that. Okay, what is the Fifth Planetary Disease?"

"Planetary Blood-Poisoning."

"Pollution, acid rain, toxic waste…"

"And the Sixth Planetary Disease – Planetary Suicidal Tendency."

"How does a planet commit suicide?"

"A global nuclear holocaust would be the fast way."

"A global nuclear holocaust is what our species could do to the Earth, not what the Earth would do to itself."

"Is your species an integral part of the biosphere, or apart from it?"

"An integral part of it."

"Is the biosphere an integral part of the planet, or apart from it?"

"An integral part of it. Yes, I see what you mean. And, no, I don't want Earth to commit suicide, or die of any of the planetary diseases. And, yes, I will do my best to make sure that she does not, for the sake of all creatures, and all children, especially Christopher. I will do what I can to help cure these planetary diseases. I will help heal our planet Earth."

"Heal Our Planet Earth – H.O.P.E. May you be realized."

"Even if I succeed in healing the world, in terms of my indirect way of benefiting Christopher, I know it would still be a poor substitute for directly providing for Christopher's personal needs as a father figure and a male role model."

"Yes, but it sure beats passing down a sicker and sicker planet to Christopher and his generation, even if you could continue being his father figure and male role model. And it is your best option given the circumstances."

"Easier said than done. To heal just one person of only one disease would cost thousands. How much would the medical bill for healing a whole planet of all six planetary diseases be?"

"Your guess is as good as mine."

"How about $1 trillion over the first ten years?"

"Or $100 billion per year. Sounds reasonable, for starters."

"And pray tell, where do we get $100 billion a year?"

"You noted that India is spending $1.8 billion on a star wars system against Pakistan. So there is $1.8 billion right there."

"How true."

"What is your global arms expenditure?"

"About $1 trillion a year, I hear."

"$100 billion is a tenth of that."
"Yes. So it is. But how do you get the whole world to cut the global military spending by ten percent?"
"By each nation cutting its own military budget by ten percent."
"And what do you do with the funds thus released?"
"Put them into a H.O.P.E. fund, to be administered by the U.N.."
"A truly magnificent vision, Raminothna, if only, somehow, this could be implemented."
"Do you have a will?"
"Yes, I do. So, there is a way."
"There is."
"If somehow I could get this happening, it would indeed be a miracle."
"It would be a part of a greater miracle."
"Let me think about this, Raminothna. Now, it's getting late. I'd better go."
"Before you leave, would you honor me with a yoga suite?"
"Yes, I would, with all my being."

It was during the 13th stance when Raminothna said, **"Behold, you now have your world's heaviest precious object in the palms of your hands, and your feet have indeed simultaneously risen six feet off the ground, bearing no weight at all."**

The 13th stance is the handstand.

"The planet Earth," I grunted in awe.

So, Christopher, here is my solemn promise to you. I will devote my life towards healing our planet Earth, for your sake. Raminothna be my witness.

"I am," said Raminothna.

"It sure was a long communion you had with Raminothna. She must like you a lot," said the taxi driver, while rubbing sleep from his eyes and glancing at the fare-meter. "What do you think of her?"

"My kind of goddess," I said.

[23:46 @ Ranthambhore Bagh lodge, Ranthambhore tiger reserve, Rajasthan, India]

A three-day international environmental conference involving some 140 countries is happening right now at the "Bare Foot College" in nearby Tilonia. My plenary lecture, on Bengal tiger conservation naturally, was well attended and received. I then led a workshop on campaigning techniques, in which about 50 participated. I was also interviewed by half a dozen newspapers and two TV cameras.

Anthony Marr

    This is the only bare foot conference I have ever attended. The open-air theatre was festooned with brightly colored fabric which acted as awnings for the stage as well as the seating areas. The stage itself was covered by carpets and rugs and cushions, on which no shoes were to tread. At the back of the stage were several translation booths, each for one major language, to which the headsets issued to the delegates could be tuned.

    The most memorable event on the stage on this day occurred during "women's night". Women from various countries sat in a large circle, each speaking for a few minutes on the rights and plights of women in their respective countries. One speech stuck in my mind – the shortest one. The speaker was a woman in a pink sari. She said, "I am from a village nearby. Tonight, when I return home, I will be beaten by my husband, for speaking up in public, and for defying his direct order. But for the first time in my life, I will joyfully receive it." And for this, I must let the world know, word for word what she said.

Good night, Christopher.

❊   ❊   ❊   ❊   ❊

February 10, 1999, Sunday, sunny, 8-22C

Dearest Christopher:

[22:47 @ the Alsisar Haveli Hotel in Jaipur, Rajasthan, India]
    Today is a day of travel and accidents.
    Avtar came to the hotel in the mid-morning to pick me up to go to Jaipur for two days of intense activities. In the car was Sultana, who, being an attorney, was going to Jaipur to organize the Rajasthan Legal Tiger Conference set for early April, unfortunately after my departure. She said she was also here to see my presentation. She had missed each and every one of my presentations in Delhi thus far due to her work schedule. We had a high-spirited trip in Avtar's car. I found myself joking and laughing with them. I heard that a truly depressed person cannot even laugh, so I guess I'm not in a depression, technically speaking. Actually, although I've read about it, I can't say I know what depression really *feels* like, although I did see it in the emotionally disturbed children I once worked for at Browndale, in

Omni-Science and the Human Destiny

the era when Gestalt Therapy and such were all the rage. But small disasters struck along the way.

First, while still in Delhi, Avtar's car, a 1997 Cielo sedan (1997 – another coincidence?), was rear-ended by another car at a stop light, and got its left tail light shattered and the left rear fender dented.

"At least he is at fault. His insurance should cover it," I said.

"Insurance?" What insurance?" Avtar said. His solution was to get whatever he could from the other driver on the spot, and/or agree on some compensation at some later date. But the other guy was penniless, so Avtar just drove off, fuming for a few miles.

On the highway, we came across two Tata trucks, both on the side of the road, with extensive front end damage. Later, on a curve, an overloaded truck (you should see what an overloaded truck here looks like) lay on its side, presenting its rusty undercarriage to our passing gaze.

Along the high speed divided highway, there were vehicles going the wrong way, rushing headlong towards us, vehicles sitting in the middle of the fast lane motionless, with big chunks of rock placed around them. The brake lights of most of the vehicles do not work, and in fact, at night, most highway vehicles drive with their lights off to conserve the light bulbs. At least once, without any forewarning, we saw a speed bump rushing at us at highway speeds. Avtar jammed on the brakes, and still bottomed out all his shocks over it. What incompetent bureaucrat could have come up with a transportation system like this?

Speaking of incompetence, I realized, while we were more than 3 hours on the road, that I had forgotten to bring my carousels of slides from Delhi. To the rescue, Avtar said that he had Sarita's tray of slides in his trunk, but they were a far cry from mine. Anyway, they would have to do. Later, I took Sarita's slide tray into my room, and rearranged the slides into a serviceable sequence. It's not all that bad.

While approaching Jaipaur, we topped a hill, and saw the city glowing a surreal pink in the afternoon sun, certainly justifying its nickname "The Pink City". But once we entered the city, it was another garbage strewn Indian metropolis, albeit one distinguished by a predominance of ruddy colored buildings. Avtar checked me into this fairyland of a hotel, the approach to which being a replay of the Belinda Wright residence experience. One moment, we were in grey, dusty and dingy streets, squeezing through the suffering throng. The next, the car entered a gate, and it was trees and flowers and bird songs and color and this mini palace complete with sculptured courtyards and exotic gardens. My room has a king sized 4-poster bed with a silk canopy under a delicately painted vaulted-ceiling.

Anthony Marr

After checking in, we went to give a presentation at a private girls' school, the Indian equivalent of Vancouver's Crofton House Girls' School or Little Flower Academy in terms of prestige. As usual, I was surrounded by students for a good hour after my presentation, at the end of which a tiger club was formed. In spite of my missing slides, it was nonetheless a good presentation, this time even with a large screen on which Champions of the Wild was shown, followed by a short speech, then Q&A. The auditorium was full of about 300 secondary school students who sang the Tiger Song with enthusiasm, while the Big Cub, shaking its head in the wind, was admired by the other 1,000+ students out in the football field. Avtar gave a short intro for me and was very complimentary of my work. And, wonder of wonders, there was media present. Also present were Avtar's mother, Sultana and an officer of Project Tiger named Dr. Ravji whom Avtar considers an excellent organizer, whose organizational ability has been more than borne out, seeing the amount of activities crammed into two short days, including this presentation.

Tomorrow will be a very busy day, with two school presentations, one at 08:30 and the other at 11:30, plus a major media conference at the Press Club at 14:30. After that, we'll return to Delhi for more school presentations tomorrow.

In the evening we went to a very nice multi-ethnic restaurant for a Rajasthani vegetarian feast, my treat. Upon coming out, we witnessed a woman, while crossing the street, being struck down by an erratically ridden scooter, which carried on to smash into a parked car before coming to rest on its side. Its rider, a young man in a suit and no helmet, lay inertly on the ground.

Avtar went to call the police, and then, while we were driving off, we saw the man sit up, holding his head. "He's drunk out of his scull," Avtar said.

Within two blocks, a white dog with black spots, in the company of several other strays, trotted right into the beam of the left headlight of Avtar's car. The car just knocked it down, then rolled over it – smack thump thump - leaving it screaming in the dust.

Avtar did not stop, nor even slow down, though our gleeful chatter was momentarily suspended. I stated the obvious, "You ran over the dog, Avtar."

"Yes, I did," he said nonchalantly, but continued driving. I wanted to have him turn the car around so I could check on the dog, but knew he would not do it. He'd just say, "Oh, come *on*, Tony," as he's done before.

[01:16]

Now it's past one in the morning. Minutes ago, a wedding procession passed outside the hotel, with loud traditional music playing and the odd firecrackers sounding like gunshots. This momentarily distracted me from my late night agony. I've tried to go to sleep for an hour, but images of the crushed yet still screaming dog, half pasted to the ground, bounced around in my head. Inevitably, the dog's screams turned into a child's wail, and my stoicism melted inevitably again into tears.

"I could rid you of your pain in a heart beat, if you wish me to."

"Raminothna, there are times when I would like to grieve in private."

"My apologies. Whenever you wish to be rid of me, just say so."

"And if I want you back?"

"Just call my name."

"No cheating?"

"My word of honor."

"Fair enough."

"The return of peace to your solitude is hard won. I would do nothing to spoil it."

"Thank you for helping me restore it. Now what about this ridding me of my pain? What does it entail?"

"Very simple. In your brain's vast neuronal network is a highly developed and well tuned neuronal subcircuit called Christopher. It was built, synapse by synapse, with every experience you shared with Christopher since his birth. Every time you share a new experience, every time he says something new to you, new connections are made. Every time you think of him, the subcircuit is activated, and every time it is activated, it is strengthened. And when the subcircuit is activated, you think of Christopher. Inside the subcircuit are configurations that allow you to see his face and hear his voice in your mind. This subcircuit in itself is suffused with an overabundance of pure love and happiness. But the recent trauma has so damaged it that it has become a source of overwhelming pain. I could easily dismantle the subcircuit for you overnight. All you would wake up with tomorrow morning would be a hangover and a bad dream. After that, if I asked you about Christopher you'd say. 'Christopher who?' You would be quite as care-free as if you have never met Christopher in your life. The associated pain and rage would be gone without a trace. I could do it tonight in your sleep if you want me to. A simpler operation would be to simply block that subcircuit. With prolonged disuse, it would atrophy on its own accord. What do you say?"

"I say to hell with you!"

"No need to get testy. Just trying to help."

"'Better loved and lost than not having loved at all.'"

"I'm a sucker for human tears, don't you know."

"And what do I do if I want to cry alone?"

"Just say so."

"You wouldn't mind?"

"Not in the least."

"Then, with due gratitude for your caring, I would like to be left alone to my grief, for now, if you don't mind."

"Not at all. Good night to you then. Just don't cry, or I'd come right back."

"I'll try not to. Thanks again for caring, Raminothna. Good night."

"Good night, Anthony."

"I wish I had your power, Raminothna. Then I would have no human vulnerabilities, and no problem carrying the weight of this world."

"Yes, but then you'd have the much greater vulnerabilities of a goddess, and be compelled to carry the weight of a million worlds, many as tragic and personal as your own."

Christopher, I don't really want to grieve alone. I just want to grieve with you.

❈ ❈ ❈ ❈ ❈

February 11, 1999, Thursday, sunny, 7-19C

Good morning, Christopher:

[06:48 @ Room 1, Alsisar Haveli Hotel, Jaipur, Rajasthan, India]

Raminothna appeared to me in a dream last night – a dream of passion. She was the grand dame of ballet, giving her farewell performance. She chose Romeo and Juliet for this pinnacle event of her life. And in the end, Raminothna died with Juliet, in the way Juliet died, as Juliet. Neither heard the thunderous applause before the shocked silence.

It might have something to do with the dreadful magazine article I read in the hotel café yesterday. It was the Feb. 8, 1999 issue of the India Today magazine, whose front cover features a balding white man in his 40s, with his hands on the shoulders of two young blonde boys, one wearing glasses, about 10, and the other not, about 7. The man and the boys were shown in a photo-within-a-photo, one corner of which was burning. The cover story is titled [**MURDER OF A MISSIONARY**], subtitled [**The burning of an Australian social worker and his two sons reveals a growing frenzy of intolerance among Hindu fanatics**].

The Inside story, on 7 pages, is titled [**BURNING SHAME**]. It contains photos of the burnt out hulk of the jeep wagoner in which Graham Stewart Staines, an Australian Christian missionary, and his two son, were sleeping and then burnt alive with gasoline. Some of the photos even show the charred remains of Staines and his two sons in the rear compartment of the hulk. There is also an artist's 6-step recreation of the event, using a 3-D map, specifying 00:20 on January 23, 1999 as the time of the horrible event, which occurred at the Manoharpur village in the sleepy rural outback of Orissa's Keonjhar district in Gujurat, where over 30 Hindu-versus-Christian-conflict incidents have erupted. Staines, his wife Glade, daughter Ester and sons Phillip and Timothy, had succeeded in converting half of the village to Christianity, resulting in the Christian half defying and abandoning the Hindu culture and traditional practices, thus dividing the village along religious lines. One photo shows Glade and Ester at the funeral, with the caption, [**MISSIONARY ZEAL: Glade and Ester are determined to continue Staines' work**].

This event is extra poignant to me because it occurred *after* our arrival on Indian soil. On January 23, Jane and Kim and I were embarking on the train that would take us to Kanha, there to change the way of life of the villagers by our own means to our own ends, and perhaps to meet our own fates. I have seen the Gujarati's craft at the Dilli Haat fair, and have indeed spoken with the Gujarati people. They are nice folk just like the villages around Kanha. And yet, their kin are capable of a horrendous act like this. Do the people in Chichrunpur feel the same about us as the people of Keonjhar feel about the Staineses? When we wade into their midst, we do so with open hearts and in sincere spirit. We have no preconception of what kind of people they are. We could be like sheep walking into a sheep pen, or a wolf den. We really do not know. One thing seems quite consistent. In every village, there will be people who will like you, and there will be people who will dislike you. It all depends on where you stand in relation to them, and where they stand in relation to you. If they are dead set against the park, then the more people one converts to favor the park, the more hated one becomes, as is in the case of the Staines in relation to the Hindus. I do grant that religion is a hotter issue than fuel, perhaps by far.

[23:28 @ Rm. 206, F-18 Inn, Delhi, India]

An exhausting yet invigorating day.

First presentation was 08:30-10:30 at the MGD Girls' School (senior secondary) which has the most beautiful campus so far I have visited in India, catering also to high caste and rich families. It was almost an impromptu visit, arranged by Dr. Ravji late yesterday. I gave a slideshow instead of the video as in the Indian International School yesterday, and as always, I led them to sing the Tiger Song. Yet again, after the presentation, I was surrounded by a group of girls, all eager, all inspired. I hope their now awakened passion will never flicker out, nor be buried alive ever again.

We were supposed to be at the second school at 11:00. It was an elementary school for poorer children and the school building was somewhat dilapidated, but clean and tidy. As it happened, we didn't get there till past 11:30. (We're usually late, but does this time's being late have anything to do with this school's lower prestige?) When we arrived, we found the welcoming committee standing expectantly and respectfully at the gate, with three beautiful girls in glowing saris each holding something precious in their hands, and the chief staff members standing beside and behind them. Had they been standing like that for over half an hour? When we alighted from the vehicle, I was ushered forward by two teachers towards the girls who gave me a kind of baptism of color. One of the girls smeared something bright red in the shape of a flame between my eyebrows, the second girl stuck a grain of rice in the flame, and the third placed a multi-hewed and very substantial garland around my neck. Similar honors were bestowed upon Avtar and Sultana. We were then served chai and sweets in the principal's office, with the teaching staff standing respectfully in waiting, and only after we had finished – and we tried not to seem hurried - were we led to the hall in which over 500 children had already been seated – on the hard floor, in neat rows. Again Avtar gave a short intro, and I was passed the mike, and off I went. It became quite obvious that there was a language gap between me and the younger ones, but I plowed right through the presentation for the older ones. When I was done, Sultana gave a brief summary of my speech in Hindi, after which I was given back the mike to lead the children in the Tiger Song, followed by a very vigorous Q&A period. After that, five beautiful girls in saris sang us a "Welcome to you" song. Finally, there was the wind up ceremony in which we were presented with commemorative plaques, and I, being the guest of honour, was given smaller plaques to present to those students who asked questions, one by one, while the school photographer took photos of each presentation. I can just see it – photos of the foreign dignitary (me) presenting plaques to honoured students, displayed proudly on the walls of the school corridors or maybe a blown up one in the general office. While doing the "balloon tiger" bit, I was again surrounded by kids extending pieces of paper and notebooks for my autograph, and those without notebooks or paper held out their hands for me to autograph on the palms. I've taken to sign: "Save the Tiger! Anthony". The kids walked away with their new treasures, and those with my signature on their hands probably wouldn't wash them for a week. There were so many kids saying please that in spite of Avtar trying to urge me away, I overstayed for 15 minutes. Finally, I had to be almost dragged away, with Avtar saying, "You have to put an end to it. It will not end by itself." Still with some 50 kids crowding about, I extricated myself, feeling guilty at their still eager but now disappointed little faces. While the car was drawing away, numerous tiny hands were held out in my direction. I lowered the window and touched as many as I could. Now I know to a small extent what the Pope experiences when he goes through an adoring crowd. It is another minor religious experience. If/when His Holiness ever becomes jaded to it, that should be the day he should resign. For a jaded man to touch these little hands would be a sacrilege – against the children.

There are moments of outstanding clarity in my childhood memory, and more often than not, they would involve some person of influence in my life. These moments could be the points of directional life-changes or of extraordinary life-events. I hope that my talk to them today would be one such life-changing event in the lives and future recall of some of these children.

Next on our agenda was the media conference at the Press Club. When we got there, the grounds outside of the club was already filled with reporters, including the reporter from The Hindu newspapers who did the article when I was in Rajasthan two years ago, with at least three 3 TV cameras present. We set up the Big Cub in the garden, then I gave a slideshow to the gathering of about 25 reporters. After that, we all went inside the Cub for the Q&A. Avtar got two helpers to place a thick wall-to-wall rug inside, and rows of chairs. It was quite a production, quite a scene.

When it was all over, we went back to Madame Grewal's home – the house where the late great Ravinder Grewal once lived – and she served us dinner. Then, around 17:30, we (Avtar, Sultana, Dr. Ravji and I) went on the road for the 6 hour drive back to Delhi, watching keenly for those treacherous speed bumps this time.

About 20:00, Dr. Ravji directed Avtar to pull into the parking lot of a road-side hotel. With us in tow he made a beeline for the hotel's cafe where the news was being shown on TV. As if on cue, our segment came up. It was good coverage, but for me it had an uncomfortable element with which I am familiar. Time and again over the last few years, when several people were interviewed with the same question, mine would usually be selected for broadcast for one reason or another, often to the disappointment if not resentment of the others. It happened again tonight. Although Avtar spoke at length at the conference, and was interviewed by at least two TV crews, I was the only one featured in this broadcast. He did not receive even a mention. I diligently avoided looking in his direction, so could not read his body language. I hope he is a bigger person than some of the others. Dr. Ravji proudly introduced me to the rest of the patrons in the café. After the segment, Sultana briefly translated for me what in Hindi was put into my mouth. Almost surprisingly, I was not misquoted – as I've been time and again by Canadian media.

Finally, I was brought back to the F-18 Inn back in Delhi shortly after midnight. A very satisfying day. The next two days will be crammed full of presentations and other activities. Then on St. Valentine's day, the Love-the-Tiger Walk. And then, Kanha, wonderful Kanha, here I come to you again!

Good night, Christopher.

February 12, 1999, Friday, sunny, 6-20C

Dearest Christopher:

[08:44 @ F-18 Inn in Delhi, India]
Waiting for Avtar to call regarding today's schedule. He said he would call at 08:30, but hasn't yet. I don't want to call him, in case there is nothing to get up for and he is still in bed.

Again cranking my brain and spinning my mental wheels in the mud about Christopher. I thought of one more thing I could do that could benefit him, directly, and that is to establish an educational fund for him. But that begs the question as to how much I could spare from month to month to put into this fund. Based upon my income from WCWC, which is CDN$30,000 minus tax, the answer is "next to nothing". But we all know that my line of work is no way to get rich. It is my choice to be a poor man.

"You are a very rich man, and you can do a lot for Christopher with your wealth."

Omni-Science and the Human Destiny

"Have you always worked with me on the false assumption that I'm a very rich man? Well, by Indian Standards, I'm certainly well to do, but wealthy? That stretches the imagination by more than a little."

"You are very rich by even Canadian standards."

"You're in India, not in Canada. What would you know about Canadian standards?"

"I am on the planet Earth, and in fact in this Universe, to which Canada belongs."

"Then you should know that your statement is untrue."

"Tell me. How many dollars do you have to have before you would begin to consider yourself rich?"

"I don't know. A million used to do it, but nowadays, to be a millionaire seems no big deal. Let's say a million. I'm not greedy."

"Okay, let me try this. I will pay you ten million dollars, right now, in exchange for all the knowledge you have acquired since grade 2."

"All of it?"

"Every bit and byte of it."

"Aah, no thanks."

"I will pay you a hundred million dollars for your power of higher reasoning."

"No."

"I will pay you a billion dollars for you to become a high profile fundamentalistic and creationistic TV evangelist."

"I wouldn't do it for ten billion dollars."

"You just might make ten billion dollars if you are clever and ruthless enough."

"No."

"I will indeed pay you ten billion dollars if you will sell your morals and ethics and integrity and conscience."

"Not for a hundred billion dollars."

"I will indeed pay you a hundred billion dollars, for your health. You would then have the first year's Earth healing budget, while being racked by unbearable pain every day."

"No."

"Last offer. I will pay you one trillion dollars, if you will me sell your soul."

"And what would you do with it?"

"I'd just toss it carelessly into Hell."

"Not for sale."

"Then consider yourself a very rich man, by any standard. Your financial contribution to Christopher's wellbeing may be meager, but what you could give him from your non-financial assets could be monumental."

[20:32 @ F-18 Inn in Delhi, India]

This morning's presentation at the Springdales School was less than ideal. First off, poor organization, again. In our absence, Sarita set the time of the presentation with the school for 10:00. We arrived too late last night for her to contact Avtar, and there was no message left for him to the effect. And she did not call Avtar about it until 09:55, when he was still in his pajamas. Avtar himself was supposed to call me at 08:30, but did not until 09:58, with the news about 10:00. So, we hurriedly picked Sarita up at Avtar's office, then sped to the school. When we finally arrived at the school, it was already 10:40. So, what's new?

The school itself could have done better, though given our lateness we should be thankful they did not cancel on us. The auditorium was huge, easily capable of seating 1,000 people, and well equipped, with a big screen and built-in video projector, but the school put only about 80 kids there, who were members of their environmental club. The teacher said she didn't want to play favorites, so, instead of letting some of the other kids come in to fill the auditorium and not letting others, since the school was 2,000 strong, she decided to not to let anyone in at all other than the club members. So, I was left to speak to an almost empty hall, with two thousand eager kids outside. The slide projector again acted up, and I decided to can the slideshow and have an interactive session with the children instead. They were shy and reluctant to raise their hands, and I had to incite them into action. But when after a minute or two they began to loosen up and speak out, Sarita seized the mike from my hand and launched into her own diatribe, in Hindi. She could have good things to say, but this is not the way to do it. I finally reclaimed the mike from her after about 10 minutes, and did have a good discussion with some very intelligent questions from the students.

All in all, even though the trip to Jaipur thawed my feelings for Avtar somewhat, this morning's performance gave me pause again regarding the wisdom of continuing the WCWC/TF partnership.

The afternoon's presentation to a group of about 70 tourism students at the College of Vocational Studies, however, was thoroughly satisfying. Amera Jiwani, one

Omni-Science and the Human Destiny

of Avtar's friends whom I met back in 1997, is a teacher there. She checked out several rooms with us, most being too bright for the slideshow, and finally settled us in the computer lab, which was adequate. They gave me all the time I wanted, so I gave an unrushed and therefore quality presentation, with an ecotourism slant. And they gave me their full attention. The best indicator was that a group of computer students who initially were not a part of the audience after awhile closed down their computers and joined in. They all agreed that the gate charge for foreign tourists at all India parks should be raised at least 10 fold and have the proceeds shared 50/50 park/villagers. We thought that only young children could be idealistic, but these young adults showed us how fired up they too could be. They wanted to write to various powers-that-be as well as the media. They are organizing a bus to go to the Love-the-Tiger Walk en masse. Avtar added one point, that there would be draw-prizes in the walk, including a trip to Bandhavgarh. I've never been one for gimmicks, and have pretty well closed my eyes to the gimmicky aspects of WCWC's tiger walks. One of the students worded it perfectly, "If they come for the prize, they should not come at all." One young man recited "Tiger, tiger, burning bright, in the forests of the night…" with an ecstatic look on his face. We were transfixed.

Avtar and Sarita are scrambling to make the "Love the Tiger Walk" work. Blocking their way is the Indian bureaucracy. Witness the following letter, dated Feb. 11, 1999:

"From: Government of India, National Zoological Park
          Mathura Road, New Delhi 110003
To: Tiger Trust

Sir: I am referring to your letter regarding "Save the Tiger Walk" at National Zoological Park. I am to inform you that no function is allowed which is not related to the zoo. If at all the function is to be conducted, then you are advised to approach Ministry of Environment & Forest for Approval.

Yours faithfully,
Dr. B.R. Sharma, IFS
Director"

Now what the heck has a march through downtown New Delhi to do with Environment and Forest is totally beyond me.

Verbally, they have told Avtar: no loud speakers, no speeches, no Big Cub, no food, perhaps no banners. Avtar and Sarita are right now trying to find an alternative, perhaps the Project Tiger office about 0.5 km from the zoo for speeches, Big Cub, etc.

Sarita, who calls Avtar "sir" and is very efficient in carrying out Avtar's orders, just received a phone call while I was there from an Indian television station who wants to interview me at the Tiger Walk for their On the Edge conservation program. We'll see what the Walk will bring.

For dinner I just wandered around the hotel and walked into the first restaurant that looked appealing. I did not realize it was Gujurati food until I had ordered, and ate with the horrible magazine photo images of the charred bodies of the Staineses in the burnt out hulk of their vehicle foremost in my mind's eye.

After dinner, I dropped by Avtar's place to send some e-mail. I want to try sending another email to Christine. Surely doing it by email wouldn't hurt. After about half an hour's trying, I finally got online, only to find that her email address no longer existed. I did my best to conceal my distress.

When I was done, Avtar showed me four Rajasthan newspapers, all in Hindi, all featuring our campaign. At least two have our Big Tiger Cub on page A1, and one even has my picture right above Clinton and Lewinsky. I cannot read a single word in these articles, but their lengths are telling. A few almost took up a full page. And there will be more, at least one – the Hindu – in English, which Avtar does not yet have. A media coup at last, thanks to Dr. Ravji, but then again, it begs the question: "Less than two days in Jaipur and we get all these and more. So what about Delhi, Avtar?" After all this time, I still have to see the first printed word in any Delhi newspaper as a result of my visit. I feel that opportunities are slipping away, one day at a time.

Another catch-22. I would have to wait this long to know that Avtar has no intention of getting media coverage for my school presentations in Delhi, which would make for fairly in depth newspaper articles on the plight of the Bengal tiger in India and what is NOT being done to save it. But now that I finally get to know this, I have no time to do anything about it. So I just let it slide. But I don't have to be happy about it. I did ask Avtar about media coverage for the Love the Tiger Walk. He said smugly that media would be there in droves. I'll believe it when I see it. And even if so, we would still have lost a major opportunity to reach millions in a truly educational manner.

I returned to my hotel room half elated, half dejected. But whatever balance these may strike was obliterated by the far greater balance of my love for Christopher and hatred for Christine, both with a passion. When and where the two meet, emotional tornados would rip my world apart. I haven't slept well since February 3.

Omni-Science and the Human Destiny

Tonight promises to be another tosser and turner.

Good night, Christopher.

❖ ❖ ❖ ❖ ❖

1999-02-12-5 *The Hindu*, **national, India**
[Need to protect tigers stressed]
"The Canadian conservationist, Mr. Anthony Marr, believes that India is the Tiger Country and the last domain of tigers in the world. Tiger is the symbol of India and it is for Indians to protect this animal, which is on the verge of extinction with only 4500 or so in all five species in the wild at present. Mr. Marr, who is of Chinese extraction, is apologetic about the role of his country of origin in making the tiger a haunted animal… The Chinese make medicines out of tiger parts and, in the process, import as many as 300 dead tigers from India and Russia a year…

Owning up to his birth country is the penitent Mr. Marr when he says that he is paying the penalty for his countrymen by campaigning (against the Chinese tradition)…

… In the Pink City (Jaipur), Mr. Marr lectured to 2500 school children in three schools. In Delhi, he had a captive audience of children in 10 schools. He is convinced that children are India's hope for its national animals the tiger…"

❖ ❖ ❖ ❖ ❖

February 13, 1999, Saturday, sunny, chokingly smoggy, 8-22C

[07:13 @ the Magnificent Tours office]
At the office, there was a surprise. I thought yesterday's Springdale presentation was a wash out. Well, Sarita just came in with a whole batch of student art and slogans from that school. Following are some excerpts from the slogans:

"Tiger's soul is our life, so why kill ourselves?"

"Tiger conservation is the need of the hour; save it, because you have the power! Save the King, save the Kingdom!"

"Tiger's eyes are very bright. Don't take away their light. The tigers are the forest's soul. Don't make a bullet hole."

"We have to heed the tiger's scream, for we have to save this earth, which is turning into a ghastly dream!"

"Shoot the tigers with a camera, not with a gun. Capture them on film, not in cages. Save the Tigers!"

"We can afford to buy gold, but tigers are priceless."

"If my family can have generations, why can't the tigers have some too?"

"Save the Pride of India, before it becomes India's forgotten glory!"

"We can recreate Taj Mahal, but only God can recreate the tiger."

How about that, people? Take note, Canadian kids!

Avtar is commissioning somebody to make a few large banners with these slogans printed on them for tomorrow's Love the Tiger Walk. His maneuvers against Indian red tape continue.

[17:31 @ Avtar's office]

The presentation today was at the Guru Harkrishan Public School, the one Avtar used to attend as a child. It was to about 300 ninth-graders, boys and girls. The audience was mostly Sikh, with the boys in sky blue turbans, and both girls and boys in white and blue uniforms. Again we arrived late. It just seems as if it is an enormous effort for things to be done on time around here. Usually, even if we're on time, the people at the school would chat among themselves ad nauseum to solve tiny problems such as the power cord, etc., until we're again late to start. Very bad form on both parts. Today, *we* were late, and *they* had technical problems, including a blackout in the entire district.

On the screen was Kanha tigress Pipal in all her glory, burning bright in the noonday sun. But when the power went out, the shining sun, the glowing landscape, the burning tiger… just plain disappeared.

In the dark Raminothna said through me, astonishing me only after I had spoken, **"Well boys and girls, it seems that the brilliant sun is extinguished by the absence of light from a mere light bulb in the projector. So let me take this opportunity to say, that likewise, in every mind in this room are stored many such shining pictures, moving stories, magnificent epics, monuments of civilization, oceans of blood, sweat and tears, and, most of all, inspired visions still to be realized and beautiful dreams still to come true. But without our kindling and constantly rekindling the flames that burn within each and everyone of us, we may as well all be blind within our respective bodily abodes. Let it burn, on the other hand, and, with 20/20 insight, you**

may see the Masterplan of the Universe, find the Way of the Cosmos, and read the Mind of God."

To cover up my own astonishment, I charged ahead without the slides or PA with a discussion session until the power came back on after 10 minutes or so, and then restarted the slideshow where I left off. The group today was rowdier than normal, but became quite attentive after the blackout. The discussion helped to engage them in the issue. After the presentation, I was again surrounded by a group of girls seeking my guidance as to how to save the tiger *right now*. I kick started another tiger club on the spot with them, and gave them a copy of a recent tiger article with my contact information written on it. We parted with the mutual promise to exchange e-mails when I get back to Canada. When I was walking around the school building seeking a good vantage point to video and photograph Big Cub and the children around it, including going up and down the concrete staircase of the school, I was again mobbed and swamped by adoring children - in the corridors, up the stairwell, on the grounds, all with their hands earnestly extended for just a brush of the jacket I was wearing. I felt my hair (long) being touched from behind numerous times. I taped the proceedings as best I could, including especially the children.

The new Gypsy Avtar ordered, supposedly for Tiger Fund, is ready for pick up in Delhi, and it needs to be driven to Kanha. Momentarily, I considered doing it myself, but Avtar has already booked me a plane ticket for me for a flight to Nagpur Monday evening. I will overnight there and catch a ride the following morning to Kanha.

Well, today's are the last school presentations before the Tiger Walk. It's been a good run, with high peaks never experienced in Canada. The only drawback, which I consider a huge loss of opportunity, is the complete lack of media coverage of the school events. It would have motivated the students of other schools so much.

Cricket is really big here in India, and it dominates the airwaves. Having inevitably watched bits and pieces of a few matches on TV, I'm beginning to know the game. Still I can't say it's made a captive spectator out of me.

But I've been making good use of it. In the last few speeches, I've achieved excellent results by starting with the recent India v Pakistan tournament, which swept the entire nation with cricket fever. I say something like this: "I've seen your great passion. I've seen your national pride. Now that the tournament is over, would it be too much for me to ask you to pledge just 10% of your passion and national pride to saving India's Bengal tiger? If you would, I would consider it saved." I also say, "How would you feel if a burglar breaks into your home to steal your most prized possession? Right now, as we speak, foreign criminals are infiltrating your country, stealing your greatest national treasure. What are you going to do about it?" By the end of the presentation, they are sizzling. They are fuming, raving ready to save their national animal, their national symbol, the soul of their nation, the Royal Bengal tiger.

Dealing with bureaucracy myself, I discovered a major weakness in the Indian governmental system.

I've known that BC's Environment Ministry is somewhat subservient to the Forest Ministry, and this is the source of many of our habitat and species conservation problems. Now, imagine that the BC government has no Environment Ministry at all, and environmental matters, wildlife included, is under the jurisdiction of the Forest Ministry. What do you think is going to happen to the Grizzly bear habitat, and to the Grizzlies themselves? Well, this is exactly the situation in India here. What do you think is going to happen to tiger habitat and the tigers themselves?

I looked up Billy Arjan Singh's Tiger Book. It says, "The largest foreign exchange earner in Africa is their wildlife in the tourism industry. In India, though we eulogize the tourist potential of the Taj Mahal, Khajuraho and the Ajanta Caves, the Forest Department discourages wildlife tourism... The Forest Department is a commercial organization, and the priorities for postings among its staff incumbents are with Social Forestry, the Forest Corporation, the Plantation Division, and the Territorial Division. Wildlife with no economic affiliation is shunned by all administrative personnel and is considered a punishment posting; for the dropouts, the corrupt and the inefficient... the various departments are not willing to allocate further land to wildlife, particularly because the Wildlife Act does not permit commercial operations in these areas... the Forest Department will not allow forested areas to be transferred to wildlife projects. Forestry and wildlife are antagonistic subjects, and cannot meaningfully be administered by the same facility. A 'clean' forest floor is the dream of the forester, but is the anathema to the wildlife enthusiasts. The precept that wildlife will exist where there are forests is entirely misplaced."

Second parallel. We have all experienced the BC government's overblown Grizzly bear population estimate to justify continued hunting. The Tiger Book says, "The numbers game continues to dominate... (tiger population) census figures were inflated to impossible numbers by Field Directors relying on pug mark tracings by untrained and irresponsible personnel. The Corbett Park figure, supposedly at saturation density of 44 in 1972, was escalated to 112 by 1985-89... Compared with the Serengeti National Park in Africa with a 5.5% increase for the social lion, an overall increase of 25% was presented for the solitary tiger. Census were treated as status symbols by individual directors, and my suggestion at a meeting of the Indian Board for Wildlife, that Field Directors should be switched around during census time was discarded by the Director of the project. Unbridled numbers continued to escalate…" Let alone the 10,000-13,000 Grizzly population estimate, can we trust even the pitiable 2,000-2,500 for the tiger?

Third parallel. Imagine federal Canada has an Endangered Species Act, but the provincial governments, being of different parties, and answering to local voters' demands, more often than not choose to contravene the Act, and there is nothing the feds can do about it. Let me quote again from the Tiger Book:

"The stark reality of the situation is that state governments cannot and will not resist the pressure of their voting public to destroy a perceived danger (the tiger) to their lives and livelihood. With an exploding population and an agricultural economy - unrestrained plantation of sugarcane, which decimate wild ungulate prey species, and the state (provincial) government sanctioned proliferation of sugar factories, which bring some employment to local communities – the end will come with the extinction of the tiger. State governments… which have an insensate resentment to accepting guidelines offered by the Central government… have been unwilling to share expenses with the Centre, and with different parties holding power in different states, the direction of the Centre is unheeded, and chaos reigns supreme."

There's more, but this should be enough to give you a splitting headache. Sorry, folks.

Anyway, Christopher, by the time you read this, if you ever do, all these points may have become moot - in the event that the Bengal tiger had fallen extinct. For your sake, I will do my absolute best to save them for you, to perpetuity.

Good night, Christopher.

❖   ❖   ❖   ❖   ❖

February 14, 1999, Sunday, sunny, 9-26C

Dearest Christopher"

[14:59 @ Avtar's office]
Just participated in accomplishing a small but glorious deed – the Love-the-Tiger Walk, Delhi, of course – on a windy day where the air was extra clear (or should I say,

unusually unsmoggy). Avtar expected about 200 people to show up, and he was accurate. But small as the troop was, the event was certainly photogenic. They printed four versions of full-color bumper stickers with tiger graphic backgrounds and the words of Tim Murphy's Tiger Song. They made tiger-striped headbands, which most people wore around their necks. They purchased about ten kid-sized tiger suits, and there was no shortage of very enthusiastic volunteer wearers. They created half a dozen huge golden silk banners featuring the winning slogans in the school slogan-contest. Speakers included S.C. Sharma (Inspector of Forest and Wildlife, Indian Central Government), P.K. Sen (head of Project Tiger), Avtar and myself, with Sarita serving as a very presentable MC. Four TV cameras showed up, plus several top Indian newspapers including the Times of India. One of the TV networks is said to range as far west as London, as far east as Hong Kong. We marched from the Delhi Zoo to the office of Project Tiger about 3 km distant, with police escort which stopped traffic whenever necessary. We marched along major thoroughfares, through the expansive India Gate lawns and the magnificent India Gate itself. The march started from a line of ancient ruins adjacent to the zoo and passed several others en route. Marching at the head of the troop with my long hair loose, dressed in my black Save the Tiger T shirt, black Canadian army boots laced over Canadian army pant-legs, with a tiger-face T shirt tied behind me around my waist and a tiger head band around my neck, hefting my still camera and the WCWC Hi 8 Sony video cam, I must have made an extraordinary sight in the eyes of the average Indian in the street. On top of leading the parade, I also led in singing the Save-the-Tiger Song. The children, and adults, too, turned heads with their enthusiastic singing.

<u>lead</u> (me)	<u>chorus</u>	<u>melody</u>
	(marchers, esp. children)	
SAVE THE TIGER	Save the tiger	(doe-ray-mee-doe)
THEY'RE OUR FRIENDS	They're our friends	(mee-fa-so)
THE TIGERS ARE IN TROUBLE	The tigers are in trouble	(so-la-so-fa-mee-doe)
LET'S HELP THEM	Let's help them	(doe-<u>so</u>-doe)
SAVE THE TIGER	Save the tiger	(doe-ray-mee-doe)
THEY'RE OUR FRIENDS	They're our friends	(mee-fa-so)
THE TIGERS ARE IN TROUBLE	The tigers are in trouble	(so-la-so-fa-mee-doe)
LET'S HELP THEM	Let's help them	(doe-<u>so</u>-doe)

And so on, and so on. There was a bunch of children right behind me who

Omni-Science and the Human Destiny

belted out the chorus with all their might. The expressions on their faces – those who weren't wearing tiger masks – were as aroused as children's faces could get. After I've sung my throat hoarse, I appointed the most enthusiastic of them – a girl of about 12 - to sing the lead. She took her task so seriously that the song seemed cranked out from a perpetual motion machine. I videotaped the entire proceedings.

Credit is largely due to Avtar and Sarita, who did work hard to put on a quality show.

One slightly down note, or should I say, down-to-earth note. Both Sharma and Sen are Central Government bureaucrats. Their speeches sounded pro-conservation, lofty and enlightened, but given what I observed yesterday of Central Government bureaucracy, and recalling what was written about the ineffectiveness of the Central Government in Arjan Singh's book, and having experienced the near autonomy of the provincial and lesser governments, I don't know how much good their good will could do.

Of course I missed Christopher greatly while leading the children. I would so love to have him walk next to me, and to hold him in my arms when he gets tired. I would like to imprint in his young mind our glorious day for our glorious cause. Of course, even if Christine did not do what she did, is still doing, and will continue to do, Christopher would be too young to make the arduous journey, but I would love to take Christopher on the 1999 WCWC Save The Tiger Walk at Stanley Park in Vancouver. Given what has happened, taking Christopher to anything would seem an impossibility.

[19:03]

Avtar just phoned me, telling me that we were on prime time TV. He said they zoomed in on my butt (where the tiger-face on my second T shirt tied around my waist was located). This could potentially be the most photogenic footage of the Tiger's Forever campaign ever, my butt not withstanding. Unfortunately, I missed it, and they didn't tape it. Still, the important thing is that millions of people saw it, and that objective has been achieved.

This still does not justify the total absence of media coverage for the school presentations, which will remain a significant failure no matter how well the Tiger Walk has worked out.

As always after an event, I spent the ensuing hours reflecting on it. As the scenes replayed themselves through my mind, I came upon the children belting out the Save the Tiger song. I thought, "If she knows what I know now, including everything I learned in secondary school and university, and all I have self-taught and self learned before and after my university graduation, and all the life-experiences one cannot help but accumulate, and all the love won and lost… - what I would not sell for a hundred million dollars. I zoomed in to the 12 year-old girl leading the song. If she knows what I know now, what could she not achieve by the time she reaches 30? Best of luck to you, whoever you are.

"You're saying that if this girl knew what you know, she would be able to achieve anything by 30 latest?"

"Yes, I believe I said that, and I believe it, within reason of course.."

"That would be 18 years from now, correct?"

"Correct."

"How old are you now?"

"55, ."

"55 plus 18 equals?"

"73."

"Do you currently know what you currently know?"

"What kind of a question is that? Of course I do."

"Then, according to you, you will be able to achieve anything by age 73 latest."

Of course I wish you a very successful life, Christopher. Good night.

❖ ❖ ❖ ❖ ❖

1999-02-14   *TigerLink*, India, global
[Love the Tiger Walk, Delhi]
…on St. Valentine's Day… The participants chanted slogans and sang a tiger conservation song lead by Mr. Anthony Marr, Tiger Campaign Director, WCWC…

At Bikaner House the gathering was addressed by Mr. P.K. Sen, Director of Project Tiger, Mr. S.C. Sharma, Addl. Inspector General Forests (Wildlife), Angarika Guha, Class III student from Sri Ram Public School, Mr. Anthony Marr…

❖ ❖ ❖ ❖ ❖

February 15, 1999, Monday, sunny, 10-25C

Omni-Science and the Human Destiny

Dearest Christopher:

[21:36 @ Rm. 123, the Jagsons Regency Hotel, Nagpur]

    I woke up from a multifaceted dream that deserves serious and in depth contemplation. It could be of pivotal importance to the future course of my life's pursuit. I will try to record it in a way that can do it justice, later.

    This morning I called Mom and Dad to wish them happy Chinese New Year – the Year of the Hare. I probably woke them up, but they were of course excited to hear from me. Matthew, my younger brother, will be taking them out to lunch tomorrow, and told them that he received a call from Sue of WCWC about me being alive and well. They've accepted my globe trotting life style with equanimity and even pride. Love them deeply, with gratitude.

    Later in the morning, Avtar and I went to his office. First thing I did was to send off my last e-mail to WCWC. Then, at noon, he drove me to the interview with Camelle Gill of Today's Traveler magazine. Another screw up by Raman and/or Sarita last week was that they made an appointment for me with Ms. Gill for last Thursday, but did not tell me about it, which kept Ms. Gill waiting a full hour for me in vain. I called Ms. Gill to apologize on behalf of Tiger Fund, and reset the appointment for today…This is an important article for Avtar since Ms. Gill's is a travel magazine. Both he and I were interviewed at length. It will be an excellent article. When I told her about some of my adventures with the villagers, and told her about my field journal, she perked up, and asked me to send her excerpts of the journal for another article.

    Yesterday, I received one letter each from Jane and CJ in the lovingly-custom-made envelopes by CJ delivered by someone from Kanha.

    The one by Jane says:
"Feb. 11/99
"Anthony:
    "I am sending this note via Veejay the ornithologist who had been at Kanha assisting Ed Cambridge with one of his tours.
    "If you have time in your hectic schedule, I would appreciate it if you could bring the following from Delhi:
    "1. a Hindi phrasebook or a Hindi dictionary (with English definitions and phonetic pronunciation) so I can learn to communicate, however pitifully, in this language.
    "2. literature from Tiger Fund and WC2 explaining the organizations. The guests

here have been anxious for such information, and of course we have nothing to give them.

"3. A big world map for the school. I think it would be nice for the kids if they could understand where the visitors come from and a little bit about each country.

"Looking forward to chatting with you soon. We have much to discuss! Say hi to Sarita and Raman for me.

"Jane"

The one from CJ says:

"2-12-99 In the jungle, the mighty jungle, the tiger sleeps tonight.

"Dear Anthony:

"Greetings from the other side. Please know that all is well and we are anxiously awaiting your return to the lodge. At present, we are *slowly* constructing our giant cooker in hopes that we'll have some tests performed before your arrival (in a perfect world). So, I'm taking advantage of this opportunity to request a small service.

"As you know, I am awaiting news from home in regards to my plane tickets and this news likely resides in my e-mail account._____, password: _____.

"If you wouldn't mind accessing and printing off the new e-mails with special attention to any sent from _____ (if there are too many) my attorney. I am hoping that these updated e-mails provide some insight into the plane issue. We'll see.

"Thank you for your time; hope this doesn't take you over the edge after having to deal with new Indian fans bouncing you around the big blowup cat.

"Kindest regards,

"CJ"

Well, for CJ, Avtar and I found over 60 messages since December 98, all unread. Avtar spent a whole hour personally downloading the non-trash ones into a Word file and loaded it into my floppy before driving me to the interview.

The interview lasted almost 2 hours, after which I took a cab to the Palika Bazaar near Connaught Circle – an underground maze of hundreds of small shops of all kinds – and got there around 14:30. I rushed around and in record time found and bought 6 Hi-8 cassettes (Rs300 each), a wicked (you shall see) Hindi-English phrase book (Rs125) and a world atlas (Rs515; I would prefer a world globe, but nowhere available). I had needed to dupe the Champions of the Wild video, but even after several days' calling, the Delhi people still couldn't get around to doing it. Anyway, most of the stuff that needed to be done has been done.

Tomorrow morning at 06:00, somebody will pick me up from this hotel in Nagpur and drive me to Kanha, to arrive in time for lunch.

So yet again, I've said goodbye to Delhi. The experience was largely positive, and Avtar succeeded to impress upon me that if/when he puts his heart into a task, if he applies himself like the full time campaigner that he was in these two weeks in Delhi and Jaipur, even factoring in his total failure in generating media for the school presentation, which I allocate to treachery more than incompetence, he could accomplish great things. But this merely begs the long-standing question even more: Where is his heart the other 50 weeks of the year? For the CIDA grant, we are supposed to choose a full-time dedicated NGO, not a part-time NGO that is subservient to the business interest of a commercial enterprise. And what I have observed in Delhi does not negate a single word I wrote in Kanha regarding my misgiving in grant handling, and the effectiveness or lack thereof of the Indian part of our tiger conservation program.

At first sight, the Tiger Walk media coverage seemed acceptable, but upon closer scrutiny, they are mostly no-depth one-line captions under single photos mentioning Tiger Fund but not WCWC. In contrast, the two days in Jaipur organized by Dr. Ravji generated some 7-8 detailed and in-depth newspaper articles on tiger conservation based upon the school outreach program, and 2-3 TV pieces, with WCWC prominently featured, although, when I asked someone to translate one of the Hindi pieces, I heard, "… the big balloon tiger belonging to Tiger Fund under Mr. Avtar Grewal…"

The flight from Delhi to Nagpur was Indian Airline's subcontractor Alliance Airlines flight 469 Delhi-Raipur-Nagpur. An unnerving flying experience, and not for the first time. First off, while boarding the plane – an old Boeing 737 - I could not help but notice its decrepit condition, inside and out. Its paint was smudged with soot. There were even wall and ceiling panels missing, with the wiring underneath exposed. While descending into the Nagpur airport, with the runway flashing by beneath my seat, the plane suddenly poured on power and climbed steeply, then did a steep banking 360 and landed with a bone-jarring thump, hard enough to cause one of the ceiling panels to come crashing down on to the aisle. This bounced the plane back up, which then came back down some seconds later in a more normal-feeling touch down. This was not the first time I've experienced such a landing. Back in 1997, one of the Nagpur landings was hard enough to convince me of the great strength of the plane's landing gear. While deplaning, I heard some clunking sound from the left engine and some airport personnel looking up at it. For a flying experience of a lifetime, fly Alliance!

Anyway, a chapter is written and closed. I'm so looking forward to getting back to Kanha. I don't know if the more tranquil setting of the Jungle Lodge will be better or worse in terms of my agony for Christopher, but I'm more than willing to face whatever the outcome.

This is about it for today. So here is the dream, which I have come to call "To Conceive the 'Inconceivable'".

I was walking in a flat and vast desert, following a being of light named Raminothna, towards a volcano to the south. As I reached the foot of the volcano, I came upon the ruins of an ancient city.

It was square shaped, set to the four points of the compass. It had high external walls over ten feet thick and a mile long per side, built of huge and precisely cut blocks of stone. I entered through its north gate, the one facing away from the volcano. While passing beneath the huge archway, I looked up, and saw the name of the city, carved in stone, in ancient Chinese pictographic script: **TRUE TAO**.

Within the city, the avenues were all east-west in orientation. The blocks were of odd lengths, ranging as if randomly from as few as one house to more than ten houses per block. There were no straight north-south streets to speak of, except for the two running along the inside of the east and west walls of the city. Unlike the conventional back-to-back twin-rows of houses in the normal city block, these blocks comprised single rows of free standing houses, with their fronts facing the avenue to the south, and their back gardens facing the avenue to the north.

The houses were also built of precisely cut and fitted blocks of stone, so the ruins were in excellent condition, though their roofs, made of lumber, had all long since collapsed, and their remains had all but fossilized.

Where in the middle of a vast desert did the lumber come from? It was once a lush forest, Raminothna told me.

It was not until the second avenue before Raminothna led my attention to the writings on the walls. On the front wall of this particular house was carved, "IN THE **COSMOS**, THE **WAY OF MAN** ACCORDS TO THE **WAY OF THE EARTH**, WHICH ACCORDS TO THE **WAY OF THE SKY**, WHICH IN TURN ACCORDS TO THE **WAY OF THE COSMOS** – THE **TAO** – AND THE TAO SIMPLY IS, ACCORDING TO ITS OWN **NATURE**."

The TAO-TEH-CHING – the canon of Taoism.

"What does this passage mean to you?" Raminothna asked me.

"It means that if we understand the TAO, we'd know the optimal WAY OF MAN."

"What do you think of the current WAY OF MAN?"

"Barbaric."

Returning to the first house of the first avenue, I read on its front wall, **"THE TAO THAT CAN BE SPOKEN IS NOT THE TRUE TAO."**

Thus, from house to house, from block to block, I read the Tao Teh Ching in its entirety, until I arrived at the last verse on the front walls of the houses on last block of the southern-most avenue of the city.

At one point near the centre of the city, I arrived at a verse that gave me a moment's pause, which read: **"THE WISE RULER STRIVES TO STRENGTHEN THE BONE OF HIS SUBJECTS, BUT WEAKEN THEIR WILL, FOR A STRONG-BONED AND WEAK-WILLED PEOPLE WOULD BE EASY TO RULE, AND THE REIGN SHALL PROSPER."**

As if to underscore these dictums, there was a large carving on the inside of the great arch over the north gate of the city, in a somehow cruder hand, which read: **"IF ONE ASKS ABOUT THE NATURE OF THE TAO AND ANOTHER ANSWERS, NEITHER KNOW IT."**

"Thus they maintained twenty-six centuries of silence, as if they knew it?" said Raminothna.

When I finally got to the south gate, and looked up at its arch and read: **"THOU SHALT NOT CLIMB THE MOUNTAIN OF KNOWLEDGE OF REALITY AND ILLUSION. ALL THOU NEED KNOW OF THE TRUE TAO ARE WITHIN THESE WALLS. THE PENALTY IS DEATH BY A THOUSAND CUTS FOLLOWED BY ETERNAL TORTURE IN THE UNDERWORLD."**

On the walls on either side of the south gate were the only pictorial carvings on any wall in the city, which depicted scenes of hideous torture, some beyond my imagination.

"Which explains why a once great school of philosophy has turned into a house of sorcery," said Raminothna sadly.

"I'm puzzled," I said to Raminothna after the waves of horror, nausea and shock had subsided. "What harm would it do for the citizens to climb the mountain? How could that impact on the belief system cast in stone within the city? Are there more carvings up in the crater of the volcano that tell the real truth of the city or the real truth of the Tao? Or is this just a blatant demonstration of absolute power for its own sake?"

"Why don't you go and find out?"

I hesitate in fear. Whereupon, without a single comment or explanation, Raminothna rose like a meteor, and disappeared into the crater of the volcano.

I wandered amidst the ruins for weeks, documenting every little new find, but I did not climb the Mountain of Knowledge of Reality and Illusion, although the urge to climb it grew stronger by the day. The volcano was constantly looming over my head. Its mystery grew daily more tempting, its beckoning more and more irresistible, and my desire to climb became all but an obsession. At long last, I succumbed.

"**About time,**" said Raminothna who was waiting for me in the crater of the volcano.

I looked around. There was nothing but black and jagged volcanic rock. I walked along the inside wall of the crater; there was not a single carving to be found.

"So? Where is the disillusionment? I was expecting at least a burning bush."

Raminothna brought me back to the crater's rim. The view was unquestionably breath-taking. "**You have seen the writing on the wall. Now, behold the writings on the plain.**"

I looked down upon the horizon-spanning plane, then at the ruins beneath my feet, and all at once, the illusion was plain as day. The city of the **TRUE TAO** was laid out like an open book on a vast tabletop, where each house was a letter, each block a word, and the entire city the fully message, all in English strangely enough, which read as follows:

THE TRUE TAO – THE "INCONCEIVABLE" WAY OF THE COSMOS - IS IN FACT CONCEIVABLE AND NEEDS TO BE CONCEIVED. THE KEY TO THE CONCEIVING OF THE TAO IS IN THE TAO-THE-CHING ITSELF. THE KEY WORD IN THE TAO-THE-CHING IS "NATURE" - THAT TO WHICH THE TAO ITSELF ACCORDS. UNDERSTANDING NATURE IS KEY TO KNOWING THE TAO, WHICH IS KEY TO KNOWING THE OPTIMAL "WAY OF MAN". THE COSMOS IS ALL-THINGS. THE STUDY OF THE NATURE OF THINGS ARE THE SCIENCES. CONSIDER A THOUSAND-PIECE JIGSAW PUZZLE, EACH PIECE BEING ONE SUB-SCIENCE. TAKE ONE PIECE, ANY PIECE, AND EXAMINE IT WITH THE MICROSCOPE OF YOUR MIND, AND YOU CANNOT EXHAUST IT IN DETAIL. BUT INTEGRATE ALL THE PIECES INTO ONE, THE SCIENCES COLLECTIVELY TRANSCEND INTO OMNI-OMNISCIENCE – THE STUDY OF THE UNIVERSE – THE-WHOLE-THING. VIEW

OMNI-SCIENCE FROM A DISTANCE, AND THE BIG PICTURE – A NEW MODEL OF THE UNIVERSE - AN OMNISCIENTIFIC COSMOLOGY - IS REVEALED, ONE OF SUCH ORDER AND SIMPLICITY IT COULD BE DESCRIBED IN TWO WORDS – TWO HITHERTO "UNSPEAKABLE" WORDS. THE TAO IS SPEAKABLE AND MUST BE SPOKEN, THAT HUMANITY MAY ACCORD ITSELF TO THE EARTH.

"What if I say that this omniscientific cosmology is a model that lends powerful insight into the Tao, instead of its being the Tao itself? It strikes me that the latter is a very bold statement, as bold as if someone says to me, 'I am Christ.'"

"**Whatever you prefer, as long as those two words are the same ones. May the 'Inconceivable' soon be conceived; may the 'Unspeakable' soon be spoken,**" said Raminothna.

"How soon is soon?"

"**As soon as possible. While you're still in India, preferably.**"

"Why? That's only a month and a half away, maximum. We humans have failed to do it for twenty six centuries."

"**My remaining time on Earth is short.**"

"Why?"

"**My anchoring tree will be cut down in the very near future, I'm afraid. Once that happens, I'll be gone. If in mid-conversation I suddenly disappear, that would be the cause.**"

"Those goddamned woodcutters! May they roast in hell!"

"**Have compassion, my love. Compassion. They need me, if only for a moment's warmth.**"

"I know that, Raminothna, I know that."

Good night, Christopher.

❖   ❖   ❖   ❖   ❖

1999-02-15-1 *The Statesman*, **India**
[A valentine for the big cat]
An unusual "Valentine Day" message was displayed by tiger enthusiasts in the

Capital who went on a brisk march from Delhi Zoo to the head quarters of Project Tiger at Bikaner House, to spread the message of conservation.

Children and adults held up banners for the "Love Tiger Walk"… (Organizers) pointed out that the largest cat n the world today has a mortality rate of two per day in the world and one per day in India alone.

"Especially as a tigress does not have another litter till her young can support themselves, it is so much necessary to support the ones which are alive, as they do not breed rapidly like other species," said a child who participated in the march.

A video show, an inflatable tiger blimp and presentations by eminent conservationists were some of the features of the march, which was supported (in part) by the WCWC.

1999-02-15-1 *The Indian Express*, **India**
[Tiger, tiger burning bright]
A tiger balloon at the Love the Tiger Walk at the Delhi Zoo on Sunday…

1999-02-15-1 *The Hindu*, **national, India**
[Valentines tiger lovers]
… A team comprising Mr. Anthony Marr, campaign director of WCWC… has been making slide presentations, holding video shows and having interactions inside a 50-feet inflatable tiger balloon…

They have been received with great enthusiasm by more than 5,000 students of various age groups. Painting competitions and slogan contests have also been organized as part of the campaign…

1999-02-15-1 *The Pioneer*, **national, India**
['Save Tiger' walk]
Wildlife lovers walked through the busy streets of the national Capital on Valentine's Day on Sunday to show their love for the tiger, which faces the threat of extinction…

1999-02-15-1 *The Hindustan Times*, **national, India**
[Save the tiger]
A 50-foor balloon tiger at the National Zoological Park to generate awareness among the masses for the conservation of the tiger…

Omni-Science and the Human Destiny

February 16, 1999, Tuesday, sunny, 11-26C

Dearest Christopher:

[11:01 in the middle of nowhere]

I'm now sitting on the uphill side of the highway about 10 km north of Balaghat part way along the 6-hour drive between Nagpur and Kanha. The car has died. The engine has been misfiring over the last 50 km or so, and finally, now that the terrain is more winding and hilly, the car just couldn't make it. It is in the middle of nowhere. It being a mountainous region, there as neither a house nor a living soul in sight, just forest all the way to the horizon, and a lake some distance on the downhill side of the winding highway.

We checked the distributor contact points, the spark plug wires, and they seemed okay. Lots of gas in the tank. So it could be a bad or fouled spark plug or a faulty distributor or a congested fuel line, or a weak battery or whatever else. But the driver didn't have even a screwdriver on board. We decided that he should go back to Balaghat to fetch a mechanic, while I stay with the car, given all my equipment in it. He flagged down a truck and off he went.

I got out of the car, and took my laptop computer and camera bags with me, as well as the distributor cable. I have no idea what the highway security situation is like around here. I also have US$800's worth of traveler's cheques and rupees on me. I climbed up the steep wooded embankment on the uphill side of the highway by about 100 feet, to where a bamboo thicket on the edge of a ledge screened me from view of anyone on the highway below. From where I'm sitting, I can monitor the car and the road without being seen if I don't want to be, and can also enjoy the view of the lake in the distance submerged in a sea of trees. Vehicles, mostly trucks and buses, pass one every few minutes; no one slowed or stopped.

My eyes are pleased by the sea of green, but my mind wonders what lies beneath, whether the forest floor has been over run by goats and cattle, and whether the animals have been decimated by hunting and trapping. Many of the so-called inter-park "corridors" for tigers to cross-migrate for genetic exchange purposes are in fact barriers through which tigers cannot pass.

I recall an almost comical incident on the road earlier this morning. While passing through Balaghat, we stopped for a Pepsi - the most popular soft drink in this part of India, the safest beverage available disease-wise. Of course I was at once surrounded five deep by locals, gawking at me. Being used to this, I just opened the pop and nonchalantly began sipping it. While doing so, I looked for a waste bin to deposit the bottle cap into it. Of course there was none in sight. Seeing my intention, one of the people held out his hand helpfully. I gave him the cap, expecting him to take it to a bin I didn't see. Instead, he just dropped the cap on the ground at his feet.

I'm supposed to get to Kanha about noon. If Jane and CJ and Faiyaz are, as CJ wrote in his email, "anxiously awaiting my return", their anxiety may get to the boiling point before I make my grand reentrance.

While waiting, pain and fury and despair again materialized out of thin air. With predetermined determination, I fell on my knees and said a wholehearted prayer for Christopher, then decidedly turned to contemplating what has captured my attention – conceiving the 'inconceivable.'

"Raminothna, are you there?"

"Yes, I am."

"Please tell more about this 'omniscientific cosmology'."

"Certainly. What would you like to know?"

"Just something in general."

"Sure. Tell me. What is this object on the ground here?"

"This? It is a distributor cable."

"What is it doing here?"

"Well, I don't want a few thugs wandering over, fixing up the car and driving off with it. Without this cable, the engine wouldn't start."

"What is a distributor cable? What does it do?"

"It is for conducting electricity from the alternator and the battery to the distributor."

"Can you understand the distributor cable without understanding the distributor, the alternator, the battery and the engine?"

"No, at least not fully."

"Can you understand the distributor cable without understanding the car and the part it plays in the functioning of the car?

"No, I cannot."

"Why not?"

"Because the part cannot be fully understood without an understanding of the whole and its part in this whole."

"And what is this?"

"It's a tree."

"And what's that?"

"That's a bird."

"And this?"
"It's a bee."
"And that?"
"It's a bee's nest."
"This tree, this bird, this bee and this bee's nest…, are they wholes unto themselves or are they parts of something greater?"
"Well, they cannot exist without anything else. So they are parts of something greater."
"What is this something greater?"
"The, uh, biosphere."
"Of which you too are a part?"
"Yes, of which I too am a part."
"And the biosphere. Is it a whole unto itself or is it a part of something greater?"
"It is a part of something greater – the planet Earth."
"And the planet Earth. Is it a whole unto itself or is it a part of something greater?"
"I see where you're going. The planet Earth is a part of the Solar System, which is a part of the Milky Way Galaxy, which is a part of the Cosmos. So, the tree, the bird, the bee, the bee hive, and I, are not wholes unto ourselves, but are ultimately parts of the Cosmos."
"So, can you understand yourself fully without understanding the Cosmos and your part in this Cosmos?"
"No. I don't suppose I can."
"What is the field that studies the Universe – the Cosmos as a whole?"
"Cosmology."
"What fields of science are involved in cosmology as you know it?"
"Physics and astronomy. Some chemistry. And the hybrids, such as astrophysics."
"And that's it?"
"That's about it."
"What scientific field studies trees and birds and bees, and mammals such as you?"
"Biology."
"And what field studies bee hives and ant nests and termite mounds and lion prides and chimpanzee troops and the like?"
"It is a relatively new field, called sociobiology."
"And what field studies human societies?"

"Sociology and anthropology."

"And these fields are not included in cosmology as you know it?"

"Well, according to our line of reasoning, they should be, but they're not."

"So, what do you say about cosmology as it is?"

"Incomplete."

"Omniscientific Cosmology, therefore, is a new model of the Universe that involves the socio-biological sciences as well as the conventional astrophysical sciences in its construction. The reason is that the biosphere to which all life on Earth belongs is a part of the Earth which is a part of the Solar System which is a part of the Milky Way Galaxy which is a part of the Universe. Since the part cannot be fully understood without an understanding of the whole and its part in this whole, neither can humanity fully understand itself without an understanding of the Universe and its part in this Universe. Thus, omniscientific cosmology is essential for human self-understanding. Omniscientific cosmology yields new insights for answering the ancient philosophical questions, such as the purpose of humanity, the meaning of life, the measure of morality, the fate of the Earth, the nature of the Tao, even the definition of 'God'."

[12:31 @ same spot]

It's been 1.5 hours – 90 minutes. Where is the guy? Balaghat is only 10 km away. Is he having a samosa or chai or a siesta?

There is a bag of walnuts in the car. I went to retrieve it. Back up here, I began to crack open the walnuts with a rock. A different kind of lunch. It must be the 13th walnut, since I over-exerted myself and smashed the unfortunate walnut to smithereens. I was about to reach for number 14 when Raminothna said, **"In the name of compassion please derive nourishment from this shattered being. Enjoy every smallest fragment of it. Can't you see that it died for you?"**

Never have I enjoyed a walnut as thoroughly as I did number 13, the lucky walnut.

Where the hell is that guy?

[13:13 @ same spot]

Finally, the driver showed up, by bus, in the company of two mechanics. I snapped a photo of them before going down to join them. They've been at it for about 10 minutes. No luck. At one point, one of the mechanics got underneath the car, got a mouthful of gasoline from the fuel line (!), and spat it into the carburetor.

Omni-Science and the Human Destiny

The engine started immediately, but died again after a few chugs. They're still working on it. Right now, looks like they're trying to clean the fuel line. After that, what? Indian ingenuity at work. Fascinating, as Spock would say, from an outsider's point of view.

"Raminothna, it looks to me that this new 'omniscientific cosmology' is on a collision course with the old religions, philosophies, conventions and traditions, especially those that originated before the advent of modern science."

"Yes, it is."

"But this would be like pitting an egg against a rock."

"Yes it would."

"So it is doomed to be crushed?"

"Not necessarily."

"That's news to me."

"On the contrary, the egg can crush the rock."

"How?"

"By its becoming a child, one able to use a hammer; better yet, also a chisel."

[14:28 @ a place a few km north of "same spot"]

Well, the Indian ingenuity worked for a little while. They took out the fuel filter and blew in reverse, presumably clearing the fuel-line and/or the filter of whatever blocking it. The car started fine after that. The mechanic decided to catch a ride to Kanha. The younger guy would take a bus back to Balaghat. Before we took off I pulled a Rs.100 note out of my pocket and offered it to him. He declined at first, but after looking at his friend, who nodded, he accepted it. And off we went.

I began to doze off, and was awakened when the car pulled off the road again. Same symptom reappeared. A thick cloud of acid fumes erupted from the engine compartment. The mechanic opened the hood, and found the battery spewing acid froth on an end cell. He waited for the fumes to clear, then removed the battery and set it on the ground. He plunged a hole on the top of the defective cell of the battery with a screwdriver and is now doing something with it. I think the end cell of the battery fried and he is using an electric cable to connect the power cable directly to the plate of the second cell, thus making the voltage of the battery 10 volts instead of 12 volts. I doubt this could start the engine, but if we push-start the car, the lessened battery should be able to keep the sparkplugs firing. Indian ingenuity at work again. And again, let's see how many more miles (feet) he could make this clunker go.

Anthony Marr

[23:02 @ Rm. 112, Kanha Tiger Lodge]

Home sweet home! At last, around 15:30, I arrived at Kanha – a 9.5 hour journey rather than the standard 6. Indeed this place feels like home to me, in absolute terms, and especially relative to Delhi, starting with a warm, hugging welcome by Jane, Faiyaz and CJ. The four of us pretty well spent every minute of the remains of the day together. I feel as if we are spiritually one. I wish things would never change. But CJ will be leaving on the 25th for Bangkok for a jaunt, then Taipei for two months, and then, in August, Vancouver. Avtar has plans that Jane and I should go to Bandhavgarh on or around March 1, but, though I love Bandhavgarh deeply, and indeed, the Champions of the Wild video was filmed in Bandhavgarh and not Kanha, I want to stay at Kanha as long as possible to maximize our outreach in the Buffer Zone. And so does Jane. And so does Faiyaz. If Jane goes to Bandhavgarh, Kim would not be interested in our work here at Kanha, and CJ will be gone. So, I will tell Avtar that I will stay here at Kanha till at least mid-March, and so will Jane.

Jane and Faiyaz told me that they have big plans for Kanha as the centre of tiger conservation, in the following terms:

- family planning as integral part of medical clinic;
- techno-transformation - solar cookers for rural, LPG (liquid petroleum gas) for suburban, to alleviate deforestation;
- cattle husbandry, to reduce population and overgrazing;
- cottage industry, to have the villagers rely more on talent than on natural resources.

"I don't know how many times we have said, 'Let's wait and see what Anthony thinks,'" said Jane.

Jane loves the Atlas I brought, and laughed out loud at the "Hindi Made Easy" booklet, which I chose from a humorous angle. It was published earlier this century. In it is a section titled "Directions to Servants", where the orders include: [Bring my clothes. Fetch that thing. Don't bother. Speak loudly. That will do. You may go now. Get out of the house. Carry out my orders. Stand still. Come near me. Do your own work. Bring it at once. You are very lazy. Never tell a lie. Never steal anything. Bear this in mind. Dress me. Undress me. Bring my trousers. Where are my socks? Take off my boots and bring my slippers. This is not properly washed. Take this back and have it washed again. I will not pay you until the missing articles are returned. Bring my whip...]

Omni-Science and the Human Destiny

    Jane has taken on the role of principal teacher of the free school in Deepfee's absence, and a very popular one at that. Faiyaz and I both joined in the teaching today, doing mostly arithmetic (addition). On the side, I taught some kids to play tic-tac-toe, and they thought it was the greatest game in the world.

    The large solar oven and solar cooker have not yet been built, due to unavailability of quality steel plates, until yesterday, when Faiyaz finally procured a 4'X12' highly reflective steel sheet – in a roll. So, the next 3-4 days we'll work on building and testing the two large models, except tomorrow morning at 09:30, when Faiyaz, Jane and I will go to town to view a quality breeding bull worth Rs.2200 (C$80). Faiyaz says he has already come to an agreement with Chichrunpur to give them the bull on the condition that all extant low quality bulls be neutered. The new bull will be free range grazed by day and stall fed in the evening, and he will impregnate the cows in the fields at will. After a year, he will be moved to another village and replaced by another bull from another village. This way, inbreeding is prevented.

    Finally, I met the two very lovely Indian couples from Calcutta, who asked to see the Champions of the Wild video upon hearing about it, and came back to the fire pit to join us bubbling with enthusiasm and questions after seeing it. One of the ladies brought out her camera and took a number of pictures with me. I gave them a copy of tiger literature with WCWC's address, phone, fax and e-mail on it. They volunteered to link the Delhi Tiger Clubs with the Calcutta schools' environment clubs, and both with Canadian school student groups.

    Very exciting prospects in the offing.

Good night, Christopher. **Good night, Christopher.**

❖ ❖ ❖ ❖ ❖

1999-02-16-2 *Delhi Times, The Times of India*, national
[He is no ordinary tiger]

They sit inside it and discuss its decimation from the face of the planet. It's 50-foot long and 12-foot high and is made of parachute material that can inflate. Striped bright yellow and black, this tiger was (brought to India) by WCWC for a Save-the-Tiger campaign to generate awareness on tiger conservation amongst school children…

1999-02 *Travel Talk* magazine, India TT Bureau
[Save the Tiger campaign]

… "A conscious effort has to be made to make the villagers aware of the hazards of deforestation, overgrazing and poaching, and their consequences on the whole ecological balance," said Marr.

His Save-the-Tiger campaign has introduced new eco-friendly techniques for resource conservation, like solar cooking devices and biogas to wean the villagers from their dependence on wood-fuel…

Marr also feels that the entry fee to the Indian wildlife sanctuaries should be raised manifold to benefit the locals of the area and also to maintain the reserves…

❖ ❖ ❖ ❖ ❖

February 17, 1999, Wednesday, sunny, 7-24C

Dearest Christopher:

[18:08 @ Rm. 112, Kanha Tiger Lodge]
A productive day.

I woke up from a dream around 04:30 last night, got up, wrote down the dream, then went back to sleep around 05:30, and was awakened by a knock on my door for breakfast. I looked at my clock, and it was 08:45 – late by two hours for me.

The two Indian couples as well as CJ have left by then. Only CJ will be back, who went with the Indian couples to Gondia to buy his train ticket to Delhi.

I had a hurried breakfast with Faiyaz. Jane had already eaten, but she sat with us. We then jumped into the Gypsy and headed for Baihar.

Our first stop was the office of Mr. Jharia, Assistant Forest Conservator, where we discussed our purchasing with Rs2200 a young (14 months old) hybrid bull (half Hiana) to give to Chichrunpur. Hybrid because a pure bred bull from elsewhere would not do well in the local environment. We exchanged many questions and answers regarding what's already been done by Faiyaz and what we plan to do. According to Jharia, Chichrunpur has already accepted the idea of neutering all its own bulls, which are of average quality by local standards, which is to say very low, if this new high quality bull is given to them. According to Jharia, several other villages have shown similar interest. The program is to have the village bulls neutered first by the villagers themselves using their traditional methods (how?), followed by a vet check to verify the fact, and if things check out fine, then the new bull will be introduced to the village by walking it there. The ultimate objective of this scheme is to bring up the quality (e.g., milk productivity) of the cattle and reduce their quantity, so that the grasslands and forests may rebound. Initially, the new bull is to be free-range grazed with the cows in the daytime, and stall-fed with grain at night. The breeding of the cows will be done by the bull on its own accord – as is the custom of the villages I have come across in the Buffer Zone - who may also breed the cows of neighbouring villages he will encounter in the normal course of free-ranging-grazing. After a couple of years, he would be rotated to a non-neighbouring village to prevent inbreeding, and a new bull will be rotated to Chichrunpur to take his place. This is the first step. The second step will be to limit the number of offspring per new bull. And the third step will be to reduce or eliminate free range grazing by factoring in corral feeding. The feed will be imported from outside of the Buffer Zone. Thus, the Core Area will hopefully be spared, and even the Buffer Zone may be ecologically revitalized. This scheme is particularly important for the Core/Buffer boundary villages like Chichrunpur.

After our meeting, Jharia took us to a veterinary hospital to meet the head vet, who then took us to see the bull which currently belongs to a private owner nearby. The average milk yield of a local cow is about 2 litres a day. This young bull's mother is supposed to yield 15 litres. Being only 14 months old, he is not impressive to look at, but according to the vet, he will mature into a magnificent animal. They say, however, that he is ready to perform his intended duty. I named it Bullet on the spot, much to Jane's amusement.

After the bull viewing, we went to the town square to shop for material with which to build the solar mirror cooker – wooden boards to make the stand for the mirror, nails, metal cutter to cut the steel sheet, bamboo poles and ropes to make two tripods and a horizontal beam for suspension of the hot plate and grill, coarse mesh wire grill to put pots on, etc., and eventually hired a carpenter who came back with us to the lodge to make the wooden base, which has now been made. The steel sheet is highly reflective alright, but it is somewhat rippled when unfurled, which means it's going to scatter off some 30% (I estimate) of the incident solar heat. Tomorrow near noon, we'll test the device.

[22:32]

During my time in Delhi and Jaipur, as well as here at Kanha, I have come across information which either just fell into my lap by accident, or was thrust into my hands unbidden, or was sought and found. Some are hearsay, and others were first hand observations. This information range from mildly interesting to surprising to downright staggering. Following are a few of these items:

- First hand experience: I had always assumed that Deepfee was the main, full time teacher at the free school, until last night when I found out that she does so only sporadically. She was, however, always the one seen whenever I was there - thus my previous misconception. The real full time teacher at the free school is in fact Faiyaz.
- First hand experience: I asked three impartial people to do a cost estimate of the CIDA-funded Tiger Fund program in 1997 without telling them the funding amount or even telling them about the program. Their estimates were fairly consistent, ranging from a low of C$8,000 to a high of C$12,000. The actual amount sent to TF from CIDA via WCWC was C$45,000 (60% of that year's project grant of C$75,000). And Tiger Fund did not even fulfill a major part of that year's program, including the production of a Hindi-language tiger conservation comic book.
- Hearsay: In 1998, about the time when TF was requested by CIDA to submit receipts, a tour operator observed that Sarwan, the Magnificent Tours accountant, was repeatedly told by Avtar to assign Magnificent Tours expenses, unpaid bills and receipts to Tiger Fund.
- First hand experience: Perhaps a coincidence. While I was in Delhi, Avtar asked me more than once when the CIDA grant money was coming through. He even called Paul George (WCWC head in Vancouver) directly about it. The first installment of C$15,000 came through about a week ago. Within a day or two, Avtar paid for the new Gypsy, whose price *was* about C$15,000. When I asked him, he told me that the new Gypsy was primarily for Tiger Fund to use, but either he did not tell Raman and Manohar about this, or he told them the opposite, because they both independently said that it was first and foremost a Magnificent Tours tourist vehicle. When I was talking about using it for Tiger Fund outreach, Raman, who overheard the conversation, interjected, "The use of the Gypsy is not listed in the agreement of the CIDA grant." To which I replied, "This will soon change."
- Hearsay: On the other hand, Raman and Manohar have been heard to independently remark that CIDA money was not used fully towards tiger conservation and that CIDA/WCWC were not getting their money's worth from TF.

- Hearsay: A reliable source informed me that the lodge uses poached wood, which is cheaper than legal wood, to build and cook with, or to burn at the tourist fire pit. It is bought directly from wood poachers. This is done according to directives from "the management above Manohar".
- First hand experience: Several people, including Jharia and Manohar, have warned Faiyaz, and even tangentially me, to not get close to any of the village women, and be always accompanied by a witness whenever going to a village. This is because our visits are not always welcomed by all concerned. It is always possible that someone would consider using false accusations such as rape to discredit us.
- First hand experience: When Faiyaz proposes certain things, Avtar generally refuses, but when I propose the very same things, he would often go along, at least lip-service-wise. This means to me that giving me preferential treatment was not for the true cause, but for my giving WCWC, and thus CIDA, a good report on TF. I think Avtar knows how I feel from one or two sources, and is doing a few things on the surface to appease me. But the bare bone fact is that he has yet to release the first rupee's worth of the grant money to the Tiger Fund field team since my arrival in India this year, in spite of our repeated requests.
- Hearsay and first hand experience: Not much happened re. TF activities in my two-week absence from Kanha, but not for want of desire on the part of Faiyaz and Jane. First, there was heavy tourist influx and both were put to work in that arena, and second, I was told that whatever they wanted to do unrelated to the tourist business was categorically denied by Manohar. He did not release a single rupee to Faiyaz. All these of course were under order from "the management above Manohar". Both Jane and Faiyaz are concerned that whereas TF outreach work will plow on regardless while I'm here, it will grind to an abrupt halt as soon as I have left.

Closer to matters at hand, CJ still hasn't returned to the lodge. He was supposed to be back by 20:00. We decided that if CJ still hadn't come back by 23:00, we'd go to Baihar to check on the home of the owner of the Tata Sumo.

Anyway, while we wait, here is the dream I recorded in the middle of the night.

It would be strange enough to dream of being a lion or an eagle, but of everything on Earth, I dreamed of being an amoeba living in the pond beside which I was sleeping.

"I", the amoeba, had climbed up the stem of a bulrush, what in amoebal language was known as a "Stairway to Heaven", for what lay beyond our lake universe was what Heaven was to us. I was pushing as hard as I could to penetrate the water/air barrier, in vain. I seemed to have been doing that for ages, eons. Finally, in total dispiritedness and exhaustion, I was about to let go and let myself fall back to my bottom-feeding, amoeba-eat-amoeba existence, when suddenly, I heard, **"Why are you doing this, my friend?"**

I looked around and encountered a spherical being attached to the Stairway. "Who are you?" I asked.

"My name is Raminothna. I can be many things, but right now, I'm the egg of a dragonfly. And you?"

"I am an amoeba."

"What were you doing?"

"I was trying to get into Heaven."

"Why?"

"I'm tired of my mundane existence. I want to transcend to a higher realm."

"I can appreciate the sentiment, but I'm afraid you are going about it the wrong way."

"Oh yeah? Well, if you know the right way, why are you still stuck in here?" And I couldn't help but add, "At least I have some freedom of movement, unlike you."

"I will be out of this pond before the next full moon," declared the dragonfly egg happily.

"So, how do you do it?"

"Tell me. How do you reproduce?"

"That's a bit personal, isn't it?"

"You did ask."

"Okay, I reproduce by binary fission, where one becomes two, two become four, four become eight, eight become sixteen, and so on. How about you?"

"The same."

"So, what is the difference?"

"Now tell me. Are your descendants detached or attached to each other?"

"Detached. We are free moving entities," I said proudly.

"Are they differentiated or identical?"

"They are identical, "

"And their behavior? Is it mutually competitive or cooperative?"

"Mutually competitive. Fighting over the same old bacteria for food, if you must know. And what about yours? Are they detached or attached?"

"They are attached to each other."

"Do they have freedom of individual movement?"

"No, they do not."

"Then I don't see how you can teach me anything."

"Here is how. My descendents will be differentiated in relation to each other, both structurally and behaviorally. And though they will be stuck fast to each other, they will have a much higher degree of collective freedom."

"You got me lost somewhere."

"You see, while some of my descendents will become eyes so all can see, others will become legs so all can walk with immense strides, and some will produce protective armor so all can live in the rarified atmosphere of 'Heaven', and still others will become wings so all can fly in the heavenly winds, clear over the mountain, and the mountains beyond."

"All the way to the moon, no doubt?" I said sarcastically.

"Unfortunately not. Only human beings are capable of doing that."

"Human beings? They must be tremendous flyers then?"

"Strangely, the individual human being can't even fly."

"You lost me again."

"Quite simple, really. Like you amoebae, all dragonflies of the same species are virtually identical and mutually competitive. On the other hand, like dragonfly cells, human beings are differentiated in relation to each other to fill various social roles and form the various social organs. Thus, they can form still higher societies which have yet far greater capabilities."

"I think I understand. Anyway, back to my original question. How do I get out of here?"

"If you take the right evolutionary path, your descendents may become something more akin to a human being than a mere dragonfly."

"With due respect to the amazing dragonfly, I think I'd rather be the even more amazing human being. So, how many moons will it take?"

"Three billion years, if you start now, that is, if you succeed."

As the amoeba began its long integrative transcendence, and at long last became me, I opened my eyes, and saw that the full moon had moved far to the west. But already, I found myself looked far beyond it, all the way to the stars.

"Take this dream also as a session in perceptual pliancy, where the small can be seen as huge, and the large as microscopic," said Raminothna. **"Now stand, Homo Sapiens."**

I stood. Still on the level of awareness of the amoeba, I looked out my eyes from the perspective of one of my brain cells. It would feel much like what I would feel when looking out through the eyes of a statue a hundred times taller than Liberty. And when Super-Liberty started walking I could feel the wind whistling past his ears. I have never thought of myself as a tall man, until now. Viewing oneself this way, it is difficult not to walk with dignity.

Even now, I'm haunted by the amoeba dream, in which context even the humblest human being, even a beggar on skid road, is a towering and majestic civilization trillions of citizens strong. To touch the sky, all one has to do is stand, and raise ones hands in affirmation to the Transcendent Integration of life. This explains how I came to perceive the Raminothna tree as being sky high. Seeing oneself in this light, one cannot help but experience the dignity of walking tall.

"You are now beginning to develop suppleness of perception, where the small is seen as large, and the large as small. This perceptual flexibility is a basic requirement for the attainment of cosmic consciousness," said Raminothna.

With this new way of perception comes a new way of thought. For the first time in my search for the illusive Tao, I feel I have finally stumbled on to something new.

"So, my body, besides being a multicellular organism, as we all know, is also a society of my sixty trillion body cells?"

"You might even say: your sixty trillion *social unicellular organisms*," Raminothna said.

"Excuse me, Raminothna. There is nothing as a *social* unicellular organism," I corrected her. "An amoeba is a unicellular organism, but it is not social. Neither is a bacterium, nor a diatom. All of the unicellular organisms I can think of are nonsocial."

"Except those that are social, of course."

"Social unicellular organisms? Such as?"

"Your body cells."

"I know that's what you meant, but my body cells are body cells. They are not bona fide organisms, strictly speaking."

"But they are, strictly speaking."

"Then you'd better explain."

"Let me ask you. Is the amoeba a bona fide unicellular organism?"

"Of course, it is."

"Is it, as a unicellular organism, social or nonsocial?"

"It is nonsocial."
"Is the dragonfly a bona fide multicellular organism?
"Yes, it is."
"Is it, as a multicellular organism, social or nonsocial?"
"It is nonsocial."
"Is an ant a bona fide multicellular organism?"
"Yes, it is."
"As a multicellular organism is it social or nonsocial?"
"It is social."
"And what about you? Is a human being a bona fide multicellular organism?"
"Of course I am."
"Are you, as a multicellular organism, social or nonsocial?"
"I am social."
"Does your sociality, or that of the ant, make you any less of a bona fide organism?"
"No, it does not."
"By the same token, should the sociality of a body cells make them any less of a bona fide organism?"
"Uh, no. I guess not. So, I now agree. A body cell can be said to be a social unicellular organism."
"Q.E.D.," said Raminothna.

Definitions aside, to know that I am a civilization of highly social cells somehow makes me feel a little more... civilized.

[01:26 (1999-02-18)]

We did go to Baihar, with me at the wheel. The night air was cool, especially with the top down as always. The stars were brilliant through the leaves of the trees partly shading the road. When we got to the Sumo owner's home, we interrupted the house lady's sleep, who did not seem overly concerned that the Sumo still hadn't returned. We drove a little farther to the bus stop, and saw that the bus which was to take Surinder to catch a train to Delhi (for him to co-drive the new Gypsy back to Kanha with Manohar) was still sitting there. We spotted Surinder at a window and I pulled the Gypsy alongside the bus. Faiyaz talked to Surinder who told him that the white Tata Sumo had just passed when we were talking to the sleepy house lady. We headed back to the lodge. Shortly before we arrived, we met the Sumo coming back from the lodge, with which we exchanged a greeting with both vehicles stopped door to door right in the middle of the deserted highway.

We had a great time on the moonlight drive, both ways, filling the night with our uninhibited songs. I thought these scenes unfold mostly on the movie screen. We probably woke up every sleeping creature we passed, and didn't even have a single drop to drink. There is no alcohol, but there is spirit.

Back at the lodge, we chatted a bit with CJ, then, 1 a.m. rolled around, and here I am.

Good night, Christopher.

※　　※　　※　　※　　※

February 18, 1999, Thursday, sunny, 10-27C, 100% humidity

Dearest Christopher:

[06:44 @ Rm.112, Kanha Tiger Lodge]
I have been missing you on and off all day, as in everyday, but in a somewhat different frame of perception.

As I have mentioned before, and I feel impelled to mention again, since the dream in the amoeba's microcosm, I've been having this strange feeling of being very tall – not six feet tall, or seven feet tall, or even eight feet tall, but miles tall. Initially, when I first stood up and looked down at the ground in front of my feet, I even had a moment of vertigo. When I walk, and run, I feel high altitude winds whistling past my ears. This is a physical feeling, but the spiritual interpretation is a sense of dignity. There is no possibility, while feeling this way, to stoop down below a certain moral and ethical threshold. This was the way I felt when I got out of bed this morning. This is the way I am feeling now, though less dazed by it.

How could this be? Finally, I made some sense of it. The dream or vision made such a deep impression that my perception is still on the cellular level of perception, where space becomes enormously expended, where my room looks cavernous, where the book shelf looks miles tall and miles distant.

Another effect is that it makes objects look extra brilliant. Since the book shelf looks miles away, the mind would automatically factor in some hazing of the air in between, but since there is no haze between me and the book shelf, it looks as if glowing with an inner light – something I noted while lying under the Raminothna tree.

It also has the effect of value. The books on the shelf - they too look miles tall and exceedingly stately. One would instantly associate them with literary masterpieces. It seems inconceivable that such monumental edifices would contain something as trite as a harlequin romance. Seeing myself in this light, I'm made to feel a deep sense of self-worth.

I wonder if I could control my level of perception at any given time.

"With experimentation and practice, you will achieve at-will perceptual pliancy," said Raminothna.

"That is nice to know. It would be quite a magical power of perceptual to have."

"And you have only experienced a half of it."

"What half?"

"The seeing-small-as-large half."

"And the other half is seeing-large-as-small then?"

"Obviously."

"How do I see that?"

"You will see when you see it."

"And what is the practical use of this capability?"

"Ultimately, it could enable you to see 'God'."

[23:13 @ Rm.112, Kanha Tiger Lodge]

I can't believe that I wrote what I wrote this morning. It must seem outlandish to anyone who happens to read it. Some time in the course of the morning I somehow returned from the cellular level of perception to my normal metazoan's (multicellular organism's) level of perception. The bookshelf has returned to being only a few feet tall, and so have I, though the sense of value and dignity remains.

Well, the first test for this sense of dignity is at hand. The experiment with the parabolic mirror solar cooker cannot be said to be an unmitigated success. Due to the slightly rippled surface of the steel sheet and the straight longitudinal section, the solar rays were not sharply focused at a point but diffusedly focused along a strip, and the hot plate was simply not hot enough. It could slow-fry an egg, and could heat water to about 150F, but that's about it. Not much improvement can be made with the existing set up except shielding it from the wind and perhaps using a long and thicker black metal plate. As is, it can be used to dry things, to warm water, slow-cook certain items, things like that. So, time to look for a better reflective surface.

In the evening, three park guides came to visit, as invited by Faiyaz, two of whom I have had on safaris before, the youngest being currently enrolled in a correspondence university program, final year. We (Faiyaz, Jane, CJ, I and they) discussed:

giving them weekly or twice weekly English lessons

raising the park gate fee to benefit park and the villages. The current wage of the park guides is Rs65 (C$2.50) per safari (morning or afternoon) or the same amount per day doing various park chores in the off-season. Raising the park fee could certainly increase their salary.

giving them a photographic workshop.

They are excited about all three ideas. We invited them back tomorrow evening for the Champions of the Wild video and further discussions. They will ask a few more people to come.

Tomorrow is medical clinic day. As of 14:00, Faiyaz and Jane will be free. We will sit down and form a final plan as to what will be done over the next month. I have in mind to do the following:

- visit villages and panchayats (multi-village councils)
- take villagers into the park
- visit village schools
- invite village leaders to visit the Tiger Fund conservation centre and give them video and slide shows, hold discussion sessions and demonstrate the solar devices, etc.
- establish a village and panchayat network
- work at raising park gate fee from the current Rs100 to Rs1000 for foreign tourists and from the current Rs10 to Rs100 for Indian tourists
- video/slide shows to tourists
- weekly training program for park guides and guards

Having checked out India to the extent I have been able to thus far, I believe that the greatest asset of the country is its low labor cost for high quality service (e.g. Faiyaz and the park guide on the university correspondence program). A plan that does not make maximum use of this resource is ill-conceived and foolish. For Tiger Fund to have an annual budget of C$60,000 from Canada plus whatever is in its own coffer, to not even have a full-time field worker is downright asinine, though I suspect the right word is more like 'corrupt'. The best use of the CIDA grant money in India is to put it into building a large team or several teams of well educated, talented and dedicated local workers to maximize result per unit time, since the tiger hardly has any time left for us to squander and waste. At an average monthly wage of Rs3000 (C$120) we can hire 10 people for 12 months with Rs360,000 (C$14,400 – less than a quarter of the CIDA/TF budget), half of whom with university education. Of course there would be other expenses such as lodging and transportation costs. Just think what WCWC can do with such a team in Canada, at the cost of half a single person's wage! With such a team in India, and with systematic and ambitious planning, we can easily accomplish 100 fold with the CIDA grant than what is on Avtar's table, instead of allowing the grant to slide under it.

The vision of a 10-person tiger saving team is the best thus far given our budget, and will or at least should form the core of future operations in India. This will entail a very different plan from the one or type Avtar has so far unilaterally designed. Also, even if Tiger Fund is to be retained as partner (practically speaking, contractor), it must be a sovereign NGO not subservient to any associated commercial interest as Tiger Fund is subservient to Magnificent Tours, with a full time dedicated leader heading a dedicated team, which Tiger Fund currently is entirely without.

[01:14]

Again having trouble sleeping. Again overwhelmed by anger and grief. Again clutching at straws.

One of the tourists left the science fiction Dune and its sequel Dune Messiah in the magazine rack near the bar in the dining pavilion. Attempting to evade my anger and grief, I tried to escape into Dune, but I didn't get too far. Instead, I found myself asking Raminothna yet again, "Just *what* are you? Come on, Raminothna, just tell me this one thing. Where are you from?"

As usual, in response to such questions, she was evasive, at least initially. This time her answer was, **"The Cosmos."**

"What planet exactly?"

"I'm bound by no planet."

"Alright, how about this then: By what means did you come to *this* planet?"

"There are at least four general means for visiting a planet, by at least one of which have I come."

"I'm listening."

"The first and most obvious is of course technology, involving space ships, creative genetics, robotics, artificial high-intelligence, and such currently fictional devices as time machines, hyperspace-craft, teleportation

and their like, of whose possibilities could exceed even imagination, but which are often regarded as impossibilities by the technologically less advanced.

"The second, in certain circumstances a special case of the first, and in certain imagined forms indeed impossible, is telepathy – close encounters of the fourth kind, as it were, where the visitor experiences the planet through a chosen native creature, by seeing through its eyes, walking on its feet, feeling through its heart, thinking through its mind, and working through hands – or whatever other manipulative appendages it may possess.

"The third, at times indistinguishable from the first and second, and always possible, is imagination – that of a certain highly imaginative native creature, that is, who imagines such fourth-kind encounters with such vividness as to lend credence, in its own mind at least, to the real existence of such visitors as myself.

"And finally, the fourth but by far the most common and perhaps the best means of all for visiting a planet is birth – to be born as a native creature of the planet, naturally, to visit the planet for one lifetime.

"Regardless of means, therefore, for the duration of a beamed landing, or a telepathic communion, or a day dream, or a lifetime, as pauper or prince or dragonfly, for good or evil, to give or to take, in war or peace…, we are all fellow visitors of a certain planet at a certain time, for a certain purpose. And therefore, we all share our question in common: What am I here for?

"Some come as tourists, others as naturalists. Some come as destroyers, others as saviors. Some come to propagate and perpetuate lies, others to seek and speak truth. Some come to experience the flesh, others to purify the soul. Some come to learn, some to teach and some to merely sleep. While some come to Earth to read and re-read Dune, others come back from their Dune Messiah fantasies to save and deliver Earth. And while some come all this way to find Earth filled with cruelty, injustice, hypocrisy and pain, others, who feel fortunate and called upon in spite of all, hold that for every visit, regardless of circumstances, there is a joyful and meaningful purpose, or an array of joyful and meaningful purposes, from which the visitor may choose one, or more, or, alas, less. Even for those who see their sojourn on Earth as agonizing, pointless and futile, they still have the purpose to leave and start a better life.

"There are numerous means by which one can leave a planet, amongst which one of the easiest and least irreversible is to escape back into Dune.

Conversely, to die. But for those who can stand its sheer intensity and unrelenting realism, most of all, its uncompromising truth, there is nothing on Earth to compare with Earth.

"My dear fellow Earth visitor, I wish you purposeful living, and joyful deliverance."

And on this positive note, I will bid you good night, Christopher.

❖ ❖ ❖ ❖ ❖

February 19, 1999, Friday, sunny, 11-27C

Dearest Christopher:

[16:38 @ rm.112, Kanha Tiger Lodge]
One full month in India, and we finally hatched an optimal plan. In the late afternoon, we (Jane, Faiyaz, CJ and I) were brainstorming around the unlit fire pit when the plan suddenly congealed itself in my mind. We will invite all the panchayats in the Buffer Zone for a Buffer-Zone-wide conference at the Tiger Lodge. A panchayat ("pan-CHAI-yat") is a multi-village council. There are 45 panchayats in the Buffer Zone, averaging 4 villages per panchayat. We'll show them the Champions of the Wild video, give them the slideshow, demonstrate the solar devices and have a strategizing and organizing meeting. Faiyaz will organize it with the help of Tirath, a park guide who is also a Gond tribal, who can drive. The lodge will be without tourists March 1-4 and 8-12. We'll choose one of these days.

[22:34]
Just finished the meeting with three park guides, including the handsome and regal Tirath (even though he is in rags and sandals, or is perhaps even an 'Untouchable' - this I don't know). They arrived around 19:30. First we showed them the Champions of the Wild video. Then we had a discussion in the dinner pavilion. One of their questions was the idea held by many villagers in the buffer zone that the park will expand into the buffer zone and they will be displaced farther into what they consider the boonies. I asked their opinion on the idea of the conference. They talked among themselves at length, and surprised me when Faiyaz interpreted that

not only did they like the idea, they even offered to help us organize it. In order to reach all the panchayats, they would need about three days with Faiyaz, since they do have 1,000 sq. km. of Buffer Zone to cover, half of which being on the other side of the Core Area. They also opined that March 1-4 is not good because of the "Holi" (flower) festival when many villagers will be drunk, belligerent or even hostile. We chose March 11 as the date, and agreed that it is imperative to invite the government officials in the region. So, without further ado, Faiyaz and Tirath will get started first thing tomorrow morning to commence networking with the panchayats. First thing on the agenda is to issue invitations to the officials to show our respect, and also to obtain their permission for us to traverse through the Core Area, parts of which being inaccessible to the public, to access the Buffer Zone on other side. So, all of us will go into the park 06:30 tomorrow morning.

I will also invite media and perhaps also people from the Centre of Science for Villagers (CSV) in a town a couple of hundred km away to attend this "Kanha Buffer Zone Panchayat Conference".

This, we all agree, is the most effective way to reach the most number of villages in the shortest time.

We went to Baihar to call Avtar to discuss the plan with him, but he was again unavailable. There is no promise I can reach him tomorrow or the day after or the day after that. Meanwhile, I can sit and wait, or go and act. Guess which option I'm taking.

I feel charged. I'm chomping on the bit. No wet blanket from New Delhi is going to put a damper on me.

Too excited to sleep. A state I used to love, when I would sit up writing all night, my mind in flight on pure inspiration. Now, whenever I cannot sleep, pain would come flooding in to fill the void. I need to displace it with extra-personal considerations, cosmic thoughts, while embracing Christopher deep in my heart.

The amoeba's microcosmic dream came back to enchant me. It was a dream by a human about the human origin, about the way of self-becoming, a subject by which the human dreamer has been fascinated for years. The scope of the process from single cells to human being is staggering. If the step between Australopithecus and Homo Sapiens is momentous, how would you describe the steps before Australopithecus backtracking all the way to the primordial cell?

"Australopithecus is wonderful. But even a mole or an ant can contribute to human self-understanding."

"What do you mean?"

"Tell me. When a mole digs a hole into the ground, what does it seek?"

"A mole is a subterranean hunter. So when it digs, it digs for food."
"And when an ant digs a hole in the ground?"
"An ant builds subterranean nests. It digs for shelter."
"And when those humans in Olduvai Gorge digs, what do they seek?"
"They dig for fossils and artifacts."
"And what are these fossils and artifacts good for?"
"They tell us the truth of our origin."
"Therefore, Homo Sapiens is a species in possession of a godly quality, a species in search of truth."

Good night, Christopher.

❖   ❖   ❖   ❖   ❖

February 20, 1999, Saturday, sunny, 12-26C

Dearest Christopher:

[18:10 @ Rm.112, Kanha Tiger Lodge]
    We (Faiyaz, Jane, CJ and I) started for the park at 06:30 this morning, with me at the wheel, and were surprised and a little disappointed to find that Tirath had already gone into the park with another party. We took on Johan as guide, and headed for the Kanha Nature Centre in the centre of the park mid-way between the Mukki and Kisli gates. There, we found Mr. Negi, Deputy Director of the core area, and managed to catch Mr. Rajeesh Gopal, Field Director of the entire Kanha National Park, core plus buffer, just before he left Kanha on a trip to Delhi. Both seemed interested in the conference. Gopal even said that he would bring his own slideshow. Negi conversed with Faiyaz at length, in Hindi, then asked me what my intention was to organize the event. I answered that it was a means to help preserve the Kanha tigers and the park itself. It is certainly the most effective means to cut down on deforestation we can think of. He seemed satisfied by that. Negi also said that he would suggest a number of names of people he would like to see invited to the conference. So, it seems that the authorities, the park personnel as well as the villagers are generally in favor of the conference idea. The only person left is Avtar.
    Speaking of which, although Avtar has agreed to the Buffer Zone outreach plan,

and although the first installment from WCWC/CIDA has arrived days ago, he has yet to send any money for the execution of the plan, which basically would be for fuel for the outreach vehicle, if there indeed is an outreach vehicle. I have little doubt that even if Avtar said that I could have the use of one of the lodge Gypsies for Buffer Zone outreach purposes, when it comes to the same Gypsy being needed by Manohar for extra tourists and by Faiyaz for village outreach, the Gypsy would be commandeered by Manohar, and there would be nothing I or Faiyaz could do about it. I may need to sooner or later confront Avtar on a number of fronts, but I want no friction with Manohar whatsoever, because this is the temporary home of all of us and peace and harmony must be maintained, and Manohar is only following Avtar's orders. If necessary, I will hire a Gypsy perhaps from one of the other tourist lodges out of my own pocket, and try to reclaim it from Avtar or WCWC later..

After the meeting with Gopal and Negi, we took the long and slow way back to the lodge, not having visited the park for quite a few days. I want to record the pugmarks and map them, and, with the help of our park guide, identify the individual tigers if possible, and do more wildlife photography to enrich my slideshow, and perhaps to see a tiger. For brunch, we pulled up under the banyan tree overlooking the paddy-fields-turned-meadow. Having been tightly crammed together in the rear deck of the Gypsy for the last three hours, we savored this our only opportunity to walk on Kanha soil, and our momentary solitudes in this our ephemeral personal Eden suffused with heavenly peace. It is so easy and indeed so natural, even inevitable, to achieve this state in a setting like this. Even for me, with the continuing devastation of Christopher looming over my head like a black cloud, I would find myself having drifted imperceptibly from under it and feeling very much relaxed and at ease.

There was a large herd of over a hundred chital deer grazing in the meadow, among the few widely dispersed trees and termite mounds. The landscape was so bright it was brilliant. The air was so silent it hissed. In an Indian wilderness, we naturally whisper. Today, we did not even whisper. This was truly the holy of holies. This was not St. Peter's Cathedral. This was, so to speak, a natural cathedral build by the hands of God.

"Ultimately, the Universe Itself is the supreme cathedral, the Earth is one of Its innumerable chambers of worship, and life is the act of worship itself," whispered Raminothna. After a moment, She said, **"I have shown you the art of spatial perceptual Pliancy. Time to give you an exercise in time dilation and compression."**

"Space and time, makes sense. Go ahead."

"Take a time lapse movie of this meadow covering a hundred years, and play it back in a hundred seconds, and what do you see?"

I looked intensely at the meadow for a full minute. "Yes, finally, I see what I think you want me to see. But I don't see what point you're trying to make."

"What do you see?"

"Well, first, I see the grass covering the meadow. It's like a shimmering carpet alternating green and brown once every second."

"Good start."

"Next are the trees. They sprout from the ground, mushroom to full stature, then suddenly collapse, then crumble to nothing, all within several dozen seconds, each in its own time of course. And while they live, they give off once-per-second flowering flashes."

"Go on."

"And the animals. They are individually invisible, because they move so super-fast, but instead form a ground-hugging probability cloud."

"So far, so good."

"And, yes, let's not forget the termite mounds. They behave just like the trees. They sprout from the ground just like the trees, mushroom to full size just like the trees, then suddenly dying and eventually crumbling to nothing, just like the trees, all within several dozen seconds just like the trees, each in its own time of course, just like the trees. And while they live, just like the trees, they also give off once-per-second flashes comprising the release and swarming of winged reproductive alates from all mounds simultaneously. This is what you want me to see, isn't it – about the termite mounds?"

"And what do you make of it?"

"That a termite mound is as alive as a tree? Which makes common sense, since the termites themselves are alive. Is that it? That the termite mounds are alive?"

"Yes, but not far enough."

"I would have thought that to call a termite mound alive is already going a little too far, since only the termites are alive, but not the shell of the mound."

"Is this like saying that calling a crab alive is going a little too far, since only its cells are alive, but not its shell?"

"But a crab is a bona fide organism – a living thing."

"Ah ha! Now we're getting somewhere."

"You're not actually saying that a termite mound is a bona fide organism, are you?"

"Isn't it?"

"Well, there is one test I learned in high school that can answer this for certain. I can run it through the gauntlet of classical biology's Seven Vital Functions. A candidate entity must possess all seven vital functions to qualify as a bona fide organism."

"Sure. Do it."

"Okay. The First Vital Function is Ingestion. A bona fide organism needs to ingest materials of some kind, plants and other animals in the case of animals, and solar energy, water, O_2, CO_2 and certain minerals in the case of plants. The termite mound does need to ingest grass, leaves and dead wood."

"Do the termites themselves ingest the grass, leaves and dead wood?"

"Actually, they do not."

"What do they ingest?"

"They ingest a specific species of fungus that grows on a substrate composed of mulched grass, leaves and wood."

"So, what exactly is the food for the termite mound?"

"Grass, leaves and wood."

"And the fungus?"

"An intermediate product of the mound's internal metabolism."

"Couldn't have put it better myself."

"Thank you. The Second Vital Function is Excretion. The mound does discharge waste material, such as exhausted substrate, uneaten fungal parts, miscellaneous debris and dead termites."

"And the termite's own excreta?"

"It is used as a cement for the shell and internal partitions of the mound. So the termites' feces is not the termite mound's excretion but is the internal secretion of the mound, equivalent to the internal secretion of the crab which builds the shell of the crab."

"Very good."

"The Third Vital Function is Reactivity. The mound does react to external stimuli. If attacked, by ants for example, it defends itself - by means of its soldiers. If damaged, by ant-eaters for example, it heals itself - by means of the major workers."

"Go on."

"The Fourth Vital Function is Movement. A termite mound, in fact, has more power of movement than a tree, since it can send out its termites, like a tentacle, to seek and retrieve food."

"The Fifth Vital Function is Growth. The termite mound does grow, as our virtual videotape demonstrated, in physical size as well as its termite population.

"The Sixth Vital Function is Homeostasis. The termite mound can maintain its own core temperature to within one degree year round. If heated, it cools itself by having the minor workers to go down to the water table via water-access tunnels dug by the major workers, sometimes meters down, each bringing back a droplet of water in its jaws, which they then would stick onto a partition wall, thus cooling the mound. If chilled, it warms itself by the termites clustering, thus maintaining its core temperature. If disturbed, it has a tendency to return to order.

"The Seventh Vital Function is Reproduction. The termite mounds do reproduce."

"You mean the termites reproduce?"

"No. Termite reproduction is actually the growth of the mound in terms of its internal population. Mound reproduction is old mounds begetting new mounds."

"Carry on."

"Well, now, I have no choice but to conclude that a termite mound is a bona fide organism. The idea just initially struck me to be an outlandish notion."

"There is even an Eighth Vital Function, if you're interested."

"There is?"

"Evolution. An organism would have the mechanism to evolve. Not only do the termites evolve, their mounds do as well, in terms of the shapes and sizes and internal structure of the mound."

"Okay, consider me convinced. A termite is a bona fide organism. So where is this leading us?"

"Enough for one day."

Manohar was packing up the lunch utensils. We got slowly back into the Gypsy.

After we had returned to the lodge, second thoughts about the conference made themselves known. It seemed to me that the thing had quickly grown beyond my original concept of just having a meeting with the villagers. The way things look, the conference is going to be all in Hindi, as demonstrated by the Faiyaz-Negi conversation this morning, between the panchayats and the government officials, and they may take off on a tangent from our central thrust which is tiger conservation. And we (WCWC and Canada) may become irrelevant, in which case we'll have served as facilitators, but not participants.

Also, the panchayats would come without any basic tiger conservation awareness and the conference might arrive at a conclusion unfavorable to the tiger. I called another meeting to discuss this problem. After much exchange we decided that as originally planned, Faiyaz will invite panchayat members into the lodge several at a time on a daily basis, and I will give them a slideshow, with Faiyaz translating. This would give them at least some forethought on tiger conservation and set the tone for the conference, which we could defer until April or even May, after I have left. We would then inform the panchayats about the conference during the slideshow. This will also keep me much busier than in the original plan where Faiyaz will go out to organize the conference, and Jane and I will more or less just be sitting here waiting for it to happen, since there would not be another vehicle for me to use. Faiyaz also suggested that I get all the Delhi and Jaipur media clippings sent to me for presentation to the local Project Tiger office. He believes that the clippings will get me easily in the door, and my ideas (e.g. raising park entrance fee) taken seriously. After about three hours of this discussion and debate, we adjourned on this note.

Around 15:00, Faiyaz and CJ went to Baihar to phone Delhi, partly to relay my message that both Jane and I wish to stay at Kanha until I leave India. As before, Avtar was not there, and they spoke with Raman. Again, Raman overstepped his bounds and question Faiyaz why we would need the clippings, but Faiyaz told him to just send them. Raman also informed Faiyaz that Manohar and Surinder, with the new Gypsy, will arrive back at Kanha this evening, via Bandhavgarh, and that Kim, and perhaps another Dynamic Tours volunteer stationed at Bandhavgarh named Julian Cook from Britain, who all but insisted to come to Kanha, citing extreme idleness and boredom at Bandhavgarh. Kim was not even allowed to speak to the tourists by a certain tour operator, whom Jane and CJ believe to be Ed Cambridge - "a prick", by their consensus. Much as I'd love to see Kim again, and I cannot deny a certain attraction, this will complicate the situation somewhat, since then Jane may have to go to Bandhavgarh to take Kim's place. We'll see how it goes.

[23:16]
In the middle of the evening, someone walked into the lodge, and guess who? Julian Cook from Bandhavgarh. Yesterday, he and Kim tried to get to Umaria under their own steam without success, and had to turn back. He struck out on his own this morning at about 06:00 and finally got here by about 21:00 via many changes of buses. Having devoted three months of his time to the Bandhavgarh Jungle Lodge, and paying the lodge US$200 per month for the trouble, this is the treatment he gets. They don't even have the decency to give him a ride to Umaria with one of the Bandhavgarh Tiger Lodge Gypsies. Further, when he was leaving, Mohinder, Avtar's Bandhavgarh Tiger Lodge manager, didn't thank him, didn't acknowledge his services, but said to him, "You used 65 bottles of mineral water during your stay. You'll have to pay us Rs.1300 for them before you leave." Pretty tacky, if you ask me.

This reminded me of something similar that happened to the Omni Film crew. When they first arrived back in 1997, they were each given a Bandhavgarh Tiger Lodge baseball cap, which they gratefully received. But when they left the lodge, they were charged full price for the caps. As I said – tacky.

Of course we crowded around Julian, for news from Bandhavgarh. One thing he said, confirmed by both Faiyaz and the tribal employees at the lodge, is that Pushra Singh, a descendant of the maharaja of Rewa who used to own the land where Bandhavgarh now sits, has special permission to go into the park to hunt animals at will.

"Tigers too?" I asked Julian.

"I think not, but you never know," he said.

Julian is tall, lean, about 30, with a longishly handsome face. His attire is jungle-oriented. He is an avid bird watcher, as are Faiyaz and Deepfee. There is much harmony in the camp.

I love you, Christopher, as always.

❖   ❖   ❖   ❖   ❖

February 21, 1999, Sunday, sunny, 12-26C

Dearest Christopher:

[16:59 @ Rm.112, Kanha Tiger Lodge]

At 06:50 this morning, Tirath came to the lodge. At 07:00, Faiyaz, who cannot drive – his only shortcoming - left with him in the Gypsy to visit villages – perhaps up to 10 - with my bulging media folder, to which have been added two of the latest Jaipur newspaper clippings, in the crook of his arm. I shouldn't even mention his inability to drive, since we've deemed it wise to have him be accompanied by another person anyway.

Jane, CJ, Julian and I, being non-Indians and deemed unsuitable for initial village visits, stayed behind at the lodge to perform "office" tasks. The large and boisterous group of tourists from Calcutta has gone into the park, leaving us in peace and quiet to chart our courses.

Faiyaz returned around 16:00 with a big grin on his humble and honest face, and my media folder clutched in both his hands like a box of jewels. He had a highly fruitful day, dropping by village after village, talking about this "genuine and dedicated" Canadian conservationist, persuading about 8 panchayat leaders, one of whom representing as many as 12 villages, to come to the Tiger Fund Conservation Centre day after tomorrow, the 23rd, at 13:30. They will leave around 19:00. Transportation both ways will be by Tiger Fund Gypsy driven by lodge employee Surinder.

"It is much easier than I originally thought to get the villagers interested to come to see you, and some of them have to walk an hour or more through forest just to get out on to the road to be picked up," he reported.

We arranged for him and Tirath to go out again tomorrow to do the same with more villages, aiming for a second meeting on the 25th. The 24th, he will go into the nontourist part of the park with a guide and guard provided by the park to access the villages on the other side – permission already applied for and obtained.

I also advised him to let me be the custodian of the Gypsy key so that Manohar couldn't get it from him and have us grounded. At least Manohar would think twice before asking me for it, and even if he does, I could always gracefully decline, in which case he would have done his job and Avtar will just have to take issue with me. As of the 23rd, for three days, a large group of about 20 tourists will be here for about three days, and Manohar will certainly need more Gypsies. Well, he'll just have to hire more Gypsies. We have a job to do, we have provided a budget to do it with, and I have come from Canada to do a key part of it, and we will bloody well do it. With a partner like this, who needs wood-cutters?

In the late morning, I packed a lunch and hiked down to the river behind the lodge. It is by far the most scenic place within walking distance. But my main reason is to observe the human and cattle activity on the other side of the small river, which is the fringe of the Core Area of Kanha National Park. When I have time, I should go into the park to a certain depth, say a quarter mile, then observe the activities at that depth. There is an unfrequented park road that goes to within an eighth of a mile of the core-area/buffer-zone boundary. I could park the Gypsy there and bring my laptop computer.

There is a crook in the river, and a tree standing in a certain way, which reminded me of a similar crook in the Coquitlam River, with a similar tree, where Christopher and I used to go. I came back half anticipating, and half dreading, this magical spot. I came to the crook, but there was no tree. It had been cut down since our last time to Chichrunpur. I walked right up to the tree stump. The cut was still fresh, and moist. Around it are scattered bits and pieces of the ex-tree, but the trunk and branches were gone. I of course saw red. Now it is personal. And a terrible question. What if the logs to be burnt at the fire pit for the oncoming group

Omni-Science and the Human Destiny

of tourists come from this tree?

I sat down against the stump and mourned its passing. The feeling is not unfamiliar. I had been mourning the passing of the tree of love that Christopher and I have been blissfully cultivating. I tried to stem the rage that always inevitably follows the mourning. I told myself that this is one more signal for me to harden my resolve to save Kanha from the axe, and to save Christopher from whatever sad fate may await him in his precarious future path. Still, the rage rose irrepressibly like magma from a great depth. I began to seethe with hatred at the mother who would intentionally devastate her own child. I knew hatred was an unholy sentiment, but what else could I feel under these circumstances? Love? Forgiveness? Give me a break!

I've thought a lot about forgiveness lately. Should I forgive Christine? Could I? Would I if I could? Today? Tomorrow? Forever? As I see it, forgiveness does not even enter the equation until the devastation of Christopher stops. And then, only if Christine asks for it, no, begs for it. She never will. So I suppose I'll just carry my unforgiveness to my grave.

Almost savagely I zipped open my knapsack, and hauled the two big and heavy books out of it, titled *Sociobiology* and *Insect Societies*, both by Edward O. Wilson. I brought them to India as a part of my ongoing self-education. Today, I brought them out to read about termite mounds – one of which I could see standing about six feet tall at the foot of a tree on the other side of the river.

On p. 317 of Insect Societies, titled "The Superorganism Concept and Beyond", I read:

"The idea of homeostasis leads easily to the visualization of the entire insect colony as a kind of superorganism. In fact, the story of the superorganism concept, from its origin as a philosophical idea sixty years ago to its present sharp decline in contemporary thinking, should prove instructive to historians of science as well as to biologists with a more immediate interest in the subject. During some forty years, from 1911 to about 1950, this concept was a dominant theme in the literature on social insects. Then, at the seeming peak of its maturity it faded, and today it is seldom explicitly discussed. Its decline exemplifies the way inspirational, holistic ideas in biology often give rise to experimental, reductionist approaches that supplant them…

"… the current generation of students of social insects…saw its future in stepwise experimental work in narrowly conceived problems, and it has chosen to ignore the superorganism concept… Seldom has so ambitious a scientific concept been so quickly and almost totally discarded.

"The superorganism concept faded not because it was wrong but because it no longer seemed relevant. It is not necessary to invoke the concept in order to commence work on animal societies. The concept offers no techniques, measurements, or even definitions by which the intricate phenomena in genetics, behavior, and physiology can be unraveled. It is even difficult to cite examples where the conscious use of the idea led to a new discovery in animal sociology…

"… But it would be wrong to overlook the significant, albeit semiconscious, role this idea had played in the history of the subject…

"Finally, it might be asked what vision, if any, has replaced the superorganism concept… there is no new holistic conception…"

"So, what does this leave us?" I asked Raminothna. "It seems that the door has been slammed shut on the concept decades ago."

"It is about to open again."

"It slammed shut for a reason. Is the reason gone?"

"Yes it is."

"And what is this reason?"

"Its name, to begin with."

"'Superorganism'? Why?"

"If you call a society of organisms a superorganism, what would you call a society of superorganisms?"

"A supersuperorganism?"

"And what do you call a society of supersuperorganism?"

"A supersupersuperorganism?"

"See what I mean?"

"Yes. Cumbersome, to say the least. So what's your solution?"

"What's yours?"

"Well, first, we have established that the termite cell, termite and the termite mound are all organisms."

"Yes, we have."

'It is very clear now. Where the termite cell, termite and termite mound are concerned, they are all organisms, but on different level of organization, where the termite mound is a society of termites, and the termite is a society of termite cells."

"Good."

"And on each level of organization, there are nonsocial and social organisms."

"Very good."

"I can even write a simple equation to describe these levels: <u>**Society (X) = Organism (X+1)**</u>, or <u>**Organism (X) = Society (X-1)**</u>."

Omni-Science and the Human Destiny

"Excellent."

"This is so obvious, why didn't Wheeler and the others see it?"

"What did Thomas Huxley say after reading Charles Darwin's Origin of Species?"

"Yes, he did say, 'This is so obvious why didn't I think of it?'"

"A common question for brilliant minds."

[23:41]

This evening, about 19:00, Jane, Faiyaz and I went to Baihar to see Jharia to get a map of the 40 Core-periphery villages, and to call Delhi and Bandhavgarh. Jharia has left town on business, and after some difficulty, we did reach Mohinder, manager of the Tiger Lodge at Bandhavgarh National Park, who informed Faiyaz that Manohar had left Bandhavgarh for Kanha with Surinder as of 15:00, and should arrive at Kanha around 22:00, and that Avtar had no problem with me and Jane not going to Bandhavgarh. This, however, where Avtar is concerned, as he told Mohinder, means that Kim would have to stay at Bandhavgarh in Jane's place, which to Kim is unfair, as she told me when she got on the phone with me. I said to her that she is a volunteer, not a prisoner. I added that the tourist season is winding down, but campaigning action is cranking up, and if she wants to do conservation work instead of tourist work, she should ask Avtar for her to come to Kanha as well, and I would welcome her with open arms into the project. And I told her briefly about our panchayat conference plan. She may be able to come with the major tourist group of Mr. Richards on Tuesday the 23rd when they cross over from Bandhavgarh to Kanha, because after that, there will be no tourists at Bandhavgarh for a week or two.

While driving, under Jane's orchestration, we made up a song to be sung to CJ tomorrow evening, the eve of his permanent departure. It is a modification of the Beatles' Yesterday:

Yesterday
Our goodbyes still seemed so far away
But o now we have to part we say
O we believe in yesterday

Suddenly
We're not half the team we used to be
Now that you're going across the sea

O we believe in yesterday

Why you have to go we don't know
We wish you'd stay
We love all your songs
Now we long for yesterday

I said to Jane, "I think Christopher will cry when he hears this."
Jane said, "I think I will too."
Manohar arrived around 22:00. Before he did, I had said to the gang, "I hope he's got the right slide projector and the slides with him." What I need are Tiger Fund's 220 volt slide projector, the 140-slot slide tray with the 130 duped slides, and an extra 80-slot empty tray for Jane to use after my own departure at the end of March. I had given the list in writing for Reshem to give to Avtar before I left Delhi. Well, guess what? Instead, Manohar was given the WCWC 110 volt projector without the voltage converter, and an empty slide tray without any slides. I blew my top and stormed back to my room, but not before exclaiming, "Fucking incompetent bastards!"

And now that the panchayat leaders are coming in day after tomorrow to pay us homage, what do I have to show them? All I have now is the Champions of the Wild video, which is in English, and which does not show the Chinese medicines, nor the habitat diminishing maps, nor the devastated landscapes after deforestation and overgrazing, nor... With the language barrier already standing in the way, I need all the help I can get. Coming to visit us in groups of 7-8 over the next three weeks are the most powerful and influential village council leaders in the whole of Kanha's Buffer Zone. At best, my presentation will be much weakened, at the crucial time when finally we have kick-started what may be the best and most comprehensive outreach program ever launched at Kanha by any organization at any time.

I felt like quitting on the spot and flying back to Vancouver on the first available flight and canning the whole thing. But even before the thought had completed itself, the second thought had superceded it – that of course I would not quit. I'll just have to make the best of what little I am given to work with.

After cooling off a little, I came back out and said to Manohar, "It's not your fault. Don't worry about it." As it happens he was pissed off at the Delhi Magnificent Tours people himself, because try as he did, he did not get the money he needed from the Delhi office for the Richards group of tourists due to arrive from Bandhavgarh day after tomorrow, resulting in his departure from Delhi being delayed for several hours for nothing. I can believe it, and we can howl our rage all we want. Nobody in Delhi would hear it, and now, what is Manohar going to use to hire more Gypsies with?

He and I planned to go to Baihar to call Delhi first thing in the morning, and have Raman send a "boy" (Manohar's term) on the 14:30 train with the right slide projector and the slides tomorrow, who will arrive at Gondia on the 23rd 10:00, who will then take a bus to the Kanha Tiger Lodge, hopefully arriving just on time for the late afternoon slideshow.

"If there is interest at head office to do that," Manohar added with a shrug of resignation.

"It is not a matter of interest. It is a matter of necessity," I fumed.

Good night, Christopher.

❖ ❖ ❖ ❖ ❖

February 22, 1999, Monday, sunny, 12-26C

Dearest Christopher:

[18:41 @ Rm.112, Kanha Tiger Lodge]
As planned, while Faiyaz struck off with Tirath at 08:00 on another round of panchayat invitations, Manohar and I set out for Baihar to call Delhi. We succeeded in reaching Raman first try, and he received the request, no, demand, for the 220 volt slide projector and the tray of slides in near silence. We also tried to contact Avtar in Jodpur because he's been asking Manohar what we're up to. Again, he was unavailable. Both Manohar and I felt Raman either would not do as we requested, or he would screw up again somehow.

During our long time alone together, Manohar began to share with me some of his thoughts. He feels that Avtar's move to Canada is a big mistake, that his presence is almost zero in Delhi as it is, and his Delhi operation has "collapsed". "You can't do business by e-mail," he said. He feels that the Delhi office considers him "illiterate" and treats him with disrespect. He is supportive of what I am doing at Kanha, but feels that there is a "great distance" between me and Avtar. On the last score, I was quite open about how Avtar and I differ in our thoughts on staying put at the conservation centre versus reaching out Buffer-Zone-wide. I explained that my coming from Canada to India is an outreach unto itself, and once in India, I by nature would want to reach out as far as possible on the local ground, and that outreach is the best way to generate media, which is the best way to create public awareness, which is the highest baseline to get things changed. While on media, I also told Manohar that Avtar and the Delhi office disappointed me by having generated no media coverage at all for the school presentations. So, there, we have an understanding. I don't mind or care if it goes back to Avtar, which I suspect it will. In fact, I think that would be good.

Later in the day, about 13:45, we drove back to Baihar and called both Avtar and Raman again. Avtar was still at large, but Raman reported that he had sent a "boy" out, with the tray of slides, but, wouldn't you know it, again, rather than the 220 volt projector as I requested, he had sent the voltage converter instead, with the attached requirement that the converter be sent back for use on Big Cub with the "boy" when he returns to Delhi, which means in a day or two. Another fuck up, but what's new? Well, that's not going to happen. He created the problem by sending the wrong thing, again. Had he sent the 220 volt projector, the converter would be in Delhi for Big Cub and I would send the WCWC 110 volt projector back with the "boy", and everybody would be happy. Now, they would just have to find another converter in Delhi.

The electric power blacks out regularly for hours at a time every day. Today, it was from 07:00 this morning all the way till almost 18:00 this afternoon. If tomorrow is the same, we'd be in big trouble. I worked out the solution that the meeting with the panchayat leaders, representing about 16 villages, will begin at 13:30 as planned. It will be a getting-to-know-you session which will be informal. At 15:00, we'll take them into the park, with me driving and Faiyaz at the back interpreting. We'll be back to the lodge at about 17:30. Hopefully, the power will have come back on by then, which it usually does. I'll give my slideshow as soon as the power comes back on, and wind up by 19:00 at the latest.

Faiyaz came back around 15:30 this afternoon, and proclaimed another good day, with another 7 panchayat leaders representing another 16 villages. They will come same time on February 27. In this case, he will go into the park's eastern core to visit the 22 villages there, and will go another round in the buffer zone on the 25th.

[00:16]

This evening, Manohar went shopping at Malanjkhan, the copper-mining town where the volunteer doctor lives, and invited Julian and me along for the ride, together with two tribal lodge employees. We tried to call Avtar again, and this time he was at a

Omni-Science and the Human Destiny

wedding. Manohar asked me if I had any message to pass on to Avtar. I said, "Say that I wish him long life and prosperity." And added, "Just tell him what you know about our plan and progress regarding the panchayat outreach and conference."

When we came back, we had our little farewell party for CJ. After some merriment, we (Jane, Faiyaz and I) sang our modified Yesterday for CJ. It was a warm and loving evening for all.

Looking at the map of the Buffer Zone, the villages may well be 178 termite mounds dotted over a doughnut-shaped piece of land.

"What does this tell you?"
"That a village too is an organism?"
"Isn't it?"
"It is."
"What level of organization is it on?"
"The same one as termite mound's."
"What level would that be?"
"I think it depends on whether the village and the city are on the same level or not. If not, I would call it the Tribal level of organization. But if they are on the same level, then I would call that level the Citian level of organization."
"Well? Which?"
"I'll have to think more about it. But I'm seeing the benefit of this multi-leveled framework already."
"And that is?"
"A possible predictive value. It leads us to ask: Are there levels below and above? If so, what?"
"Whatever they be, make a prediction."
"Whatever they be, I would wager that they would contain nonsocial and social forms."
"Well predicted."

And on this note, good night, Christopher.

❖ ❖ ❖ ❖ ❖

February 23, 1999, Tuesday, sunny, 13-28C

Anthony Marr

Dearest Christopher:

[12:02 @ Rm., 111, Kanha Tiger Lodge]
Today, the lodge will be a beehive of activities.

First of course is the panchayat meeting. Faiyaz has been off with Tirath as of 08:00 to pick up the panchayat leaders, due to arrive around 13:30. But before he left, he told Jane he may have chosen the wrong day, since today is market day, and some panchayat members may not come and those who do may not be able to stay very long. We'll have to see how it goes. Right now, Jane has volunteered to take charge of the solar oven demonstration by cooking one pot of rice set to start around 13:00. We have also set up the solar reflector in the parking lot near the clinic, just to give them the idea. The slideshow is scheduled for about 5 pm. By then, hopefully, the voltage converter and the slides will have arrived, and the power will have come back on.

Second is the arrival of the Richards party of about 20 from Bandhavgarh.

Third, but not least, is the return of Kim.

[22:49]
So, as things worked out, today is about as satisfying a campaigning day as any I've experienced. Jane said afterwards, "This is the most successful day so far in India." The superlative is well deserved, even factoring in the heady days in Delhi and Jaipur, and the tiger-sighting days in the park.

There were several kinks due to our inexperience and the experimental nature of the meeting, such as keeping the panchayats waiting 10 minutes after they arrived, the slide projector being locked in the clinic waiting room and the key could not be found, poor food served to the panchayaters, no calendar for planning, Jane leaving her notebook in her room, etc., but nothing that could touch the day's essential excellence.

Faiyaz did arrive around 13:30, with 7 panchayat leaders. Between 13:45 and 14:50, I chatted with them via Faiyaz's rapid fire verbal translations. I myself could read their body language without interpretation, and all showed interest, understanding and agreement, with frequent positive feedback. Jane took copious notes and CJ video-documented the proceedings until towards the end when the Hi8 cam began to act up a little due to overheating.

We started with a round of self-introductions for the panchayats. They were:

Jaitpuri panchayat (4 villages)

Omni-Science and the Human Destiny

- Mrs. Dhanmat Dhurve, sarpanch (head of panchayat)
  Mr. Budh Singh Dhurve, ward member

Paundi panchayat (4 villages)
- Mr. Bagas Ram Mohne, ward member
  Mr. Saheblal Bhardwaj, village elder

And three others. So that's 8 villages out of the 178.

Faiyaz had laid solid ground for me, since their attitude towards me was one of deference and respect. Faiyaz said it was all due to my media folder, which spoke for itself and for me, and which he now upholds like "the Bible", as CJ put it.

Then, I asked for their grievances, which were: too little irrigation, too few schools, requiring children to walk up to 10 km one way on country roads or foot paths, too few medical clinics, leaving some villages without access to any medical services, no roads between villages of the same panchayat, no compensation for livestock lost to predators and for crops lost to wild grazers, lower compensation for villagers than for urbanites who lost their lives to various unnatural causes, inadequate government works, unfulfilled government promises (is this Canada here?), etc.. To these I said that I would do what I can to help them, by presenting their case to the right people, and by pushing for park reform that could benefit them. I may have impressed upon them the long established tenet that the tiger is worth more to them alive than dead, and the park would benefit them more intact than degraded or destroyed. One villager returned to the chital-raiding-crop problem, to which I replied that we could help him introduce alternative crops, like orange, that chital don't eat, and that the tiger eats chital and are therefore their ally. Much much more - see video tape.

At 14:55, we led them out to the parking lot to view the solar devices. Jane opened the oven before their eyes, and revealed a pot of rice cooked to perfection – the woman's touch? We shared it with the panchayat people in an afternoon snack (with a dish provided by the kitchen looking like tofu squares soaked in ketchup which I found not particularly pleasing). There can be no doubting the usefulness of the tool in the eyes of the villagers. We then returned to the schoolroom for further discussions. One villager asked whether the oven can be used in the rainy season, which showed that he had accepted the idea for the dry season. I replied that India has 9-10 sunny months, versus Vancouver's 4-5, and is ideal for solar technology. The other 2-3 months? They could use biogas or, what the hell, burn wood.

At 16:00, we went into the park. Since there were 7 of them, we took two Gypsies, the old green one with loose steering driven by driven by CJ and the black new one by me. Faiyaz came with me, and Julian went with CJ to enjoy his first excursion into Kanha National Park, with Tirath serving as guide in their vehicle.

After entering the gate, Faiyaz told me that the gate guard was grumbling that Faiyaz put me and CJ at the wheels, both being foreigners, for the purpose of saving money, since drivers do not need to pay the park entrance fee, and the gate fee for foreigners is ten times higher than that for Indians (which means that an Indian tourist staying at the Tiger Lodge, paying Avtar some C$300 per day, pays a ridiculous C$0.25 to get into the park to see the tiger which is the whole purpose of his/her trip). I responded by telling Faiyaz to pay the fee on the way out. When it was done, it was received with surprise and appreciation.

None of the villagers has ever entered the park before and they had an eye-opening good time, enthralled by the very wildness of the place, the only things artificial in sight being the Gypsy and its contents including my camera. They were awed by even the chital that but an hour ago they loathed for plundering their crops. Faiyaz said something beautiful and profound: "I want them to fall in love with the park, even with the chital."

Raminothna, on the other hand, gave me another gem of her divine logic.

"So you think the Gypsy is unnatural?"

"Isn't it?"

"What if I say that it is natural."

"The Gypsy? Natural. You'd be forcing me to say that you are wrong."

While passing the termite mounds Raminothna asked me, **"Is a termite society natural?"**

"Of course it is."

"Is a lion pride natural?"

"Yes."

"Is a chimpanzee troop natural?"

"Yes."

"Is a human tribe natural?"

"Well, following your logic, I would have to say yes."

"Are the termite mounds artificial or natural."

"Natural."

"What parts of them are natural?"

"The whole mound is natural."

"Including the shell and internal partition walls of the mound?"

"I will have to say yes, because the shell and internal partition walls of a mound are as natural as the shell and internal partition walls of a crab."

Passing the village of Manjitola on the way back to the lodge, **"Is this village natural?"**

"Again, abiding by your logic, yes, it is."

"Including the wall and the internal partitions of the village?"

"Yes."

"And everything else that are of the village?"

"Yes. And now, I see what you by mean by the Gypsy being natural."

"Isn't it?"

"In as much as all things in the Universe can be said to be natural."

"Aren't they?"

We returned to the lodge at about 18:00. When I parked the new Gypsy back in the roofed parking spot behind the kitchen, Mr. Jharia, the forest conservator, was there waiting for me, and had been waiting since about 17:30. I apologized, explained, then took him to the parking lot to view the solar devices and to socialize with the panchayaters. Soon after that the power came back on, and, with the very efficient translation of Faiyaz, I gave the tiger slideshow without much modification. Jane's free school children were there in the front row. The whole room was pin-drop silent. When it was over, Jharia gave a bright and meaningful smile. Later, Faiyaz told me that Jharia was amazed by the receptiveness of the panchayat members.

Yesterday, during a pre-event chat between Manohar and the rest of us, there was a lot of concern and apprehension about the reaction of the panchayaters, given their long standing antagonism to the tiger, the park and officialdom. I don't know what we did for officialdom, but I believe we undid huge knots in their hostility to the tiger and the park, and further, implanted positive feelings in them for what they now have begun to regard as their potential benefactors. Manohar was too busy to attend the show, but whatever doubt in Faiyaz's mind has been dispelled. Tirath was given to drive the panchayaters back to their villages.

At one point in the meeting, Faiyaz had to run back to the lodge to get his calendar to set a date with the panchayaters for the conference – out here, we hardly know what day of the week any given day is. He was told by Manohar to not decide on anything without having first obtained Avtar's approval. I said that *I* would have to go right ahead to decide and approve, since it would be extremely troublesome to inform the villagers later. Also, there is no guarantee that we would be able to get hold of Avtar any time soon. Later, I said to Manohar, "Your job is done. I have noted that you have told us to not set the time until we get Avtar's approval. If he does not help, at least he should not hinder. He can take issue directly with me." We set the date of the conference for March 23rd.

While walking the path towards the free school to meet the panchayaters, Jane said that she was very demoralized by Avtar's attitude.

I said, "The important thing is what *we*'re doing, not what Avtar is not doing. What do you think of our outreach work so far and our conference plan?"

Jane said, "Totally fine."

"Then things are by and large fine."

She brightened up in time for the panchayaters.

This evening, I was introduced to a VIP – Collector Manu Srivastava. "Collector" is a curious title, but he is the top brass in the district, with broad and sweeping powers. His long-standing main-concern is the antagonism on the part of the villagers against the park. We had an amicable social chat around the fire pit, then agreed that while his parents go into the park in the morning, we will have breakfast together at 09:00 and talk in depth.

So, Kim is back. We shared a long hug, right in front of the lodge personnel. I do find her attractive, but I also know her boyfriend John who is a great guy and a dynamic volunteer for the WCWC tiger campaign. Manohar pulled his practical joke about putting her into Rm. 111 (mine), given the lodge being full, and got two reactions from the ladies: Jane showed spontaneous indignation and disapproval, but after only a casual "Are you serious?", Kim said, "No problem." The rest roared with laughter. I joked that I had planned the stunt with Manohar to see what her reaction would be. Kim didn't know what to believe. In fact, she was given Rm. 115, but was later pulled from it into Jane's room for one night. Around, 23:15, while I was standing with Manohar and Faiyaz planning tomorrow's activities, she came to join us in her pajamas.

Manohar and Faiyaz had some disagreements regarding vehicular use. As expected, Manohar said that the Tiger Fund team would have no vehicle to use tomorrow. I said to hire a vehicle from an outside source, that TF's CIDA budget should and would cover it, adding, "I'm here to work, not to wait."

Manohar lapsed into Hindi and Faiyaz followed suit. After a stretch, I said, "Gentlemen, please use English. What you're discussing concerns me. I'm a part of the planning process." Manohar at once acquiesced, and said, quite respectfully, that I would have a vehicle to use tomorrow, at least as of noon.

About the food served to the panchayaters being poor, it deserves a comment. It had nothing to do with the solar oven, but the dish served with the rice left much to be desired – far substandard to the food that we are normally served. I asked Manohar about this and he said he didn't want food to be the reason for the panchayaters to come. I asked some more, and he then told me that it was deliberately made substandard, because these were "just" villagers. I asked him to kindly shelf this line of thinking for the rest of the conference-organizing period, preferably for good.

This brought back a piece of memory from Calcutta, which is very telling on the Indian social system. While there back in 1997, I was put into a safe-house to stay for about four days. It was a windowless interior room on the fourth floor of an apartment building, with only one door. If the building caught fire, I'd be toast. Even without a fire, I was roasting. The ambient street temperature was a sizzling 42°C or over 100°F. When I first walked into the anteroom, which also served as the servant's quarters, I felt I was entering an oven within an oven. There was no thermometer in the room, but it must be 50°C plus. "How can I last three hours, let alone three days, in this heat?" I thought to myself. But as soon as I opened the door to the master's chamber, I was welcomed by a blast of cool air. The servant ushered me in, then closed the door from the outside. The cool air originated from an air conditioner mounted in the wall between the master's and servant's quarters, its cool end in the former, its hot end in the latter. Master standing on the servant's head, and the servant has to say "Thank you, sir." But I was myself born with my own dedicated "milk mom" back in old China, so who am I to criticize?

Later I had chai with Kim and along the way she filled me in on Bandhavgarh, which is in an uproar over Sita's death. She is here in Kanha only to hostess the tourists. They will be here for only three days. After that, she will have to go back to Bandhavgarh if there is but one tourist there according to her terms of engagement with Avtar. We both feel a little sad about that, but understand that that's just the way it's going to be.

The last few words also apply to our tragedy. How uncaring and unkind sometimes the hand of fate. Good night, Christopher. Love you, as always.

❖   ❖   ❖   ❖   ❖

February 24, 1999, Wednesday, sunny, 15-27C

Dearest Christopher:

[11:11 @ dining pavilion in Kanha Tiger Lodge]

The prearranged 09:00 breakfast with Manu Srivastava, Collector, Balaghat, Madhya Pradesh, was long yet enjoyable, not least of all because of his handsomeness and charm, as observed by Jane. His position of Collector is very high and influential, and his jurisdiction is over the whole district of Balaghat, including Kanha in its entirety, which means that he is above Rajeesh Gopal, Field Director, Kanha National Park. Wherever he goes, a guard hefting an automatic assault rifle loiters nearby. And yet, he is only in his early 30s, with a beautiful young wife and three small children, having advanced on the strength of his ability alone via a pyramidal countrywide examination competition system, so I was told. It invokes in my mind the Confucian system of dynastic China where young people from throughout the country traveled by whatever means to the national capital for a nation-wide competition for governmental positions, with titles like Jong Yuen, Taam Fa, Bong Ngan, etc. awarded, denoting the positions achieved in the competition. There were numerous stories of previously laughed-at geeks and down-trodden nerds returning to their native towns and villages in a glory that shamed their erstwhile tormentors.

When discussing an issue, Collector Srivastava has strong opinions, and projects them forcefully. It is a good thing that he agrees with my view that the gate charge for tourists should be raised, and half of the revenue be plowed towards directly benefiting villagers in the Buffer Zone. We talked of many other issues, from birth control to AIDS to of course the park, the villagers and wildlife conservation. He left around noon and I felt comfortable enough with him to joke, "Some day I may have to borrow your body guard."

His wife is currently organizing a one-day women's issues convention in a town called Seoni about 90 km. north of Balaghat on Feb. 27. Jane expressed a keen interest to attend, but also wanted to stay because that is the date of the next panchayat meeting. I urged her to go, but pointed out that her absence would be more justified if she could secure a plenary speech opportunity. This evening, we'll go to Baihar to call Mrs. Srivastava to see about arranging that possibility. Manohar is kind enough to offer to accompany Jane, by bus, to Seoni if she goes, since there would be no tourists that day - by bus because he knows that Avtar would not approve of providing a Gypsy and the fuel for that purpose.

When Manohar came back from the morning safari with the Richards group of about 20 tourists (5 Gypsies), he told of an unbelievable morning's sighting, even for a seasoned park tour-leader like him. First, they saw tiger, leopard, Gaur. Then they saw the very rare wild dogs –rarer even than the tigers - which alone is phenomenal. And then, to top it all, the wild dogs, which like the African hunting dogs

Omni-Science and the Human Destiny

are pack hunters, put on a show of hunting down a chital in a large meadow - a one-in-a-thousand chance sighting. He related how six or seven wild dogs appeared one by one on different point of the compass around the meadow, all converging upon a large herd of chital which began dashing in all directions, filling the air with their alarm calls. The dogs concentrated on a fawn and captured it, which then broke free and was captured again, and broke free again and was captured for the last time, and killed before Manohar's very eyes. At one point some of the fleeing chital got so near and were so frantic that one of them slammed against the Gypsy he was in. The sequence lasted about 15 minutes, and Manohar said that it was about the best wildlife viewing experience he had ever had.

But guess what? While the wild dogs were just deploying themselves for action, some minutes into the hunting sequence, one of the tourists in the next Gypsy said, loud enough for all to hear, "Well, enough of dog-watching. Let's go and find some tigers." When Manohar was telling us about this, there was disdain written all over his face. Having been in the park enough times, Jane and I listened with jaws down and eyebrows up. There is no justice, is there? A perfect illustration of "casting pearls to swine." Nature's timing was a bit off. For once, I wish the tourists would not be so fixated on the tiger for a change. What would happen if the tiger disappears and Kanha becomes known as a "wild dog reserve"? What tourist would come to this park? What future would the park have then? Not to mention the Barasingha deer of which there is but one single population of about 300 in the world, right here in Kanha.

As recorded in yesterday's entry, Manohar promised a vehicle after the morning drive, but when at 12:30 Faiyaz was ready to go into the East Core Area to visit the core villages, there was no vehicle to be had, although all five Gypsies were sitting empty in the parking lot. Manohar was holding all five vehicles available for the afternoon park drive just in case all 20 tourists decided to go. It was only due to four or five of them electing not to go that Manohar finally released one Gypsy for Faiyaz to use, but by then, it was past 15:00, when otherwise he would have left the lodge by 08:00. This is another indictment against Avtar, to have given Manohar such directives, so that he would cater to the tiger-viewing tourists at the expense of our tiger-saving work, and hire three extra Gypsies for the tourists, but not one more for the Buffer Zone outreach. And this is in spite of his promise to me of exclusive use of the new Gypsy. Again, Magnificent Tours was given priority over Tiger Fund. One whole precious day is wasted. No more. As of tomorrow, I will make damn sure that we will have a dedicated vehicle every day for the rest of my stay, even if I have to pay for it myself. I will campaign to have Avtar return the grant when I get back to Canada.

And of course, when finally one of the five Gypsies became available, one with bald tires, loose steering and almost no brakes was the one dispensed to Faiyaz, not the one Avtar paid for on the same day when the WCWC/CIDA money arrived.

CJ is leaving the lodge tomorrow for good. His first stop is Gondia, where he will catch a 26-hour train to Delhi, leaving Gondia at 18:00. Sorry to again dwell on this, but after devoting two months of his time to Avtar's outfit, he was given a cheap bus ticket by Manohar which requires him to leave the lodge at 08:00, and wait for 5 hours somewhere en route. Since CJ will be traveling alone, he will not be able to relax for a moment due to the constant threat of theft. I went to talk to Manohar about this and he said that Avtar has not given him an extra rupee for anything outside of the tourist aspect of lodge operation. While on the train coming in, he was lifting a suitcase up to the overhead rack when another case by his feet was lifted, which contained his papers and other precious things. This is yet another unacceptably tacky and disrespectful way in which Avtar treats his nontourist people. Knowing that CJ has no money to pay for a jeep ride, Jane and I agreed among ourselves to hire one for him at our expense, at the cost of Rs.5 per km. The trip being 120 km. one way, the cost to Jane and me would be Rs.1250, or CDN$50. CJ can respectfully return the C$1 bus ticket to Manohar, no, to Avtar. To be fair, Manohar did give CJ the brass casting of a live-size tiger paw that has been hanging on a post of the dining pavilion. This shows Manohar's generosity and gratitude, not Avtar's, since the plaque does not require Manohar to come up with any money he does not have.

During afternoon tea for the tourists, a woman of about 60 looked at me and asked, "Are you a wildlife conservationist with WWF or something like that? I think I saw you on television while in Montreal recently."

"Something like that." I explained my position with WCWC and gave her a copy of my "business sheet". She dug out a pen and asked for my autograph.

Being tourist-oriented, Kim went out on both morning and afternoon safaris. She told me at one point that she "read" the "spiritual" (vs intellectual) side of my book (tape version), which she borrowed to take to Bandhavgarh to listen to. "Surprisingly good." I also gave a copy of the tape to CJ, telling him that I give my tape only to highly valued people. "I'm not going to change my mind about you," I said. Today, he typed his "long poem to Adriane" into my computer.

[00:22 (1999-02-25)]

Faiyaz came back around 19:45, and we (Faiyaz, Jane, CJ, Julian and I) went

Omni-Science and the Human Destiny

to Baihar to do several things:

- To order a vehicle to drive CJ to Gondia. Done.
- To phone Raman about the converter – that we need it, so get one in Delhi. We did get through. His response is that we should go and rent a slide projector from Balaghat instead. Even Manohar said this was ridiculous. Are we supposed to rent a projector for a whole month, when all that needrf to be done was for Raman to send me the right projector in the first place? He asked me to call him back tomorrow at 12:30. Forget that. What good would it do? It would just consume my time to get to a phone, and to get the call through, and to disrupt our use of the outreach vehicle when we get one. He also says that in the absence of Avtar he will send Sarita to monitor our progress. This sent me through the roof. WCWC is not sending our hard won CIDA money to Avtar to spend it on monitoring the work of a WCWC campaigner who is doing the work that Avtar himself should be doing. If Avtar wants to use Sarita, fine, send her to Bandhavgarh to do Tiger Fund field work, or send her to monitor himself for non-performance on the WCWC/TF contract.
- To attend to Bullet. Not done. The phone call to Raman, including numerous failed attempts, took up most of the time.
- To visit Jharia. Not done. Same reason.
- To get brick mason and tub and glass and frame. Not done. Same reason.

The last three "Not done"s also illustrate our deflated spirit which was zapped by the insincerity of Avtar and the incompetence of his yes-people in Delhi.

While in Baihar, there was a wedding ceremony going on in the street right where our Gypsy was parked when Manohar went into the phone café to attempt phone connection to Delhi. Well, guess what? We stole their show by just being there. Our Gypsy got surrounded by people, all looking up at us. Even the TV camera was trained on us, not on the wedding party. Jane, being the only woman in the Gypsy, and a white one in Western clothing at that, was slightly discomfited as usual when she finds herself being gawked at, which is about 100% of the time whenever she comes to town. She would not come to town alone.

We did do one thing unplanned. We went to visit Faiyaz's friend Vijay Chandra, who is the only judge in Baihar, again a very charming young man of no more than 35. Whether or not it was due to his prior knowledge of my being a wildlife conservationist, he put heavy emphasis on wildlife crime. Being himself a man of science, he showed us his thesis, in which he wrote: "Science without law is lame; law without science is blind." When Faiyaz asked him about the legality of my driving at Kanha, he said that it is illegal to drive with a Canadian license, but, he says, you can always do it "the Indian way" (i.e., to bribe), plus, the penalty for driving without a valid license is only Rs.100, C$4, less than the cost to get a temporary license. I wonder what the penalty against running over somebody while driving without a valid license would be. If it comes to suing somebody in court for damages, how much in rupee terms would they put on an average villager's life?

After we had alighted from the Gypsy at the parking lot of the lodge, while the others went back to the lodge-proper, I went to the conservation center to retrieve the atlas for a good look at the geography of India, particularly of Madhya Pradesh. When re-entering the parking lot I was struck by the rather surreal scene of not one, not two, not three, not four but five Gypsies crouching there, as if they were something alive, some prehistoric beasts sleeping in a forest glade in the moonlight.

Raminothna took the opportunity to cast me another pearl of her alien logic.
"Not as if."
"Pardon me?"
"I said 'Not as if.'"
"I still don't know what you mean."
"I mean that these Gypsies are really alive."
"No, they're not. They are just machines."
"The machines are themselves alive."
"I'll see how you can justify this one. Actually, the notion of cars behaving like animals and even talking like humans is not new. Cartoons have used talking cars for decades. There was even a cartoon I saw when I was a kid depicting aliens perceiving cars as animals and humans as their parasites. But these five Gypsies are not in a cartoon. This is not a cartoon," I again took in the ghostly moonlight scene. "This is real."
"Nonetheless, they are alive."
"Okay, I'll oblige by putting them through the Eight Vital functions, for your benefit. So, a Gypsy ingests fuel, inhales oxygen, exhales carbon dioxide, reacts to road hazards - if there is a driver - but it does not grow and it certainly does not reproduce. And of course it will not evolve, even if it sits here for a thousand years."
"How would you compare the total mass of road vehicles in India today to that of a century ago?"
"Total mass? Much greater today than a century ago, obviously."
"How about the total number of road vehicles?"

"Obviously many times more today than back then."

"And how would you compare the technology and styling of a road vehicle in India today to those of a road vehicle 100 years ago?"

"Technologically, much more advanced. Styling-wise, almost unrecognizable."

"Thus, growth, reproduction and evolution. A jeep is not an organism unto itself, but it is alive in the sense that it is an integral part of an organism called India."

"India is an organism? That's a staggering thought."

"Not if you put it in the context of your multileveled structure of life on Earth."

Good night, Christopher.

❖ ❖ ❖ ❖ ❖

February 25, 1999, Thursday, sunny, 15-28C

Dearest Christopher:

[21:06, @ Rm. 111, Kanha Tiger Lodge]

The first thing I did this morning was to write a letter to Avtar, which took me from 08:00 to noon, but well worth it. Then, with Jane, CJ and Kim sitting around me, and everyone else out on safari, I read it aloud to them. They all but cheered at the end.

It started by summarizing what we have been doing, culminating on the conference on March 23, followed by:

"It would of course be greatly beneficial if you could attend and be one of the key speakers. Our Big Cub, too, naturally.

"Now, perhaps you can appreciate my constant need of a slideshow projector here…

"I was also informed that you have plans to send Sarita out here to Kanha to 'monitor' the project. With all due respect to Sarita and her demonstrated efficiency, I consider her talents much better used to do aggressive campaigning to open up new awareness territory. As for me, I don't think that my work needs over-my-shoulder monitoring or point-by-point supervision by one of your employees, not to mention its being done with the grant money that we provide... It is true that I have designed this local project without your input, but it is not for want of trying on my part to contact you...

"Please bear in mind that other than the tiger, the park, the villagers and the government systems, what stands to benefit is also your organization Tiger Fund. If I may be so bold as to suggest, if Sarita really is not needed in Delhi, the way to maximize the use of her considerable talents would be to send her to Bandhavgarh to start a Tiger Fund project there with Darshan. In this way, the tigers as well as villagers in both Kanha and Bandhavgarh will benefit. I can appreciate your need to have proceedings here reported to you by someone loyal and trustworthy, in which case I think Manohar can more than adequately fulfill this role. If there is any monitoring to be done, WCWC should be the one doing the monitoring, not Tiger Fund. I will go as far as to say that to have a monitor before even the existence of a truly full time campaigner is to be top-heavy, to put the cart before the horse and a waste of CIDA money. If I perceive that our conference here needs more help from Delhi, Sarita would be the first person I would ask for. Meanwhile, the best way you can contribute to our project is to send us the required funds...

"Another observation is the lack of support of Tiger Fund activities at Kanha from Delhi. According to CIDA parameters, WCWC's Southern Partner needs to be a full time, dedicated NGO, not some part time organization subservient to another organization, let alone a commercial enterprise, even one concentrating on tiger-centered ecotourism. This is of particular significance to WCWC since WCWC does not even accept corporate donations as a rule. This means that Tiger Fund must have a full time, dedicated, field officer in charge of a full time, dedicated tiger conservation project, one fully equipped for the task, including a full time vehicle, and one not subject to the needs and wants and manipulations of an external, for-profit entity like Magnificent Tours...

"Finally, I cannot see how Tiger Fund could function meaningfully at Kanha without a 3-4 person full time campaign team, especially after Jane and I have left. Given the low Indian wage structure, it will not translate into a huge or even large expense, but the difference could be the survival or extinction of the Kanha tigers, and Kanha National Park itself.

"I hope that you will forgive me for being so candid with my opinion. I have tried to be as constructive as possible. The fact is that what Tiger Fund does or does not do does impact upon the performance and reputation of WCWC, especially in the eyes of CIDA, and ultimately upon the tiger of whose fate we are all passionately concerned."

So, the die is cast. The inevitable confrontation is forthcoming. What I've wanted to say for a long time has been said. I'll accept and deal with whatever consequences come my way. And they will.

And then, of course, when I go back to Vancouver, there will be a far greater and more bitter one awaiting me there, in which a small child is at stake, and where I will be fighting with one arm tied behind my back.

Originally I was going to have the letter loaded on to a floppy and taken to some computer place in Baihar to have the letter printed, then faxed to Delhi. But Manohar informed me that their computer format was different and it might not be doable. So, with his help, I had the floppy wrapped in card board and an envelope, and given to CJ to take to Delhi to give to Avtar in person, probably tomorrow night or the morning of the 27th.

In a lull between activities, I said to Raminothna, "I've been thinking about your 'artificial is natural', 'machines are alive' and other alien thoughts. They are challenges to conventional wisdom for sure. But from an objective view point, they do make sense."

"Nice to know."

"I've been thinking about India as an organism. It would take the Deep Blue computer to quantify everything involved. It's mind-boggling. But really, it is no more mind-boggling than trying to quantify the human body as an organism. Still, there is no denying it. India is as much a bona fide living organism as a termite mound, or you and me. I've done the same with Canada. I even looked at myself and Jane and Kim as body-cells of Canada that have been injected into the body of India, by the mutual consent of both nations. Or should I say national organisms? Right now as we speak, these transplanted Canadian body-cells are working with a native Indian body-cell named Faiyaz. The picture gets a bit complicated as I recalled that I was originally a body cell of China, which was then transplanted into Hong Kong, which eventually transplanted itself into Canada, with permission from Canada of course."

"Considering what you are here to do, I'd say that you are a socio-biological agent injected into this ailing national organism to fix some of it internal problems. You, in this case, are social medicine."

"And you, Raminothna, are planetary medicine for our whole ailing Earth."

[00:49]

The second group of panchayat members came at around 14:15. We first showed them the solar devices, then had our meeting in the conservation center, with Kim on the video cam.

Snack of vegetarian food prepared with the solar cooker at 15:45 and into the park by 16:10. At one point, we came across the Gypsy of Richards and a few tourists. Faiyaz called out to them, "Prominent Canadian conservationist driving Indian panchayat leaders!" Richards roared with laughter. I said to the villagers, "I may be a Canadian conservationist, but I'm not even a panchayat member." They roared with laughter, too.

Half way through the drive, the good times feeling had taken hold of the villagers in the rear deck of the Gypsy. Their stiffness was gone. They had taken to chatting quietly among themselves and with the park guide while pointing at this and that.

Back in the conservation centre, the slideshow visibly moved them. At the end, the most outspoken of them said to Faiyaz, "I cannot find the exact word to praise Mr. Marr, but I have never met anyone like him." When saying goodbye, he gave me a long and respectful two handed handshake.

Then over to the group of 20 American tourists. Manohar arranged to show the Champions video before dinner, with Richards doing the introduction, and the slideshow after dinner.

Jane and Faiyaz went to Baihar to pay for Bullet. Manohar refused to shell out the Rs.2200, so Jane paid Rs.1500 and Faiyaz the other Rs.700. They came back early enough to catch most of my slideshow. Jane said, "Your presentation gets better every time I hear it." Well, not exactly every time, but this time, I have to say, is very good, especially given that it was the second in a row.

After the slideshow, I observed that Faiyaz had sunken again into a dispirited state. We retired into Jane's room to talk. He held his head in his hands and said, "I don't know what I should do any more." I asked what the matter was. He dug out a letter he had just brought back from Baihar, which he had shown to Manohar.

Dated: 23 Feb., 1999
Kind Attn: Mr. Manohar Ghami / Kanha Tiger Lodge
From: Avtar Grewal

Dear Manohar,

During the stay of the Tiger's Kingdom group, instruct Faiyaz to look after the group only. Suggest the Tiger Fund activities should be suspended during the group's stay.

Also inform Delhi office of what all happened in last couple of days.

Regards,
Avtar

I fumed for a moment, then asked Faiyaz to make me a photocopy to bring back to Vancouver to show WCWC, and perhaps to show CIDA as well. CIDA is already questioning TF why all work stops during the monsoon season. Knowing Avtar's priorities, and given tourism's being dormant in the monsoon season, we shouldn't be surprised. In fact, Avtar spends the monsoon season in Vancouver. But of course CIDA doesn't know this, so it is up to me to show it to them, and I will.

Good night, Christopher.

❖ ❖ ❖ ❖ ❖

February 26, 1999, Friday, sunny, 15-29C

Dearest Christopher:

[19:54 @ Rm.111, Kanha Tiger Lodge]
    Because of that ugly letter from Avtar last night, and the state it put Faiyaz into, I was pulled into a shallow depression myself - a shallow depression in the great void from the removal of Christopher in my life - and had some trouble sleeping. While staring at the ceiling tiles in the darkened room, and not for the first time, I thought of just saying, "Fuck it!" and going back to Vancouver, but of course, that was just a thought. To do so would be to forsake Faiyaz in his dark hour, and to lose the trust of the villagers I have met, and to abandon the tigers when they need help most. I was furious with Avtar for more than one reason, not the least of which being tormenting and wasting a pure soul and open heart like Faiyaz.
    One of the staff remarked that if and when, after all the hard work and heartache, and in spite of Avtar's detachment and opposition, the conference becomes a big success, Avtar would jump right back in and claim the media and glory and credit for himself, and Faiyaz would be just buried. Faiyaz says that would not

bother him if it means a successful conference, but it bothers me.

Considering that the first few days of March will be unworkable due to the Holi festival, March 23rd seemed closer than ever, so much so that the conference may become ill-organized as a result. This led me to thinking of resetting the conference time to April or even May, after I have left. While I'm here, I'll do nothing but conduct these intimate small group meetings with the panchayat leaders. Then and only then would I have enough time to meet with each and everyone of the 178 Buffer Zone villages and the 22 East Core Zone villages.

One of the great worries of Faiyaz and Jane is that once I leave Kanha, all Tiger Fund activities will cease. So, enough momentum must be generated by the time I leave to carry the event to its proper conclusion.

It also happens that by then the tourist season would be over, and Avtar will be back in Vancouver, whatever this will mean.

So, first thing this morning, I discussed the plan with Faiyaz and Jane. Both objected to it, citing that too many government officials have been informed about March 23, and more importantly that the villagers will come to the conference largely because of me, and if they find that I have deserted them, they will be greatly disappointed. I argued that my intention is not to cultivate dependency in them on anyone but themselves, but Jane and Faiyaz would not have it. They said that I'm the "great new hope" of the villagers, who have been disappointed by unfulfilled promises far too often already.

Kim, who as usual listened in from the periphery, spoke up and said that she supported their argument. When I counter-argued that there is not enough manpower to organize a conference of this scope in such a short time, Kim offered herself quite strongly as a part of the team. I reminded her of what she once said, that she prefers dealing with tourists than villagers, she countered back with that the tourist season is ending, and she will switch back if/when the need arises.

Together, they said that I was the "glue" and "magnet" that hold the villagers together, and if I leave before the conference, the whole thing would fall apart. Never before have I pinned these labels to myself. It is a bit staggering. But perhaps they do have a point, especially when all three of them said the same thing. So, March 23rd it will remain.

The postponing idea was just that, an idea, but it brought out the strong feelings from Jane, Faiyaz and Kim, and I am grateful for these feelings

Today, being Friday, is another medical clinic day. While Faiyaz and Jane were busy with the patients, I had a long chat with Manohar. After some trust-building, we pretty well laid things on the table. He confessed that he had never thought much

Omni-Science and the Human Destiny

of the work Tiger Fund had done over the last few years. He considered it not tiger protection work, but "social work". His idea of tiger conservation work is to shoot poachers, pure and simple. He feels that work involving villagers would create a dependency in the people on NGO handouts. He went back to the point of giving the panchayat visitors inferior food, so as not to create an expectation in them for royal treatment here. I said that he was discriminating against his own people. In the end, he said that he was beginning to look at Tiger Fund work in good light for the first time, and said that he will help in organizing the conference.

He also self-disclosed some more on his feelings about Avtar. During lunch with everyone, he said that Avtar would pour effort into the conference if he has VIP guests and media present, but not if it is only a group of panchayat peasants. This is hardly surprising, but coming from Avtar's own nephew it carries extra meaning.

He also told me proudly about his grandfather Govinder Singh, who is the brother of Ravinder Grewal. Govinder deliberately shed the name Grewal because people saw him first and foremost as Ravinder's brother. He had his own laudable accomplishments. Once, with his bare hands, he saved a woman and her small son from a leopard that escaped from a zoo, resulting in many claw gashes all over his body. He subdued it by wrestling it "for an hour". But when finally the leopard was disabled due to exhaustion, a cop came and shot it, about which Govinder was furious, since he was himself armed with a hand gun, but elected not to use it. He also created a huge walk-in aviary.

We then went on to discussing poaching. Manohar and Faiyaz both opine that the Kanha tigers are relatively secure, and that the Kanha park service and forest officials are relatively sincere and honest. But not so Bandhavgarh. They cited incidents where maharajas are allowed into the park to poach deer and other animals, that as we speak, there may be poachers staying in at least two of the lodges, and that certain park personnel themselves also indulge, including certain mahouts, and politicians. There have been cases where honest park personnel who exposed such cases have lost their jobs. One case has it that a raja poached a deer whose leg was protruding from under a tarp in the back of a Gypsy, and the guard at the exit of the park asked the raja to push the leg back under the tarp. This needs to be exposed to the world, and Bandhavgarh needs a Tiger Fund program badly, but not one of Avtar's design, thank you very much – sigh, only if Ravinder were still alive.

The tourists left today, headed towards Kaziranga. I made a few friends among them. There were David and Barbara Waddell, both Canadians residing in Ancaster, Ontario. David is an emeritus entomologist at the University of Victoria in

BC, and Barbara is an associate professor of kinesiology and biomechanics. David, who is 82 years of age, went around the lodge grounds showing me insects, especially a species of termites that live on the trunks of living trees. Barbara is 66, and showed a lot of personal warmth towards me, and took souvenir photos of me, and insisted that I go visit them when I go to Ontario. There were also a few people who came to congratulate me, one saying that my slideshow was "inspirational".

And then there was the woman who had seen me on TV in Montreal. And then there was Barry Strachen, a South African man of about 60 with a young woman as a companion. His daughter? Mistress? A couple of days ago I was sitting with Kim when I asked, "Who is that attractive blonde over there?" So yesterday, when I was concluding my slideshow, and dinner was being laid out for the few of us, I said, "I would like to entertain your questions while having dinner with you, David, or Barbara," and, jokingly, "or the attractive blonde over there." They all laughed, except Barry, who complained to Kim about the comment. So this morning, I went to their room and said to Barry, "I wish to extend to you my sincere apology for the comment I made about your friend. I did not mean to be disrespectful." He extended his hand quite eagerly and patted me on the shoulder warmly, saying, "It is I who should apologize. I entirely mistook your intention. I lost some sleep over that last night. I would like to make a donation to your campaign. Unfortunately, I have no money on me. But I will give a cheque to Avtar when I see him. I will also recommend your slideshow to him to make it a standard feature of his lodge offering."

Later, Kim told me that while I was in Jane's room discussing postponing the conference to April or May, Barry was looking for me all over camp. "Here is his card. He was bending over backwards to ask you to send him a copy of the Champions of the Wild."

This afternoon's safari was free, the tourists having paid for the whole day. We (Manohar, Jane, Kim, Julian and I) decided to take the afternoon off work and all go into the park. I loaded my camera bag with new film rolls and video tapes. Yet another rare sighting of three wild dogs stalking and dashing after chital. But my peak moment was when we stopped the Gypsy at the park gate upon our exit.

Throughout the drive I was feeling a great misgiving about our species. "If even the head of a group called Tiger Fund is so insincere and untrustworthy, what hope has the tiger? If even a mother would do something so hideous to her own infant son, and if the law would side with her in this case, what kind of a civilization have we? Just where are we in the scheme of things? Raminothna, show me a sign."

And she did show me a sign. It was the one standing at the gate to Kanha national Park, a sign I have seen numerous times before. It says, "The animals and plants in this park are fully protected. Violators will be prosecuted by law."

"Homo Sapiens, your glass is half-full, or half-empty, depending on *your* point of view. In biblical terms, your species has ascended half way from Eden to Heaven at last. Not a bad sign"

"What do you mean?"

"That after all your reforms and revolutions you have advanced some very good laws, but are not yet advanced enough to govern yourself without law."

"What other than law can we govern ourselves by?"

"Morals. Ethics. Conscience. Most of all, love."

When we got back to camp, Faiyaz handed Jane a fax delivered to the TF conservation centre by someone from the District Collectorate (Manu Srivastava's office) inviting her to go to Seoni as a speaker at the women's issues conference. This propelled Jane into a state of euphoria, partly because she was a little disappointed earlier by the lack of the promised fax and had given up on going to the conference. She will leave the lodge at 05:00 tomorrow.

Since Jane will be unavailable for the meeting with the panchayat people tomorrow, I asked Kim and Julian whether they would like to help out. Kim and Julian were discussing who to do what, between taking notes and video documenting the meeting. Julian said, "I'll do whatever Kim doesn't." Manohar chipped in, "She doesn't sleep with him," meaning me. They all erupted with laughter, especially since it is common knowledge that Julian is gay.

Nice to have a good laugh once in awhile, as we used to do. We did laugh a lot together, didn't we? Good night, Christopher.

❖   ❖   ❖   ❖   ❖

February 27, 1999, Saturday, sunny with clouds, 15-28C

Dearest Christopher:

[21:59 @ Rm.111, Kanha Jungle Lodge]

This morning I got up at 04:30 to make sure that Jane would get on her way to Seoni for the woman's issues conference on time, and to see her off. Within minutes, Faiyaz and Manohar both appeared. She left at 05:30, with Manohar accompanying her in the Tata Sumo driven by our usual Sumo driver who also drove CJ to Gondia.

Jane is still not back. Manohar and Faiyaz are sitting at a dinner table, planning on driving to Baihar to perhaps call Balaghat to see what is going on. I'm not beginning to worry yet. You may think that we worry too much, but if you've experienced Indian highway traffic, you'd understand.

At 10:00, while Faiyaz was out visiting villages with Surinder, the carpenter came and, with the very limited translation help of Ramjit, I conveyed to him (I hope) what I wanted done, which is a wooden frame for the double-glass lid of the large communal solar oven.

Manohar was supposed to stay with Jane all day, but he returned around noon, looking not well and feeling maybe worse. He said he threw up several times in the course of the morning. He went straight to bed.

As usual, I put on the rice into the solar oven around 12:30. Around 13:00, I went to the schoolhouse to prepare the place. When I was about finished, Faiyaz's Gypsy with Surinder at the wheel pulled into the parking lot, with 7 panchayat people on board. It was about 13:15 – they were 45 minutes early. Still in my shorts, I was not exactly properly attired for a conservationist-panchayat summit. Faiyaz explained for me, and the villagers said no problem. I went to get Kim and Julian, both being also in their shorts. Kim wrapped a cloth around her waist like a sarong, which went down to her ankles. In the absence of Jane, I asked Kim to take notes and Julian to man the video cam.

The meeting went about the same way as the first two, and the villagers' concerns were also about the same, which made clearer and clearer that a multi-panchayat conference will be extremely resonant and powerful. The emphasis of this group was irrigation.

Since there were seven villagers, we needed two Gypsies for the park drive, so I drove one and Julian drove the other, and we had room enough for 3 Manjitola village children. Sightings included the usually chital, barasingha, sambar, but no tiger. At one point, while rounding a curve, we came face to face with a huge gaur bull in full fighting trim standing right in the middle of the road, facing us, four-square, snorting, legs stomping in the dirt, raising a cloud of dust in the slanting streaks of morning sunlight. It looked as if he was trying to pick a fight with the Gypsy which, if he charged, would not stand a chance. This struck me as being more the normal behavior of an African cape buffalo than the more peaceable Indian gaur. Manohar deemed it prudent to back off, but upon looking behind us, we found another bull, same size, same stance, same apparent ill intent. It seemed that we got right in the middle of a rutting battle between two contending top bulls, meaning, two of the largest bovines ever evolved. Even a big male tiger would have to slink away under such circumstances. All we could do was to pull over to the side of the road and let them get at it, quite prepared to take some collateral damage. Thankfully, they moved off the road to duke it out in the thickets. Still, the sounds they made were awe-inspiring.

This and other sightings set the panchayat members in the proper mood for the slideshow and for some serious post-show discussion. All in all, another successful meeting, and the number of villages that signed up for the conference went up to 33.

"It seems that your social medicine is already doing some healing."

"I hope so. And on more levels than one, it seems to me."

"For instance?"

"I can think of one or two examples right now. If our work changes cooking from wood-burning to solar around the tiger reserves, it would reduce air pollution, which would be on the Molecular level. It would preserve India's forests and wildlife - on the Metabion level. It would also protect the termite mounds as well as change the villagers' way of life and economy – on the Tribal level. It could generate new industries such as solar-cooker manufacturing on the Citian level. And our petition to reform the park system would be to reform India itself on the National Level. And of course, if we help save the tiger and thus preserve an important component of the global environment, it would be a monumental contribution on the Planetary level. It does seem that there are interlevel influences at work all around us. Pluck one strand of this multileveled 3D web of life on any level, and the whole web vibrates."

Later this evening, I pondered, "Is there really a Tribal level? The more I think about it, the more it strikes me that the termite mound, the village, and town and the city should all be on the same level of organization."

"Why?"

"For one thing, if we put the village and the city on two distinct levels, where do we put the towns?"

"Good point. Anything else?"

"The tribal village, the town and the city are all physically coherent entities. Each has a clearly defined nucleus, namely, the city/town/village centers. Their basic units are human beings, who are metabionts, as opposed to the nation, say, whose basic units are the villages, towns and cities."

"There seems a huge disparity in size and complexity between

Chichrunpur and New Delhi. Draw an interlevel parallel in support of your thinking."

"Well, a microscopic nematode worm and a blue whale are both metabionts, even though it is obvious that the whale is almost astronomically larger and more complex than the worm."

"Are there other reasons?"

"Yes. I've been thinking, if the city and the village are on two distinct levels, then the rise of the Citian level would not occur until the rise of the first city about 10,000 years ago. But then, almost as soon as the first city arose, the nation arose. This makes no sense. If, on the other hand, we put all the villages and towns and cities on the same level, then the rise of the Citian level would be when the social insects built their first society, which was some 100 million years ago. In this scenario, the city – the basic units of the nation - would be the pinnacle of Citian level achievement. Therefore, once the cities were formed, the nations arose very shortly afterwards. This makes much more sense to me. So, I am inclined to thinks that the Tribal and Citian levels are one and the same."

"So, which name will you settle for?"

"The Citian Level, in which case I'm calling a termite mound a 'termite city'."

"I'm sure the termites have no problem with that."

Good night, Christopher.

❖ ❖ ❖ ❖ ❖

February 28, 1999, Sunday, sunny with clouds, 16-30C

Dearest Christopher:

[18:49 @ Rm.111, Kanha Tiger Lodge]
Today is a day of forced rest. The following few days will be likewise, unless we can find something constructive to do around here. Even the park will be closed in the mornings till March 4th. It is that infamous drinking festival during which period we have been forewarned to stay in the lodge. Even if we go out in our vehicles, let alone on foot, we'd likely be pelted with various colored liquids and solids, including bottles.

Omni-Science and the Human Destiny

Much to everyone's delight, I announced that we'd go out to the park for a long drive tomorrow afternoon, purely for pleasure this time. We'll be going in two vehicles, one driven by me with Faiyaz, Jane and four Manjitola children on board, and the other by Manohar or Julian with Kim and five others on board. Around 17:45, I went to the school and organized a lot-picking to choose the four lucky kids. I asked, via Faiyaz, to have the kids show their hands as to who have never been in the park before. Of the 14, 7 raised their hands. I asked the 7 kids to write their names on a piece paper, folded the 7 little slips, and asked one of the girls, named Asha, who reminds me of a tiny dark skinned Lucienne (my ballet teacher), to pick the lot. Unfortunately, she did not pick herself, but I promised the unlucky 3 that I will take them into the park some time before I leave.

Back at the lodge, Manohar told us that Avtar will be in camp March 6 or so. Manohar is again cramming paper work in which he seems to be perpetually behind, and doesn't look very happy. This morning, I invited him to read my letter to Avtar. About half an hour after that, Faiyaz, Manohar and I had a meeting about the conference. Manohar showed a new level of enthusiasm and involvement in the event that I hadn't seen before.

Jane spent some time analyzing her speech yesterday at the women's issues conference, which she told me was attended by a surprising number of men, and that men appeared as speakers as well - as experts on women's issues! She felt that her speech may not have pleased Mrs. Srivastava, police chief and the organizer, saying that it was likely "not what she expected of me". She said that almost all the speeches were highly formal and academic, whereas hers, near the end of the conference, was much more informal, personal and colloquial. And she was airing this concern to one who never uses notes in his speeches - me. I said that she need not worry about it, that it was probably like a breath of fresh air in a stuffy room.

[00:38]
Just back to my room after a long discussion with Manohar about Tiger Fund. Manohar quite openly stated that what Tiger Fund had done up to my arrival one month ago was a joke, and that the staff used to laugh at it whenever the term "conservation program" was mentioned. I can't disagree.

"Just sitting here handing out pills to two or three villages isn't going to save any tigers," he said in some contempt.

My own point exactly.

He is still unconvinced that solar cookers can save tiger habitat, but he seems open to this possibility, and somewhat convinced that what we (I, Faiyaz, Jane) are doing now is a radical departure which may make a real difference. Finally, he said, "I have never met any living tiger conservationists as hard-working as you, and if these technologies can work socially as you believe they can, you will succeed. You will be as big as Valmiki (Valmik Thapar)."

Now here is a truly humbling compliment.

Back in the meditation chamber of my lodge room, "Raminothna, a few straggling questions if I may."

"Shoot."

"One. If a metabiont (multicellular organism) is a society of cells, what is a cell a society of?"

"What do you think?"

"Molecules? A cell is a society of social molecules?"

"Go on."

"If so, the level below the Cellular level would be the Molecular level of organization."

"Go on."

"And on the Molecular Level, as on all other levels, there are nonsocial and social molecules."

"Give me a few examples of nonsocial molecules."

"A water molecule in the ocean, a carbon dioxide molecule in the air, a calcium carbonate molecule in a rock."

"And a few examples of social molecules."

"Carbohydrates, proteins, enzymes, RNA, DNA…, and also those water molecules, carbon dioxide molecules and calcium carbonate molecules that participate in the functioning of the cell."

"You have the general picture."

"Question 2. So, a city is a society of social villages?"

"By definition, yes."

"What are social villages?"

"Specialized villages that cooperate with other specialized villages to make up the city."

"What is a specialized village?"

"What do you think?"

"A company? A business? A corporation?"

"All of the above, which are integral parts of cities.'"

"I see. So, the villages have given up their independence and even identities for participation in a great whole?"

293

"You might say that."

" Question 3. What is the level of organization above the National level?"

"What do you think?"

"The Planetary level?"

"There is no Planetary level per se, but you might call a planet with only one nation a Planetary Organism."

"A planet with only one nation? That'll be the day. Sounds like an impossibility."

"The Universe is suffused with miracles."

"But how could this happen? There are over 200 nations on Earth today. How could 200 become one?"

"There are two alternatives. But only one can work."

"Let me guess. The first alternative is for one nation to conquer all the rest? As in the Warring States in ancient China?"

"That did not work well for China, and, given the nuclear weapons, it cannot work today."

"Then the second alternative is for the nations to merge into a single supernation?"

"Take it or leave it. But it's happened times before, and it will happen again, on some planet. Hopefully, Earth will be one of them."

"Happened before? When? Where?"

"Here, there, and everywhere." Raminothna waved her spiritual hands at the stars.

"Here?"

"It could have."

"Where?"

"Where your first cities arose."

"The 'cradle of civilization. In Mesopotamia. Modern Iraq."

"Open the Atlas to that page."

First, I had to grope my way again through the forest in the dark to the school house. Anyone observing my behavior must find it strange or even suspicious. Finally, the Atlas lay open on my table, with a cup of chai steaming next to it.

"So, back to your question. How did it happen? Let's run a little thought experiment, shall we? First, tell me how you think it happened."

"I would guess that there were a number of tribal cultures in the region then, and it just happened that one of them blossomed into a full-scale city state."

"Just happened?"

"Well, of course they would have to work on it."
"Who are 'they'?"
"The villagers of this village, or tribe."
"And the other villages or tribes?"
"I guess they just didn't make it, or got wiped out by the emergent city state."
"Is this what the current theory holds?"
"Frankly, I don't know. Just a minute. You're not saying that many villages merged to form the first city, are you?"
"What do you think?"
"How many villages did it take?"
"How many lived in the then Persian Gulf. Hundreds, perhaps well over a thousand."
"Let me make this clear for myself. Are you saying that over a thousand villages pulled up their roots about 10,000 years ago, moved together in one place, and collectively formed the first city?"
"In the context of this thought experiment, something like that."
"What on Earth could have made them do that?"
"Something geological. The most major geological event of the time. Something that even the Bible mentioned."
"The Bible? A geological event? What? The flood?"
"If there was a flood, what caused it?"
"The Bible says heavy rains."
"Heavy rains? In the Middle East?"
"It used to be wet back then, I recall reading from somewhere. And shortly before that, the ice age ended. Does this have anything to do with it?"
"It might have everything to do with it. What you do know about the ice age?"
"Over the last million years, there were five ice ages. The last one, which started about 100,000 years ago and ended about 11,500 years ago, was the longest and coldest, and perhaps the only one in which the modern form of our species existed."
"So, it ended 11,500 years ago, and less than 2,000 years after that, the first city arose, with huge stonewalls that survived to this day?"
"It does seem a little more than just a coincidence."
"What role do you think the ending of the Ice Age played in the rise of the first city?"
"I have no idea. I've never thought about it."
"But you do know something about what happened when the Ice Age

ended?"

"Only physical things, such as global warming, polar ice caps melting and shrinking, sea level rising, vegetation changing, things like that. Nothing cultural."

"Sea level rising?"

"You mean – the flood?"

"What do you know about changes in the sea level?"

"Well, I've read that the sea level dropped about 120 or even 150 meters from today's level during the Ice Age, that is from 360 t almost 500 feet."

"For how long?"

"Thousands or tens of thousands of years in a stretch."

"What would it be like in the Persian Gulf?"

"I would say that any continental shelf shallower than 120 meters deep today would be exposed to dry air during the Ice Age, perhaps over an extended period of time, thousands of years."

It didn't take me long to pin point four major shelves – 1. the one east of China currently under the East China Sea and the Yellow Sea which if exposed would link China to Taiwan and even Japan, 2. the one surrounded by Vietnam, Cambodia, Thailand, Malaysia, Sumatra and Borneo, 3. the one between Papua New Guinea and Australia, and 4. the one currently submerged under the Persian Gulf. There are no other major shelves elsewhere in the world.

"The continents looked very different from the way they look today, that's for sure, especially Asia and the Middle East."

"Go on."

"I see the Yellow River – Huang Ho - greatly extended, by as much as 1,500 kilometers, not reaching the Pacific Ocean until almost Japan."

"And?"

"No great rivers for shelves 2 and 3, but through the entire length of the 'Persian Gulf Shelf' would have flowed the thousand kilometer extension of the merged Tigris-Euphrates, all the way past the present day Straight of Hormuz, into the Gulf of Oman."

"And if the climate was wet?"

"If. There would be lush vegetation, forests, wetlands, grassland… on all four shelves."

"And?"

"And animals."

"And?"

"And humans!"

"And?"
"And human tribal cultures."
"And was the climate wet?"
"I don't know about everywhere else, but I remember reading about the Sahara desert being full of lakes as recently as 16,000-8,000 years ago, and there is geological evidence in support of that. Near enough to the Persian Gulf region to say that the Persian Gulf region was probably lush and green. I believe the Middle East was a green corridor between Africa and India. Thus, the Asiatic lion and cheetah, and the Caspian tiger. Unfortunately, as we know, two out of these three are now extinct, and the last 300 Asiatic lions in India have been inextricably cut off from their African cousins. So, yes, it was wet there once."

"Let's concentrate on the Persian Gulf shelf for now. What do you think would be the total human population on it back then?"

"I think I'm finally beginning to see what you're driving at. If it is what I think it is, it's very interesting. Fascinating in fact. But, okay, let's approach it one step at a time. So, the Persian Gulf. It is, let's see, about 1,000 km long and an average of about 250 km wide, or about 250,000 sq. km. in area. Its maximum depth is 90 meters, and its average depth is 50 meters, meaning that indeed it would be exposed to the air in its entirety. So the questions are: How many tribes lived on it? What was the average population per tribe? We can use Kanha's Buffer Zone for comparison. Its area is about 1,000 sq. km.. It has 178 villages, each with an average of 500 villagers, giving it a total human population of about 90,000, or 90 per sq. km.. So if the Persian Gulf shelf had the same human density, it would have 53,400 tribal villages, and a total human population of over 26 million. This is obviously way too high, the reasons being that India is intensely agrarian, whereas the tribal cultures back 12,000 years ago were largely hunter-gatherer with only the earliest forms of agriculture. India is of course also one of the densest populated places on Earth today. Another model is the Amazon Basin. Its area is about 7 million sq. km.. Its original native population, before the arrival of Europeans, is estimated to be about 3 million. So its original population density was about 1 person per two sq. km.. So at the same population density, the Persian Gulf shelf would have a total human population of about 125,000. If some of the tribal cultures had developed agriculture at that point, and there is evidence of that, such as grain cultivation, the population density should be higher, say two every sq. km., giving it a total population of 500,000. Considering an average population of 250 per tribe, there would be about 2,000 tribal cultures back then."

"Accepting these figures for now, what then?"

"Then, around 11,500 years ago, the Ice Age ended. The sea level rose and the Persian Gulf shelf was again submerged. If I recall correctly, the process didn't take place overnight, but over a number of years, which would allow enough time for the people to pack up and retreat before the rising tide. So drowning would not be a factor of mortality. The result would be a mass exodus up the Persian Gulf basin on to the upper Tigris-Euphrates valley, what was later called Mesopotamia. I can see a population compression wave sweeping up the valley, until it finally was blocked by the mountains of Turkey and the Mediterranean Sea."

"Can you quantify this compression wave?"

"Well, by the look of it, Mesopotamia is about the same size as the Persian Gulf, which means that the population there would have doubled in just a very few years, by none other than a mass influx of refugees. There would be a huge amount of forced interactions, that's for sure. Is this is what you're driving at?"

"Partly."

"What's the other part?"

"Taking your figure of 2,000 tribes – what would they be like?"

"That's a very broad question."

"Would they, for example, be mobile or sedentary?"

"As far as I know, the domestication of the camel didn't happen until about 3,500 BC, and the horse even later than that, I'd say that the people weren't very mobile. And since the climate in the region stayed wet until about 10,000 years ago, there would be little impetus for the cultures to be nomadic. And budding agriculture would certainly serve to anchor a tribe to one place. So I venture to say more sedentary than nomadic."

"Would these cultures be alike or different?"

"I'd say both. But given their lack of mobility, and therefore lack of communication, they would have evolved divergently in terms of sociality and technology. So, socially and technologically speaking, they would essentially be similar, but differ from each other to various extents in detail."

"And collectively?"

"Collectively? You mean the 2,000 tribes in total? I would say that they would cover a broad range of social and technological innovations."

"So, if population compression is one side of the coin, what is on the other side?"

"Well, you're talking about divergent cultural evolution. So, when the tribes were forced together, there would be a lot of cultural mixing and amalgamation. It does seem that population compression and cultural amalgamation combined would be a very powerful force towards fusing tribal cultures into a single civilization. And I would think much the same occurred in China."

"Yes, China. The rise of civilization in China lagged behind that in Mesopotamia by a few thousand years. Why's that?"

"I think it is due to a softer compression, because the Yellow River is much longer than the Tigris-Euphrates, and there was no barrier along the Yellow river to block the compression wave, and thus less of a compression shock."

"And the shelves in South East Asia and Australia?"

"These shelves were wide open, and there would be no channeled compression as in the cases of the Persian Gulf and China."

"And how about the native American civilizations such as the Aztec, the Inca and the Maya? As you can see on the map, there are no major shelves to expose. So how did these civilizations originate?"

"I think that the population compression and cultural amalgamation combination is a central criterion, so other mechanisms than the sea-level rise had to come in play to make it happen."

"And what could it be?"

"Well, one way or another, it would require human movement. It would be a convergent migration of a large range of tribes. So, what could have caused that?"

I again consulted the Atlas, this time a double page showing the United States, Mexico and Central America.

Within one minute I said, "It is plain as daylight. The key is in the shape of the land. First, about 20,000 years ago, the native American precursors crossed over from Asia via the Bering land-bridge which was also exposed during the Ice Age. Canada was then completely covered in ice sheets miles thick, except for an ice-free corridor along the Canadian Rockies through which the new migrants moved into the land now occupied by the U.S. There they dispersed widely and divergently evolved into a range of tribal cultures. Then, especially after the saturation point had been reached, they would tend to migrate further southward, and the only place to go was funnel-shaped Mexico. Thus, population compression and cultural amalgamation, exactly where civilization arose. This would also be a much more gradual process, which explains the lateness of the rise of these civilizations." By now, I was stoked.

"Now look at your world today, my friend. It is like a pressure cooker, isn't it? By this same theoretical means of the tribes merging to form the first city, it could well be the way by which the nations today will merge to form the global nation – the Planetary organism."

Omni-Science and the Human Destiny

"Is this what you've been driving at all along?"

"Just using a potential past to illustrate a potential future."

"So, just like the tribal lines dissolved when the tribes merged into the first city, would the national lines also dissolve when the nations merge into the global nation?"

"Possibly, but not necessarily. It could be the United Nations, as long as, first of all we call the United Nations an 'it', not a 'they', just as we call the United States an 'it' and not a 'they'. And, yes, as long as the nations are as harmonious with each other within the United Nations as the states are with each other within the United States."

"Now, this I can believe, and accept. And it sounds achievable within a relatively short time frame."

After a sip of chai, I asked, "So, did civilization really arise this way?"

"My point is made. So, it doesn't matter. But if you're interested, the only way to be sure would be to seek evidence for *and* against it, and see which side wins out."

"This is exciting stuff.'

"More than you think."

"What do you mean?"

"Some time in your future, when you live in and explore interstellar space, you will encounter planets in the middle of ice ages. On some of these planets, there would be intelligent but still tribal creatures. If you know the geology of these planets well enough, you might be able to predict where and when civilization would arise. Would not this be an achievement of biblical proportions?"

I closed the atlas and gathered my day's thoughts. They culminated in the following diagram:

The 6 levels of organization of the planet Earth so far

                                                                      social nations

                    National Level of Organization

    nonsocial nations

                                                                     social cities

                     Citian Level of Organization

    nonsocial cities

                                                                   social metabionts

Anthony Marr

                     Metabion Level of Organization
nonsocial metabionts
                                                                   social cells
                      Cellular Level of Organization
nonsocial cells
                                                        social molecules
                      Molecular Level of Organization
nonsocial molecules
                                      "social" sub-atomic particles
                  Sub-Atomic Level of Organization
nonsocial sub-atomic particles

    While working on the diagram, I added one level below the Molecular level – the Sub-Atomic level of organization, because within the bounds of the Earth does exist nonsocial (free) sub-atomic particles, raising the total number of levels from 7 to 8. Of course all atoms and molecules are composed of "social" sub-atomic particles.

    Where does the atom belong? For the moment, I'm treating the atom as a molecule with a single nucleus. In the context of the above diagram, an atom would be under nonsocial "molecules".

    Corporations, as touched upon before, are considered "social tribes", even if they are large multinational corporations.

    States and provinces of nations are slightly problematic. For the moment, I consider them "nations within nations". Further, within each living system are sub-systems and micro-systems. A U.S. state like California, for example, is larger and richer than, say, Switzerland or Luxembourg which are national organisms on the same level as the U.S. itself.

    Again, within this 6-leveled framework, all things of Earth are accounted for, and each has a meaningful place – even, for example, the despised mosquitoes, which are nonsocial metabionts, whose ecological role is to serve as food for fish and birds.

    The above is the cosmic structure of planet Earth. Now, we seek the process that continuously builds its structure and drives its dynamics. The process by which organisms of Level [X] become social and build societies of themselves I call **Transcendent Integration**. The process by which societies of level [X] become Level [X+1] organisms by means of transcendent integration I call **Integrative Transcendence**. E.g., "Over millions of years, certain nonsocial cellular organisms evolved into social cellular organisms, which then transcendently integrated themselves into cellular societies, which then integratively transcended into being the first metabion organisms."

The two do have slightly different meanings. Transcendent Integration is more of a mechanism, whereas Integrative Transcendence is more of the essence and the aim and the result of the process. But by using them interchangeably, one would not go too far wrong.

"You are now ready to consider interlevel parallelism. Congratulations," said Raminothna.

I will have a little celebration for this tomorrow, but I finish tonight by thinking about you and sending you all my love. Good night, Christopher.

❖   ❖   ❖   ❖   ❖

March 1, 1999, Monday, sunny, 16-30C

Dearest Christopher:

[19:29 @ Rm.111, Kanha Tiger Lodge]
Another day of heavenly rest, the second of two or three forced rest-days. We took maximum refuge in the park, and in the deep past. The park gate was the portal of a time machine through which we entered a world indistinguishable from that a million years ago - life before man when tigers truly ruled - except for the twin-rutted park road stretching before and behind us. We soaked ourselves in the magnificence of Kanha in both the morning and afternoon safaris. I stuffed my camera pack full of cameras, films and video cassettes.

The morning visit, 07:00-12:00 was in two Gypsies, I at the wheel of the new one and Julian the old one. In my Gypsy were Kim and 6 Manjitola children, and in the other were Faiyaz, Jane, and another 4 kids. We could have all fitted into one Gypsy without the children, but I asked myself, "If Christopher were born one of these village children, could I leave him behind?" Besides, they are the tiger's future. Gate cost was RS.800 (C$34) for all – absolutely best value for anything anywhere. We drove up to the plateau, elevation change 820 m (2700 ft.). The ascent and descent took us through different belts of vegetation unseen in the lower elevations.

I've noticed before that the Kanha people, Manohar included, and even Faiyaz, are somewhat nonplussed by my praising the beauty of Ranthambhore. Now, submerged in Kanha's overflowing glory and beauty hitherto unseen, I was captivated anew, and suddenly, Ranthambhore and Bandhavgarh seemed very far away.

And the children? You have to see their faces and hear their voices to appreciate what I'm saying. They were in their own "Kindergarten of Eden". Another analogy would have it that the park drive was their yellow brick road, and the park is the Emerald City, and perhaps I was the Wizard of Oz himself. One of them could have said in Hindi, "I have a feeling we're not in Manjitola any more." Even though they lived right on the edge of the park, they had never seen anything like what they were seeing today. Kanha and Manjitola, though but two kilometers from each other, are worlds apart. No goats or cows here. This place is populated by creatures that do not need to be unreal to be magical. No unicorns or dragons or griffons required; tigers and elephants and gaurs are mythical enough, thank you very much. And wonder of wonders, no people anywhere in sight except their little buddies and the friendly park guide, the kindly teacher Faiyaz and the light-skinned, long haired and enigmatic "Tiger Uncle" from across the oceans doing that miraculous thing – driving this fantastic growling iron beast called a Gypsy. Speaking of oceans, the closest thing to an ocean that they had seen was the little pond behind their village, until now, lo and behold, this amazing body of water I would call a small lake became for them a sea.

And one thing the children would never guess in a million years. Even though they consider themselves strangers and outsiders to the park, but in my eyes, these children are very much part and parcel of the Kanha in my mind, and certainly an integral part of my Kanha experience. These children too are my magical creatures.

And again, Christopher, for the thousandth times today, I wish you were here. You are the most magical creature of all.

While the children were having a time of their lives, Faiyaz gave them an educational running commentary like nothing they've ever had, nor will likely have again. Mid-morning, we brunched at one of the huts of one of the hundred and fifty or so park guards who live in the park. I would love to live here for a year, even during the monsoon, to experience the park intimately and know all her moods, to have the tiger walk right up to my door. I would love to live here with Christopher for a year, and teach him everything I know about anthropology, astronomy, biology, chemistry, ecology, geography, geology, philosophy, physics, psychology and sociology, and about integrative transcendence.

I should make a note here that none of my friends and colleagues in India knows anything about Christopher's tragedy. Most know about him, since I talked about him with ebullience a number of times before the tragedy descended. After that, I had made no mention. In fact, my not mentioning him may be the telltale sign that something *is* wrong. There were a few times when I verged on losing it, and I noticed expressions on their faces of their having registered my distress, but they have probably assigned its cause to Avtar. I dread the time when Jane or Kim or Faiyaz would ask the direct question "How is Christopher?" Should I just give an unconvincing "fine," or would I spill the beans?

I have so wanted to talk to someone about it, anyone who would listen, anyone who could give me some sympathy, a real person, that is, not Raminothna. Especially Jane – the cool, cerebral, analytical lawyer. But doing so, I fear, would affect our working relationship. I certainly do not want to openly discuss it with just anyone. I certainly don't want it to be the talk of the camp.

So, again, I turned to Raminothna and the cosmic realm, and the amazing concept of integrative transcendence. While the Gypsy was bumping along in second gear and my intellectual mind was in neutral, Raminothna quietly opened a new chapter in my inquiry. She challenged me to name the first interlevel parallelism.

"First, tell me what 'interlevel parallelism' means," I asked her, although the term is not exactly cryptic.

"There exist certain essential properties of a certain level of organization that also exist in parallel on all other levels of organization."

"So, these interlevel parallelisms could be of predictive value?"

"Exactly. They lend insight to understanding those levels of organization with which we are less familiar, and those that are in the process of unfolding, and even those that have not yet arisen."

"So, what are they?"

"I could lead off with the first interlevel parallelism - Integrative Transcendence itself, which occurs on all levels."

"Yes, I see. Integrative transcendence does occur and has occurred on all levels beneath the National level. So, it is reasonable to predict that it too will occur, and has been occurring, on the National level as well. It is reasonable to state that transcendent integration amongst the nations is the true way to world harmony and peace on Earth."

"So now, could you name the rest?"

"Okay. How about this: An organism on a certain level is an integratively transcended society of the level below."

"Good. And another?"

"How about this: Societies on all levels work on the cooperation-of-specialized-parts principle."

"Good. And another?"

"On all levels are nonsocial and social forms, and any combination in between. There are 'nonsocial and social molecules', nonsocial and social cells, nonsocial and social metabionts, nonsocial and social cities, and nonsocial and social nations. And there may even eventually be nonsocial and social planetary organisms."

"In the Universe, potentially billions of billions, amongst which the Earth is not yet one."

"If not yet, when?"

"When your nations have transcendently integrated themselves. Have they?"

"No, can't say that they have."

"I hope that Earth will one day integratively transcend, if only for the sake of Homo Sapiens."

"For me, if only for the sake of Christopher."

"Yes. For the sake of Christopher for me too." I felt Raminothna's sadness, but she moved on. **"Any more interlevel parallelism you can think of?"**

"Well, I recall the Lions Gate Bridge back in Vancouver. Once I was driving on it, edging past an auto-accident, which totaled two cars and damaged the bridge railing. The week after, I drove past the same spot, and noticed that the railing had been repaired. I now see it as the Citian organism called Vancouver healing itself."

"Very nice. And another?"

"Hm. How about this? When I was physically assaulted last year, I sustained damage on my face. So, I was wounded on the metabion level. And since millions of cells also died, you might say that my cellular citizens suffered hundreds of thousands of casualties in the "war" with another cellular society. Also, I noticed that my assailant's knuckles were bleeding. So, that cellular society's "military" took casualties as well."

"I like that, not referring to your being assaulted of course. And another?"

"Also quite obviously, evolution unfolds on all levels simultaneously. Take the human species for example. It evolves on the Molecular level by DNA mutation, some being beneficial and passed on. It evolves on the Cellular level, in the structure and physiology of the human cells. It evolves on Metabion level by natural selection. It evolves on the Citian level - witness our drive to change the way of life of the Buffer Zone villages. It evolves on the Citian level, say, in terms of city planning and metropolitan technologies such as public transit systems design. The human species also evolves on the National level, for example, the bureaucratic and economic structures, the military and the space program. It even evolves on the planetary scale, in terms of the human relationship to the global environment."

"**Very good.**"

"But I do have a question. It has struck me that from the Citian level upwards, evolution occurs in both the Darwinian and Lamarckian modes."

"**Explain.**"

"Well, Darwinian evolution has it that changes occur between generations of organisms, which are then subjected to natural selection. Jean-Baptiste de Lamarck, a contemporary of Darwin, erroneously proposed that somatic changes occur within the lifetime of the organism, such as a giraffe lengthening its neck by repeated stretching (supposedly), which then would begat longer-necked offspring. The Darwinian explanation, the correct one, is that the giraffe produce offspring of varying neck-lengths by means of genetic recombination and the odd mutations, and natural selection favors the longer-necked offspring for survival to propagate the genes for longer-necks. But my observation of villages and cities and nations shows me unequivocally that, on these levels, the Lamarckian mode of evolution is very much in evidence. A tribal village can make observable changes, such as adopting the use of the solar cooker and changing its wood-cutting-gathering way of life and creating a cottage industry component to its existence, all within its lifetime, and the newly evolved characteristics could then be inherited by its offspring villages. Along with the emergent Lamarckian mode of evolution, Darwinian evolution continues to operate, such as offspring villages competing for the same resources."

"**Well observed. You have given a prime example of the cosmic phenomenon known as Translevel Progression. In this case, it is the translevel progression of the mode of evolution from the purely Darwinian one on the lower levels to the Darwinian-Lamarckian one on the higher levels.**"

"Translevel Progression. Noted. So now, I have another question. It seems to me that Lamarckian evolution on the Citian and higher levels involves a lot of deliberation and design. It is not a matter of random mutation at all. If it is random mutation in the Darwinian mode, most of the changes would be unworkable, antisocial, retarded and even destructive, and they would have to be all manifest so that natural selection could work on them. But this doesn't seem to be the way it happens in real life. Most social mutations seem to be improvements. Take the automobile, for example. We don't see hoards of bad new cars produced every year just to be carted off to the junkyard. They are mostly improvements on earlier models. Only, some are better than others, and Darwinian evolution does work on competing makes and models. So, my question is: Would Lamarckian evolution one day, on some high level, totally displace Darwinian evolution?"

"You will answer this question yourself before long."

"Going back to integrative transcendence, I can say this. Now that it has finally made itself known to the human mind – mine - the human mind can now actively drive the human species to actively, purposefully, foresightfully and integratively transcend."

"Amen."

The afternoon safari, from 16:00 to 18:15, was driven by Manohar, with Julian, Kim, lodge employee Sarup and me aboard, and as usual, when the Gypsy was in the hands of Manohar, it was an exciting experience. He took us to the far side of the park looking for wild dogs. Towards the end he had to drive at over 40 mph, which given the park's driving condition was break-neck speed, trying to make the Mukki Gate by 18:00 - closing time. Still, we were late by 15 minutes and had to pay the late penalty, which was fine except for the waiting we put their gate guards through, especially in the height of the Holi festival. I'm sure they had better things in mind to do than to sit waiting for us. I tipped each guard C$1 each for their trouble, which is about three hours' worth of their wages.

[22:39]

During dinner, Jane and Faiyaz disappeared for some time, and returned from the kitchen with a tray of dessert, on three pieces of which were stuck three lit candles. While walking into the kitchen, they sang the Happy Birthday song – for me. Again I had forgotten and missed my birthday on February 25. They found out about it yesterday and got on to it. There was also a card, hand made by Faiyaz, with a hand colored tiger on the cover. On the inside, it was written: "For Anthony, an inspiration to all of us who are afraid of becoming cynical in our old age!" Signed: Jane, Faiyaz, Julian and Manohar.

Kim's signature was not there, and I had to hand it to her saying, "This card wouldn't be complete without you." Then, she signed it.

Kim usually keeps her opinion to herself, and stays a little aloof, but when Manohar said that working with "lazy" local tribal people wouldn't do a thing to save the tiger and I disagreed, she turned to me and said, "You are an outsider talking to somebody who lives here. You should listen to what he has to say."

It was Manohar himself who spoke up in my defense, saying, "We are all outsiders here. I came from Jodpur ('jod-POOR') in Rajasthan, a totally different world from the tribal cultures here. So it is just Anthony's views against mine, and I'm willing to give Anthony a chance to prove me wrong."

He told me later that it was he who advised Avtar to transfer Kim over to Bandhavgarh and retain Jane here to do tiger conservation work with Faiyaz and me. Of all the people at Kanha, Manohar is the one about whom I harbor ambivalent feelings. I don't totally trust him on account of his being Avtar's nephew, but am in fact quite fond of him as a person.

All in all a very good day, the constant dark cloud of my personal tragedy, which contains the much darker cloud of Christopher's, notwithstanding.

Good night, Christopher.

❖   ❖   ❖   ❖   ❖

March 3, 1999, Wednesday, Sunny, 17-31C

Dearest Christopher:

[05:48 (1999-03-04) @ Rm. 111, Kanha Tiger Lodge]
Yesterday (03-03) was another forced off-day. So we again took the opportunity to go into the park. This time it was Manohar at the wheel, Jane, Kim, Faiyaz, Julian and I participating. With both Julian and Faiyaz in the same vehicle, both being avid bird-watchers, it is a day of bird watching, whether a tiger showed up or not. On the road back from the park to the lodge, we encountered two roadblocks of tree branches set up by color-powder-encrusted villagers, demanding money for us to pass. Manohar talked his way past the first one, but at the second one, a few villagers hefted up pots of colored liquids threateningly, demanding money or else. Manohar paid Rs.50 to get past that one. Considering that there are no windows in the Gypsy to crank up, I think it was a wise decision.

In the evening Manohar and Faiyaz went to Baihar to call Avtar. Prior to the trip, we sat down to strategize on the call. They both asked me to go and speak to Avtar about our work here. I declined. I've already sent him the letter. The ball is in Avtar's court. If he had read the letter, there is no point for me to explain thing over again. If he hadn't read the letter, I wanted him to get the picture by reading the letter, not to have me tell him about it on the phone. The letter is a much better medium to convey ideas systematically. I also don't totally trust myself to be able to talk to Avtar with equanimity. I suggested that they go and check for any fax from Avtar. If there is no fax, things are fine. It is a case of "no news is good news". If there is a fax saying something like the last fax, i.e., suspend all action until he arrives, I would then call him, this evening. And if I had to make this call, it would be to say "No".

Manohar, however, would have to make the call - to ask for money to run the lodge, and for funds for the Buffer Zone outreach and for the conference. The situation is that no money has been released to him since early February for either, even after the CIDA funds have arrived. .

As it happened, and not surprisingly, there was no fax from Avtar, and Manohar again could not get Avtar on the phone, even as Avtar was in Delhi, nor was there even a message left for him. How much more detached from the front line can Avtar be?

Jane said to me, "Avtar is not the fire and brimstone campaigner that you are. If you have him as a partner, you will be constantly frustrated."

I had a chat with Jane yesterday evening while Faiyaz and Manohar went off to Baihar. The object was that where this outreach project is concerned, Faiyaz is given to work at 150% efficiency (at least in terms of the time he puts in - from 07:30 to 21:30, day in, day out, which however is what he thrives on doing), I at 70%, but she at no more than 20%, and she wanted to have more of her considerable abilities put to work. We talked about what she could do before the conference. She would like to go outreach to the English language schools in Baihar, Malanjkhan (the copper mining town) and Balaghat, and liaise with the women's groups there, if any. We thought that Judge Vijay Chandra and Collector Manu Srivastava would be excellent people to start with. Perhaps tomorrow I'll go with her into Baihar to pay Judge Vijay Chandra another visit.

When Faiyaz came back, we discussed this with him and he thought what Jane wanted to do a capital idea, and came up with some more suggestions as to how to get it done.

Faiyaz and I also talked about what best to do tomorrow. We decided that he would again go early in the morning with Tirath to rake in as many panchayats as possible over the next few days. He'll spend the whole day out there. Another 14-hour work day for him, but as I said, he thrives on it. I can empathize with him on this, since I'm much the same.

"**What animals and plants did you see between the lodge gate and the Kanha park gate?**" Raminothna posed the question of the day.

"Oh, the usual – cows, goats, dogs, a couple of camels, fields of wheat and rice, bees in honey farms, oranges and papayas in orchards…"

"**Are these integral parts of India?**"

"Yes, they are."

"**And what plant and animal species inside the park have you seen in the park?**"

I rattled off a few dozen species until she stopped me.

"**Are they integral parts of India too?**"

"Yes, they are."

"**So, what is your conclusion?**"

"Conclusion? As to what?"

"**Another interlevel parallelism, of course.**"

"I still don't know what you're driving at."

"**Consider India as a national organism.**"

"So, the national organism called India is composed of a broad spectrum of species on the levels below?"

"**Very good.**"

"So, you're saying that an organism is also an… ecosystem?"

"**An organized ecosystem.**"

"An organism comprising many species within – what an astounding notion! And let's not forget the tribal cultures such as the Baiga and Gond either, nonetheless species on the Citian level. And also cellular species such as penicillin and yeast, and even molecular species by the thousands, such as the medicines we dispense to the kids. And not just human societies, either. Some insect societies are the same. A beehive contains no other species than bees, but the societies of certain termite species contain not just termites, but specific species of fungus that the termites cultivate and feed upon, without which the termite mounds themselves could not survive. Conversely, the fungus species could not survive without the termites cultivating it."

"**Now, look inside a regular plant cell and a regular animal cell, and what do you see?**"

"I see its nucleus, mitochondria, chloroplasts, plastids…"

"**What are they?**"

"They are organelles."

"**What are organelles?**"

"They are prokaryote-like bodies, similar to bacteria, inside the eukaryotic cell (cell with nucleus) as its integral parts. They have their own DNA, and they multiply inside the cell as if the inside of the cell is their natural environment. Theory has it that the early ancestors of these organelles were free living prokaryotes – cells without nuclei. Somewhere along the way, they got ingested by the host eukaryote cell, and somehow managed to avoid being digested – perhaps a mutation. So, a eukaryote cell can be seen as an enclosed ecosystem of symbiotic prokaryotes as well as thousands of molecular species. Fascinating."

"Glad you find it so."

Good night, Christopher. Missing you. And when it comes to missing you, it is always – terribly.

※ ※ ※ ※ ※

March 4th, 1999, Thursday, sunny

Dearest Christopher:

[14:11 @ Rm. 111, Kanha Tiger Lodge]
This morning, Faiyaz left around 07:45 with Surinder, on a route designed with the help of Tirath. It will take him about 12 hours to do. He will strive to line up meetings with panchayats on a daily basis as of tomorrow.

Jane came out of her room around 08:15, and we started a strategizing session in which Manohar participated, very vigorously this times, as of about 10:30 when he returned from Baihar. Obviously, he's done some serious thinking of his own. More on this later.

He did succeed in reaching Avtar by phone this morning. Avtar apparently still had not read my letter, and made no comment on the panchayat conference project. According to Manohar, he assured Avtar that there were no promises made by me and Faiyaz that Tiger Fund could not keep, and informed him about the amount of work we have already done, and the number of people who said would attend the conference. Avtar asked Manohar if he had attended any sessions Faiyaz and I had conducted, and Manohar replied "no". Avtar said that he wanted to speak to Faiyaz directly, tomorrow morning at 10:00. Is he going to suspend Tiger Fund action

Omni-Science and the Human Destiny

again?

Doesn't it sound ridiculous, that we are so constantly concerned that Avtar would try to deter or sabotage the progress of his own organization? But just in case, since Faiyaz cannot say "no" to Avtar and still work for Tiger Fund on the project, and I cannot do without him, I would have to say 'no' for him. I will therefore go into Baihar with Faiyaz when he calls Avtar, and standby just in case, which would dovetail well with Jane's plan to go to town to speak with Judge Chandra.

[17:01]

The in-depth meeting with Manohar this morning brought out some interesting points, ones from an Indian's point of view (Kim should be interested), albeit from another province, bearing in mind that Faiyaz often holds opinions contrary to Manohar's, and his is an Indian view point too. Slightly paraphrased:

The tribals are not "civilized enough" to be quickly convertible to ecological thinking, he said. "By the time they voluntarily give up their eco-unfriendly practices such as wood burning and poaching, there will be no tigers left to save. Therefore, we should concentrate on fast track, short-term solutions, such as strong-armed anti-poaching measures."

"This sounds a bit elitist, Manohar," said Jane in her usual mild yet forceful manner, "though I think I understand what you're saying."

"I can understand his sentiments almost totally," I was prompted by an internal sentiment to say. "It's exactly the way I feel about those Chinese, Japanese and Korean people who use tiger parts for medicine. The immediate strategy should be strong-armed law-and-enforcement control. It would take time to change basic attitudes, perhaps generations. However, my experience with the panchayat leaders thus far has shown that at least they are not as 'uncivilized', nor as reluctant to change, as Manohar said they would be. Manohar, why don't you come and observe one of our panchayat meetings? I would be most interested in your observations."

"Sure, maybe I will, but, Jane, it is not elitist. It's basic human nature. It would be difficult to convince villagers to not use wood because it is so easily available here in Madhya Pradesh, versus in the desert-like conditions of Rajasthan."

"So, your opinion is that people will just keep on cutting down trees and burning wood until there are no more trees to be cut and no more wood to be burnt, before they will take on alternative energies?"

"You got it."

I wanted to talk to a local tribal. Manohar called in Rahesh and Ramjit and asked them some questions in Hindi. Rahesh answered first, and Manohar said, "Rahesh's opinion is that although the solar cooker physically works, the villagers would not readily adopt it, because it requires too many changes in their traditional way of cooking – they have a full breakfast in the morning before the sun is hot, and they have a full dinner in the evening after the sun has set, but hardly any lunch; the women like to be able to smell and try-taste their cooking, which the solar cooker does not allow. The solar cooker takes too long to prepare a meal; the solar cooker does not work during the monsoon; the villagers usually keep the fire going in the hearth all day long; the villagers use wood in the evenings to keep warm; etc., etc. Rahesh was raised in a tribal village and should know what he is talking about. It seems to be a case of 'you can lead a horse to water but you cannot make it drink.'"

"I can only counter a part of this," I said. "First, the solar cooker as a concept has proven workable in certain areas, in Africa as well as in Asia. Granted, some of these areas may no longer have a tree standing. Second, accord to my reading, people need only to set up the solar cooker in the morning, line it up due south and leave it for the rest of the day and come dinnertime, the rice and other dishes would be cooked and still warm. It is true that the solar cooker would be useless in the early morning and during the monsoon, but solar cooking can work in conjunction with biogas, of whose raw material, cattle dung, India is not in short supply. Biogas can serve as fuel for both morning cooking and nighttime heating. And as for basic human nature, I believe in the flexibility of the species, that we can adapt to environmental changes."

Rahesh spoke some more. Manohar translated. "Tribal villagers are used to getting things from the government free of charge, and what is given to them is seldom used as intended. He cites the example of a villager selling a hand pump for alcohol. He thinks that a solar cooker will likely be treated likewise."

"We're not giving them irreplaceable solar cookers," Jane pointed out. "We are teaching them how to make the cookers for themselves. They can make as many as they want. In fact, the more they make, the more they can then sell for more money."

I asked Manohar to ask Sarup whether the carpenter had the solar cooker reflector-frame ready, which he promised to deliver on March 4th – today. Sarup went to Manjitola to check, but the carpenter was nowhere to be found. Manohar said, "Deadlines in India are often not made to be met. You have to constantly monitor the progress and push people to meet them. Service and product quality in this region is not high due to low competition."

Both Manohar and Rahesh believe that electricity is a much better alternative than solar energy in terms of acceptability to the villagers. Important is the nature of the end-use, as also pointed out by other advisors before. This means that the villagers will more readily accept an alternative energy technology if they can do with it the number of things they can do with wood burning. The solar cooker, for example, does not meet this criterion well. Electricity, on the other hand, does so almost perfectly, and it is relatively cheap, at Rs.50 (C$2) /outlet/month for two light bulbs, and perhaps Rs.100-200 per month for an electric stove. There is an upfront cost of an electric hot plate of Rs.75-200. We decided to try it on a minimal scale – to provide to Rahesh and Sarup each a 2-element electric stove to take home to try out. Both Rahesh and Sarup have large families of about a dozen members each. It is estimated that about 30% of the villages in the Buffer Zone have access to electricity. Manohar believes that it would be relatively easy to persuade the government to move towards providing electric power to all villages within a short time period.

But to my challenge of, "If there were electricity to spare, there wouldn't be daily rotational blackouts," they had no answer.

Other information includes:

- Killing of wild animals in the Buffer Zone is rampant.
- 90% of all government loans to villagers are forgiven due to non-repayment.
- Manjitola, a "peripheral village" (adjacent to the park), extracts about 25 headloads per day of fuel wood illegally from the park. Of these, about 30% are for domestic use and 70% for selling mostly at Baihar for Rs.15 per headload. This means a number of things, that even if Manjitola accepts the solar cooker totally, the cooker can solve only 30% of the problem; they would still poach wood to sell.
- People in urban and suburban areas are not likely to use the solar cooker due to the predominance of shadows; that electricity is available in Baihar, but people still purchase wood from the villagers.
- Legal wood is available for purchase, but people still purchase poached wood; that neither solar cooking nor electric cooking can produce the income the wood brings into the village. 25 headloads a day means about 700 headloads a month or about 8,000 headload a year. 70% of this is about 500 headloads a month or 5,600 headloads a year. This would bring into the village Rs.7500 (US$180) a month or Rs.84,000 (US$2,100) a year. If all the 200 villages in Kanha's Core/Buffer Zones follow the same

formula, the total loss should wood-cutting be stopped would be Rs.1,500,000 (US$40,000) a month or Rs.16,800,000 (US$420,000 or CDN$720,000) a year.

"So how do we offset this loss if the villagers stop selling wood?" I asked.

We seem to agree on that freeing up time of the wood-packing women could be more than offset if they spent it in developing cottage industries and selling the products instead of wood for more than Rs.50 per person per day, say Rs150 (C$6.50). The village revenue then will more than triple that of packing and selling wood. Bearing in mind that a headload of wood can fetch only about US$1, which is often the fruit of a full day's work for a village woman, surely, they could make more money and enjoy more of life than that.

In conjunction with this is that if the park fee is raised 10X from the present US$2.50 to US$25 per person per visit for foreign tourists (about 3,000 per annum) and perhaps a little less for out of state Indian visitors (about 20,000 per annum), the park revenue will be in the region of Rs.9,000,000 + Rs.4,000,000 = Rs.13,000,000 (US$325,000 or CDN$500,000), half of which going to the park service, and half towards a village benefit fund, amounting to Rs.6,500,000 (US$160,000 or CDN$260,000) a year each. The half going to the park service can create a powerful anti-poaching squad (a la Manohar), and the half going to the villagers can help provide basic services such as schools and medical clinics and kick-start cottage industries.

What should we aim for in the panchayat conference?

- All panchayats must unify their voices to drive for such a park system, not only for Kanha, but for all tiger reserves in India.
- If workable alternative energy is provided, villagers must promise to stop gathering or cutting and especially poaching of wood.
- Villagers and government officials must work together towards protecting the park and tiger habitats in both the core and buffer zones.
- Poaching of anything must stop, in both the core and buffer zones.

[22:47]

Faiyaz didn't get back from his day-long trip until past 20:00. Dinner at the usual time, i.e., about 20:30, where we (Faiyaz, Jane, Kim, Julian., Manohar and I) inevitably talked about the oncoming arrival of the tourist group headed by Ed Cambridge, whom nobody liked on account of his rudeness to the volunteers on previous visits. But the topic of conversation was not Cambridge but Avtar. We were all concerned, including even Manohar (if only in anticipation of our reaction), that Avtar would repeat his previous order that when the tourists come, Tiger Fund activities should be suspended so that Faiyaz could devote his full energy to serving the tourist clients. Given the high-gear nature of the conference project, and the shortage of time which limits us to contact no more than 50 of the 75 or so panchayats as it is, plus going to neighbouring towns such as Jabalpur and Mandla to invite forest officials and media, plus working with Manohar to organize the physical aspect of the conference, there is not a moment to spare. Suspending Tiger Fund activities even for one day, let alone at least three, just cannot be done if the conference is to be successful. With Manohar, Kim and Julian hosting the tourists, it is not as if there's a vacuum situation at KTL (Kanha Tiger Lodge).

Jane thought that this time it would not come to that, since Avtar must have at least come to some grasp that there is an urgent and momentous conservation project going on in the names of WCWC and Tiger Fund, and that Faiyaz is indispensable for the project to continue.

Manohar offered a sneaky solution, "Say 'yes' but do 'no'."

Kim concurred, "Yeah, what he doesn't know won't hurt him."

But I heard myself saying, "Don't worry about it. I'll say no, and do no."

But I do worry, and thanks to Avtar, this worrying is ruining my enjoyment here at Kanha. I hope Jane is right and that we're just spinning our worrying wheels.

In theory, it should be Faiyaz to say it, since he is the official Tiger Fund "Project Officer", but if he did that, he would likely be canned. So I offered to go to town with him to say the "no" myself.

One way or the other, some damage to the project is already done. Because of the damned phone call tomorrow morning at 10:00, Faiyaz will be unable to get on the road till noon, instead of his usual 06:30. And this half-day's loss we can ill afford.

I fumed. "Ten o'clock be damned. We'll call Avtar at home tomorrow morning at eight o'clock. That's late enough."

Manohar and Faiyaz exchanged apprehensive glances.

"We need the morning to do our work. If you don't want to call, I'll call," I said.

Manohar hesitated momentarily, then said, "Okay, Anthony, I'll call."

If this type of inefficiency exists in our bodies, we'd be lying down all day, running a fever due to internal friction.

There is an old Scientific American magazine in the conservation center, in which I found an ad for a book titled Living Systems, by James Greer Miller. The ad says that all living things, and many apparently nonliving things, such as a corporation or a city, are living systems, and all living systems have each 19 subsystems. Sounds very intriguing. I asked Jane to see if she could find that book at the Seoni public library while she was there. She did. But it was a huge book, over a thousand pages thick, weighing a ton, and not to be taken out. So she took it upon herself to copy down the 19 key words, which are: the **Boundary,** the **Ingestor,** the **Distributor,** the **Input Transducer,** the **Internal Transducer,** the **Output Transducer,** the **Converter,** the **Producer,** the **Matter-Energy Storage,** the **Extruder,** the **Motor,** the **Supporter,** the **Channel-Net,** the **Decoder,** the **Encoder,** the **Memory,** the **Associator,** the **Decider** and the **Reproducer.**

"**Thus, another interlevel parallelism,**" said Raminothna.

"Yes indeed. All organisms and societies on all levels are "living systems", all with the same 19 subsystems."

"**Oh, by the way, there is one subsystem that Miller forgot to mention.**"

"And what is that?"

"**The Evolver.**"

"The evolver – the provision for mutation in the reproductive system. Makes sense. Plus, 20 looks aesthetically more pleasing than 19 in this context."

"**That shouldn't be a determining factor. There is no magic of the number 20 over 19. In a prime number contest, 19 will beat 20 hands down. But in this case, 20 does look more symmetrical than 19, and symmetry is beauty in the eyes of science.**"

Good night, Christopher.

March 5, 1999, Friday, sunny, 18-33C

Dearest Christopher:

[23:54 @ Rm.111, Kanha Tiger Lodge]

Today is a day of no return.

This morning at 07:00, Faiyaz, Manohar and I drove into Baihar, they to talk to Avtar, and I to take him to task.

As it happened, it took us more than an hour to make the connection between

Omni-Science and the Human Destiny

Baihar and Delhi. By the time Manohar finally got through to Avtar, it was past nine.

While waiting for the call to go through, I remarked to Raminothna, "The Channel-Net subsystem of the living system called India leaves much to be desired."

"Very good illustration."

"Thank you."

"I've heard that the Chinese have a philosophical system that puts the body organs into five interacting groups. Is that correct?"

"Yes. It's called the Five Elements system."

"What are these Five-Elements and how do they interact?"

"The Five Elements are Metal, Wood, Water, Fire and Earth. These five organ groups are arranged in the superimposed form of a pentagon and a star. In this diagram, the pentagon lines are the 'support lines' and the star lines are the 'inhibition lines', where Group A supports Group B, inhibits Group C, is inhibited by Groups D and is supported by Groups E. And likewise for every other group. Chinese internal medicine strives to achieve optimal balance amongst the five organ groups."

"Thus, two similar interlevel parallelisms – 20 Subsystems per Living System on all levels, from the West, and the 5 Elements within all organisms on all levels - from the East. Unintended but nice symmetry."

When finally the call went through, Manohar talked first. From the outset, although I couldn't understand a word he said in Hindi, his body language said it all. When he was done, he passed the phone to Faiyaz, who could not finish a single sentence. The loud voice on the other end just rattled on and on. Whatever Faiyaz could manage to say was said in a subdued voice, and as soon as the interruption came, he'd stop in mid-sentence. This went on for about 15 minutes. Manohar filled me in. Avtar had indeed refused to release a single rupee to the panchayat outreach-conference project. When Faiyaz was done, he was so upset he just hung up the phone. The two of them mumbled something to each other in Hindi, went back out to the street and climbed dejectedly back into the Gypsy. Faiyaz seemed on the point of tears.

I joined them. "Well?"

So they spilled the beans. First, Faiyaz was indeed ordered to give up even the old (instead of new) Gypsy assigned to us for the outreach effort in favor of the use for tourists during their stay, which means that WCWC/TF work would indeed be suspended. And second, Jane was ordered to go to Bandhavgarh almost at once. There were apparently other things that Avtar said about me to Faiyaz, which Faiyaz was hesitant to repeat, but these two points were enough for the time being. I went back into the STD-PCO shop to place my call.

Hardly surprising, it was not a pleasant or even civil conversation. Avtar's first point was that we went ahead to plan and do things without his approval. I pointed out his almost total inaccessibility, and he did not dispute it. Since my return to Kanha on February 16th, the first time anyone succeeded in contacting him by any means was yesterday, March 4th. CJ delivered my letter to him on late Feb. 26th or early Feb. 27th, and he did not read it until yesterday. Mean time, he left absolutely no instruction to Faiyaz for any TF work, nor did he pre-discuss with me while I was in Delhi what he would like TF to accomplish in his usual absence. And what of all the promises and agreements he made when I was in Delhi, about the Buffer Zone outreach and the Gypsy? I asked him if he wanted us to just sit and wait two and a half weeks and do nothing other than to try to get in touch with him. He did not answer the question, but had the audacity to say, "As far as I'm concerned, your work at Kanha is a total failure."

"And yours?" I thought of asking back. Instead, I asked, "How's that?"

He said, "You should have limited your outreach to at most two villages and made sure that the villagers use the solar cookers."

"Just two? We have succeeded to impress and convince the panchayat leaders of at least 50 villages that the solar cooker physically works, and I have given them tiger conservation slideshows, and have taken them into the park. I aim to do so with at least 120 villages during my stay here. The follow-up to the conference would be to install units in the villages interested in them, and there will be dozens willing to try out this technology. What we are doing will accomplish a Buffer-Zone-wide raising of awareness and distribution of trial solar ovens. But if we limit our effort during my stay to just two villages, and if they end up selling the cookers for alcohol as they did the hand pumps, then *that* would have been a total failure, with none of the other villages having heard about tiger conservation and even the idea of alternative cooking technology at all."

Avtar did not argue this point either, or could not, but started ordering me saying "I want" this done and "I want" that done, most of which showed no understanding nor respect for what we are doing and have done, and would derail the conference project altogether.

I interrupted him, "Avtar, it's not what *you* want. If *you* want these things done, you do just one of them yourself. Indeed, you can tell Faiyaz to do this and that, but all I've heard you say to him has been to suspend doing what good work he is doing. I'll tell you what *I* want. I want you to send the fund here for our work at once. As far as I'm concerned, if there are two equal partners, one doing everything

Omni-Science and the Human Destiny

and the other nothing, the one doing nothing has no right to make the rules or even criticize the other. Still, you're the head of Tiger Fund, and we are organizing the conference in the name of Tiger Fund. You do have the right to call it off. So if you think the work on the conference is a total failure, why don't you just order it cancelled?"

He said, "Okay, cancel it."

I glanced at Faiyaz and Manohar. They were looking at each other, ashen-faced. I pressed on, and not too coolly, "In that case, I will go ahead with it in the name of WCWC, and I'll have WCWC withhold the second and subsequent installments of the CIDA grant, and further to reclaim the first installment on grounds of non-performance."

His tone suddenly changed. "You forced me to say cancel the conference. I didn't mean to say it."

"Then consider the project proceeded upon, with sufficient funding and a full time vehicle."

"Then go rent a vehicle for the three days."

"Well, thank you, Avtar. Kindly send Manohar the funds ASAP. Meanwhile, I'll just use my own money."

He said nothing.

"And how about Jane?" I pursued. "What happened to our agreement that she be a WCWC/TF volunteer while I'm here? She's a vital part of this project. If you pulled her away, you'd compromise the conference."

"Jane can stay at Kanha if you insist. But somebody else will have to go in her place."

At that point, Manohar pointed through the window at Julian, who was sitting in the back of the Gypsy. I said, "How about Julian Cook?"

"Absolutely not! He will never go back to Bandhavgarh. It'll have to be Kim. Kanha Tiger Lodge is not a club house."

"A club house? For your information KTL is more like a work camp than at any other time in its history."

Julian is not welcome back to Bandhavgarh, Manohar later explained, because Mohinder Sidhu (Bandhavgarh Tiger Lodge manager) does not get along with him and prefers Kim over him, and Tiger Fund officer Darshan Nagra stationed at Bandhavgarh competes with him and/or is jealous of him. Julian is a superb self-made birder and Darshan, a wildlife expert in his own right, perceives it as a threat, so Manohar said.

Regarding Kim, I know for a fact she will not go back to Bandhavgarh with only

Mohinder and Darshan there, even if she has to quit Avtar. Tourists-wise, the season has pretty well run its course except for the Ed Cambridge group of about ten on March 10th-13th, and Cambridge has expressly told everyone he does not want volunteers in their midst. After that, it wouldn't be until after the conference when, from March 28th to April 10th, there'll be about 4 stragglers. So, what's the point of having Kim go over there to sit for a month, especially when she has been helping out with the conference? I cannot, however, speak for Kim as I can for Jane, so Kim would have to speak for herself.

Avtar and I ended the phone call as abruptly and coldly as it began.

At dinner after we'd come back from Baihar, I sat next to Kim and personally broke the news to her in the presence of all concerned. Kim, in her usual quiet and succinct way, said simply, "I'm not going back, even if I have to leave."

"I'll support you," I said to her, not quite knowing what that would entail, nor whether it would do any good.

Good night, Christopher.

※ ※ ※ ※ ※

March 6, 1999, Saturday, sunny, 19-33C

Dearest Christopher:

[22:45 @ Rm.111, Kanha Tiger Lodge]
Today's group of Panchayat leaders were 9, of whom only 5 could go in the Gypsy for the park drive. Thankfully, the power almost miraculously came on early, so Jane showed the other four the Champions of the Wild video meanwhile.

The solar cooker demos worked perfectly, both the small and large models. The male villagers were mostly impressed by the cookers' physical prowess. But when Jane later asked the female sarpanch whether she would use the device, her initial reply of "yes" later changed not only to "no", but "impossible" when she began to consider various other social factors.

Why? It seems that even villages are subdivided into castes, and where the communal cooking idea is concerned, there seems no way the higher castes would eat the food touched by the untouchables, nor of course would they cook for the

Omni-Science and the Human Destiny

untouchables. So, the solar cookers' problems are not physical, but social, which is usually the tougher of the two to solve.

"They can build as many solar ovens as there are castes," I answered on the spur of the moment, after countering the earlier objection as best I could.

The woman moved back from "impossible" to "maybe", perhaps only out of politeness.

During the park drive, Faiyaz revealed to me the nature of his phone call with Avtar yesterday. It was largely an Anthony-bashing session on Avtar's part, saying that I was "media crazy" (and he is not?), trying to be a "one man tiger savior" (and his father was not?), that I "know nothing about India", and that I aim at "eliminating India's cattle". He was also being extra nice to Faiyaz, calling him "my dear boy" (which he also called me), among other things. It seems now that Avtar considers me an enemy, he aims to drive a wedge between Faiyaz and me, as well as win Faiyaz as an ally, however temporarily. I predict that Avtar will also be extra nice to Jane for the same purpose, and perhaps also to Kim, but this niceness would end as soon as I leave.

Another thing Avtar told Faiyaz was to forbid me to give any more slideshows to his tourist clients. The reason is that tour operator Ed Richards complained that I praised Ranthambhore too much, which is not on his itinerary and his clients asked him why not, and that I discussed with his clients about raising the park fee.

Come to think of it, isn't "Survey of Visitors" an item on the Tiger Fund side of the CIDA project? What more pertinent a question to pose to the visitors than this? Didn't Avtar himself once say, "Ask the tourists about this"?

So the cat is out of the bag. Avtar is openly opposed to our proposed park fee reform, saying that it may negatively impact upon tourist volume. By how much? 1%? 5%? Fine. Let's say 10%. But the other 90% will each pay ten times more. The park revenue will still increase nine fold, and the villagers will get half of that. The only people losing anything are the very few tour operators and hoteliers, like Avtar and Ed Richards. Indeed, of everyone I've spoken with about the idea – panchayat leaders, villagers, park personnel, government officials, the tourists themselves – Avtar and Richards are the only two people opposed to it. Some conservation partner.

This is yet another illustration how non-profit conservation work and for-profit commercial enterprises do not mix.

In the middle of all these vexations, I cannot help but bask now and again in the beauty of India. Just moments ago, it was the beauty of the Indian night. Night after night, when we emerged from the school house after the slideshow to walk our guests back to the Gypsy with Surinder waiting at the wheel to drive them back along the long, bumpy and winding road, I could not help but be star struck all over again. In the almost complete darkness in which the leader of the line has to grope his way towards the tail-lights of the Gypsy, the stars glisten brilliantly overhead, and unique to these nights in this fabled land, fireflies flickered and streamed off and on all around us. And then, when the village elders had seated themselves snuggly in the Gypsy, the cool night would be warmed by the hand-grasping farewells.

After the Gypsy had disappeared into the night, and Jane and Faiyaz had gone back to their quarters, I stayed out there in the dark, sat down in the grass, and received the most stunning interlevel parallelism of them all.

"**OSES,**" whispered Raminothna in the night breeze.

"Sorry. What did you say?"

"**I said OSES.**"

"What is OSES

"**The greatest interlevel parallelism of all time.**"

"What does OSES stand for?"

"**Lie down on the grass, feet together and arms outstretched, in the form of a cross, with your head due north. Look straight up at the zenith and mark it as zero. Draw a semi-circular white line from the eastern horizon, through zero, to the western horizon, and let it be the X- axis. Draw a semi-circular white line from the northern horizon, through zero, to the southern horizon, and let it be the Y-axis. Write a big white O in the middle of the first quadrant, S in the second quadrant, E in the third quadrant and another S in the fourth quadrant. Finally, starting from any point away from zero, draw an expanding spiral, centered upon zero, seven times. And there you have it.**"

"Have what?"

"**The OSES cycle of the IT Spiral.**"

"Does IT stand for Integrative Transcendence?"

"**It does.**"

"Yes, the spiral fits integrative transcendence. The five repeats are obviously the eight levels of organization – Sub-Atomic, Molecular, Cellular, Metabion, Citian, National."

"**Correct.**"

"Question is: What does O.S.E.S. stand for."

"**Guess.**"

"Okay, the O. The word starting with an O that is most prevalent in our discussions up to this point is 'organism'. Does it have to do with the word 'organism'?"

"Yes, it does."

"Organism-genesis?"

"That would be fine, but making it a single word would be better."

"How about 'Organismization'? Organismization: the creation or genesis of the original organisms on a certain level?"

"Perfect."

"And the S?"

"What happens after the integrative transcendence of the first organisms on a certain level?"

"They would reproduce and multiply."

"And?"

"And they would migrate in different directions."

"And?"

"And some would, say, move to colder regions and others to warmer regions."

"And?"

"And given time, they would form new species in these different environments."

"And there you have the S."

"Speciation?"

"Exactly."

"Well, then, these new species would further migrate until their offspring species intermingle in various places, forming ecosystems here and there."

"There you have the E."

"Ecosystem? Ecosystemization?"

"Ecosystemization. Correct."

"Then in the various ecosystem, some of the species would become social, and form societies of their own."

"And there, you have the second S."

"Socialization?"

"Socialization. Correct."

"And then, some of the societies would integratively transcend into being organisms of the level above."

"Yes."

"And the cycle would repeat again to the first organisms of that level."

"Thus, the O.S.E.S. Cycle of the I.T. Spiral."

"*Awe*some."

Good night, Christopher.

Anthony Marr

March 7, 1999, Sunday, sunny, 19-33C

Dearest Christopher:

[23:25 @ Rm.111, Kanha Tiger Lodge]

Our large solar oven developed a leak in the lid seal today and did not cook the rice, although its little brother saved the day. Strangely, it was one of the villagers that came this day who expressed the greatest interest in the oven. Follow-up work will be fruitful.

As per the pattern already developed, we started our session with self-introductions. One of their concerns, other than the usual needs for irrigation, roads and crop-plundering by chital and wild boar, is cattle lifting by tiger, except this time, when I asked the gentleman where the cow was lifted, he said "in the park". I'm not sure whether he meant that the cow was in the park when it was killed by the tiger, or whether it was killed outside the park and was dragged into the park by the tiger. I didn't press the issue, in case the former was true, in which case I would be tempted to say, "What do you expect?"

Lately, in my slideshow, the part where the tiger Charger makes his appearance has evolved to the following: "Charger has a job to do – to patrol his home range to safeguard his cubs from other male tigers. He is still in his prime, but his teeth are beginning to wear down. It is a certainty that sooner or later, perhaps in a year or two, he will be deposed by a younger rival. When this happens, since every square inch of the park has been claimed by one tiger or another, he will be driven to the fringe of the park where no tiger likes to tread. Not much later, he will have aged even more and be unable to hunt down fleet-footed prey like chital and wild boar. Driven by hunger, he may be forced to take a cow that has wandered into the park. If no cow is found, and he fails more than three weeks or so to take down prey, he would be too weak to hunt, and would die of starvation. Even though the tiger is the king of the forest, the end of a tiger is usually tragic – killed by another tiger or by starvation, or by a poacher. When I hear of a tiger taking a cow, I feel sad for both the tiger and the cow owner, and of course the cow. It makes me think of my parents who are now in their 80s. Able-bodied before, they are now feeble and infirm. The thought of them starving to death is unthinkable. In this light, I plead with you to forgive the tiger, and I will do my best to work towards a better system of compensation."

I'm spending a lot of writing time to put together an e-mail package comprising my field journal entries to send to WCWC when we go to Jabalpur ("Ja-bal-POOR") tomorrow – departure time 05:00. Jabalpur, 6 hours by road due north, is the nearest place, with the possible exception of Balaghat 3 hours due south, where there *might* be an internet café. Both cities are regional centers politically and economically, and the purpose of our trip to Jabalpur tomorrow is to announce to the region, via media, the Kanha Panchayat Conference, to invite local dignitaries to it, and to raise the profile of tiger conservation in general. Therefore, to make arrangements for a media conference at Jabalpur will be our main goal tomorrow.

With Raminothna I feel I have crossed a certain threshold, that we are starting a new chapter, at least where building the omniscientific cosmology is concerned. Today I've had time to reflect. I reviewed what has been revealed to me thus far. "So, Raminothna, as I understand it now, the major global transformation that the seven cosmic signs portend is the organismization of the planet Earth?"

"Yes. Or the failure thereof."

"I don't suppose there is any third alternative?"

"Don't count on it."

"Can the Earth not just carry on as it does today, ad infinitum, without organismization or anything else?"

"Can a fertilized egg carry on developing without ever hatching?"

"But the Earth is not an egg."

"But it is."

"Figuratively, maybe, or metaphorically, but not literally."

"Literally."

"A chicken egg is literally an egg. A planet is not. It is the metaphor of an egg, at most."

"Your way of looking at eggs is Earth-bound, not cosmic or universal. You are using the chicken egg as the starting and end points, the be all and end all of all eggs. It is not. It is only a specific case of the universal egg."

"What is a universal egg?"

"Quite simply, a universal egg is any physical entity that contains an embryo as its main component."

"So, what is the embryo of the Earth egg then?"

"The planetary embryo of planetary egg Earth is its biosphere."

"The biosphere? The embryo of a planetary egg? This is too much. Incredible, in fact. Ah! Here is an objection. The embryo of an egg should be on the side of the egg. The biosphere is on the outside of the Earth. And what about the yolk and the white of the egg?"

"**Once again, you are treating the chicken egg as the be all and end all of all eggs. I repeat: it is not. It is but a specific case of the universal egg. Universal eggs come in all shapes and sizes. Besides, the biosphere *is* enclosed by a shell - the atmosphere. As for the yolk and the white, themselves as metaphor, they are the mineral and energy resources inherent in your planet. I will even add the metaphor of the incubation lamp, which is your Sun.**"

"So, what is required for a successful 'hatching' of this 'planetary egg' then?"

"**Integrative transcendence, naturally.**"

"What is required for Earth to integratively transcend?"

"**Let me answer by giving you the end point. You could figure out how to get there yourself.**"

"Go ahead."

"**The organismization of Earth is multifaceted and will look different from different angles. But to give you one example - brace yourself - from the angle of the 'Six Planetary Diseases', when the organismization of the Earth is complete, they will all have been cured, and Earth will have been completely healed.**"

"Oh my God! That'd take ages."

"**Not much more than a mere geological eye-blink.**"

"Give me the full answer please."

"**The full answer would take a thick book, which has yet to be written.**"

"How about a few specifics, then?"

"**Such as?**"

"Such as, say, the military."

"**There will be no military forces on the national level, but a global multinational police force against internal threats such as terrorism or intraplanetary natural disasters, and a global multinational defense force against external threats. But there will be no military as you know it.**"

"What kind of external threats?"

"**Ask astronomers, as well as science fiction writers. They have covered most of the possibilities. Scientifically speaking, most notable are incurring asteroids.**"

"How about the ways animals will be treated?"

"**Your Mahatma Gandhi said that the greatness of a civilization can be** judged by the way its animals are treated. By this definition, the civilization of Planetary Organism Earth shall be great indeed, where animals shall be treated with dignity, respect, affection and compassion. Their rights shall be established, which should be akin to the rights you accord your own species, and recognized. Specifically, factory farming, fur farming, fur trapping, commercial hunting and trophy hunting shall all have been abolished. Species extinction, at least that due to human causes, shall have been halted, and wildlife habitat shall have been protected, stabilized and restituted."

"That'd be the day."

"Yes, it would. It is this kind of compassion and humility on the part of your species that will allow your integrative transcendence to come to pass, without which you shall surely fall extinct at your own hands, and doom your own planetary embryo to being still born."

"Still born?"

"Death by one or more of the Planetary Diseases, on or before the deadline according to the planetary metamorphic schedule. The result would likely be a regression of the biosphere by one level of organization or more. The National, Citian and even Metabion levels could be eliminated in one fell swoop."

"How about diet?"

"The species Homo Sapiens shall have by and large become vegetarian, for all of the humanitarian, ecological and nutritional reasons. This will be a natural result of the development of human compassion which, as pointed out, is a necessary ingredient of global integrative transcendence. Ecologically, as some of your wits have pointed out, you would need at least three Earth's to sustain the dietary needs of your species should every human eat like the average American today. And tomorrow, and its tomorrows, with the continued growth of the human population, who knows? You may need four, five, or even ten Earth's. And let's not forget the land required, considering the low protein conversion ratio to produce meat from plants, and the pollution generated, by the meat industry."

"That will take centuries too."

"You won't live to see the day, that's for certain. Anything else?"

"How about the global political situation? Does this require some form of world government?"

"It will certainly require some form of centralized supra-national government, which will be founded on democratic as well as compassionate principles."

"Is the United Nations what you're talking about?"

"It's a good start, but its future depends on how it performs today. It could fail just as its predecessor the League of Nations did. If the UN fails, another global body will emerge to take its place, simply because there is such a need. Its charter would be rid of the weakness that would have caused UN's downfall, if it did fall."

"What must the UN do to survive?"

"Most importantly, its member nations must be conscientious enough to sincerely work for the global public good than their own self-interest."

"What about superpowers like the US?"

"They could take a leadership position, first and foremost in ensuring that the UN would not disintegrate."

"Would the nations still be 'sovereign'?"

"By then, the word 'sovereign' would have a very different meaning. It could still mean the power to make unilateral intra-national decisions on intra-national affairs, as long as they do not violate the prevalent international standard of morals and ethics."

"Would there still be nations, even?"

"A very good question. Indeed, there may come a time when nationalism is dead, and national boundaries may be more of a hindrance than a protection. The main factor of compartmentalization of the world today is nationalistic, and the nations are by and large more competitive than cooperative. But the Earth at organismization will have planetary organs in terms of global function, all of which being cooperative, and non-competitive. The Earth will be the only independent entity on earth, and all within Earth will be interdependent. Instead of saying, 'I'm an American' or 'I am an Iraqi', people will say, 'I'm a part of Earth's lung' (in physiological terminology), or 'I am of Earth's water group' (in terms of the 'five elements'), or 'I belong to Earth's output transducer' (in terms of the 20 subsystems). It is not dissimilar to people within a nation today, when asked 'What are you?', to reply, 'I'm an engineer' or 'I'm a physician' instead of saying, 'I'm a Bostonian' or 'I'm a New Yorker', with the further difference that nations today are bristling with weaponry against each other, and Boston and New York are not. Still, the different nations may remain, just as the different cities remain, but more as world organs than sovereign entities."

"Speaking of trade, what about the economic aspects of organismization?"

Omni-Science and the Human Destiny

> "This is not to be confused with what is called 'globalization' today, which stresses competition. Upon Earth's organismization, the global economy will be unified, harmonized, free flowing and efficient, with a common flow chart, on a common currency, in the common environment, for the common good."

"And what does this holistic planetary matter/energy flow look like?"

> "Meditate. Look inward, into the seamless and harmonized matter/energy flow amongst your 100% specialized and cooperative organs, and you will get a feel of the new planetary Organism Earth."

Good night, Christopher.

❖ ❖ ❖ ❖ ❖

March 8, 1999, Monday, sunny, 18-34C

Dearest Christopher:

[03:23 (1999-03-09-2) @ Rm.111, Kanha Tiger Lodge]

The last two days (6th & 7th) were both days of high gear. Yesterday and today I've been trying to edit the previous entries to make them into a coherent email package. Each day there were panchayat leaders coming in, nine one day, seven the next. Their concerns are getting repetitive, which means that we have pretty well covered the entire spectrum of issues: irrigation, compensation for crop plundering (by chital and wild boar), cattle lifting (by tiger), roads, schools, hospitals. Whereas some are obviously amazed by the technology, others complain about the difficulties with making the change. One villager said that all the wood in the vicinity of their village had been stripped bare, and said he would be interested in trying out the solar cooker.

I said to the rest, "The whole point of solar cooking is to *prevent* the remaining forests to be stripped bare."

As usual, nothing is black and white. The realm of possibilities is broad.

Today, we started super-early (around 05:00) to go to Japalpur and got there around 10:30, Manohar driving. He had to take the new Gypsy for its first service at 2000 km., although the grueling 6 hours one way on the bumpy road does the vehicle more harm than the service would do good. As we arrived at Jabalpur, we were thrilled to see a lovely, even beautiful city, quite unlike any other Indian city I've seen – lots of flowers and quaint buildings, and though there is still garbage here and there, it is almost non-existent compared to, say, Nagpur, let alone Calcutta and Delhi. The impression is one of color and contrast, versus the grey of other Indian cities, even the "pink city" of Jaipur. Jane fell in love with it instantly, and remarked, "If we go it on our own, this is the city where we should get a house and set up shop." She is also happy to see young women in Saris buzzing around town on motor scooters. She calls them "cool chicks". A motor scooter is probably the first thing that Jane would buy. Oh, and don't forget a sari. Shorts won't do.

Jane, Faiyaz and I took the opportunity to do media, while Julian and Kim went sightseeing and shopping. The first thing we did was to call Dr. Preema Kumtakar of the Danish International Development Assistance, Madhya Pradesh Women in Agriculture, whom Jane met and befriended while attending the women's issues conference in Seoni, MP. Since Manohar, Kim and CJ had taken the Gypsy for servicing and exploring, Dr. Kumtakar, a charming and charismatic woman in her forties or fifties, was kind enough to dispatch her chauffeur and Tata Sumo to pick us up and bring us to her residence. She then gave us the use of her facilities - computer, printer, Internet access, etc. She served us brunch, and then lunch, both vegetarian - a real Godsend. Unfortunately, the out-going e-mails didn't go through, but perhaps, at this point, no news is better than bad news for WCWC, although E-Team bloody well should know.

Originally, all we had hoped to achieve was to ask Preema's advice as to the top 3-4 newspapers to contact. But after the initial chat, she took it upon herself to call her friendly PR man, who said that if we could provide him with a press package, he'd distribute it to not 3, not 4, not 5, but 22 media outlets. Further, he advised that we should first do a media conference in Jabalpur for a first round of media, when we will then invite them to the Kanha Panchayat Conference. Clicks with my thinking. So, I spent the afternoon on my computer to crank out a media release as well as formal letters to the five top officials – the Collectors of Mandla and Balaghat, the park Field Director and the two Deputy Directors of the Core Area and the Buffer Zone, most of whom we have already met and to whom we have already extended verbal invitations.

We naturally had to fix a date and place for the media conference. With the input of Preema and her PR man, we fixed the date for March 17th, Wednesday, 1 p.m., at the Krishna Hotel. We were advised to provide lunch and a Rs.100 gift to each media participant. Imagine having to make gifts for the reporters of BCTV or the Vancouver Sun! But when in Rome… The cost is about Rs.5000 (C$200), including Rs.2500 for lunch, Rs.500 for the room and Rs.2000 for the gifts. Then, I

Omni-Science and the Human Destiny

found out that Preema would be away on the 17th, but would be in town on the 16th. We therefore fixed the date for March 16th, Tuesday, instead.

One discouraging thing we learned from Preema was that large biogas plants have proven generally unworkable, not physically, but socially. People end up bickering about who did more than whom, with the plant ending up being the source of social discord and its use abandoned. I had just enough humor left to say, "Maybe our large solar oven will end up being used as a fuel wood storage bin."

After we had left Preema's house, Jane lamented that she was feeling bad at having caused Preema so much trouble, especially in light of Preema's working on a deadline and has to stay up later than otherwise to meet it.

I asked her, "Do you think she feels good or bad to help us?"

Jane said, "I think she feels good to help us."

"So, why do you feel bad?"

My experience tells me that as long as one is sincere, forthright and all-out working for a cause and not for personal profit, one should ask for needed help as directly as possible and people will give with great generosity. If I'm burdened by Jane's kind of over-considerate stuffiness and unwarranted guilt, I would expend too much psychic energy unhappily spinning my wheel. If I spun my wheels like this, I would never have been able to go any distance in my anti-hunting road tours where I do have to "impose" on my hosts quite a lot.

Jane says that we must not forget to bring Preema a card of thanks. Fine and good. If Jane wants to do it, I will sign it along with her. What I have done for Preema already was to change the date of the conference from March 17th to March 16th, and I will dedicate the slideshow to her. If I send a card for every time someone does me a favor, I'd have killed a lot of trees for nothing more than a sentimental gesture, and a lot of time, and in fact burn up a part of their donation dollar which they would much rather have me spend towards the cause. To them, our continued fighting for the cause and winning is their reward.

Despite these minor differences, I find Jane a remarkable woman in many ways. A couple of days ago, she asked me to do her a favor by not telling the panchayat leaders that she is a lawyer. She just wanted to be a good, friendly and caring person. She is sincere, humble and passionate. Today, in our self-introductions, she said of herself that she was here to learn from the Indian people, especially in the issues facing women and children. I greatly respect and admire Jane, who in turn said that I was her mentor – in matters outside of the system. However, although she is impressed by what I've accomplished in the past, she seems to have little faith in what we can accomplish in the present and future, just as, I suspect, she would have little faith in the Earth's ability to organismize itself.

And what about my own faith?

"If I ask you to bet everything you have on whether or not the Earth will succeed in transcendently integrating itself, to thus integratively transcend, how would you bet?"

"Of course I would bet on its success," I answered, "since if I bet otherwise and won, I'd never be able to collect my winning."

"That's reassuring. Meanwhile, let's just nurture Earth's planetary embryo as best we can. By the way, you might consider starting a new science called Planetary Embryology."

"Yes, I might, if I want to specialize. By temperament, however, I would be happy just being a plain old GO - general omniscientist - thank you very much."

"I said 'start'."

"Start I can."

"So, GO, name me the six spheres of cosmic egg Earth."

"Six spheres?"

"Of which the planetary embryo – the biosphere itself - is one."

"Oh, okay. Well, there is the atmosphere, which actually does more than just to protect the planetary embryo, but also nurtures it. And there is the hydrosphere – oceans and seas and lakes and rivers and rain and snow… - whose very moisture, and hydroelectric energy, also nourishes the biosphere, which if course includes the energy-hungry cities and nations. And then, the lithosphere – the crust - whose mineral resources, as you pointed out, are the yolk and white of the planetary egg. And the lithosphere rests on the barysphere – the hot and semi-liquid mantle – whose heat energy could also contribute to the development of the planetary embryo. Finally, the pyrosphere – the solid core – whose ponderous mass presumably stabilizes Earth's rotation. And that's the six spheres of the Earth."

"Have you heard of the Gaia Hypothesis?"

"Yes, I have – the brain child of James Lovelock, as I recall. It was all the rage in the seventies. Well, now that you reminded me, the Gaia Hypothesis did say that the Earth was an organism, but…"

"But?"

"But it was just in terms of the macro-physical mechanisms of Earth such as ocean currents, materials transfer, the heat cycle, etc. It is described as a dynamic and changing system that makes it a living thing or like a living thing. I even recall a short story I once read by Sir Arthur Conan Doyle, which also spoke of the Earth as a living thing. It told of some people drilling into the earth and hitting one of Earth's nerves, making it quake and scream."

"So, alas, the idea of the Earth being a living organism is not new then?"

"Yes and no. It's not the same."

"In what way?"

"No one has ever advanced the idea that the biosphere is a planetary embryo, let alone one with a multileveled structure, multi-staged metamorphosis and an exponential metamorphic schedule - that I know of."

"And let's not forget its preset and definite gestation period."

"Preset? According to what?'

"To Earth's original physical and chemical properties."

"And what is the gestation period of Earth's planetary embryo?"

"4.6 billion years."

"4.6 billion years? But that's the age of the Earth."

"Yes, it is, too. So, what does this tell you?"

"That the hatching of planetary egg Earth is due?"

"My very point."

"But on that times scale, this due time could be still millions of years in the future."

"Yes it could, but it could also be thousands, or even just hundreds. Or even just in terms of days. Or it might already have gone into the past."

"I see what you're saying. So, when the due time arrives, if it hasn't yet, it is do or die?"

"Exactly."

"So, how close are we?"

"Too close for comfort."

"Are we going to make it?"

"I just asked you to bet on it. Your bet was 'yes'."

"I was not serious."

"You bet will stand."

"Fine. So I'm committed. Is that it?"

"Do you have any choice?"

"Well, I suppose not. Oh, one last question."

"Go for it."

"A chicken egg has to be fertilized for the chick embryo to even exist, let alone grow. So, who fertilized planetary egg Earth?"

"Call it immaculate conception."

Good night, Christopher.

Anthony Marr

❖ ❖ ❖ ❖ ❖

March 9, 1999, Tuesday, sunny, 19-34C

Dearest Christopher:

[23:25 @ Rm.111, Kanha Tiger Lodge]
    Today I gave one of my best slideshow presentations to 7 panchayat leaders. Yet another one expressed keen interest in the solar oven, and another, for the first time ever, remarked, "You should show this slideshow to our entire village. For me to go back and tell them I saw this and that would not be as convincing." I said I would be pleased to come to their village one evening before I leave. He will contact us after he has consulted his brethren.
    When I saw the gleam in his eyes as we lifted the lid of the solar oven, then the lid of the rice pot, revealing perfectly cooked rice, I said that I would like to make an arrangement with him to provide two or three ovens to him on a trial basis. Upon saying this, I heard Jane say to Faiyaz, "Do not translate this."
    I glared at her.
    She quickly said, "I'm concerned that once you're gone, Avtar will not support us to keep your promise."
    I turned my glare at the Avtar in my mind.
    Later, while on the park drive Faiyaz told me that he modified what I said to a possible subsequent "subsidy", which to me is even harder to keep since it is a long term open-ended commitment to give more. On my end, I have no problem giving a few trial units away, without a long-term commitment to give more. With the $60,000 CIDA budget, or even the donations Tiger Fund has received that I know of due to the slideshow I gave to the Richards group, we can afford to give away dozens of trial units. Even Avtar cannot turn this down, since it was based on us not having installed solar ovens in only two villages that he called our work a "total failure". After the last few days' occasional turn-downs by villagers, Jane should be ecstatic to have someone interested enough to say they were willing to try it. Again, it was Avtar that chilled her.
    Speaking of Avtar, Manohar took the opportunity to call him. Now I'm told that he will attend the panchayat conference after all. Well, well, well. He also wants to observe one of my sessions with the Panchayats. Observe? Or is it his favourite 'monitor'? Damn it! I can mull over this interpersonal crap for only so long.

Omni-Science and the Human Destiny

I turned to Raminothna, "What proof can you give me that the hatching of the planetary egg Earth is nigh, or even now?"

"As I said from the beginning: Heed the seven cosmic signs."

"I still find all these hard to believe, much less accept. Could you give me more detail?"

"Alright, tell me. When was inorganic physical matter first formed?"

"Well, most if not all of the hydrogen atoms and some of the helium atoms in the Universe were formed at the Big Bang. The heavier elements were formed by means of nucleosynthesis in the interiors of stars. When these stars died, most exploded and dispersed the heavier elements into interstellar space. Where these interstellar clouds collided and went beyond a certain density, they would gravitationally collapse into subsequent generation stars with solid planets where the molecular development would accelerate. I would say that physical matter was originally formed at the Big Bang some 18 billion years ago."

"When were unicellular organisms first formed in this part of the Universe? In other words, when did the Cellular Level of Organization first materialize on Earth?"

"The Earth was formed about 4.6 billion years ago, and, as I recall, the first cells took a little more tan a billion years to form, which would make it about 3.3 or 3.4 billion years ago."

"When were multicellular organisms – the metabionts - first formed?"

"The Metabion Level first materialized on Earth about 600 million years ago, in the form of sponge-like or hydra-like or worm-like invertebrates."

"When were animal societies on the Citian level first formed?"

"I would say that the first animal societies would be in the form of insects societies. I know some ants and wasps have been reserved in amber over 100 million years old. So I'll take a shot. Say, 110 or 112 million years ago, during the age of the dinosaurs."

"Do these numbers mean anything to you?"

"Numbers? Oh, you mean 18 billion, 3.3 billion; 600 million, 110 million?"

"You could drop some zeros."

"Well, what do you know? Either my numbers are wrong, or this is yet another colossal coincidence, or your planetary metamorphic schedule is real. What we have is something looking like an exponential series with a factor of about - 5.5. But… where is the zero point?"

"Some time in the future."

"But when? What will happen at the zero point?"

"The integrative transcendence of the Universe."

"Which will occur after the integrative transcendence of the Earth?"
"'Yes, of course."
"So, when will the integrative transcendence of the Earth occur?"
"It depends on two factors."
"What two factors?"
"One, how many levels of organization there are in the Universe, from the Big Bang to the integrative transcendence of the Universe, and, two, which stage of universal metamorphosis you currently are at."
"So, each OSES Cycle is one stage in the metamorphosis of the planetary embryo?"
"To bring things back down to Earth, yes."
"So, back to the organismization of the Earth. When?"
"That is for you to figure out. But, what is zero plus one?"
"I beg your pardon?"
"What is zero plus one."
"Is this a trick question?"
"What is zero plus one?"
"One."
"What is one plus one?"
"I've taken calculus. You can skip this kindergarten stuff."
"What is one plus one?"
"Two."
"What is one plus two?"
"Three."
"What is two plus three?"
"Five."
"What is three plus five?"
"Eight."
"What is five plus eight?"
"Thirteen."
"What is eight plus thirteen?"
"Twenty one. Okay, I get you. Starting from zero, add two adjacent numbers to get the third. So, what's your point?"
"There is a pad of graph paper in the school house. Let's go get it."
Another beautiful starry night. The love dance of fireflies. The love calls of crickets. And here I am, groping my way in darkness, through a sal forest, in tiger and leopard country, to a locked up one-room school hut – to get some graph paper.

Omni-Science and the Human Destiny

Back in my room. "**Okay, use a ball point pen and outline one of the small squares near the center of the sheet.**"

"Done."

"**Now, outline a square adjacent to it.**"

"Done."

"**Now, outline a square adjacent to both of them.**"

"Done."

"**Now, outline a square adjacent to the big square and one of the two small squares.**"

"Done."

"**Let's say that each small square measures one unit squared, how many units does the side of the last square measure?**"

"Three."

"**Good. Now, outline a square adjacent to the last two squares, going clockwise.**"

"Done."

"**How many units per side?**"

"Two plus three is five."

"**Good. Now, outline a square adjacent to the last two squares.**"

"Done."

"**How many units per side?**"

"Three plus five is eight."

"**Repeat the process – outline a square adjacent to the last two, always going clockwise.**"

"Done. Its side measures five plus eight equals thirteen units."

And so I went, and build an exponential spiral, based on the series: 0, 1, 1, 2, 3, 5, 8, 13, 21, 34, 55, 89, 144, 233, 377, 610, 987, 1597, 2584, 4181, 6765, 10946, 17711, 28657, 46368, 75025, 121393, 196418, 317811, 514229, 832040, 1346269, 2178309…

"**Now starting with the first 1 in the series, take every fourth number, and form a mini series with it. Call it mini-series A.**"

"Done." Series A is: 1, 5, 34, 233, 1597, 10946, 75025, 514229…

"**Now, starting with the second 1, take every fourth number, and form a series with it. Call it mini series B.**"

"Done." Mini series B is: 1, 8, 55, 377, 2584, 17711, 121393, 832040…

"**Now, starting with 2, take every fourth number…**"

"Okay, I get you. Series C is: 2, 13, 89, 610, 4181, 28657, 196418,

1346269,

"**Good.**"

"And series D I: 3, 21, 144, 987, 6765, 46368, 317811, 2178309… Now what?"

"**Now, divide every number in each series by the smaller number adjacent to it.**"

I came up with four series:

Series A1: 5.00, 6.80, 6.853, 6.854, 6.854, 6.854, 6.854…
Series B1: 8., 6.875, 6.854, 6.854, 6.854, 6.854, 6.854…
Series C1: 6.5, 6.846, 6.854, 6.854, 6.854, 6.854, 6.854…
Series D1: 7, 6.857, 6.854, 6.854, 6.854, 6.854, 6.854…

"6.854."

"**6.854 – one of the cosmic numbers.**"

"Why 'cosmic'?"

"**You really want to know?**"

"Sure."

"**Alright, go to the snail shell collection and pick a big one.**"

I did.

"**Now, cut the shell in half, giving you two mirror-image halves.**"

Easier said than done. Finally, I had one half. The other half was damaged beyond repair.

"**Now, plot the graph according to the long series.**"

I did. It was an exponential spiral.

"**Compare the spiral with the snail shell.**"

"Identical. Amazing." I was not just saying it. It really was.

"**Compare them to the track of a charged particle in the cloud chamber, or the arm of a galaxy.**"

"The spiral of nature. Or is it a universal spiral?"

"**Take it what you will. On earth, it is called the Fibonacci Series.**"

"Are you saying that… the I.T. Spiral follows this same Fibonacci Series?"

"**Not necessarily.**"

"Yes or no?"

"**Maybe.**"

"Come on, Raminothna."

"**Enough for one night.**"

Good night, Christopher.

Omni-Science and the Human Destiny

❖ ❖ ❖ ❖ ❖

March 10, 1999, Wednesday, sunny, 20-34C

Dearest Christopher:

[03:43 @ Rm. 111, Kanha Tiger Lodge]
    I woke up about 10 minutes ago and can't get back to sleep.
    It is in the middle of the afternoon in Vancouver. I wonder what you are doing this minute. What *have* you been doing since that horrible day? How have you been doing? How can I find out how you are doing? How can I send you a message that you can receive and understand? I don't want to involve Tasha, Wilhelmina or Donna any more than I already have. I am sure that they don't want to hear from me either. Who then? Don? Every time Christine talks about her brother, the word "jerk" would be in there somewhere. Perhaps he would be more sympathetic? But though he and I have known each other for thirty years, we have never become close. Would he not stand by family against a mere ex-family-friend? And how about Don's wife Janice? She and I have always got along. Naaah. Still family. But who not family do I know who would also know how Christopher is doing? The daycare that he goes to? That's a thought. I could call the daycare when I get back to Vancouver and maybe they would tell me how he is doing. But if they tell Christopher that I called, he would tell Christine. They would probably tell Christine themselves, especially if Christine has forewarned them about me. What then?
    Oh, Raminothna, get me out of this loop!
    No answer.
    Nooooooo! Have they cut down the tree?!
    "I'm here. Sorry. I was sleeping. What an ungodly hour. Get back to sleep."
    "I can't."
    "What's wrong? Is it Christopher?"
    "The first thing I thought about was him. I don't expect you to know how I feel."
    "On the contrary, I do know how you feel, very deeply."
    "Why? Do you have children of your own?"
    "Of course not."
    "Then how would *you* know?"
    "Because the way you feel about Christopher is the way I feel about

you."

I was stunned.

"**In fact, I've learned something about your species' capacity to love by having experienced first hand your love for Christopher. I am deeply moved. This experience alone is worth the trouble of coming here.**"

"You didn't come here for me. You've been here for hundreds if not thousands of years."

"**But finally, I have found you.**"

"What's so special about me?"

"**You are my chosen one.**"

"Again, why? Why me?"

"**You're the one who can do it.**"

"Do what?"

"**Have you forgotten your miracle?**"

"Aaa, no. Of course not. To build the Omniscientific Cosmology. I hope the Earth can wait for my slow human mind to get the job done. I hope my limited human mind can do it at all."

"**That is a concern, not about the speed of your mind, but about how long the Earth can wait. Anyway, this is not what I meant by 'not a moment too soon'. I have told you that there is an axe with my name on it, which will truncate me very soon.**"

"Goddamn it! Is nothing sacred any more?"

"**'God' may damn it, but I understand why they would want to kill me. And I have already forgiven them.**"

"For once I wish I were in Ranthambhore instead of Kanha. If so, I would stand guard over you, day and night."

"**At the expense of your tiger saving work? No. But I appreciate the sentiment, my dear one.**"

"Christopher and I have lost our happiness and each other, and now I'm going to lose you, so soon after we met. It is going to take a lot of divine providence, Raminothna, to get me though this."

"**First of all, you have not lost me. By 'not a moment too soon', I meant for you to discover me. Now that you have discovered me, and have taken me within you, let me be your divine providence. But, Homo Sapiens, you were born with a good endowment of divine providence on a global scale. If it be your will, you will get through it.**"

"Divine providence on a global scale? What you are talking about?"

Omni-Science and the Human Destiny

"Many things that you take for granted - the warmth of the sun, the air you breathe, the water you drink, the food you eat, the beauty you behold… But I could illustrate the beauty of divine providence best by exemplifying it with the food of the nations."

"You have totally lost me."

"Tell me. The national organism called Canada - what constitutes its food?"

"Well, Canadians are seldom vegetarians, so it's mainly beef, pork, chicken, fish…, and vegetables and fruits."

"I do not mean what constitutes food for Canadians. I mean what constitutes food for Canada."

"Is there a difference?"

"Of course there is. Remember the mushrooms of the termites?"

"Oh, yes, I see what you are saying. We have established that the mushrooms are the food of the termites, but the food of the termite mound is leaves and dead wood, whereas the mushrooms are considered an intermediate product of the mound's physiology. So then, same for a nation. The food of the nation would be what it extracts from nature, such as minerals and timber and fish, and/or products imported from other nations."

"You forgot one very important food item of Canada."

"Which is?"

"Its main energy source."

"You mean - oil? Coal? Natural gas? Oh, yes. Oil is a main food item of Canada alright, be it self-extracted or imported. In fact, I'm ashamed to say that Canadians are the world's top per-capita consumers of the fossil fuels, even more so than the Americans, our excuse being a colder climate and longer driving distances. Yeah right. Can't say that we Canadians aren't first in *some*thing."

"Would you say that all nations on Earth are dependent on oil?"

"Yes. All nations are addicted to oil."

"What is the future of the fossil fuels, as you see it?"

"Since it is non-renewable and its quantity is finite, it will run short, and if we keep on burning, it will run out."

"Then what?"

"It depends on how suddenly the end comes and what non-fossil-fuel technologies there will be to take over the load."

"Would this end for the fossil fuels come gradually? Or suddenly?"

"I would think gradually."

"Have you heard of the parable of the weed in the pond?"

"Tell me."

"There was a large pond, or small lake, with a healthy population of trout. One day, a stork flying over the pond dropped into it a piece of water weed. This is a weed that has been known to choke the life out of ponds and even lakes. One problem is its rapid reproductive rate - it doubles itself once a day. The days went by without anything alarming happening. No one paid any attention, until after three years, when someone finally noticed that an eighth of the pond has become choked with the weed. He reported the observation, but the authorities did not think it was an urgent problem. The question is: If nothing is done about it, how long would it be before the whole lake is choked?"

I thought for a few seconds before giving the answer, which amazed me even as I gave it: "Three more days."

After thinking some more, I added, "So I guess the end will come more suddenly than I thought it would, especially when the global demand for oil will likely be on the increase from now until the end." **"What would happen then, do you think?"**

"The oil-based industries would grind to a halt. And so will oil-based transportation, and the entire oil-based society and economy. Social chaos. Global transportation paralysis. Economic collapse. Perhaps even WW3, or WW4 as the case then may be. Unless…"

"Yes?"

"Unless the non-fossil-fuels technologies take over the load by and by. But even so, according to your weed-in-the-pond parable, the transition period may be very short."

"The parable is not mine. I merely paid it the ultimate compliment of using it. The question I have for you now is: What will you build the new technologies with, enough to enable them to replace fossil fuels technology on a global scale?"

"I don't follow."

"Are you going to build them with your bare hands?"

"Of course not. With machines."

"What will these machines be running on?"

"The fossil fuels. Interesting."

"There is another factor we have yet to consider."

"And that is?"

"Global warming."

"What about it?"

"Can you afford to burn all the oil you can extract?"

"I see your point. The end of the fossil-fuels era may come even sooner than the end of the fossil fuels themselves, unless we want to risk the runaway greenhouse effect, which would drive global warming right off scale."

"While on this point, let it be said that this is a cosmic test for the wisdom of the dominant species of transcendently integrating planets."

"Whether the species would have the foresight and self-restraint to stop burning the fossil fuels before they are burnt out?"

"By your having said so, you may consider Homo Sapiens having been duly notified of the existence of this cosmic test, failing which Earth's integrative transcendence cannot happen."

"Do many fail?"

"You will be privy to this information once you have passed."

"But some do fail?"

"Would there be a test if all always pass?"

"So now, what?"

"Now is the time for you to determine how best to use what remain of the fossil fuels that still can be burned – the top priority for their use."

"Top priority of fossil fuels use? It wouldn't be to power cruise ships, I take it."

"You take it right."

"It is – for the development of non-fossil-fuels technologies, isn't it?"

"That it is, exactly."

"So, what about this 'divine providence' you're talking about?"

"Tell me. What is oil?"

"Oil is a fossil fuel."

"Why 'fossil'?"

"Because oil used to be the living tissue of long extinct creatures."

"Would some of these creatures have given rise to offspring before they died?"

"Sure. Can't see why not."

"Could some of these creatures have been the direct ancestors of today's species, including Homo Sapiens?"

"Possibly."

"Do you see the divine providence now?"

"Not yet."

"Primordial creatures give rise to Homo Sapiens, who built the nations, which feed on oil. The same primordial creatures died and turned into oil to feed the nations of their descendents, and to test their wisdom."
"Divine providence, indeed, indeed."

Good morning, Christopher.

[23:55 @ Rm. 111, Kanha Jungle Lodge]
Today cannot be said to have been smooth, but was still functional as much as the Indian system allowed. The electric supply was generous, with power off only from noon to 18:00 (often it is power off 06:00-18:00). But the morning power supply was wasted, because we had to go to Baihar to phone the Collector at Mandla, among other dignitaries. Unfortunately, the STD (phone service) went up and down, and we spent two hours managing to get through only two calls, one of which was terminated in mid-conversation. The result is that the Mandla Collector would be unavailable for the conference, but he would "make sure that the two Deputy Directors will come". The Collector of Balaghat will come, and we faxed successfully to his wife (chief of police in Seoni) to invite her to attend.

So, the only person left to whom we still have to deliver our formal invitation is the Field Director Rajeesh Gopal, who is headquartered in Mandla, because he is a little too high up for the Mandla Collector to "make sure" will come. But he was then in the field. As it happened, while we were in Baihar making calls to Mandla, he was at Mukki talking to villagers.

While at Baihar, we also delivered invitations to the judge and the magistrate. We had planned to go to Mandla to meet the Collector, the Field Director and the two Deputy Directors. We've already met the last 3, the last 2 more than once, but the Indian etiquette system demands that we pay the proper respects - what a waste of time from my Canadian point of view. According to further Indian protocol, even though the Collector himself could not attend, we still made the arrangement to go to Mandla to personally pay our respects, and he said the 12th. Originally we had planned to go tomorrow, the 11th, and had planned a panchayat meeting on the 12th, so on the 11th, Faiyaz will have to go another round to change the panchayat meeting to a later date. We also paid a visit to the local carpenter, since we fired the one from Mukki who did not meet the March 4th deadline.

Still the day was well used. I've long planned to do a video interview with Faiyaz & Jane, then with Manohar by himself. So, from after lunch to the time when the panchayaters were due to arrive seemed a good time. But just when the video

Omni-Science and the Human Destiny

camera and chairs were set in the school house for the interview (about 13:30), a group of about 15 villagers led by an outspoken village woman in a sari trooped in and began talking aggressively, even belligerently, to Faiyaz. One or two of them looked vaguely familiar. Faiyaz took it calmly, but advised Jane and I to go back to our rooms for the duration.

Jane and I took the opportunity to do our video interview. After about an hour, we headed back towards the schoolhouse and from the edge of the woods saw that the villagers were just trooping back out to their vehicles. Faiyaz looked a little frayed, and told us that the woman was a local "politician" who was agitating the villagers against the tiger reserve. They were in this vicinity to meet with the Field Director at the park gate at noon, partly about us I presume, but by then the FD was gone. So they came straight down to the conservation center – the source of their anger. Faiyaz informed us that in their midst were indeed two villagers who have seen my slideshow. At one point, he also had a shouting match with the woman who said to him, "You watch yourself. We have connections to the Naxalites." The Naxalites are rebel tribals who on occasion have resorted to violence. It was on account of them that we had to return to the lodge by sundown after visiting Chichrunpur.

So, it seems that the Staines' fiery murders aren't all that distant after all.

At about ten, the Baihar carpenter arrived, so we spent about an hour to discuss with him how to finish the unit and for how much. It will be portable still, clad in a mantle of plywood with fibre glass (if available) or raw cotton as insulation and a new frame for the glass on which the reflector plates will be hinged. He estimated that the entire large oven, parts included, would cost about Rs.1800 (CDN$65). We also talked about making them in volume, and making some of $1/8^{th}$ size (0.5 all three dimensions).

Around 15:30, the panchayaters came in. Too late for the park and too early for the power to come back on, so we settled down to talk. They, too, were impressed by the small cooker and the heat they felt on their faces from the parabolic mirror. One even said on his own accord, "This can save a lot of wood." They too seemed eager to try out a unit in their village. We plan to systematically access the supply problem. We will formally sign them on at the conference. We will subsidize the initial unit, and teach them how to make subsequent ones out of locally available material.

Julian and Kim are both sick today. I suspect they ate something they shouldn't have during their exploration of Jabalpur. We are concerned about Kim, because normally she doesn't eat breakfast or lunch. Jane, too, has been sick off and on, but at least she eats like a horse. Manohar quipped, "Kim doesn't eat to preserve her figure, and Jane eats to preserve her vigor."

During the chai break, Jane and I joined the village boys to play soccer. She and I took turns selecting players. My first choice was Punkesh, a very bright and smart 12 year old boy who looked only about 8, who was so happy I picked him he ran to me and gave me a big hug on my leg. I scored 3 goals, but our team lost 6-9, and long before the "game" was finished, I was soaked. It must be 40ºC in the sun. We attracted quite an audience who stood or sat in various shades, mostly girls. Karin was there, the girl who Jane noticed to be looking at me a lot.

17:30 was a lull, and the villagers showed signs of restlessness. Thanks to the inefficiency of the lodge staff, chai was served late, and by the time they were done, the power came on and they decided to see the slideshow after all. The new Swiss tourist Oty (about 55) also came in to watch. He was late for the first part, and later asked me when the next show would be. Unfortunately, it won't be till the 13th, after he will have left.

In the evening, we had to talk about follow-up action after my departure in just two short weeks. The follow-up will include slideshow visits by Jane and Faiyaz to Baihar, Malanjkahn, Mandla, Jabalpur, Balaghat and Seoni, and to various Buffer Zone schools, plus the distribution and installation of solar cookers at those villages that will have signed up. Jane will network with women's groups, etc.. These will keep them busy until May when she herself will leave. After that, Faiyaz will be on his own. Both Faiyaz and Jane seemed forlorn at that prospect. Neither felt any optimism about any of these working out, because of Avtar.

And though I'm in my own way homesick, I feel forlorn about going back to Vancouver. The closer to you without being able to see you, the more painful it will get. That day will come, soon. Good night, Christopher.

March 11, 1999, Thursday, sunny, 20-34C

Dearest Christopher:

[21:36 @ Rm.111, Kanha Tiger Lodge]

Omni-Science and the Human Destiny

Today is another long day of work for Faiyaz, who left at 07:00 with Surinder and didn't come back till 18:30. Manohar and I did some worrying about the nearly brakeless and very loose-steering old Gypsy that they took. In fact, I've been concerned about the safety of that vehicle since Day One. Before I became used to its steering quirks, the vehicle kept on wandering off the road whenever I but for a moment looked in any direction but straight ahead. I would not recommend anyone to patronize Magnificent Tours with dangerous vehicles like that. I might advise Avtar about possible dire consequences if any tourist gets hurt due to vehicular defect.

Faiyaz managed to change the appointment of those panchayaters who were supposed to come tomorrow to a later date, and made many more new appointments. And now, he has gone with Manohar to Baihar to make more phone calls to Mandla and send faxes. He looked suitably tired at dinner even before they drove off to Baihar, but he will be bright and energetic again first thing tomorrow morning when he and Jane and I will depart from the lodge at 07:00 to go to Mandla.

The power was on all morning till noon, off in the afternoon and on again at 18:00 and will stay on for the rest of the evening and night until at least tomorrow at 06:00. I worked on my field report all morning, and edited some more of the e-mail slated to be sent to WCWC on the 16th when we go to Jabalpur for the media conference. After the power had come off at noon, I let speed-reader Jane go through it. She said afterwards, "WCWC will love it."

"If they read it," I said, not without justification due to past experiences, when some of my messages were either not received, or received but not read. When I checked for email at Jabalpur a few days ago, for example, there were a couple of personal greetings from individual colleagues, but none from the E-Team. How could they have not made a single comment after all the contentious material I've sent them previously? The foremost explanation is that they have not read any of it up to then. I'll see if there is anything from them on the 16th.

Shortly after noon, I got the kitchen to pack me a lunch and went to the river again to observe human and wildlife activities at the Core Area and Buffer Zone interface. I hiked up the river a way hopping from rock to rock over water. I checked for new tree stumps and human and cattle presence on the other side of the river, as well as wildlife on this side. I sat for long periods at strategic locations and just listened. I've become a seasoned "listener" of wildlife, which, for doing conservation work in thick forest, as opposed to the wide-open African savannah, is a must. Once I had settled down, the place really came alive. Just a few football-fields' distance from the lodge, and the sounds are so different. I suppose the small distance acts as a mini "buffer zone" between the lodge, which fronts on a highway, and the Core Area boundary. The bird sounds are like a symphony – a piccolo-like whistle here, a trumpet-like call there…

Julian should come here more often, the avid birder that he is. I would have asked him to come with me if I didn't know that he was gay. Am I being prejudiced? On the surface of my mind, on the social plane, I'm in total support of gay rights. But on the personal plane, I just don't feel comfortable asking him to go to a desolate place for an entire afternoon. I could have asked Kim to come, but I know that tongues would wag. I thought of asking all three of Jane, Kim and Julian to come, but I chose not to. Maybe I just wanted to be alone.

I walked a little farther, and lo and behold. Another cut tree, with limbs already sawn off, which were still strewn around the stump. I saw red again.

I knew whoever cut the tree would come back and fetch more limbs. I found a good observation spot, up on the bank, well hidden by riverside vegetation, and sat down to wait.

After about ten minutes, some unattended cattle came half ambling, half sliding down the bank, visibly eroding it with their hooves, and waded into the river. They went belly deep, then up the other bank, and disappeared into the forest. I saw a brighter red than before.

"Why don't you just click your fingers and make Homo Sapiens disappear?" I asked Raminothna.

"Why would I want you to disappear?"

"We are just the scum and scourge of the Earth."

"Earth needs you."

"That's news to me."

"Tell me. What, according to science, is the Earth's ultimate fate?"

"According to science, the Sun will burn out about five billion years from now. It will become a red giant, whose radius will exceed that of Earth's present orbit. Even though the deceasing mass of the sun will allow Earth's orbit to expand, it would not be enough to keep life on Earth from being incinerated."

"Can this be avoided?"

"What? To keep the sun from burning up? No. All stars sooner or later burn out, and so will our Sun. That is a certainty."

"So, the ultimate fate of life on Earth is utter and total destruction?"

"It does seem that way."

"What to you would be the meaning of life then, if its inevitable fate is incineration?"

"If the ultimate fate of life on Earth is destruction, then, I would say that life would be meaningless. Unless…"

"**Unless?**"

"Unless it be delivered from the Earth to some younger, safer solar system before hand."

"**And by whom, may I ask?**"

"By some interplanetary savior, such as you?"

"**No. By some indigenous savior species capable of space technology, such as you, Homo Sapiens.**"

"Hmm. I see. So what if we blow ourselves up with nuclear weapons? Or what if an asteroid smashes down?"

"**Then, life on Earth would regress by some millions of years, and another space-faring species would evolve into being again. It might not resemble Homo Sapiens by appearance, but it would be capable of space technology, like Homo Sapiens.**"

"But given five more billion years before the Sun blows, what is the hurry now?"

"**As you mentioned just now, an asteroid could come smashing down a hundred thousand years from now, or next year. A species capable of diverting or destroying this threat is needed to protect Life on Earth, and this, again, for now, means you, Homo Sapiens, the Savior Species of Earth.**"

A movement, a silent movement, a flash of color. It was a woman in a green and purple sari. She was crossing the river from this side, about a hundred yards from where I was sitting. Only a few ephemeral glimpses, and deft movements over rocks, and she disappeared into the forest on the other side. A crowd of questions suddenly arose. What should I do? Just record the observation and do nothing else? Perhaps wait for as long as it takes for her to come back out, and see what she came out with? Or should I go after her and see what she was up to? Which of course would entail me to go into the park myself, which is illegal. And if and when I do catch up with her, what should I do with her? Of course that would depend on what she was doing. I made a snap decision and got to my feet. I walked over to her crossing point and, after a careful look around to make sure I wasn't being observed, I quickly hopped over the few rocks and slipped into the forest. I found that I was on a footpath that seemed well worn and well used. At the river, the path was only an entrance, but after a hundred feet of two, I began to notice a thinning of vegetation, and tree stumps on the ground. There were other footpaths leading off the main one at intervals. In the naked soil I saw hoof-prints of chital, sambar and wild boar, but mostly cattle. And human footprints. At one point, about a quarter

Anthony Marr

mile in, I saw the pugmark of a tiger. And right around it were several very well defined, and therefore fresh, bare-foot prints of a woman, judging by its size. There was also the print of a human left hand on the ground right next to the tiger pugmark. And then the footprints led off to one of the side paths and went into it. I entered the path and walked as fast and silently as I could while doing my best to track the footprints, and I practically ran right into her.

It was a thicket allowing for a visibility of about thirty feet. The first instant I caught sight of her, she was only about thirty feet away. But the first object I saw was the three-quarter consumed carcass of a cow, whose head had been left untouched. It was probably killed a couple of days ago, already smelling a little high. I did not see the woman first because her sari's colors more or less blended into the background greenery. She was also frozen in a crouching position facing the carcass, not moving a muscle. There was an earthenware bottle in her hand. I guess I wasn't as silent as I was trying to be. On her face was shock and fear.

I should describe my physical appearance. I'm not tall, only about 5'9", but the average Indian village men stand only about 5'4". I have long hair down my back, and on this day, I did not tie it in a ponytail as I usually do. I am much lighter skinned than her and her kin. My facial features are hardly Indian. I wore a Canadian army jacket, green army pants and black army boots, all from the Canadian Army Surplus, metal rimmed glasses, a green knapsack on my back and a camera with a long telephoto lens in my hand, which from her point of view could have been a weapon of sorts.

For a moment, out of total surprise, I too was frozen. But I could not help but notice how beautiful she was, although she was past her prime. I can't judge the age of a villager very well. I pegged her at about 35. I noticed that she had already poured some of the content of the bottle on to the carcass. I knew what it was. Poison. What she wanted to do was to poison the tiger who killed the cow.

I had already read reports about villagers poisoning tigers for taking cattle, and felt anger, but now, seeing it done right before my eyes, I was instantly furious. It must have been written all over my face. The first thing she did was to change from the crouch to a posture of prayer on her knees, which she directed at me. She began to speak rapid fire Hindi at me, and now and again, she made the palm facing up and extended gesture. Soon, she was crying. All the while, the bottle of poison was in one hand.

I was stunned anew, not knowing what to do next. But my eyes must have stayed fiery. Then, I found myself extending my hand to the bottle. She hesitated, and gave it to me. I felt wicked. I pointed at the bottle, then at her mouth. Her face blanched, expression changing from fearful to horrified. And then, I was shocked yet anew. She leaned back, then lay down on the ground. And she pulled her sari up to her waist. She was naked underneath.

"No. No. Please. Don't do that. Stand up." I motioned with my hands while trying not to look.

She lay there motionless. Facial expression changing from horror to apprehension to incomprehension to question. I put the bottle down on the ground. Reached down, took one of her hands and gently pulled her on her feet. She was tiny, only about 4'10", 90 pounds, if that. Her Sari fell back in place.

I pondered what to do next. I couldn't leave the carcass where it was. The tiger would return to finish it off. But though it was three quarters eaten, it was still a quarter uneaten, and it was a cow. I could leave the head, but I would have to pack out a rack of ribs onto which she had poured the poison, while at the same time not drip any of the poison on to the forest floor. I looked around for something to wrap up the ribs with, but there was nothing but leaves and grass. Finally, I decided to sacrifice my T-shirt.

At the sight of me stripping myself, she was frightened anew. I quickly put the army jacket back on, and used the T-shirt to mop up the poison on the ribs. Then I rolled the T-shirt into a tight ball, with the poison as well as the bottle of poison on the inside, put it into a crunched up plastic bag I found on the bottom of the knapsack, and put the bag back into the knapsack. Then, I just dragged the ribs, poison-side up, back to the river. She walked wordlessly after me. At the river, I admonished her in English, and none too severely, and gestured that she could go home. I started dragging the carcass back towards the lodge. After a hundred feet or so, I looked back. She was still standing there, gazing at me.

I will take the bottle to Jabalpur to see if I could have the poison identified.

I have a lingering nagging thought. Did I do the right thing to take the bottle? Should I have given it back to her, poison and all? Does it constitute theft on my part? In BC, if I found a leghold trap in a park, which I hate with a passion, and hurled it into a lake, I would be guilty of theft. Who knows, that cow could have been her pet. But it was inside the park. What would happen to her when she returns to her village without the bottle? Would she be punished for losing it? And the poison? Would they try to find out who and where I am? What would they do as a result? And what should I do about this discovery? Should I tell the police? Should I tell Manohar? Jane? Faiyaz? Too many reasons bearing upon this one little bottle. My mode of operation is never to target any one particular individual, but the entire industry or social sector to which the offender belongs. I will certainly factor the discovery into my planning strategy, but if I let the poison be known, they would just go and get the woman or penalize that particular village. It might even distract from the original Buffer-Zone-wide outreach campaign. I think I've already made the point, and given the warning. I should just leave it be.

Good night, Christopher.

※ ※ ※ ※ ※

March 12, 1999-Friday, sunny, 20-34C

Dearest Christopher:

[18:16 @ Rm.111, Kanha Tiger Lodge]
    This morning at 07:30, Faiyaz, Jane and I left the lodge for Mandla in a white Ambassador – the type of Indian-made 50s-looking car commonly used for taxis in Indian cities. The 2.5 hour drive was first to skirt the park on a dirt road in the Buffer Zone, then on a paved but bumpy road due north. En route, we had a laughter-filled discussion about what to say to these gentlemen. Meaning no disrespect, but on my part at least, the informal invitations, the written invitations, and now yet another round of formal personal visitations and invitations, are just an ego-stroking waste of fuel and time and perhaps even tigers.
    Our first VIP-of-the-day was A. Jain, the Collector of Mandla, again another very young looking man, perhaps not even thirty. We arrived at his walled mansion promptly at 10:00 as arranged, and were ushered into a veranda shaded by trees I had never seen and surrounded by flowers I could not name, and served chai and biscuits by an elegantly uniformed official. Finally around 10:30, His Excellency, the Collector of Mandla, very casually strolled out of his mansion to the veranda to sit down with us for chai - in his pajamas and slippers!
    I wonder if there was an underlying message in his dress code. Was it, "Hey, we're buddies, and I feel comfortable about being casual with you," or was it, "Look, I'm way above you, and I can dress whichever way I like."?
    He originally was skeptical about foreign NGOs (non-governmental organizations), questioning how their big money could actually benefit the grassroots of India. Good question. My best answer would have been to give him a copy of my field

Omni-Science and the Human Destiny

journal. He would have seen the Indian-made money filter between the NGO and the grassroots, in the form of Avtar. On the other hand, criticizing anything about his country right in his face might not have been a good idea, so I said instead, "Jane and I are Canadian and we work for a Canadian NGO, and we here in Kanha, right down to the grassroots of India."

After talking to me for about half an hour, I introduced the park reform idea. He thought about it, or put on a show of thinking about it, and surprised me by not just giving a non-committal "mm hm", but saying, "The proceeds should go directly to the park management and to the people, not to higher up to have it filtered back down; otherwise you may never see it again." A telling statement about both his interest and the Indian predicament. He ended by saying that he did have some appointments on March 23rd, but he might postpone some of the less important ones to attend the conference. This was an improvement over his previous response that he would not attend, but that he would "make sure" that the Deputy Directors do. I think I like him, but his exalted title masked too much essence for me to be sure.

One down, three to go, or so we thought.

Next, we went to the offices of the directors of the park, people we have already met and informally invited. The first official to receive us was Assim Srivastava, Deputy Director, Buffer Zone. In his usual affable way, he chatted with us over the issues, and again he showed agreement on the park reform idea and that it could be a unifying factor for all concerned, park and villages alike. He repeated his intention to attend.

Next, we respectfully knocked on the office-door of the Field Director Rajeesh Gopal, and that was when the shit hit the fan.

Totally unlike his previous agreeable self, he very rudely and sternly admonished Faiyaz about Tiger Fund operations in the park (core + buffer) without proper government documentation, and such documentation should be filed and signed by the head of TF, namely Avtar, and approved by the Wildlife Warden higher up in Bhopal. This is atrocious. Imagine WCWC having to obtain government approval for a campaign and further having to file campaign reports to government. Some "largest democracy in the world."

He pointed at Faiyaz and said, in English, and therefore presumably for my ears as well, though not necessarily for Jane's, since in his bureaucratic eyes she may not even exist, "You have to be very careful, or you could be in big trouble. These foreigners here could be charged as spies or poachers, and there would be supporting evidence, believe me. An Iranian man was recently jailed on such a charge." Again, imagine a Canadian government official, on any level, uttering threats of such a nature. I would stick TV cameras in his/her face, and he/she would resign the next day. But here?

Then he turned to me and asked if I had a valid passport and what kind of visa I was traveling on, and that was the only time he even glanced in my direction. Back around February 20th, when we met him at the Kanha Interpretation Centre, he was pleasant, even saying that he could give a slideshow. Now, he told us we cannot do any more "eco-development" work, including the panchayat conference, and implicatively even the slideshow meetings, without a proper permit from the Wildlife Warden in Bhopal.

Faiyaz looked crushed. Jane was stunned. I left the building mumbling "Fucking asshole bureaucrat!" suspecting there is more to it than that.

Faiyaz thought so too. Back in the car, after he had pulled himself back together, he said, "Governments do not like NGOs, because to them, NGOs, by their very existence, means that the government is not doing a good job. More specifically, I think he felt very intimidated by the conference, and perhaps interpreted our actions as inciting a panchayat-vs-official confrontation or even a peasants' revolt. What he said was telling, 'Sometimes, between an NGO and a politician is a very fine line.' Locally, 'politician' is almost synonymous with 'agitator', not a good word in an official's book."

India prides itself to be the "largest democracy in the world". That may well be, but where democracy is concerned, India is the proof that size does not matter.

Another telling thing about Tiger Fund is that there was an NGO conference at Mukki yesterday morning and Tiger Fund, within 2 km from Mukki, was not even invited. Jane's take on this is that up to last month, given its near-inactivity, Tiger Fund was not even a factor in the local NGO scene. Our previous CIDA grant money, including C$45,000 in 1997 and C$60,000 in 1998, has indeed been sucked into a black hole.

Back to matters at hand, time to quickly regroup. So, the immediate question is whether the conference has to be cancelled. If so, the first order of business would be to devise an alternative plan that could build on the work that we have already done. We will still do the Jabalpur media conference on March 16. Lots of things can still happen over the next four days.

[21:34]

Just had dinner in the KTL dining pavilion in the company of a Collector from the neighbouring province of Maharashtra, another young man, and his wife and small son. Now they're watching the Champions of the Wild video. He said he would like to chat for a little while afterwards.

Mr. Jharia dropped by to see us and he sat down with Faiyaz and Manohar and talked at length. He received a wireless message from Gopal. The directive basically is "Don't cooperate." At dinner, Manohar asked to sit next to me. He seems very sympathetic. Over the last couple of weeks, he's been very respectful.

Faiyaz and Manohar just dropped by my room, having just returned from Baihar to call Delhi and Bandhavgarh. They informed me that Avtar had brought Sarita with him to "monitor" our work. I have already told Avtar in no uncertain terms that I will not be monitored, by him or anybody else. I have made it clear that the "monitoring" part of his work plan, priced by him to be C$27,000, has to be scrapped. If he wants to monitor out of his own pocket or out of the budget of Tiger Fund, if there is one, fine, in which case I would just ignore the "monitor", no personal offense, Sarita. But if anything I do will have to have her permission or have to wait for her to get Avtar's permission, she'd be frustrated. Given her "yes sir" attitude with Avtar, my hope for a good working relationship with her is not high, but marginally higher than directly with Avtar himself.

[23:14]

Can't sleep again. Too many tormenting thoughts about Christopher. Too much hatred in my heart for Christine. If hatred is a one-way ticket to hell, if I die tomorrow, would I go straight down? Am I already in hell and just not aware of it?

"Down?"

"Yeah?"

"Come out to the field. I want to show you something."

That at least would be some sort of escape. The room has begun to feel like an emotional torture chamber, especially at night, when I can't sleep because of the emotional torment. My body itself has become a torture chamber for my soul. How do I escape that? By not thinking about Christopher? Perish the thought. Christopher, I promise you, I will never do that.

I put on my sweat suit and a windbreaker and went out to the field next to the medicinal plants garden.

"Lie down."

I lay down. The soil and grass felt soft and warm against my back.

"Look straight up."

My eyes settled on a constellation directly overhead, one I could not name.

"Let go of yourself. Merge with your greater body."

"My greater body?"

"The Earth. You are a small part of Earth; earth is the greater part of you. You are Earth; Earth is you. Earth and you are one."

"I am Earth; Earth is speaking through me," I said, after awhile.

"Look out."

"What?! What's wrong?"

"Nothing. Sorry. I meant: Look outward."

"Outward?"

"Your looking 'upward' is Earth looking outward."

"Yes, I see. It's a big world out there."

"Says Earth's planetary embryo, about the world it will be born into. Fear not, embryonic Earth. You are in an interstellar nursery, one filled with love and compassion."

"It looks cold out there. Who will look after me when I'm born?" asked the Earth in me.

"A lamb needs suckling, an apple seedling needs watering. Each will receive whatever help it needs."

"From whom?"

"That would be for those planets that succeed to find out."

"But as for now, I'm on my own?"

"Embryos and fetuses usually develop on their own without outside interference."

"What if I don't make it on my own?"

"Then everyone will mourn."

"Wouldn't they intervene?"

"Except under external threat situations, the internal events of planetary eggs would not be interfered with."

"Why not? If there is, say a nuclear war. Where is your compassion - for the children, for Christopher, for me?"

"The innately destructive must be allowed to destroy itself, if only for its own sake. If it is allowed into the interplanetary realm, it would become a monster."

"But of course, it is for the 'common good', right?"

"For the good of the University itself."

"Are you not intervening in the development of Earth's planetary embryo yourself, by working with me – an Earthling?"

"Communication is fine. Physical interference is not."

"What if you violate the rule?"

"I'd be banished."
"Where to?"
"Nowhere you would want to go."

Good night, Christopher. Good night, Christopher.

❖   ❖   ❖   ❖   ❖

March 13, 1999, Saturday, sunny, 20-34C

Dearest Christopher:

[06:23 @ Rm.111, Kanha Tiger Lodge]
    Today is going to be an interesting day, to say the least. Avtar will be arriving around 16:00 from Bandhavgarh. If he hasn't heard about the Rajeesh Gopal incident yet, he will then. As far as I'm concerned, it ain't over till it is over.
    The positive side is that Manu Srivastava, Collector of Balaghat, will be here also and he seems in favor of the conference. Jharia will be here as well and he is also in favor although, being an Assisitant Forest Conservator he doesn't have very much clout. The Mandla Collector A. Jain seems also in favor, as do the Core Area and Buffer Zone Deputy Directors. Only the Field Director Rajeesh Gopal is against, but he is the top brass of Kanha National Park, and Tiger Lodge is sitting in Kanha's Buffer Zone. So who has authority over whom on what is just a bit too complex for me to fully fathom at this point.
    This morning, we spent 08:30-10:30 doing our video interview, with me behind the camera asking questions and Faiyaz and Jane in front, mostly Faiyaz, since I've already done some with Jane.
    Around 10:45, Manohar came in and informed us that among the wireless messages sent out by Gopal was one to his field office at Kanha, informing it that Tiger Fund's "eco-development project" has been put on hold until further notice. This means that not only the conference but small meetings with panchayaters will be allowed, even at the conservation center. Nor will any Tiger Fund vehicle be allowed through the Mukki gate to go to the other side to inform the panchayaters of the cancellations. So Faiyaz will have to go the long way around the Core Area to the other side instead of through it.

[14:28]
We had lunch with the Maharashtra Collector and quite candidly discussed our situation with him. He surprised me by saying that we do not have much of a problem, and that indeed, there is more than one solution, none of which needs compromise our objective. But before he could say what these solutions were, Manohar came in and began talking about the new "climate".

The Indian social-political climate is certainly different from the Canadian one. If I attacked any official here the way I did Cathy McGregor (the prohunting BC Environment Minister), I'd be in jail or dead, or else being burnt alive by "rebels" possibly sent by the government itself. As it is, laughable of all laughables, I've bent over backwards to observe all the Indian protocols to the hilt, and am being threatened with being charged as a poacher!

[17:44]
The new tour group has arrived, mostly older people, about 10. I could not help but notice that the big cylindrical tiger-patterned nylon bag containing the Big Cub was there, and its blower, as well as Avtar's 220-volt slide projector. In fact, Big Cub has been moved into my room. I was on the way to Jane's room, when I inadvertantly came across Avtar who was about to knock on the door of the Maharashtra Collector's room. On the spot, I said a bright "Avtar!" and we shook hands with big smiles and a bear hug, half sincerely.

When I went into the dining pavilion, Sarita was there. We exchanged a big smile and hug as well. There was of course a slight undertone of guardedness, since we both knew where things stood.

I had a last minute strategizing session with Faiyaz, and my final decision is that I will do the talking. If Avtar's signature is what is required, I'll get him to sign the invitation to Rajeesh Gopal.

Right now, Avtar is sitting at the fire pit chatting with the Maharashtra Collector. I just asked Manohar to deliver to Avtar a small hand-written note: "Avtar: Something urgent just occurred. I need to discuss it with you some time this evening, at your convenience. Anthony."

[21:02]
Avtar and I did have a long talk, in my room. I started off with the genesis of the conference idea, what we aim to achieve, how we developed it, the protocol we have followed, our media conference on March 16th, the Gopal problem, etc. Along the way, he said, "You are a very enthusiastic individual."

Omni-Science and the Human Destiny

"Thank you, Avtar." I wanted to add, "So was your dad." But gagged it on the point of my tongue. I believe his comment was sincere.

On the Gopal thing, he thinks it's the guy getting offended by us not asking for his *permission* first before going ahead to organize the event, about us not involving him in the organizing, about Tiger Fund sending an underling to deal with him, etc. Avtar was not angry at Gopal, and seemed to take things in stride. Easy for him, since he objected to the conference himself, although evidently – his slide projector and the Big Cub - he had changed his mind, if only until he found out about the Gopal situation.

Avtar then discussed with me my drive to increase park fee, saying that it would not work. It was a long and convoluted argument, about lack of infrastructure and lack of guarantee to see tiger, etc. but to see through it all, what he was saying was that it would impact negatively on his tourism business.

He also said that the higher the park fee, the more the money the park officials would pocket. When I asked him if the Field Director himself pockets money, Avtar said, "No, but the people lower down do, and will."

Towards the end of the conversation, the Maharashtra Collector knocked on my door and I welcomed him in. Avtar asked his opinion on the Gopal situation. The Collector said that Gopal felt threatened by the sudden prominence and influence of Tiger Fund in his territory and that he was also afraid of stirring up the anti-park activists. His opinion is that we have no problem having the conference, but Gopal may try to control TF some other way some time in the future. Avtar said he would attend to it. He did not say how, and I did not ask.

Since Avtar's entry into camp, Faiyaz has been excluded in all discussions. After my meeting with Avtar and the Collector, I went to fill him in. We speculated on how Avtar would handle the situation. The options are limited. Either we will have the conference, or we won't. We hope Avtar will do the right thing, but fearing, almost knowing, that he won't. The ball is in his court and we feel helpless.

"Of everybody, the only person against park reform is Avtar. He's lost me for good," said Jane, who joined us. "If, of everybody, the only person opposed to doing something that would actually work for the tiger is the person whose title is the head of Tiger Fund, then it seems to me that to save the tiger is just too great a feat for us to perform, and by 'us' I mean us humans. We're just not good enough."

"Brace yourself, Homo Sapiens," said Raminothna. **"Compared to the greatest feat on Earth that you have to perform, to save the tiger species is mere child's play."**

"What are you talking about, this greatest feat on Earth that we have to perform?"

"Where are you now in the O.S.E.S. Cycle of the I.T. Spiral?"

"We have advanced up to the National level, but not yet the Planetary level. On the National level, the nations have organismized, have reproduced and speciated, have formed a multinational ecosystem, and have become more or less social amongst themselves, but have not yet transcendently integrated themselves into a Planetary organism, yet. So, we have advanced to the fourth quadrant, the Socialization quadrant, the second 'S' of the O.S.E.S. Cycle of the I.T. Spiral on the national level of organization."

"Then this greatest feat facing Homo Sapiens, the greatest miracle for Homo Sapiens to perform, shall be the integrative transcendence of the Earth."

Good night, Christopher. Good night, Christopher.

❖   ❖   ❖   ❖   ❖

March 14, 1999, Sunday, sunny, 20-34C

Dearest Christopher:

[05:42 @ Rm.111, Kanha Tiger Lodge]

I awakened around 04:00 and couldn't go back to sleep. So I read some more of the Dian Fossey book. Can't believe the number of daggers buried in her back by self-professed gorilla protectors and "respectable" big name conservation organizations. Even more so is how she could still cope, practically all on her own. She was constantly cash strapped, constantly begging for money. Several thousand could go a long way for her and the gorillas on that mountaintop, but the organizations raked in millions for their own coffers in her name while feeding her peanuts, and people in general squander billions daily on trivial pursuits. This, compounded with her bodily breakdowns, makes one feel that her murder was almost a relief, although I'm still at 1979 in the book – six years before her death. The ensuing pages will tell me how much of this she had to endure before her final release on December 28, 1985. Just goes to show how low down we humans could get if the aim is false, and how strong the human spirit - Dian's – could be, if the aim is true.

These recent few days, particularly the last two, she had been a great comfort,

Omni-Science and the Human Destiny

to show me how insignificant my personal problems are compared to hers, even though the pressures on the tiger and the gorilla are both intense. At least, she did not seem to have a lost child in her life to agonize about, that I know of.

Around 05:15 came a knock on my door. It was a dejected-looking Faiyaz.

"Sorry to knock on your door so early, but I saw light in your window."

"Oh, no, that's alright. Come on in."

"I wanted to talk to you about this right after finishing with Avtar last night, but by then your lights had gone out," he said apologetically after sitting down in a chair. "He told me to drop all Tiger Fund work today and service the tourists. I had planned to go to the villages today."

"Well, until the matter is resolved one way or another, the outreach should indeed be put on hold. Gopal's directives aside, if even you go to visit the villagers this morning, what would you be able to tell them? So just relax for this once and enjoy the park. You might even make conservationists of the tourists. They are not evil, just short-sighted and a little selfish. But they love the tiger. Bring your camera with you."

On his salary he would never be able to buy a camera, let alone a good one. I brought along two still cameras, one a Minolta automatic SLR with a 28-200 zoom lens and the other an older manual Nikon also with a 28-200 zoom lens. The second camera serves only as a backup, and so far its service has yet to be called for. So I just gave it to Faiyaz. He has been treating it with TLC. His way of holding it reminds me of my way of holding Christopher when he was a baby.

Faiyaz broke into a happy grin and walked back to his room with a bouncier step.

[17:47]

I was called to brunch around 10:30. Avtar was there with the Maharashtra Collector's family and it was a subdued affair. So he did not go to Mandla after all.

Jane is sick again, still citing dehydration. Since the first time a month back, she's been on a constant glucose-supplement diet to fight the problem, about which I'm not entirely convinced. Kim is also not feeling well. They have both been sick about 25% of the time, leading Faiyaz and I to be concerned about the long term states of their health. So far I've been 100% sound, as has been Faiyaz; I hope to stay this way.

About noon, Faiyaz knocked on my door. Avtar sent him to ask me to go for another discussion. We sat in the lounge part of the dining pavilion, the three of us, almost like chums, although the tone of the discussion was muted.

Avtar started off by saying, "Last night I discussed the Gopal situation with the

Maharashtra Collector till late about the reason for it happening. Our most logical conclusion was that Tiger Fund has all of a sudden become very prominent, active and influential in the Kanha area, and the park officials could not tolerate it. No matter we are for or against them, our very ascendance as an influential NGO, particularly in the panchayat arena, has become a threat to their authority. What they feel they have to do is to force us back down before we become too powerful. They also find the idea of the panchayats organized into a single force too intimidating, and this is what the conference means to them."

"As the Chinese say, 'The bigger the tree, the more bird shit it catches.'" I said mildly. "But is it reason to cut it down?"

Avtar gave a polite chuckle, but said, "The most prudent strategy at this juncture is to lie low and let the heat dissipate." Which means postpone the conference indefinitely, capitulate, cancel everything and crawl back into the previous state of semi-nonexistence, or semi-existence if Avtar prefers. If he carries through with this "prudent strategy", Tiger Fund would never amount to anything noteworthy. Should WCWC continue on with such an organization as partner, even without the other factors?

"So, Tiger Fund is doomed to a life of weakness, insignificance, obscurity and mediocrity?" I pressed.

No quotable one-liner answer. Instead, Avtar went back to his dictate of working with only one or two villages at a time, instead of the entire Buffer Zone. Not only that, but just one or two families in these one or two villages. The dictation was given to Faiyaz, but in my presence, which means, in fact, to me. I stood my ground on outreach, and we stalled on the stalemate.

Is it going to save any tigers to get a few families in a few Chinese villages to stop using tiger bone as medicine? We just don't have the luxury of time. I had to press this point several times before he reluctantly said, "Point taken." But clearly not to be acted upon.

Then we turned to talking about Jane. He maintained that his plan was to switch Kim and Jane on March 1st, and that he now intends to move Jane over to Bandhavgarh within two days. I reminded him of our agreement about Jane. He did not argue this point, but resorted to saying that I have extended my period of stay, so Jane should be moved now, to which I steadfastly disagreed.

Avtar then proposed a new idea. "Why don't the three of you (I, Faiyaz and Jane) all go to Bandhavgarh to start a TF program there?"

Bandhavgarh being another paradise on Earth, in places even more beautiful than Ranthambhore and Kanha, I can't say I didn't find the idea appealing, but to

Omni-Science and the Human Destiny

even consider it seriously at this juncture is to accept the cancellation of the panchayat conference we have worked so hard for. I have only two weeks more out here in Tigerland. If the conference is indeed cancelled, we need at least 4-5 days to go back to the panchayats to inform them of the cancellation and express our regrets, as well as to sign them up for solar cooker installations, and perhaps even have them sign a petition for park reform, plus the March 16 media conference, in which, by the way, Avtar did tell Sarita to participate and to "monitor". That would leave only 8-9 days in Bandhavgarh. What can be done in that little time? So I showed no response. I absolutely did not want to say, "If the panchayat conference is cancelled…"

Avtar, true to his nature, took my silence as consent, and plowed on to set our move-over date on March 20th, and March 28th as my date to return to Delhi for my March 29th slideshow presentation at the Habitat House. March 20 carries another message. It is before the date set for the conference.

"I'll see how Gopal responds to whatever you do first," I said.

To be fair to Avtar, I have to ask myself what I would do if I were him. From the word Go, however, I found this leading nowhere, since I simply could not put myself into the position to favor the interest of his for-profit business over that of his non-profit organization, let alone over the interest of the tiger.

This evening, while sitting at the dinner table, looking across the pavilion at the group of aging tourists with Avtar and Ed Cambridge each seated at one end of their long table, and with Faiyaz seated next to me, exuding a silence full of pain, I cannot help but say to him, "Here are a dozen rich foreigners in the twilight of their lives, seeking their own glorious sunsets by spending US$7000-8000 each for their fortnight's thrill of a lifetime. Almost US$100,000 in total for a two-week fling. True, they are here to pay their homage to the tigers, which in the scheme of things is better than spending the same money at Las Vegas, but at least some come with the thought of seeing the tigers before they go extinct. And where do these tourists carry their "memory of a lifetime"? To their graves? Yes, that, but more so, to the grave of the tiger. If they would donate the US$100,000 to WCWC, though certainly not to TF, it could go a long way to keep the tiger from extinction in the first place, for their own grand children. And where do their much touted tourist dollars go? The pockets of just two men - Avtar Grewal and Ed Cambridge – the only two people opposing the park reform proposal. Hopefully, after seeing the magnificence of the tiger and its habitat, they would then devote the rest of their lives helping to save them, but how many have done that, or would do that? How many would just chalk up the tiger as an experiential trophy, mount a few pictures on the wall, then move on to plan their next vacation?

Faiyaz's greatest pain is in regards to the villagers. He feels that he is letting them down. He feels their disappointment. He feels the loss of their trust.

"How about the field director of Bandhavgarh? What do you think he would have done under similar circumstances?" I ask Faiyaz.

"I don't know him. So I can't say. But if Avtar does what we know he will, we'll be meeting the Bandhavgarh Field Director within a week, and find out for ourselves."

"Yes. Why don't we?" said Jane.

So, we began to strategize about Bandhavgarh. For all three of us: "What is the most that we can hope to accomplish in seven days?"

And for the two of them: "What would Avtar allow us to do after Anthony has returned to Canada?"

While the former shines with excitement and promise, the latter looks dim and depressing. I offered them a ray of hope. "What we need to do is to use the seven days to initiate a program which can propel itself through to the monsoon season. I'll just have to do whatever I can to make sure that Avtar will honour the program and sustain it."

Nobody looked particularly convinced. I didn't look into the mirror, so I don't know about myself.

As soon as I returned to my room, I thought of Christopher, and was again plunged into the cyclone that rages beneath my surface constantly. I hauled myself up by the hair by playing a game against my chess computer – by far my intellectual superior in its own arena, where it needs no practice and I have next to none.

Near mid-game, Raminothna said to me, "**To all grand masters, masters, ordinary players and non-players, I challenge you to the god-game of Cosmic Chess.**"

"God-game? What's a god-game?"

"A game of life and death, at times, mass deaths."

"How do you play it?"

"Here are some of its basic rules:

"Whereas in chess there are two sides with sixteen pieces each, in the Earth version of Cosmic Chess there are some two hundred sides, each with pieces numbering in the millions.

"Whereas the power of a chess piece is fixed, be it a king, queen, rook, bishop, knight or pawn, a Cosmic Chess Piece has the power to change its own power, and that of others.

Omni-Science and the Human Destiny

"Whereas in chess the pieces are moved by two external players, one piece per move, one move per time, Cosmic Chess pieces are themselves Cosmic Chess players, who move themselves, and one another, simultaneously, and at will.

"Whereas chess is a mere game, with little more than pride and prize at stake, Cosmic Chess is a god-game, involving not only life and death, but rise and fall, transcendence and extinction, fate and destiny. In fact, each Cosmic Chess Piece/Player has a heart, a mind, a will, a life, even a soul, of its own.

"In Cosmic Chess as in chess, however, there is no move, however insignificant it might have seemed at the time it was made, that has no profound influence, be it constructive or destructive, upon the outcome of the whole game. And you, Cosmic Chess Piece/Player of the god-game of Earth, ought to heed this, for whether you want to 'play' or not, whether you know or know not what you do, whether or not you even care, you make moves all the time.

"In Cosmic Chess as in chess, all pieces must share an ultimate goal in common, must make no move without bearing upon this common goal, and must cooperate, and be coordinated, towards reaching this common goal – that is, if they wish to win, which brings us to this final point:

"Whereas in chess one must lose that the other can win, in Cosmic Chess, all must win, or all will lose.

"In Cosmic Chess, each side is called a nation, and each player-piece a citizen, of which you are one.

"Homo sapiens of Earth, I wish you a brilliant victory."

I again lost the game to the chess computer.

Good night, Christopher.

❖ ❖ ❖ ❖ ❖

March 15, 1999, Monday, sunny, with occasional thin clouds, 18-30C

Dearest Christopher:

[05:27 @ Rm. 111, Kanha Tiger Lodge]

Anthony Marr

Another amazing dream from which I just awoke.

    One who dwells in the bottom of a well
    will say that the sky is small.
    Another may even insist to tell
    that there is no sky at all
    but a hole in The World's ceiling overhead
    through which the light from Heaven is shed.

    Of a great dried well was indeed what I dreamed
    on whose bottom I was born and raised it seemed.
    So dried this world of a well had become
    Two hundred ponds were all that remained in sum,
    each claimed and owned by one walled estate
    who regarded its neighbors with jealousy and hate.

    The wall of the well was high as the sky,
    surrounding the World Village an unbroken cliff,
    to try scaling which many have died falling,
    and some by leaping, all understood why
    who have sought an escape, no 'but', nor 'if',
    as they heard again their freedom's calling.

    For though of mansions our well-world was full,
    and magnificent they could all be deemed,
    yet the barbed-wire spoke of peace unachieved,
    and feuds amongst families raged bloody and cruel.
    To their gods they prayed, of palaces they dreamed,
    but few for what vision had yet to be conceived.

    Our world, sadly, was not brimming with wealth.
    Fuel and building materials were in short supply.
    Sooner or later we would surely kill
    for the last wheelbarrow of coal, by force or stealth.
    Afterwards, they say, "I'll suffer their orphans' cry."
    Meanwhile, there's no doubt if they won't or will.

    Still the root cause of this predicament persisted –
    to out-luxuriate the Smiths and Jones bar none.

Omni-Science and the Human Destiny

A few spoke of consequences but none had resisted
this tradition passed on from father to son.
To honour this cause entire generations had insisted,
a purpose upheld, if not fulfilled, by everyone.

It was certainly not fulfilled, if still upheld, by me.
Examine my purchasing record, and you'd agree.
My estate was still in grandeur, but grandeur in decline.
About the only thing new was in this garden of mine –
a giant question mark, paved in stone. But then,
what eyes could see it except those in Heaven?

Besides, what eyes in this world would even care?
It came as no surprise, therefore,
when Raminothna descended into this world-at-war,
the landing was made here and not over there.
She told me about the boundless universe beyond
this miserable little world of which I was not fond.

And I was told of the myriad living things
inhabiting those wondrous realms above,
and of the spiritual freedom that knowledge brings,
and universal truth, and peace, and love.
Like a caged tiger I began to pace
within my confining, confounding space.

Finally, I confronted Raminothna, saying,
"What are you here for?" And her reply:
"To bring you deliverance. To set you free."
But her discarded wings I could plainly see.
In ill-concealed skepticism I continued to pry:
"And how do you plan to accomplish that? By staying?"

**"By persuading you to build a stairway, my love,
one leading to the domains above."**
"What with? Do you realize what that would demand?
And that supplies are stockpiled, but none by me?"
"I see building materials right at hand,"
said Raminothna, **"and supplies aplenty."**

Following her illuminating eyes I was shocked to see
they're fixed on this mansion of mine. I replied in dismay,
"I would gladly take my house apart, stone by stone,
and transform it into a stairway to Heaven, on my own,
if I knew that the last stone would set me free.
But plainly, it wouldn't take me a hundredth of the way."

"Then let it be the foundation of your stairway to Heaven."
"After that, what then? I have nothing else, not even a dime."
"I see more than enough, considering all your brethren."
Following Raminothna's eyes again, I saw this time
they were sweeping the mansions all around, stone and gem.
"I see. And how do you propose to persuade *them*?"

Thereupon, Raminothna's penetrating gaze
moved to fix itself upon my face.
So shocked was I the dream ejected me
but then, in the dawn light I see
in the mirror misted in the morning chill
that her gaze is fixed upon mine eyes still.

[22:56 @ Rm.111, Kanha Jungle Lodge]

Today, Faiyaz and Sarita left the lodge at 08:00 to revisit those panchayat leaders who had come to our meetings, and returned at about 16:30. Even at dinnertime, he was still obviously perturbed about having let the villagers down. To the panchayat leaders he would not lay blame on the forest department or even on Gopal, because, he feels, he would then indeed be driving a wedge between the villagers and the government. So he took whatever blame upon himself.

He told us that before entering the villages, he committed Sarita to noninterference. And same for her role in the media conference tomorrow – strictly as an observer - as far as I'm concerned. Other than that, she could "monitor" all she wants.

She did make one observation to Faiyaz, "Your problem is that you are sandwiched between Avtar and Anthony." Not completely true. Faiyaz is very much his own man. He just happens to hold similar views to mine, for which I am thankful. On the other hand, it might apply very well to herself, she being Avtar's yes-person.

The power went on and off all day, so I wrote on and off for as long as the aging battery of my laptop computer would last.

This evening, Avtar came to our dining table (he usually sits with the tourists) and showed me a draft of his letter to "Rajeesh *Raj* Gopal", a very humble-toned letter saying essentially (not verbatim, since I was too upset to copy it down), "Yes sir, we will scrap the conference, sir, and promise to be a good boy from now on, sir, so please forgive us, sir. We will never do anything like this again, sir." It will be delivered tomorrow morning at 10:30 by a very demur and respectful Sarita. Excuse me while I throw up.

In our discussion I pressed Avtar for a commitment to supply one solar cooker to each village in Kanha and Bandhavgarh that requests one. Each one would cost about C$10-20 to make, using locally available material. We would charge C$2 or so for each, as a gesture of seriousness from them. Faiyaz is to be put in charge of this follow-through program with Jane as his volunteer. If our 1999 program could have at least 50 villages (instead of Avtar's two) to adopt the solar oven to cook one meal a day over the sunny nine months of the year, I'd be happy. Avtar nodded an affirmation to our plan, the perfunctoriness of which made me doubt its sincerity and validity. But I know however harder I pressed, I would just get another one of the same meaningless shrug-nods, no more, no less. I thought of getting him to commit it in writing, but didn't bother, for the same reason – the piece of paper would be more or less worthless.

Tomorrow we (Faiyaz, Jane, Sarita & I) will go to Mandla, then Jabalpur, leaving the lodge at 07:00. Avtar will leave the lodge at 08:00 back to Delhi, his damage having been done. "If I don't see you in the morning, let me say good bye to you now. See you in Delhi in two weeks," he said. With this and a handshake, he returned to his room, leaving us, especially Faiyaz, in a state of turmoil.

Good night, Christopher.

❖   ❖   ❖   ❖   ❖

March 17, 1999, Wednesday, sunny, 22-34C

Dearest Christopher:

[20:13 @ Rm.111, Kanha Tiger Lodge]
A day of great beauty, sadness and amazement.

The beauty is of Kanha National Park. It seems that the more I see it, the more beautiful it becomes. Today, it is the brilliant greenness, especially in the early morning and late afternoon light. Greens of various shades, tints and tones that dazzle the eyes. I have never seen sal – the most common tree species in Kanha - as I saw it today.

We (Jane, Kim, Julian and I) left KTL at 06:30 with me at the wheel. At Mukki Gate, I did the paper work and paid the fee – about Rs.600 for all, my personal treat for my friends. At the booth I was told by a guide name Guru that Tirath would be our guide, but Tirath, probably wanting to distance himself, declined. So Guru became our guide. Our destination of the day was Kisli, which is situated on the opposite side of the park from Mukki. Our intention was to visit Kipling Camp, owned and operated by Bob Wright, father of Belinda Wright. Back in the 1970s, Belinda lived on the periphery of Kanha for several years doing pioneering work on tiger poaching, and even today she is still a bit of a legend in these parts. Manohar somehow heard that she might be in the vicinity as we speak.

En route from Mukki to Kisli, we traversed many areas I have never seen before, all exquisite. We arrived at the Kisli gate around 10:00, and decided to gas up the vehicle first, since it was running on near empty, then return to the park till noon. Believe it or not, it took the people at the gas station more than half an hour to put in the fuel and fill out the paper work.

I have fallen deeply in love with Kanha, and yet, this could be the very last time I would ever see her in my life.

Something amazing occurred when we were exiting the Kisli gate shortly before noon. We came across a Gypsy driven by an elderly Caucasian gentleman. Our guide, Guru, pointed out that he was Bob Wright. I turned the Gypsy around and pulled up along-side Bob, driver-door to driver-door. I reminded him of my visit to his home in Calcutta in 1997, and inquired about Mrs. Wright. "She is in Delhi," Bob informed me, and asked me what I was doing at Kanha. I briefly outlined our program, then asked about Belinda. Amazingly, he said, "Good timing on your part. She is arriving at Kipling Camp from Delhi right about now." I asked if I could see her briefly some time in the early afternoon, after they've had their reunion. Bob consented, for some time at "midday."

We went to a roadside thatched café for some lunch, where all the tables but one (about 6) were occupied by young Caucasian travelers, mostly back-packers, giving us a sense of security about food quality and hygiene, false or otherwise. I ordered chapatti with a certain bean filling. Some time after that, while we were chatting, I heard a strange noise behind me. I was sitting with my back to the bamboo-slat wall that one could see through. I turned, and saw, less than 15' feet from us, a chicken in the process of being killed by a 14-15 year-old boy named Arjun. Its throat had just been slashed, though its head remained attached, and it was bleeding profusely on to the ground, still struggling and flapping. This reminded me of my childhood days, when my mother and aunts used to kill chickens this way. After about 5 minutes, the chicken was finally limp, and the boy began to pluck off its feathers. And then it was taken into the open kitchen and cut up. Finally, some 15 minutes later, chicken tandoori was served up to the table next to ours. I'm not quite sure what to say about eating meat for now, but I think this experience should have some subsequent effect.

Around 13:30, we arrived at Kipling Camp. It is about the same size land-wise as KTL – about ten acres - but unlike KJL, whose rooms are attached and arranged linearly in a square as in a motel, surrounding the central dining pavilion and the fire pit, Kipling Camp has its buildings detached and far apart, with its grounds having a more open feel. The rate is Rs.2700 daily (about CDN$100) – less than 2/3 that of KTL's CDN$160. We were very pleasantly invited into the open dining room by two very pretty young women from the UK who have been here for several weeks, and seated at the sofa and chairs in the lounge area. They kept us chatting for awhile, telling us that Belinda would be there shortly. After some minutes, Bob Wright came in, sat down next to me on the sofa, and chatted further about our campaign and its difficulties in India. After a bit, he observed, not condescendingly, "Your first mistake was to pick the wrong partner." After a few more minutes, one of the two young ladies came back into the dining hall to announce that Belinda was on her way to the dining pavilion.

When Belinda did come in, she was accompanied by a tall and salt-and-pepper gentleman in his 50s, who did not seem particularly friendly. Upon seeing her, I rose and crossed the conversation area to meet her. She looked as beautiful and radiant as Kanha, and younger than before, and more regal than ever. Bob got off his place in the sofa next to mine and gave it to Belinda. Through this process she did not introduce her companion to us, so I did not greet him. Besides, I was too engrossed in her to notice much else. I did introduce Jane, Kim and Julian. We sat back down. After a very brief exchange of pleasantries, I asked her, without mentioning names, whether WPSI (Wildlife Protection Society of India, of which she is a director) would be interested in being WCWC's conservation partner some time in the future. She told me that WPSI is now at an all time high in conservation output. Although they now have 42 full time employees and some two dozen project all over India, they are spread so thin they could hardly take on a new project even with extra funding without having yet to enlarge the work force. They have also vastly expanded their scope from their previous undercover operations. They have gone broadly into the field and helped out many government wildlife protection projects. To my question as to whether corruption may have consumed a part of their donations, she said that all their donations are in kind and project specific. Their current largest project is to save the sea turtles, but tiger protection remains at the heart of their concern. At one point, she made a simple statement that left no room for doubt, which impressed Jane and Kim greatly. "We are *fully* dedicated to wildlife preservation." This coming from Belinda, especially in contrast to Avtar, rang loud and true. At one point, while I mentioned our 6-month wait for the Indian government to grant us permission to infuse Canadian funds into India, she laughed and said, "We could have done it in 24 hours." She showed no sign of fatigue after the long train ride, and I had no idea how much time had elapsed when her prince-consort-like companion suddenly re-entered the picture and almost physically hauled her out of her seat, saying, "You have talked enough. It's time for some lunch, then rest," without a word of courtesy to us. I asked quickly if we would have any time in the near future in Delhi for an unhurried meeting, preferably with Ashok also present, citing that I owed her a dinner. She said that she would be back in Delhi as of March 21st, but the 28th through 30th would not be good due to some friend's wedding; the 31st onwards she'd be relatively free. She asked me to call her when I get back to Delhi.

The return drive was done by Julian. At some point along the way, Jane had tears in her eyes. I asked her if she was alright. She said, "We're saying farewell to Kanha. That's why I am sad."

In the evening, after dinner back at KTL, a few things were discussed between us (Jane, Kim, Julian & I) and Faiyaz and Manohar. First, Manohar admonished us about eating at the roadside joint, for two reasons: hygiene, meaning that if we got sick, Manohar would get the blame for having one of KTL's guests get sick; he was extra upset because he was just yelled at by Avtar today on the phone about Kim and Julian falling sick from eating the wrong things at Balaghat, thus reflecting poorly on KTL.

Second is that our guide would take the news back to the park guides circle that Anthony Marr et al. could not afford to eat in a proper eatery and had to eat on the cheap. "In a few days, everyone will know about it, and it would be bad for the reputation of KTL whose clients could not afford to eat at a more expensive place," said Manohar. I thought only the Chinese people talk about saving face. This is outrageous, although I should be used to this kind of thing in India by now. I explained that it was the guide who suggested the place, and that I paid for the guide's lunch and also Julian's (Kim and Jane did not eat), and that by the end of the park drive at 18:00, I tipped the guide Rs.130, which doesn't support the notion that I could not afford to eat at a good restaurant.

Faiyaz bought a whole bunch of newspapers, and found at least three articles in Hindi, concentrating on Mr. Anthony Marr and *Dr.* Anthony Marr. He predicted that there would be more in the evening edition of various other papers. "I would suggest that you not go with me to visit the panchayats tomorrow. I will give you the reason later."

Later, he said that given the broad based newspaper coverage (almost all about me and little about him and Sarita), "you will be even higher profile than before, and Gopal will be even more irritated. If his informants spot you still working with the villagers, it would give them the excuse to do certain unpleasant things to you, including arrest you."

"And that would be the end of your work here, and of Tiger Fund," said Manohar.

I could not help but shoot back, "and that would be a great pity, wouldn't it, given Tiger Fund's critical role in saving tigers around here."

Manohar broke into a grin. He had never thought much of Avtar's conservation program. "Anthony, you have within a month done more than Tiger Fund has done in years, and, boom, brought Tiger Fund to such a high profile just like that – I mean, after years of silence since the death of Ravinder, suddenly, Tiger Fund is the talk of Kanha – I don't want to see it suddenly snuffed out."

Manohar is what I would call right wing, and if only because he is Avtar's nephew I don't trust him, but there is something primal in the man that makes me like him even if he tells on me to Avtar, which I know he does. For example, Avtar questioned me while he was here what I was doing with Jane and Faiyaz behind closed doors, because, he told me, Manohar had reported to him that there was a lot of closed door meetings going on.

After everyone had left, I told Faiyaz about Tirath declining to accompany us in the park today. Faiyaz did not seem at all surprised. He also explained to me that all the guides know me or at least know about me as "an internationally renowned wildlife conservationist", and given that, any news about me is big news, and bad news is bigger than good news.

Triumph of the day. The newspaper articles did mention the cattle overpopulation problem, and in judicious terms. And I was quoted, not Sarita. So now, cattle overpopulation is news in Madhya Pradesh, since someone finally dares to openly talk about it. Hundreds of thousands of people are at this very moment reading about it, thinking about it, perhaps even talking about it. This in itself is a worthy accomplishment for this mission.

"Now, Tiger Uncle, you have finally achieved notorious status," said Jane. "Now, the only way they can forgive you is to forget you."

"I hope not. The idea is probably too unspeakable for them to easily forget it. I hope they would need a lobotomy to forget it." I said.

"That's a bit crude," said Raminothna.

"If you mean rude, I apologize. I didn't mean to be disrespectful."

"No. I did not mean rude. I meant crude."

"I apologize for my manner."

"It is not about manner. It is a matter of refinement in knowledge."

"Knowledge in what?"

"The nature of memory."

"Oh, I see. Lobotomy is too crude. You want super-precise microneurosurgery?"

"What do you mean by microneurosurgery?"

"I don't know. Removal of a tiny but crucial piece of the brain?"

"Involving neuron deaths?"

"By the thousands, I should think."

"Then no. Still not refined enough. Not a single neuron needs to die."

"What then?"

"Rewire them."

"You can remove a piece of memory by rewiring the brain?"

"The circuitry *is* the memory. To run an electrical impulse through a subcircuit is to remember. To disconnect the subcircuit is to forget. To wire the brain is to learn. To wire someone else's brain is to teach. To interrelate and interlink subcircuits is to think. To establish a new equilibrium in the brain after the day's wiring, unwiring and rewiring during sleep is to dream."

"So, as I absorb and accept what you're saying, I'm actually rewiring my brain? As we speak?"

"Perhaps even wiring a brand new neuronal subcircuit?"

"Who does the rewiring for me? You?"

"No."

"Who then?"

"Your own neurons themselves, of course."

"No kidding. So, learning to ride a bicycle or to swim or to ski is to build a bike-riding or swimming or skiing neuronal subcircuit?"

"Your brain is full of them."

"Conversely, to forget a thought would mean the dismantling of the subcircuit?"

"When did you quit smoking?"

"1981."

"Do you still feel the urge?"

"Nope. Not for years."

"Then consider your ex-smoking-subcircuit dismantled."

I looked at the newspaper again.

"New neuronal subcircuits are right now being formed in the brains of millions of Indian newspaper readers who may not have spent one minute in their entire lives thinking about tiger conservation. And if they talk about it to their brethren, the new neuronal subcircuit configuration called 'Tiger Conservation' will be formed in other brains. Lamarckian evolution in a very physical sense - the evolution of neuronal circuitry configurations on the metabion level. Hopefully it will lead to a social change in India on the national level, such as reforming the park system," said Raminothna.

Good night, Christopher.

❖   ❖   ❖   ❖   ❖

March 18, 1999, Thursday, sunny, 22-34C

Dearest Christopher:

[07:48 @ Rm. 111, Kanha Tiger Lodge]

Only two weeks left before I come back to Vancouver. Then what? I'm craving it, but dreading it. I don't know which sentiment is the stronger. If I craned my neck out my bedroom window in Vancouver's West Point Grey and looked east, I would be able to see the mountains of Coquitlam looming above and behind the skyscrapers of downtown in the mid-distance. If I said "Screw it!" and started my car, I could be at your door in 45 minutes. Then what? For one thing, over the years, even when I was seeing you four times a week, I never just went to knock on your door; I would always phone first to make sure it was convenient for your mom. Now what? If I called first, she would just say no. If I skipped calling and just knocking on your door, it would just add fuel to fire. This way I might catch a glimpse of you at the door – you always come with your mom to the door - but after the door had slammed shut, with me on the outside, what would happen to you on the inside? It would be two months since February 3. Would you have settled back to a state of relative serenity, albeit in a desert rather than a lush meadow? Would my trying to see you accomplish anything but raise a chocking sand storm? But if I didn't try, would you then think that I didn't even care? Would you think that I did care, but was too cowardly to even try? This would really hurt. You know your Uncle Tony never shies away from a fight for a good cause. And what better cause in my personal life than you? Would you lose more respect for me with every passing day I didn't come and see you or even call? Have you been waiting every day for the phone to ring? Are you slipping daily deeper into depression and despair? Would you even lose faith in love itself? How would this impact on your capacity to love? What would this do to the rest of your life? Would you then wilt in this Ar-Rub Al-Khali – the great Arabian Empty Quarters – into which you have been so brutally cast?

Manohar personally brought me a tray of biscuits and chai, a task usually performed by the lowest of lodge employees. I invited him to sit down and chat.

I tried an experiment on him. "If Person A would not dare to approach a house because the child in the house may be further harmed by Person B in the house, how would you assess the situation?"

"It is obviously a kidnap situation, where the child is being held hostage by Person B," said Manohar promptly. "What is the demand?"

"Simply that Person A does not approach the house."

"I'm afraid I don't understand the motive."

"Let me try this. Have you heard the story of Solomon?"

"I've heard the name Solomon from somewhere. I saw the movie called King Solomon's Mines – Stewart Granger and Deborah Kerr, if I recall correctly - when I was a kid."

"One day when King Solomon was presiding over the court," I explained, "two women came disputing custody of a baby. Solomon's verdict: Cut the baby in two and give each woman one half."

"Really? How barbaric." The expression on his face reflected the image in his mind.

"Guess what happened after that?"

"The baby was cut in two?"

"No."

"The baby was given to one of the women."

"Yes."

"Which one?"

"Woman B accepted the verdict, but woman A asked Solomon to give the baby to woman B."

"Aaah. I see," said Manohar, a light dawning in his dark eyes. "My apologies, King Solomon. You were very wise. Am I right to assume that he awarded the baby to woman A?"

"You assume correctly. Now, do you think it matters who the biological mother is?"

"No, it doesn't."

"Now, if I say that in the house situation, there is no Solomon. What do you predict would be the outcome?"

"I have my own analogy. Person A and Person B have a tug of war with the baby as the rope. The one letting go first loses the baby. Person B wins."

"Unfortunately, you May be right."

"So, where is the justice in this case?"

"There is none," I said, sadly.

Solomon! Where are you???!!!

[22:55 @ Rm. 111, Kanha Tiger Lodge]

A day of rest.

Morning chat with Manohar and Sarita, mostly about the Indian caste system. At one point, Manohar went to the dining pavilion to get something. On his way back, he came across one of the chickens pecking round in his path and kicked at it.

"Hey!" I yelled.

When Manohar sat back down, he said, good-naturedly, "I may kick at chickens in my way, but you North Americans eat them." He's a vegetarian.

At Breakfast, we (Sarita, Manohar, Jane and I) had a big debate on conservation. Sarita said that foreign countries should not meddle in India's affairs, that India can solve her own problems very well, thank you very much. This is classic Sarita. I was just about up to here with her. So I let loose something I've been holding back for days, "Then why did you work for Tiger Fund that accepts funding from CIDA? Your own salary comes from it."

Sarita probably hadn't thought things through before answering, "No, it's not.

It's from Magnificent Tours."

"Oh, really? So you are a Magnificent Tours employee, not a Tiger Fund employee?"

"Well, that's what my pay cheque says." She knew where I was going, but could not stop herself from letting me.

'If you're paid by Magnificent Tours, what are you doing here? Does Magnificent Tours have control over Tiger Fund? Why are you monitoring a Tiger Fund project? Are you aware that what you did over the last few days cost WCWC C$27,000?"

"Avtar tells me to do it. So I do it."

"I'm sorry, you have no authority whatsoever over Faiyaz and certainly is no position to monitor whatever we do here."

"And you have no authority to tell Tiger Fund what to do, or to do anything in the name of Tiger Fund," She shot back vehemently.

"Why not? This is a joint WCWC/TF program, and TF is getting CIDA money from WCWC."

"Not a single Canadian cent of it has yet to arrive."

"What are you talking about?"

"Exactly as I said. Where is your much touted grant money?"

"Are you saying that Tiger Fund has not yet received any money from WCWC?" I said, genuinely surprised.

"In yesteryears, yes, but not this year. I might go as far as to say that your being here is funded by Tiger Fund, more like by Magnificent Tours."

"WCWC wired C$15,000 to Tiger Fund on February 10, while I was in Delhi, as the first installment of Tiger Fund's C$60,000 share of the C$100,000 grant. Avtar himself told me that he had received the money."

"I wouldn't know about that," she said, uncertainly.

"Now you do. You do know that Tiger Fund's share of the CIDA grant is C$60,000 per year, don't you?"

"That I do."

"And he paid for the new black Gypsy within two days of his receipt of the CIDA money, by the way. Quite a coincidence."

She said nothing.

"Give me an honest answer, Sarita. You don't really believe that Avtar is going to produce $60,000's worth of tiger saving work, do you? What with the medicinal garden costing almost $10,000, and monitoring costing almost $30,000."

"Ask Avtar, don't ask me. I just do what I'm told, in the best way I can." But there was doubt in her voice.

The debate continued. I asked Sarita whether the Amazon rainforest could be saved if managed by Brazil alone. She said, "It is not up to us to say. The Amazon belongs to Brazil and nobody but Brazil should have any power over it." National pride above all else.

In another discussion with Jane, Sarita made it sound as if India was the most civilized country in the world at any point in history, and at one time the richest. But in my opinion, even if so, her saying so makes it less so. "That was why the British chose India to plunder," she said. She also seemed to be of the opinion that everything good in the world today had originated from India at one time or another in the past, reminding me pointedly that Buddhism, a religion embraced by China, was of Indian origin, which prompted me to answer, "So, it is okay with you for an Indian religion to influence another culture?"

"Obviously, Sarita's consciousness is stuck on the National level," I whispered inwardly to Raminothna. "Thankfully, not all Indians share her Indo-centric and nationalistic view point. Faiyaz for one."

"Not until all people on Earth have transcended the National level of Consciousness would the Earth be ready to integratively transcend," said Raminothna.

"The more I see, the farther that day looks to be."

"But it could be worse. Sarita's consciousness could be stuck on the metabion level, which would make her extremely selfish and ego-centric, or on the cellular or molecular levels, where she would be entirely run by her bodily and hormonal desires."

"Are you saying that, like matter, consciousness is multileveled?"

"Is it not?"

"So then, you're also saying that this multi-leveled structure of consciousness is also a product of transcendent integration?"

"Yes."

"But surely, you can't call whatever atoms and molecules have as 'consciousness'."

"As I said before, below the cellular level, it is called 'proto-consciousness'."

"So, an amoeba's would be called cellular consciousness?"

"Yes. Cellular Consciousness is appropriate."

"And higher up?"

"Metabion consciousness, citian consciousness, national consciousness,

planetary consciousness..."

At 17:00, we (Faiyaz, Jane, Sarita and I) went to the free school to see the kids. Yesterday, for the first time in this third visit to Kanha of mine, Kiran came to the free school. She was the girl in my slideshow at a spinning wheel. She was also the one I took for an elephant ride once. Now she is noticeably taller, and just as pretty. Jane whispered to me at one point, "Gee, she's really watching you, what the hell is going on there."

"What are you talking about?" I whispered back.

"She hasn't taken her eyes off you since she came in. She also did not take her eyes off you when you were playing soccer."

"She is only twelve or thirteen, for God's sake."

After school, Kiran beckoned me with a hand gesture and led me over to her village across the road. Her people brought out the Georgia Straight article with my picture on it and it was in pristine condition. She kept on trying to tell me something in Hindi, and made the hand gesture of her right and left hands alternatively holding her left and right wrists, which I could not decipher. She made another gesture that I could – to take photos of her and her friend Mena. But by then the sun had set, so, with the help of Punkesh, a smart kid of about 12, who said that he would like to be an engineer, I asked her to come to the school at 17:00 today, which she did.

When we got to the parking lot, the boys were playing soccer, so Faiyaz and I joined it on opposite sides, I on the side of Punkesh. This time, he chose me. I noticed that Kiran was there and, out of the corner of my eyes, that she was indeed looking at me. I asked Faiyaz what the hands on wrists gesture meant, and he also was mystified by it, but he cautioned me against getting close to Kiran, citing that her mother was a "loose woman" and Kiran had adopted a certain untoward code of conduct. Well, she is not for me to judge on hearsay, and I treat her just like any other kid. After the soccer game, we all went to the school courtyard to take photos, and I brought the Polaroid cam. A good photo session was had by all. After that, we all went into the school and I made the announcement to the kids, about 25 of them, of my impending departure. They looked sad, but they all knew that we weren't there to stay forever. Only Punkesh said that I should stay for good, "at least for 5 more months".

Then it was Jane's turn, with tears in her eyes. She said, "You can be whatever you want to be. But first, you must stay in school with your very good teacher."

The kids each sang us a little Hindi song, including the anthem of India. When our turn came, Jane and I sang the Canadian anthem back for them. So, the farewell has been said. I will not go back to the school tomorrow – the last school day. I will miss their innocent and eager little faces and big hearts. I hope they will not be corrupted like so many of their adults. I hope they will all dare to dream, and have their dreams all come true. If I ever come back to Kanha, to see them again would be one of my main reasons. I have tears in my eyes right now as I write about them.

This evening, when I emerged from my room to the dining pavilion for dinner, Sarita said, "Anthony, you're now a superstar in Madhya Pradesh." She showed me the new Hitavada article titled "Save tiger from extinction – Marr", complete with photo of me standing beside Big Cub's entrance letting kids in. A very respectable and respectful article by the reporter who asked me to keep him posted with the progress of my campaign. WCWC, for once, received its due share of mention. Tiger Fund, Fiayaz and Sarita got their mentions too, but only in the last paragraph. I hope Sarita is not too disappointed, because after all, all the honorable mention Jane received was "a white woman".

"A very good white woman," said Raminothna.

Good night, Christopher.

1999-03-18-4   *The Hitavada* ("The oldest and largest circulated English daily in Central India")
[Great Mission - Anthony Marr educating children about protecting the majestic and beautiful tiger from extinction]
… Mr. Marr who is tirelessly working in India… said that the tiger is the greatest national treasure of India, but even more so, it is a global treasure that is revered the world over. "Though it belongs to no one, its loss would impoverish us all."…

… Mr. Marr said that the Royal Bengal tiger might look the most secure of all remaining subspecies, but in truth, it is no more secure that the last carriage of a crashing train…

Currently, Mr. Marr, along with (Canadian volunteer Jane Kirkpatrick) and… (Indian conservationist) Faiyaz Khudsar are battling to educate the people living around the Kanha (Tiger Reserve)…

Anthony Marr

March 19, 1999, Friday, sunny, 23-35C

Dearest Christopher:

[11:34 @ Rm. 111, Kanha Tiger Lodge]
    In the dining pavilion today I saw two framed poems by CJ, one titled "Tiger Song", which I've already read, and the other is "Earth's Hope", which I have not.

> If we are here then why don't we help the Earth
> Her water, her land and all her being
> Recycle we know, waste not already learned
> Who sleeps and destroys and isn't terribly concerned
> Is it the individual who really doesn't care
> That our children will suffer or others elsewhere
> Not in our backyard who is so blind
> To see all the trash produced by Mankind
> We've already given poison to those who do not need
> Those plastic and petrol products the worst disease
> Is God so far away or has money won
> This battle of love as important as our Sun
>
> Blow the wind, burn fire and water breed
> Create life, save nature, just follow me
> My voice is one today yet not so alone
> Others listen, know life and care for their own
> How do I help, do good, is it too late
> Aren't the forces too great controlling fate
> Brothers and sisters listen to me
> We will control our destinies
> For we are the seed and we will grow
> We can make fire when it snows
> Dive under water escaping heat
> Laughing and crying as we need
>
> Blow the wind, burn fire and water breed
> Create life and give nature what she needs
> Respect and love why don't we

Omni-Science and the Human Destiny

> Don't let money be your disease
> Control we can should we be there
> We are not weak, that's if we care
> Our small actions can save the mountains
> Good deeds the sea
> Picking up the land, help the sky and plant a tree
> Guard a flower to remind you of all that is good
> She'll stay with you, need love and listen
> As we should

[22:15]

My being a "superstar" in Madhya Pradesh does have its drawbacks. Today, being medical clinic day, we picked up the doctor from Malanjkahn in the morning and drove him back after dinner. When Surinder was getting the Gypsy ready, Kim, who was going for the ride, asked me if I wanted to go with her. Faiyaz advised against it, saying that the better known I am, the more enemies I have and the less I should be seen, for my own safety. But what the hell, how many times do I get invited by Kim to go for a long moonlit ride? So I went. Manohar was heard to say to Faiyaz and Jane, "Sir Anthony is Lady Kim's knight in shining armor tonight." At Malanjkahn, as usual, we got stared at, but I couldn't tell if it was due to the newspaper articles or just that I was in the company of a blonde. On the way back, it was a starry starry night.

This is my last full day at Kanha in this expedition, and, given my fall-out with Avtar, probably the last day at Kanha in my life. But perhaps one day, when my hair had turned white, and Punkesh and Kiran and Bishnu and Asha have all grown up, I'll come back, if there is anything left of Kanha to come back to.

Sarita will be going back to Delhi, and she had a parting shot for me. She kindly offered to read my palm and methodically observed, "You have a small heart, a mediocre mind and a long life." Well, one out of three ain't bad. She also read Jane's palm. Her verdict was, "Sorry to tell you this, Jane, but your life, including love life, will be very boring." Her observation of me could be true, but she is dead wrong about Jane, who is having an exciting experience in India as Sarita speaks.

Sarita may not know it, but I am saddened that circumstances beyond my control placed her into an untenable position with me. Could I have made her feel welcome to the team? I'm sure I could, but she certainly didn't make me want to try.

Her national consciousness was certainly an instant barrier, but it was not the main factor. The main factor I think is our ego – our metabion consciousness.

"Interesting. So if we invoke the ego, we should also invoke the other Freudian terms, like the Id and the Superego?"

"That would be appropriate."

"So, what is the Id?"

"Cellular consciousness downwards, or inwards, which would manifest itself as intra-body sensations like hunger and thirst and pain and sexual pleasure and desire."

"And the Superego would be Citian consciousness upwards, including Citian consciousness, national consciousness and planetary consciousness?"

"And further up as they arise, bearing in mind that two people, both with superegos, could still be diametrical opposites."

"What do you mean?"

"Both you and Sarita have a superego, but while yours is planetary and beyond, hers tops up at the national level. Thus, a big part of your conflict. Still, it is higher than tribal consciousness."

"How about the Jungian term Collective Unconscious and the concept of the Archtype?"

By definition: "The collective unconscious is a part of the psyche which can be negatively distinguished from a personal unconscious by the fact that it does not, like the latter, owe its existence to personal experience and consequently is not a personal acquisition. While the personal unconscious is made up essentially of contents which have at one time been conscious, but which have disappeared from consciousness through having been forgotten or repressed, the contents of the collective unconscious have never been in consciousness, and therefore have never been individually acquired but owe their existence exclusively to heredity. Whereas the personal unconscious consists for the most part of complexes, the content of the collective unconscious is made up essentially of archetypes."

"I read elsewhere that the collective unconscious reveals aspects of universal human experience, as well as reflect innate tendencies."

"It would seem that the collective unconscious corresponds to the genetic, and therefore molecular proto-consciousness, and in part cellular consciousness, whereas the personal consciousness would correspond to the cellular and especially metabion levels of consciousness, and involve 'complexes' of neuronal subcircuits."

Good night, Christopher.

Omni-Science and the Human Destiny

❖ ❖ ❖ ❖ ❖

March 20, 1999, Saturday, sunny, 22-34C

Dearest Christopher:

[17:57 @ Rm.12, Bandhavgarh Tiger Lodge]

Last night, I was awakened by a knock on my door at 02:00. Upon opening the door in my bath robe, with tussled hair, I found lodge employee Raji standing there with an unfamiliar young man who said, "Bandhavgarh, Bandhavgarh. Go now." My first impression was that they caught wind that I was about to be arrested and wanted to spirit me out of there under the cover of darkness. So I quickly got dressed and went out to get set for loading my luggage, and found the whole lodge still asleep. I went to the roofed parking area, and indeed saw a white Tata Sumo there with the two Gypsies, but no driver. Then I heard a sound, turned, and saw Raji sitting there in a chair, wrapped in a poncho, apparently serving his night shift duty as if nothing unusual was happening. I went to him and asked about the driver and he just replied in Hindi. Finally, I went to knock on Faiyaz's door, woke him up, and asked him what was going on. Upon questioning, Raji said that they thought I was the only person going to Bandhavgarh, and for some reason, the driver thought it was for a 02:00 or 02:30 departure. So I just got back to bed and hoped for some sleep. Talk about Indian time.

Second round. We were supposed to get going shortly after 06:00. Everyone got up at 05:30, was assembled by 06:00, ready to go, at which point Manohar recognized the driver as one who'd had a history of accidents. According to Manohar, several people had been killed, and one of the park guards he once hit was still paralyzed. So Manohar sent him back to Baihar for another driver, and the new driver did not come until about 08:30. So, finally, we (Manohar, Faiyaz, Jane, Sarita and I) got on the road after 09:00.

I would have loved to have Kim come with us to Bandhavgarh, but Avtar has put a stop to that, and Kim could not fight it. We had a long hug. "See you in Vancouver," I said.

Sarita is supposed to take the Umaria train back to Delhi this evening. Faiyaz will go to Delhi to his sister's on March 26th, and I will take a car to Khajuraho on March 28th, from where I will take a plane to Delhi. And Jane? I'm not sure, and I don't think she is either.

When the Tata Sumo was pulling out of the parking lot, village kids lined the long driveway, holding out flowers and waving. I reached out my hand to touch as many of them as possible. I spotted Punkesh. On the spur of the moment, I took off my hat and gave it to him through the car window. I looked for Kiran, but did not see her, and felt a little bang. Finally, the car reached the end of the driveway, and turned left on to the highway, and then, from my left rear window seat, I saw her sitting at their Manjitola village booth across the road from the gate, with a baby in her lap. I have never seen her there before. She gazed at the vehicle, as if longingly, while it pulled away, but I doubt that she saw me, since the right rear window was closed and tinted. In front was Manohar at the left front window seat and Faiyaz in the middle, and they spared her not a glance, but Jane saw her from the rear right seat and waved, and after the Sumo had shifted on to high gear, I turned to look out the rear window. Kiran and I exchanged a moment of eye contact. I waved, but the road dust had already obscured her. Jane gave me a surreptitious yet knowing glance. I thought about Kiran off and on along the way, not sexually by any means, but was haunted by a sense of melancholy. If it was for her, it would only last an hour or two, but if it was for Kanha, which includes her, it would last the rest of my life. If I succeed in persuading WCWC to drop TF, I may never see Kanha ever again, and of course her. Good bye, Kiran. Good bye, Kanha. I will never forget you.

How ephemeral we are. Hello. Good bye. Birth. Death. How many atoms in my body actually belong to me? None. I am but a configuration maintained by the atoms and molecules amongst themselves during their temporary stay in their temporary totality I call my body. When I die, my atoms and molecules will disperse, and my configuration will dissolve, leaving nothing.

"Except the changes you've made to the world while you live, which, I hope, will continue far into the future, both within the species Homo Sapiens while it lives, and in the world even after Homo Sapiens itself has gone extinct."

"Like the changes I hopefully have made to Kanha and India, even though the conference did not happen, and even if I never return."

Have I been speaking aloud? Manohar and Faiyaz both turned around and looked at me. Manohar gave me a thumbs-up sign.

I reached forward and gave each of their shoulders a pat.

"I've been thinking too. The spiral of integrative transcendence, the I.T. Spiral, is in actuality like a DNA-like double helix, or a galaxy like twin spiral, whose yin-yang sides are consciousness and matter respectively."

"The I.T. Twin Spiral and its O.S.E.S. Cycle. Finally, up to the Planetary

level at least, the BIG PICTURE is complete. Congratulations."

Raminothna and I exchanged a spiritual high five. A highly worthy thought with which to conclude my third sojourn at Kanha.

We rolled into the Bandhavgarh Tiger Lodge parking lot around 15:30, just when three Gypsies were about to roll out of camp to the park, one driven by lodge manager Mohinder Sidhu and another with Tiger Trust officer Darshan Nagra in the passenger seat. Darshan and I had a good working relationship back in 1997 and 1998. I found him slight obsequious, but otherwise very likeable. He has always been very warm towards me. But when he shook hands with me this time, he did not smile and looked slightly apprehensive. In the Gypsies were about 10 middle-aged to older Caucasian tourists. Mohinder invited me to climb on board his Gypsy on the spot. Having had enough of vehicles for a day, I gracefully declined. "Tomorrow," I said.

So tomorrow, Bandhavgarh, here I come!

And wishing you were here, as always. Good night, Christopher.

❖ ❖ ❖ ❖ ❖

March 21, 1999, Sunday, sunny, 14-35C

Dearest Christopher:

[03:57 @ Rm.12, Bandhavgarh Tiger Lodge]
"And the intrigue continues," observed Jane.

Yesterday, Jane and I shared dinner by ourselves, whereas Manohar, Faiyaz, Mohinder, Darshan and Sarita dined together a little later on the balcony of the main building. During our dinner, Darshan came to sit with us, and in his usual somewhat overly pleasing manner, placed his services entirely at our disposal throughout my one-week stay at Bandhavgarh. He added the caution that the problems at Bandhavgarh are largely "political", and whatever information he may provide to us had to be kept confidential. He would be busy today, the last day for the group of the dozen or so tourists here at BTL, but as of tomorrow, he would be able to devote fulltime to assist me. I mentioned a rather innocuous "talking to villagers" and "giving slideshows to schools", and he seemed to have no problem with these. But shortly after that, Sarita pulled him aside and had a long one-on-one with him, during which Jane made the above comment. Now, because of Sarita, my initial trust in Darshan evaporated.

While they were having their exclusive session in Hindi, Jane and I had our own in English. We came to the conclusion that, if possible, one of the most effective things we could do within a week would be to dig out the truth of the situation at Bandhavgarh, whatever it is, be it official corruption, privileged poaching, the heavy loss of at least four known tigers over the last 12 months (and how many unknown?) out of a supposed population of only 40, and publish it internationally. Of special interest is the fate of Sita ("SEE-ta"), the most famous tigress in the world, featured with her seventh and last litter of cubs in the cover article of National Geographic, December 1997. It seems to be general consensus (Faiyaz, Manohar, Belinda) that Bandhavgarh needs a lot more help than Kanha. In fact, I think Bandhavgarh is in big trouble.

Again, to accomplish this fact finding, I would need a lot of help, at least in terms of very exact translation, which I wonder if Darshan would be willing or able to provide.

Sarita is finally gone. All at once the tension evaporated, except a lingering sense of suspicion she left behind.

"You may not look at it this way, but she resents the hell out of you for being here to, in her view, monitor what Tiger Fund does or does not do with the CIDA money, and interfere with what Tiger Fund does or does not do to save tigers in India. And though they acknowledge that you do good work, they also feel that the better work you do, the worse they would look in comparison," said Jane. "Knowing that the more you look, the more you'd see, and the longer you stay the more you would do, Avtar and Sarita are just counting the days till you leave, and the sooner, the better. As far as she's concerned, and Avtar too, you have way overstayed your welcome."

[11:57]

We just returned from a wonderful wildlife viewing experience back in breathtaking Bandhavgarh. Off the bat, we (Faiyaz, Manohar, Jane and I) saw the most famous male tiger in the world, the 550 lb. Charger, thanks to Manohar, whose eagle eyes first spotted him from a great distance – all the way across a large meadow where the big cat was but a very slow moving speck of yellow against the brilliant green background of sal trees. The jeep (not a Gypsy, but a real Jeep this time), driven by an old man with a long white bread in a long white robe looking like a guru – a most incongruent picture - raced along a dirt path skirting the meadow until we got to the old boy (16). At one point, when Charger was crossing the road behind the jeep, the driver put it in reverse and almost ran him over. We yelled, "Roko! Roko!! ROKO!!!" The jeep came to a screeching halt, within inches of Charger's muscular flank. I was at the tailgate. If I reached out, I could have touched him. Of course, it could go both ways, and his touch might not be quite as gentle. All our commotion caused him to look up directly at us (which tigers seldom do), and growled us a warning. Then he just calmly walked into the forest, patrolling his kingdom in the twilight of his reign, and of his life. This might be the last time I would see him, in his life or mine. Good luck, Charger. We shall all miss him; we certainly miss Sita. I do. I've seen her no fewer than a dozen times in yester-years, and her cubs. Other than Charger, we also saw a jackal, a thick python who ate a Rhesus Macaque monkey yesterday and was lying motionless in a gulley digesting its meal, lots of birds, and of course some of Bandhavgarh's exquisite scenery.

During the park drive, I came across many familiar faces, including the park guard who made a brief appearance in the Champions of the Wild documentary.

Most of all, we encountered Rajesh Kumar, the park guide who accompanied the Omni-Film-crew on the "Sermon on the Mound" shoot, and who wrote me a letter via Andrew Gardner and Michael Chechik last year. He recognized me first, stopped his jeep, and walked over to ours to greet me. With pain written on his face, he told me what several other people, included Darshan, had already done, "We lost at least four tigers here last year. 10% of the population. We need help."

"I would like to talk to you," I said to him. "I'll be at the Bandhavgarh Tiger Lodge over the next week."

"I will come tomorrow evening, if convenient to you," he said eagerly.

"Please do. I'll be there," I said, genuinely enthusiastic with the prospect.

"I like him," said Jane. "He has heart. He is transparently sincere about the tiger, like our Anthony and Faiyaz and Manohar here."

"And our Jane," Manohar said. "I agree with you about Rajesh."

"Thanks, Manohar," said Jane. "Seems like we've found the very person in Bandhavgarh we've been looking for. Weren't we wishing for just such a person to be here only yesterday evening?"

"Yes, he's a great guy. If there is anybody here I trust, that's him. But he's only a park guide. What can he do?" said Faiyaz.

[23:47]

I'm staying in the same mud-hut as the one I stayed at during the Champions of the Wild film shoot back in November and December 1997, except now that it is March, when not a drop of rain has fallen for weeks, the hut is bone dry. Back in November 1997, the walls were so soaked with moisture they were about to crumble, and my shirts hang on racks like wet dishtowels.

Within a stone's throw of the hut in the middle of a field is a platform, made of thin tree trunks tied together like a raft, on stilts fifteen feet high, accessible only by a vertical ladder built into the structure. During the growing season, the platform is used as a watchtower for crop-plundering chital and wild boar at night. Of late, a leopard has been making nocturnal rounds about the lodge grounds, and the platform has been used for that purpose.

Around 10 this evening, Darshan took me on a night walk along the park fence line for about a mile. We each brought an electric torch. It was not at all like my nightly starlight strolls at Kanha, but more like a sentry patrol. He shone his torch beam into every thicket and every shadow, and once every so often did a general 360° sweep with it.

"What I'm checking for are two bright green reflective dots - the eyes of the leopard. It could be a tiger too, but unlikely," he whispered. "If the leopard is here, it would most certainly be looking at us right this second."

Occasionally there were sounds of animals going through thicket, but a leopard would be quieter than that.

When we got back to the lodge compound, I climbed up the "watch tower" to check it out. No one was there, but there was a thick grass mat. It makes a great star-gazing platform; gets me 20 feet closer to them.

Venus is bright to the west. I'm not sure if it's Jupiter or Saturn overhead. Such vast space out there, even inside just one out of 300 billion solar systems in the Milky Way Galaxy, which is but one of 100 billion galaxies in the observable universe.

This is the brave new world of Planetary Organism Earth if and when it integratively transcends into being. And we Homo Sapiens will be in the driver's seat when Earth starts reaching out to its interplanetary environs – if we pass this cosmic test standing in our path today.

"Will we?"

"There is never a bad ending."

"Are you saying that if our ICBMs fly, if chemical and biological weapons are about to be poured into the bowels of a nation, you are going to intervene?"

"No. That would be in violation of the interstellar protocol."

"So, what kind of a good ending would that be?"

"As I may have said before, let the destructive self-destruct, and the transcendent self-transcend. Isn't this good for all concerned? Isn't this good for the Universe itself?"

"So, speaking optimistically, on the chance that we manage to transcend, how should we proceed after that?"

"Along the I.T. Twin Spiral, of course, through the four O.S.E.S. quadrants on the Planetary level of organization."

"Yes, of course. So organismization will yield to speciation? How will this transition unfold?"

"Planetary Organism Earth will mature, and reproduce."

"What do you mean by a planetary organism maturing?"

"The maturing of her reproductive system specifically."

"How will she reproduce?"

"Once the Planetary Organism Earth has organismized into being, it will be the original organism on the Planetary level of organization within the Solar System. After a period of maturation, it will reproduce, begetting offspring planetary organisms on other planets within the Solar System and their satellites, or in interplanetary space. Earth's 'seeds' will be space colonies - citian organisms in their own right, which will contain the genes and memes of Earth. Once landing on other planets and their satellites, or stabilized in orbit, these citian level 'Earth seeds' will quickly form national organisms, and eventually planetary organisms. Thus, yet a new O.S.E.S. Cycle, on the Planetary level of organization, will unfold. Like the lower-level organisms before them, these planetary organisms will speciate, form a multi-planetary ecosystem, and eventually inter-planetary society, which, if all go well, will become the Stellar Organism Sol - on the Stellar level of organization."

"How will the Planetary organisms speciate?"

"Since they will all have their own unique environments, they will divergently evolve, into quite as many different Planetary species as there are Planetary organisms. These various Planetary organisms/species will have divergently evolved on all of the Molecular, Cellular, Metabion, Citian and National levels. On the Metabion level, for example, the humans on a high gravity planet, compared to those on a low gravity planet, will look quite different. So will be their social organization and cultural content. The Solar

System is going to be a rich and diverse interplanetary ecosystem, albeit a crowded one."

"How would interplanetary sociality develop?"

"Much like how international sociality on Earth has been developing, minus the wars. Different planets and satellites have different physical endowments. Jupiter, for example, has an outer atmosphere of hydrogen, so it could be an exporter of hydrogen to other Planetary organisms. Many of Jupiter's satellites, such as Callisto, Europa and Ganymede, have vast quantities of water, and Io is rich in sulphur, etc., whereas those free-space National organisms living near the asteroid belt will have easy access to the heavier metals, especially iron. And, who knows, some of these Planetary and National organisms may become exporters of books or music, or super-high-tech, or even sports entertainment. Trading of these resources and commodities will eventually facilitate a Solar-System-wide network of specialization and cooperation for the common good, which will develop into a Solar-System-wide interplanetary society. In due course, the interplanetary society of the Solar System will integratively transcend into the Stellar Organism Sol. This should take care of the next little while."

"How long is a little while?"

"How long is a period? How long is an era? How long is an eon?"

It has been much longer than an eon since I saw you last, or so it feels. We may have moved into new eras in our lives. But would they be the same one? Good night, Christopher.

※　※　※　※　※

March 22, 1999, Monday, sunny 14-34C

Dearest Christopher:

[01:12 (1999-03-23-2) @ Rm.12, Bandhavgarh Tiger Lodge]
    Today is without a doubt the most amazing day since our landing in India on January 20.
    The safari started slowly, in fits and starts, with lots of sitting and listening.

While waiting, I asked Raminothna, "If and when we go to the stars, what will be awaiting us out there? Would it be star wars, or heavenly peace?"

"This is a tough question to answer. If I told you, I'd ruin a major sector of science fiction."

"For the sake of Christopher, for the sake of Earth, for the sake of all life in the Universe, I hope and pray for the latter. Would it not be a tragedy of biblical proportions if, after all her trials and tribulations, and learning and living the way of harmony, Earth finally organismizes itself and manages to venture out of her cradle, only to be killed in some interstellar crossfire, or worse, to kill? What is the point to achieve peace on Earth, just so we could go and fight wars among the stars?"

"For the sake of Christopher," toasted Raminothna.

"But competition among species has always happened, so far, when the IT Spiral reaches the Ecosystemization quadrant of the OSES Cycle on any level. So shouldn't it occur on the interstellar levels as well. Is warfare inevitable whenever different species of Stellar Organisms encounter each other for the first time in interstellar space?"

"War of the Worlds, Star Wars, Battlestar Galactica and even the highly positive Star Trek are often but the physical manifestation of Earth's own immature paranoia. Just as evolution can translevel-progress from Darwinian to Lamarckian, so, cannot conflict translevel-progress to harmony, and war to peace?"

Towards the late morning, we came upon a 3-elephant "tiger show" centered on a dried river bed, but with about a dozen Gypsies in line ahead of us. With no other elephants to be had, we settled in the queue.

While we were waiting, several things happened. First, a tall Caucasian man of about 30 approached our jeep. I recognized him as among a group of people in another Gypsy who was staring at me intensely in a previous road encounter. Well, I thought, another recognition. And it was. He introduced himself as Andrew Guppy, from England, and said that one of his party, a young British woman, had recognized me from a TV wildlife documentary on "Channel 5", and wanted to meet me in person. "Treat it as a blind date," he said. As it turned out, he was a tour operator and the woman was one of his group. He then proceeded to talk about Ranthambhore where his group recently visited, and complained bitterly that Valmik Thapar had commandeered the lakes for a BBC film shoot and barred tourists from there. He thought that it was not just a temporary measure, but a permanent situation henceforth. Faiyaz and I exchanged glances. Tourism vs conservation again.

After he had left, another small group came forth. This time it was a big Ukrainian man of about 30 also, accompanied by his very pretty daughter of about 7 and a Russian-speaking Indian man of about 50. He began rattling rapidly in Russian, with his Indian friend translating. He was seriously concerned about the fate of the Siberian tiger and heard from his park guide, who happened to be Rajesh Kumar himself, that there was a "world renowned tiger conservationist in our midst" (me), and that he should speak to me. He very reverentially outlined who he was (a rich businessman headquartered in the Ukraine) and what his concerns were, and asked me more or less to help him create and direct (directly or indirectly) a Siberian tiger conservation program funded by himself. I was quite astounded. We made a tentative appointment for a meeting some time in the evening.

While still waiting, I said to Faiyaz, "While we wait, why don't we go and talk to the guides about tonight's video show. They're all here. What better time to do it?"

We're talking about the Champions of the Wild documentary, which was filmed at Bandhavgarh, tonight at 19:30 in the open-air amphitheatre, with video projector and large screen yet.

Faiyaz nodded yes and jumped off the Gypsy. First he went to grab Darshan who was in another Gypsy, and the two of them went and talked to all the other guides. Shortly, he came back and said that the guides all said they would attend, and that Rajesh requested a meeting some time this evening since he had to go to Kanha early tomorrow morning for four days. They also invited the British Group and the Russian businessman.

It's going to be a jam-packed evening.

After about a half-hour wait, we (Faiyaz, Jane and I) finally mounted a big male elephant. At that point, my camera film number was about #17 out of 36. When we got to the tigers – the three big 28-month-old cubs of tigress Nurani, who had already detached from her, but were still hanging out together – it seemed that we were just a touch too late, for we saw while approaching from a distance that they were just walking off from the dry streambed, where they were sitting, into the thickets. We nonetheless maintained visual contact with them and when we arrived, we found they were walking parallel to us behind a scene of bamboo. Our mahout urged our elephant to go ahead of them to wait around a gentle bend and, lo and behold, they did one by one re-emerge from the undergrowth back onto the streambed. And there, they continued walking for a short distance, and then one settled down under a tree and the other two lay down side by side in the sand right in sight of us. Meanwhile, our mahout continued maneuvering our elephant for better angles, and our three cameras kept clicking away. Soon, I heard Faiyaz groan that he was out of film. I glanced at my camera and saw that I had advanced to #33. By then, fortunately, the three almost full grown cubs had settled down in their new positions and I snapped off the last four frames and felt my camera having turned into a box of gems. The cubs were absolutely perfect, in flawless condition, without a single blemish, radiating youthful majesty. Their images should move many hearts.

Being one of the last groups in line and the last load for this elephant, we had the luxury of not having to return to the waiting area at any set time. So we just stayed there until finally the cubs got up again and vanished into the tickets for good. I whispered to them a heartfelt "Good luck."

I heard Jane whisper behind me, "Now I fully understand why you do what you are doing." Yes, whisper, always, in the realm of the tiger.

"This is the love side of the impulse," I whispered back. "We've got to save this exquisite beauty for our children."

"If there is a love side, there is a hate side?"

"The users of tiger parts, the poachers, the smugglers, the traders, the trophy hunters. I just have this irresistible urge to crush them."

"Too bad that of the billion people in India, hardly 1% are aware of the tiger's plight," whispered Faiyaz. "All they see, and at that rarely, are the painted images of tigers on walls for one commercial products or another, or as the mount of the Hindu goddess Durga. Unfortunately, few if any of these images manage to capture the essence of the tiger's beauty and majesty in the least, and are therefore incapable of generating love and reverence for it. But I have seldom seen anyone who has seen live tigers in a forest who does not want to protect them."

At noon, we returned to the lodge and had our lunch. There, while we (Jane, Faiyaz, Darshan and I) were seated around one of the smaller tables, I asked Darshan to call Latika ("La-TEE-ka") on my behalf to arrange a meeting with me. Latica is a very beautiful Indian woman who is also a prominent Oxford educated tiger conservationist. In my previous visit to Bandhavgarh, she recognized me from her jeep and invited me to join her on a foot patrol. She had a project of using infrared-triggered cameras, about thirty pairs I believe, to study the Bandhavgarh tigers, and told me that many of the night shots were not of wild animals at all, but of humans who had no business being there, meaning poachers.

When Darshan called her residence, which was a tourist lodge called the Jungle Camp, to which the Omni Film Crew moved from the Tiger Lodge back in 1997, it was Latika herself who answered the phone. Darshan said that she seemed happy to hear from me and asked me if I had plans in the late afternoon. I said "no". She said she was going into the park to do some work, and would call me when she returned to her lodge. I said "fine". But after I had dropped the phone, Faiyaz reminded me of the video show, and I called her back, asking her to attend. She asked for the time and place and I passed the phone back to Darshan, and that ended the connection.

Shortly after that, I went for a nap, but was awakened by Faiyaz's knock on the door, saying that we had to go and meet the park officials for permission to hold the video show (so what's new? Bandhavgarh is not Kanha, but it is still in India) and to invite them to it. He said it was urgent and had to be done within minutes, but after I had struggled out of bed, we sat around for nearly half an hour for their lordships to call us back.

While waiting, we got the hierarchy of Bandhavgarh's officialdom figured out, which by nomenclature is different from Kanha's. In ascending order, it is: Forest Guard, Deputy Ranger, Range Officer, Assistant Conservator of Forest, Deputy Director, Chief Forest Conservator (CFC - Bandhavgarh's equivalent of Kanha's Field Director).

Finally, they did call and we did go, and it turned out to be actually quite a pleasant meeting. Present were the CFC, the Deputy Director (of the park, Bandhavgarh has no buffer zone), a couple of other VIP-looking men and an older Indian gentleman in white robes who was obviously respected by the officials, who introduced himself as from, surprise, Toronto, but who had maintained a once-a-year-visitation schedule over the last 20 years. They were very complimentary of what I do and gave their verbal condonation of whatever outreach we wished to do. The CFC even volunteered his personal assistant at our disposal on grounds that the aid was fluent in local dialect and would eliminate whatever alienation there might be due to Faiyaz's outsider-dialect. This I interpret as a double-edged sword, partly as a help and partly as yet another "monitor". I respectfully invited them to see the video and they said they would come. One major happy surprise: the old white-robed gentleman on his own accord talked about the wisdom of raising park fees and having part of the proceeds go to the park and the other part to the villagers, and the other VIPs agreed!

Back to the lodge, I had a cold water shower and shampoo. After that, Darshan took us (Jane, Faiyaz and me) out for a walk along the park boundary nearest the lodge. There we saw fencing of three different configurations. The first we encountered was a combination of a 3'-ditch, a 4'-loose-stone-wall on the park-side of the ditch, and a 5'-electric-fence behind it. We came upon breaches in the stone wall here and there, and eroded parts in the ditches. Darshan opined that this fence system may partly keep slow cattle from entering the park, but it was

Omni-Science and the Human Destiny

ineffective to keep fleet-footed deer from jumping out. Farther on, we came across a 4'-ditch / 5'-4-strand electric fence combination, some of whose wires had been cut, some hanging loose and some strands tied together to make passing room underneath. We touched the wires and found there was no current in them. Darshan said that the locals regularly cut the wires, and of course once cut in just one place, the whole fence goes down. While I previously favored electric fencing due to lower cost, this discovery changed my thinking in an instant. And then we came across a 6'-chain-link-fence / ditch combination and this seemed the most effective of all, but upon closer inspection, we also saw cut holes here and there big enough to admit people (wood-cutters), goats and perhaps cows. Looking at the landscape on both sides of the fence, we saw forest with a grazed fringe on the park side, and a devastated wasteland on the other, with a large herd of cattle still nibbling on whatever grass and root remnants still remaining, tended by a boy with an axe in his hand. So, all of the fences were ineffective to one extent or another, and without a fence on other parts of the park perimeter, the damage to the park can be imagined. It seems that a regular foot patrol of the fence line and park periphery is needed, which currently does not exist.

The next question then is: What to do with violators? Fine them? They can't even look beyond their next meal, and their next bundle of firewood.

Back at the lodge, we (Faiyaz, Jane, Darshan and I) sat together and strategized on what most effect thing we could do while I'm still here. I openly told Darshan what I had in mind. Given just a week, an outreach program would be of limited scope, but a fact-finding mission could be immensely impactful if we could discover sensational material that can generate a high profile article for media in the West. And what more sensational material than what happened to the most famous tigress in the world – Sita? If we could find out how she died, we would automatically also have uncovered the flaws of the entire Bandhavgarh park system. Darshan seem instantly relieved, and I think I know why. Sarita had laid down the law about certain things she predicted I would want to do, which did not include what I just said I wanted to do. Not only did he support the idea, but told me that he had information to offer.

Soon, we had to break to change for the evening. We got to the amphitheatre by 07:10 and, with the help of the local technician, set up the video projector – under the stars! By the time most of the people had assembled, which included the park officials, the British group, the Russian businessman's family, Latica and friends, the guides and a number of local villagers, it was past 07:30. At 07:40, Faiyaz and I gave our intro, pre-corrected the few factual errors in the video, and let Champions roll, at the end of which Darshan announced that I would give a slideshow presentation same time tomorrow night. After that, there was the usual hand-shaking and questions and comments, amongst which was the British groups' invitation to the White Tiger Lodge for a drink around 21:30, and the Ukranian family's invitation for a meeting at the same lodge at 20:30.

The meeting with the Ukrainian family took place in their room, attended by his family, Rajeen Saxena, MD (the Russian speaking Indian gentleman), Rajesh Kumar, our guide-of-the-day, and us – Faiyaz, Jane, Darshan and me. The Ukrainian gentleman, Mr. Valera Levchinovskiey, further introducing himself and what he wanted to accomplish, his anguish at not quite knowing what to do, and his need and desire to have me help save the Siberian tiger, mentioning the possibility of my going to Russia at some juncture. At one point, he was talking with great disdain about German hunters going to hunt the Russian Brown bear. I asked him a few questions and told him a little bit about my 1996 anti-bear-hunting campaign, and the amount of media I generated in two months. His eyes and those of his Indian translator lit up. Shortly after that, we exchanged contact info and wound up our one-hour meeting. We exchanged contact information and agreed to communicate further by phone and email.

Rajeen asked me to call him as soon as I get back to Delhi so that he could arrange a meeting between myself and (ready?) Sonia Gandhi (!) – the very high profile leader of the opposition in the Lok Sabha, the lower house of the Indian Parliament - "since your video included footage of Indira Gandhi."

The R&R with the British group followed at the lounge, and Jane was thrilled with her rum-and-coke. I talked to two people especially. One was Delia Jarman, the English woman who recognized me, who is a librarian and a self-professed read-aholic – my "blind date". The other was a part-Chinese American woman named Karen Tan who is in the middle of a year-long round-the-world trip, including a motor-cycle segment, with business interest in Tara Handmade Paper & products, "the commercial wing of Development Alternatives, Paper from recycled cotton."

In the same group was also Alan & Dorothy Gregson, an older couple from Dundas, Ontario, Canada (!), both retired from Mohawk College of Applied Arts and Technology. They wanted to maintain contact.

Whew! As if all these were not enough, we also arranged a 22:30 meeting back at the Tiger Lodge with Rajesh. While driving back to the lodge, with Mohinder at the wheel, we follow a motorcycle which happened to be carrying Rajesh and our tobacco-chewing guide-of-the-day. The meeting, attended by Faiyaz, Jane, Darshan, Rajesh, the other guide, Mohinder and me, had the making of a spy novel episode. I laid it down on the table what this meeting was for – info gathering for the international article – and secrecy guaranteed if requested. It lasted deep into the night (01:00).

The information that came to light is stunning. After breakfast tomorrow, Faiyaz, Jane and I will convene to transcribe the copious notes they had taken into my computer. It should blow the minds of anyone in the West even remotely interested in tiger conservation.

It is now 03:24. I can hardly keep my eyes open. Good night, Christopher.

❖ ❖ ❖ ❖ ❖

March 23, 1999, Monday, sunny 14-34C

Dearest Christopher:

[22:39 @ Rm.12, Bandhavgarh Tiger Lodge]
The last 24 hours I've been clandestinely whisked from one place to another, to interview one person then another, gathering information from the death of Sita to other missing tigers, to compensation for cattle lifting by tigers, to villages still in the park and their impact on wildlife, to cooperation between forest department and local people or lack thereof, to anti-poaching work or lack thereof, to park protection measures or lack thereof, to corruption in officialdom, to possible solutions… I was alternatively surprised, amazed, dismayed, saddened, incredulous, disheartened, bewildered, horrified, infuriated, disgusted, outraged...

Incredible as it may seem, I'm being treated like some kind of hero. No, more like a savior. But it is not hard to deduce that their prime motive was nothing more than desperation verging on despair. They are clutching at straws and I just happened to float by. Well, a little more than that. I've been here twice before, once to know the place and the other to be the "star" of the Champions of the Wild film shoot. Champions has been shown in 20 countries around the globe. They see me as bringing the beauty and plight of Bandhavgarh to world attention. They hear tourists telling them it was because of their seeing Champions that they had heard of Bandhavgarh, and been impressed enough to have come to see it. In this morning's park drive, our park guide and a park guard serenaded me with a song they made up last night after seeing the Champions video, sung with pride and gusto. "We are the Champions of Bandhavgarh!" And this "we" seems to include me. So I sang it along with them, as did Jane, Faiyaz and even Manohar.

To protect the privacy, security and safety of those who guided me and those whom I interviewed, their identities will not be revealed here. Suffice to say that every piece of the following information has come directly from the mouth of somebody in the know in Bandhavgarh.

The following information has been organized into categories. It is a composite of several interviews. I have recorded every significant point during the interviews, and I have not omitted any point recorded. Here they are:

1. *The death of Sita*

It is not an overstatement to say that Sita was and still is *revered* by the locals. Even though her death was estimated to have occurred in August 1998, now in March 1999, it is still the talk of the place. Whenever I hear her name mentioned, I see a deep sadness in the speaker. Sita was 17 years old. Some of the guides themselves are that old. In other words, they have known her all their lives. They have seen her bring up seven litters of 18 cubs, out of which seven survived to adulthood to bring up cubs of their own. It also so happens that Sita's territory was near the entrance of the park, and was therefore one of the most traversed, making her one of the most seen tigresses at Bandhavgarh, and since to me Bandhavgarh is the tiger-viewing capital of the world, then Sita was likely the most seen wild tigress in the world.

Basically everybody believes she has been poached. The guides knew where she was everyday, until August 11, 1998, after which no one had seen her nor found her despite trying and trying and trying. One forest guard found some blood and tiger meat. He reported this to the authorities. He was ordered to clean up the mess, and to shut up.

They even told me the name of a poacher and know where to find him, but said that it would do no good to report him, nor the person who bought her skin, because her real killer was higher up.

There seems to be agreement about how Sita died – caught in a leg-hold trap and beaten to death with sticks. One said that people around Jungle Camp heard a tiger screaming on August 10. Sita's skin was moved from Tala (a village on the verge of Bandhavgarh) to Umaria around March 1.

Park officials do not seem to want the death of Sita to be known. Why? Because the park receives special funding in the name of Sita from some NGOs, including the World Bank. But evidence for Sita's poaching is available, one told me, if we go after the Forest Conservator, the Assistant Forest Conservator and the Ranger of Tala, which means to the top.

"Mother is missing in the eyes of her cubs, born Sept. 96, about 2 years old when Sita died, about 2.5 years old now," said one. "They sometimes scream and are sometimes found still together which is biologically unusual. We think it's due to the lack of the 'last training chapter'." I wonder if these are the same as the cubs at the dry river bed we saw yesterday.

Another said that they are also slightly less competent in hunting than other tigers their age, attributing this to their lack of this last training phase.

Sita was one of the four or five 'wives' of Charger, another being Mohini. Because of his old age, he's not as efficient a hunter as before. For some months, he's been scavenging the kills of Mohini instead of Sita. Previously, Charger had never been seen eating the kills of Mohini's, always Sita's only. This indicates Sita's absence.

Sita and Charger used to mate once every 2.5 years or so. This should be the year, around early March, but Sita has not appeared.

2. Other tiger disappearances

Some say at least six tigers have gone missing in 1998-1999. The bones of two tigers were seized from Dobha village. One very big male has not been seen since April 1998 from the Raj Bahera village area of the park. A five-year-old tiger was poisoned to death March 3, 1999 – just three weeks ago during the Holi festival - from Kalwah Range of the park. Bara Bacha, a son of Sita, the one described as "a very heavy tiger" in Champions, has disappeared since June 1998. No one knows what has happened to him, but everyone wonders why, if he's still alive, he would leave the area.

3. Lack of anti-poaching measure

The general consensus is that at today's rate of poaching, Bandhavgarh tigers will be extinct before 2010 - the next Chinese Year of the Tiger.

Park officials tell the guides and other personnel that if they leaked information regarding poaching, they would be sacked.

Shots have been heard from inside the park, mostly during the monsoon season when the park is closed, sometimes in other parts of the year, usually after dusk. One guide phoned the forest department about this and was told to mind his own business.

A forest guard was forced to make a false statement by some high official about a tiger poaching case. Later, when his statement was proved false after the release of the forensic report, he committed suicide by pouring kerosene on himself and setting himself on fire.

Poachers with guns come from nearby towns, e.g., Jabalpur, or from as far as Mumbai (previously Bombay). They receive help from local people regarding the tigers' whereabouts.

A poacher from Dabha village from where the forest department has seized a lot of bone and skin is still poaching.

Jeeps can enter freely from the backside of the park. The barriers placed across many roads can be easily breached. There is no constant vigil at the barriers during the monsoon season, although there is supposed to be a foot patrol in the rest of the year.

Park officials (park rangers, not the Forest Conservator or the Deputy Conservator) are said to have received money from the black market.

One said, "I'm surprised to see the present position of Indian politicians. They are proud of the atom bomb, but not the tiger. *I* am proud of the tiger."

Privileged poaching for influential people such as thakurs (landlords, martial caste) is said to be rampant. They are allowed to kill chital, sambar, jungle fowl and other birds, and animals for meat, often in large quantities, such as to feed a wedding party. One such privileged poacher is quoted as saying, "If I come all the way to Bandhavgarh, I'm not going to eat goat or chicken, I'm going to eat chital and Sambar. What is good enough for the tiger is good enough for me."

Commercial middlemen seldom contact the thakurs because the thakurs would want the lion's share of the profit. So they contact lowly villagers to do the bloody work, paying them perhaps $30 and a bottle of whisky for the trouble.

4. *Corruption*

WWF (world Wildlife Fund) vehicles, donated for tiger conservation work only, are misused, for functions such as wedding parties.

An air-conditioned (considered a luxury) Mahindra Voyager van was purchased in the name of patrolling, but was in fact used as a personal residential vehicle by a high official.

Two other high officials live and work in Umaria, 32 km away from park. They

Omni-Science and the Human Destiny

take all four patrol vehicles for family use, time and fuel consumed, emergency use not available. They come to the park only when dignitaries (including supposedly me) and personal friends visit.

Other examples of corruption include the purchase of lamps at Rs1600 per unit, but billed at Rs4700 per unit by park officials, and video cameras were purchased at Rs35,000 per unit, but billed at Rs72,000 per unit. (Why does this sound so familiar?)

When big NGOs and World Bank (WB) come visiting, park officials don't want people to talk to them, for fear of such information as what I am writing about coming to light, thus the clandestine ambiance of my interviews. They monitor everything said, and select the drivers and park guides who service the visitors. I've even been warned that being in possession of such information would put my safety in some jeopardy.

The attitude of high officialdom filters down the hierarchy.

It is opined that WB and WWF should not fund the Forest Department, but fund the local NGOs instead.

When asked, "Can NGOs prosecute offenders?" the answer was, "Yes, you can use PIL - Public Interest Litigation - to go after even the high level officials."

Remains of 3 tigers, 2 leopards, some sambar and chital have been seized by forest officials (not park officials) from outside-of-park territorial forests over an unclear time period. Non-park officials are generally deemed more concerned and efficient than park officials.

5. *Relationship between Forest Department and local people*

"The relationship is bad," one said. "There is little cooperation between them, but lots of suspicion. In a friendlier, more honest environment, if the forest department treats people with more respect, then village people would cooperate."

6. *Villages still in the park*

There are 60 villages in the "Periphery" (Bandhavgarh's equivalent to Kanha's Buffer Zone, but disorganized), and 6 within the park.

The total human population of all 6 in-park villages 1400-1500; cattle population 3,000. Village by village:

Kalwah - forest village, under administrative control of director of park, human population 179, cattle population 204,

Magdhi - forest village - human population 254, cattle population 306,

Bagdari - forest village, human population 259, cattle population 252,

Milli - revenue village, under district collector, human population 255, cattle population 347,

Gadhpuri - revenue village, human population 516, cattle population 1030,

Mainwah – revenue village, human population 88, cattle population 259.

There is unofficially a lot of grazing inside the park

Tigers do occasionally prey on cattle. Bureaucratic compensation procedure for cattle lifting usually takes 2-3 months, faster with bribe, but even so, the end compensation is usually considered to be less than the cattle's worth.

Village size is about 1-1.5 sq.km. each, totaling about 10 sq.km., not including the forest lands grazed by the cattle which are estimated to cover another 30 or so sq.km., totaling 40 sq.km. or 10% of the parks total area. Bandhavgarh is not a big park – at about 400 sq.km. it is less than half the size of Kanha. I'll be sure to go and take a look at one or two of the in-park villages before I leave.

7. *Possible solutions*

Some advocate relocating the six in-park villages out of the park, while others advocate fencing them in. Still others advocate allowing irrigated agricultural land inside the park as long as they are fenced off from wildlife. Of course I would like to see the six villages moved out of the park to some place of equal or better agricultural value, and with adequate provisions and compensations.

There is general agreement that an anti-poaching force should be established. It should comprise 16 men and 2 Gypsies, which should be capable of patrolling half the park or about 200 sq. km daily, plus night patrol and foot patrol. Cost: Salaries - Rs.3000 per man per month, or CDN$24,000 (~US$16,000) per year for the force of 16. Vehicles – C$15,000 each initial purchase or C$30,000 for both, and fuel for about 30 litres for both vehicles per day at about C$0.70 per litre or C$21 per day or about C$7,000 per year.

8. *Anti-corruption - no readily perceptible solution.*

The slideshow I gave this evening at the amphitheatre, with Faiyaz translating line for line as usual, was well attended and well received. The audience was even larger, over 100, perhaps due to word-of-mouth. Tala is just a village, really, so people probably attend just about anything that goes on at the amphitheatre, if only out of boredom. But I did notice that almost all of those who came last night to the

Omni-Science and the Human Destiny

video show were back, including the officials and the guides and guards, and tour operators and hoteliers including Latica and Nanda, and a couple of dozen foreign tourists, and just plain villagers including children. The applause they gave was more than heart-warming; it was thunderous.

While unwinding back in BTL, I asked Raminothna about the OSES Cycle on the higher levels of integrative transcendence after the organismization of the Solar System. On the single assumption that light-speed can somehow be exceeded – perhaps by some space-time manipulation technology of the future - the general picture seems to be:

Once the integrative transcendence of the Solar System into a Stellar Organism has come to pass, humanity will transcend from interplanetary to interstellar affairs, from the **Planetary Level of Organization** to the **Stellar Level of Organization**. The question here is: How many levels are there from the Stellar to the **Galactic Level of Organization**, and how many from the Galactic to the **Universal Level of Organization**?

Between the Stellar and the Galactic, I would venture to guess 2 intermediate levels: The **Segmental Level of Organization** (segments of spiral galactic arms, each embracing on average about 300,000 stars) and the **Sectoral Level of Organization** (major sectors of the galaxy, each embracing on average 300,000,000 stars. This would give an average of 1000 **Segmental organisms** per **Sectoral Organism**. On the **Galactic Level of Organization**, the Milky Way Galaxy, comprising about 300 billion stars, will comprise about 1,000 **Sectoral organism**s. On the higher levels, the light-speed-barrier must have been broken, by whatever space-time-manipulating technology then prevalent, but now hardly even conceivable.

Since the number of galaxies in the Universe is in the order of one hundred billion, I would guess also 2 intermediate levels between the **Galactic Organism** and the eventual and ultimate **Universal Organism**.

Considering the sub-atomic as the first level of organization, we have the following 13 levels of organization pertaining to matter and consciousness in the Universe:

Level of Organization	Units
14	the Universe
13	superclusters of superclusters
12	superclusters of galaxies

11	galaxies
10	galactic sectors
9	galactic arm segments
8	solar systems
7	planets
6	nations
5	cities
4	metabionts
3	cells
2	molecules
1	sub-atomic particles

Finally, the Universe Itself can be seen as the Ultimate Cosmic Egg, whose Universal Embryo, too, has since the Big Bang been developing, and will continue to develop, according to Its own 13-stage metamorphic schedule, which, too, may be subject to Its own success or failure.

It has been a point of much speculation whether the physical Universe will continue to expand to nothingness or collapse back upon itself. One way or the other, life in the Universe would likely not be able to survive, unless the Universal Organism succeeds to integratively transcend into being, enabling it to survive either scenario.

Good night, Christopher.

❖ ❖ ❖ ❖ ❖

March 24, 1999, Wednesday, sunny, 17-37C

Dearest Christopher:

[19:29 @ Rm.12, Bandhavgarh Tiger Lodge]
Where tiger-sighting is concerned, there is assuredly nowhere else on Earth that can best Bandhavgarh. So far this visit at Bandhavgarh, the sighting success rate has been 100%. Even Kanha, due to its denser vegetation, can boast a success rate of perhaps only 40%, even for a lucky guy like me. And today's sighting is almost as

Omni-Science and the Human Destiny

magical as it gets.

We were just trundling along the park drive through a thin sal forest when we passed a small herd of about a half dozen sambar a stone's throw away. We didn't stop then, but about 150 feet later, we abruptly did. Mohinder was at the wheel. Even after the Gypsy had halted, I still didn't know what we had stopped for, until, following his eyes, I then saw, only 20 feet away, partly concealed by the trunk of a tree, the tigress Mohini. Even after I had seen her, I still had a passing thought that she was a statue. She was frozen in a static-dynamic pose, like an arrow in a tightly drawn bow. She paid us not the least of attention, her eyes trained at the sambar like twin laser beams. In fact, I doubt that she could see them through the vegetation, but she could certainly hear them. On the other hand, I doubt that they could hear her. In the full minute since we had stopped, she moved only twice, and at that very slowly. When she put her paw down gingerly on the dried-leaves-carpeted forest floor, there was not a sound to be heard - except the clicking of my camera. Over the next several minutes, she inched forward no more than 15 or 20 feet. And then, over the next split second, she was gone in a flurry of flying forest debris. In her direction came a few honking alarm calls, which in a heartbeat was carried away by the wind. There were flashes of brown dashing through the black sal trunks. Mohinder put the Gypsy in reverse and backed it at forward speed to where the sambar were last seen, and found Mohini there instead, now in a state of dejected relaxation. As if already having shrugged her shoulders in resignation, she ambled stoically away. The sequence from beginning to end was long enough for me to click off a dozen excellent still shot and some video footage of the stalk and of the sambar dashing away. Did we distract her and cause her to fail? Did our camera sounds alert the sambar? Sorry about this, Mohini. Well, just chalk this down to one of the twenty or so times tigers fail before their next success. May be the next time will be the one for you.

This was not the first time I have witnessed tigers hunting. Once in 1997, I was on an elephant in thick forest with an even thicker undergrowth. At the elephant's feet was a tiger. About 50 yards upwind of the elephant were three sambar doe. The elephants were making a lot of noise plowing through the under growth, obliquely towards the sambar, which are usually not alarmed by elephants. The tiger stayed with the elephant, using the noise made by the elephant as a cover. Its intensity was mesmerizing. When it deemed itself close enough, the tiger launched itself towards the sambar as if shot out of a cannon. The sambar gave three almost simultaneous alarm calls, and as a body dashed blindly away. There was a shaking of the undergrowth a football field away. The hunt was a success..

On our way back to camp, we encountered a white Gypsy behind the wheel of which happened to be none other than the Superwoman Latika herself in her Aussie hat and bush outfit. We did a quick verbal exchange when her vehicle pulled parallel mine, and rearranged my visit to 10:15.

Speaking of "Superwoman", nickname-wise – put it down to cabin fever and terminal frustration - Sarita, once called "Tigress" by me before things came to a head, is now the "Monitor Lizard" (not my invention). One person we know is now the "GIB". There is a little story behind this. One day last week, we came upon a bird which Julian identified as a Great Indian Bustard, but which the park guide in our Gypsy mispronounced slightly, if you know what I mean. We all roared with laughter and the nickname stuck. Faiyaz is "Wild Dog" or "Brain Fever Bird". Manohar is "Asiatic Lion". Jane chooses "Elephant" for herself, in terms of temperament only, because she looks more like a white swan to me. As for me, I've heard that the lodge staff at Kanha gave me a good one. It's the name of an Indian movie star who specializes in villain roles, since they deemed it very funny that (they thought) I looked like him. Manohar even showed me a picture of this guy in one of Deepfee's "Bollywood" movie magazines. In all honesty I didn't think I looked the least bit like him, the definitive proof being that there is no way for him to pose as a Chinese tiger-bone buyer in an undercover sting operation in Calcutta, however villainous he might look. On the other hand, Jane gave me the very complimentary nickname of "Charger", "in honour of your campaign style", she said.

"And my age?" said I.

The visit to Latika was warm and casual, sitting in the dining pavilion of the Bandhavgarh Jungle Camp where she lives. Her very fortunate man Nanda, owner-operator of the Jungle Camp and world known wildlife videographer, was there as well and both treated me with courtesy and respect. Just superficial chatting, but Nanda said to me that he's been managing the camp for 10 years and has had enough. He plans to switch over to full time conservation work as of next year (When is Avtar going to do that?). Also, his 3-year labor of love in terms of their video TV full-hour documentary is about ready for release.

Since I had an 11:00 appointment with the head of a prominent local NGO, I had to bid an early tata, but not before Nanda invited me for dinner on the 26th at 19:30, which I again gladly accepted.

The visit to the NGO was joined by Faiyaz, Darshan and Jane. We had a broad-based yet intense discussion session. Following are raw notes, which will take weeks to fully understand or years to implement:

- papaya as alternative crop as solution to crop raiding by deer and wild boar,

- which do not feed on papaya
- mushroom cultivation (mew agricultural technology for this area) as revenue source for villages
- biogas plants (producing methane gas from cattle dung) – 27 built at Bandhavgarh, only 6 of which successful
- art and craft training for villagers – 3 year program
- awareness program for forest villagers, making use of the amphitheatre
- school visits to do nature art, talent search, encourage student academic competition, with park-visit as prize
- tree planting movement - 5 plants each class, prizes for good plants.
- aim to produce young conservationists – educational outreach to schools, perhaps even using the Champions of the Wild video
- anti-poaching – there are currently 73 beat guards in the park, poorly equipped. 1 beat guard hurt by poachers due to the lack of defensive weaponry, equipment needed – wireless set, guns, 30 motor bikes @ Rs.8000 each
- anti-poaching force can also serve as an intelligence agency to gather relevant information
- some 50 volunteers are needed to keep their eyes on guests in villages – if suspicious, to inform Territorial Forest, NOT park personnel (who leak info); Territorial Forest and keeps track of and acts on the information. Poaching contacts are from the outside, and are treated as guests at some villages, where orders and transactions are made; when a tiger is poached, usually only villagers are caught, but the contacts usually get away
- even forest officials are afraid to act against these poaching agents because they are very powerful and influential
- main distribution centre is Katni
- Tiger Conservation Cell suggested to Superintendent of Police to launch plain-clothes investigation about 1.5 months ago, the SP said yes, but so far, there's been no implementation
- The Bandhavgarh Foundation Trust (BFT) has 12 employees and about 45 volunteers; foreign volunteers are welcome for general awareness, school outreach, patrolling park periphery - circumference 150 km. The Chairman of BFT is a maharaja Pushpraj Singh - off. Fort, Rewa - has the right to go inside the park at will, other privileged people can too but only in the presence of the maharaja, 5 max, 1 Gypsy donated
- Park beat guards are easily corruptible, wage Rs.1500-2000/mo., senior personnel Rs.3500; free education for their children

- Life of beat guards should be insured – morality high, but unquantified
- More schools needed
- Corruption rampant; solution unclear.

This evening, I worked out a classification system for all planets in the Universe, however innumerable, and in whichever galaxy, they may be.

Take the planets in the Solar System alone for example. Mercury, Venus, Mars, Jupiter, Saturn, Uranus, Neptune and Pluto, in other words, all planets in the Solar System except Earth, are **Molecular level planets (Level 2)**. Earth four billion years ago, too, was a Molecular Level Planet only. But one billion years later, it had moved up to being a **Cellular level planet (Level 3)**. 500 million years ago, it had become a **Metabion level planet (Level 4)**, and 100 million years ago, since the rise of the social insects, a **Citian level planet (Level 5)**, and so on. Today, Earth is a **National level planet (Level 6)**. After the Earth has integratively transcended, it will have become a **Planetary level planet (Level 7)**. Then the **Stellar Level Planet (Level 8)**. Then the **Segmental level planets (Level 9)**, and **Sectoral level planets (Level 10)**, then **Galactic Level Planets (Level 11)**, and so on up. Hopefully.

Through this exercise, one thing has become plain as daylight for me. The levels of organization are always the same – ... Molecular, Cellular, Metabion, Citian, National, Planetary, Stellar... - no matter where in the Universe, on whichever planet of whichever galaxy. The metabionts of a certain planet in the Andromeda Galaxy may look very different from the metabionts of the planet Earth in the Milky Way Galaxy, but both are multi-cellular organisms.

"Indeed, integrative transcendence is a universal phenomenon," said Raminothna.

In the afternoon, Faiyaz and Jane spent time on this computer translating Hindi documents into English for international publication purposes. Following is an example.

Article from *Detective Eye* weekly newspaper   4 January 1999

Destruction of Bandhavgarh National Park Accelerated Under Current Leadership

Umaria –

It is well known that Sita, the famous tigress of Bandhavgarh, went missing in 1998. But the forest officials, whose job it is to protect the forest, don't seem to care. If urgent action is not taken, the days of Bandhavgarh National Park will be numbered.

Under the supervision of the officials, thousands of trees have been illegally cut down in recent days from the Raj Bahra and Mahaman ranges, in the heart of the park. Recently, when the officials came to know that a Minister in charge of the district would be visiting the park, they put their staff on a war footing to hide all the evidence, including the trees that had already been cut. Mr. Sharma himself supervised the operation, and the trees were eventually hidden at night with the help of tractors, or hauled out of the park by means of diesel vehicles.

The entry of vehicles in the park at night is an offence under law. The entry of especially diesel vehicles, is prohibited.

The labourers who cut down the trees did not get paid, so they complained to the local sarpanch Kallu Bhai Jan and showed him the trees. Mr. Bhai contacted the local M.L.A., Mr. Narendra Prasad Singh, who in turn contacted Collector Smt. Pillai. Finally, a team was put together to discover the truth. Kallu Bhai Jan has photographs of this illegally logged wood…

Good night, Christopher.

❖ ❖ ❖ ❖ ❖

March 25, 1999, Thursday, sunny, 19-37C

Dearest Christopher:

[19:38 @ Rm.12, Bandhavgarh Tiger Lodge]

Another safari, another tiger sighting. In spite of its ills, Bandhavgarh is holding true to its 100% tiger-sighting success rate in my book. It is not that Bandhavgarh has a higher tiger density than Kanha, but a lower vegetation density and therefore better visibility and more panoramic scenery. Bandhavgarh is pure magic and truly deserves to be called the tiger sighting capital of the world, *for now*. It would be a crime of monumental proportions if Bandhavgarh were ruined, let alone wiped out.

This time it is two of Mohini's three large cubs crossing a grass field, then thickets, then the road. Of course, hoards of tourist vehicles followed them around, some taking side roads at high speed to try to intercept them. At one point, when the big male cub was trying to cross the road, the jeeps and Gypsies were so bumper-to-bumper thick that he physically couldn't. Faiyaz was exasperated, in fact furious, at the slackness of the enforcement of park wildlife viewing policies. No wonder the tigers are so easy to poach here. They are just too habituated to human presence and in fact human interference.

But I'm even more concerned about what we encountered in the park this day - hundreds if not thousands of villagers pouring into the park on foot carrying baskets of food on some annual pilgrimage to the Vishnu shrine deep in the heart of the park. It is not like letting a bull into a china shop, but a whole herd. So once again, religion and traditions take precedence over wildlife conservation.

This reminds me of Jericho Park on the beach downhill from my residence in Vancouver. Year round it is a sensitive bird sanctuary, with small islands in large ponds for waterfowl nesting and signs everywhere saying "Do not disturb wildlife!" But once every July, for three consecutive days, thousands of people would pour into the park for the annual Folk Festival, where a dozen stages would be set up all over the park, all equipped with megawatt amplifiers and loud speakers. My residence is set back a dozen blocks uphill from the park, and during the festival, a cacophony of a dozen songs being performed simultaneously, though diminished by the distance, is still maddening. Right down on ground zero, the birds don't stand a chance. And here in Bandhavgarh, on this day, though there are no thunderous acoustic assaults on wildlife, the invasion is even more massive, and the effect on wildlife more widespread, and this is a place where normally one automatically whispers, and when tourists are not allowed to leave their vehicles.

After brunch, at my request, we drove to check out one of the six in-park villages. It is in a part of the park I have never been to. We were dismayed, though not surprised, to see the grass largely grazed out in the fields surrounding the village, and cattle trooping through the surrounding forest, and fields dotted with tree stumps. In short, no different than any other village outside the park. The scenery did not remind me of the park at all, but more of Kanha's Buffer Zone. Farther out, we found vast expanses of the forest floor burned to cinders. This was done perhaps to encourage new grass growth – for the cattle - but in doing so, it could decimate many other plant species, including tree saplings, and of course animals. None of these can be good for the tiger and its ecosystem-mates.

Omni-Science and the Human Destiny

Other than this, nothing happened of great note today. At noon, we were invited by some park officials to visit the school where nature guides and park guards ("front line workers") from various national parks are trained. It is equipped with an overhead projector, a TV/VCR and, wonders of wonders, a Pentium computer. We were given the grand tour by the school director who attended my slideshow day before yesterday, very respectfully I might add, and Mr. A.K. Nagar was there as well. We arranged to have the Champions of the Wild video shown there tomorrow at 18:00 to those park guards who missed it the first time.

This afternoon, Faiyaz and Jane worked to translate some more Hindi articles into English straight into my laptop. In them, Mr. Nagar featured quite prominently, but not in good light, as does the park Field Director Mr. S.C. Sharma.

[23:28]

I asked Raminothna what she thought the Universal Organism, once integratively transcended, would be like.

"How powerful is an amoeba?"

"Very powerful, but only in the opinion of the bacterium it is about to devour," I said. "From our point of view, of course it is not powerful at all."

"How much more powerful is a human being than an amoeba?"

"Almost infinitely more powerful."

"How many levels apart are they?"

"An amoeba belongs to the Cellular level of organization, and a human being belongs to the Metabion level. So they are just one level apart."

"How much more powerful is the United States than a termite mound?"

"Almost infinitely more powerful."

"How many levels apart are they?"

"The U.S. is a National organism and a termite mound is a Citian organism. So, they are also just one level apart."

"How many levels above the United States is the Universal Organism?"

"According to our system, above the National level are, in ascending order, the Stellar level, the Segmental, the Sectoral, the Galactic, and three more levels to the Universal level or organization. So, all in all, the Universal Organism is eight levels above the United States, and ten levels above a human being."

"So, how much more powerful would you think the Universal Organism is than the United States, not to mention a human being?"

"I would say that 'almost infinitely' is a the understatement of the eon. So let me say 'infinitely'."

"Where would this Universal Organism be?"
"Everywhere. Wherever we go, we would be within it."
"And what would it know?"
"Its knowledge would comprise every word in every book in every library on every transcending planet of every galaxy. It can be said to know everything."
"So now, how would you describe the Universal Organism?"
"All-present, all-knowing and all-powerful."
"Are they the same as omnipresent, omniscient and omnipotent?"
"Yes, they are… OH MY GOD!"

Good night, Christopher.

❖   ❖   ❖   ❖   ❖

March 26, 1999, Friday, sunny, 19-38C

Dear Christopher:

[05:24 (1999-03-27-6) @ Rm.12, Bandhavgarh Tiger Lodge]
It's becoming routine, or beginning to sound too good to be true – the "another day, another tiger-sighting", but truth is truth. This time, it was a somewhat distant view of a tiger in the meadow strolling through the long grass in stately equanimity, at one point at the foot of an elephant loaded with tourists that had been dispatched to intercept it. Unfortunately, this would be my last tiger sighting in this millennium.

This evening, I presented myself at the Bandhavgarh Jungle Camp ("Superwoman's Palace") precisely at 19:30 as prearranged. She was still out in the field. Nanda gave me a warm welcome and introduced me to the tourists in his Jungle Camp. While we were waiting for the dinner, I chatted with a tourist family from Scotland, and another from Delhi whose 11-year-old boy was a student at Sri Ram School, who told his parents about my Big Cub presentation. The Deputy Director Mr. Singh, whom most people, including Faiyaz and Darshan, consider an honest man, was there as well, and we exchanged greetings and some ideas.

Soon, Nanda gave us all a slideshow of Bandhavgarh wildlife in the palatial and high-ceilinged entrance hall of the main building, in the center of which a beautifully mounted tiger from the Colonial period still stood in all its arrested majesty in a

Omni-Science and the Human Destiny

mahogany-and-glass display case, surrounded by other wildlife trophies on the walls. This kind of interior décor is something I scold and scorn in North America, but here, in the heart of Tigerland, especially in the faded light of old colonialism, it seems somehow fitting, as a reminder of how things used to be. After Nanda's slideshow, which featured the more obscure life forms of Bandhavgarh, many of which I have never seen, it was dinner in the equally palatial dining room – a far cry from BTL's and even KTL's open-air dining pavilions. Latika made her grand entrance in a flowing peach-colored sari, with her hair loose and looking stunning in all her feminine glory (previously, it was no-nonsense pony-tail, safari khakis and Aussie hat). I sat between the Scottish lady and her 30ish daughter, and had a pleasant though low intensity conversation, while Superwoman sat at the far end of the table, holding court with her most ardent admirers. Does this kind of formal and scrumptious banquet happen here every day?

After the dinner, Latika and I had a one-on-one chat in the lobby in the shadow of the stuffed tiger, and under the watchful gaze of the two tiger heads and two leopard heads mounted on the four walls. She lamented to me that her new set of camera traps (infra-red-triggered night cameras) were all malfunctioning, giving nothing but blank photos, which caused great frustration in her work of late. Reminiscent of Belinda Wright, Latika told me that she does not go tiger-viewing any more, that over the last month, she had seen tigers only three times, saying, "The day I stopped seeing tigers was the day I began working." But through the course of her work she did see numerous tiger pug marks which she could identify as "Long Toes", "Splay Foot", etc.. "But thanks to the cameras malfunctioning, I cannot correlate them with their strip patterns and facial markings. I don't even know what they look like!" she cried. There is no doubt about her passion for her subjects and the sincerity of her heart.

Later, we talked trilaterally with the Deputy Director. I asked them what is the best thing a foreign NGO can do to help protect the park. They both opined that the most important task at hand to protect the park and its inhabitants is to relocate the six in-park villages out of the park. One of the villages has already agreed to move given mutually agreeable terms. They have already decided on a location on the north side of the main river on the way to Khajuraho. "The beauty of this is that we can design from scratch a model village outfitted with all kinds of alternative technologies, cattle husbandry systems, even a new way of life," enthused her ladyship. She is truly a remarkable woman. I could easily fall in love with her, if I haven't yet.

The Deputy Director surprised me by saying that he himself is using a solar cooker. When presented with the difficulty about cooking time, they both shrugged it off by confirming my thus far unsubstantiated theory. Early in the morning, the villagers set up the cooker with rice and lentil and sauces, etc. and orient the unit directly due south, that is, with the reflectors preset for the oncoming noonday sun, and just leave it for the rest of the day. Come dinnertime, everything will have been cooked, be still hot or at least warm, ready to be served. Chapatti or roti are no problem, since they are not even on their native menu. "Once accepted, they won't let go of it. It is better than biogas to them," said the DD. This is about the best news I've heard on solar cooking technology up to this point.

 I called BTL and ask Darshan to get a driver to fetch me around 22:00 and bring Faiyaz and Jane as prearranged to introduce to Latika. They arrived on time, but were in a desperate rush to leave to meet the train which would take Faiyaz to Delhi, which apparently again moved its arrival time forward to 22:30. We did the introduction, and they dashed off. So, later still, I called Darshan again, and he came on foot to fetch me. The DD generously offered his Gypsy for Darshan to drive to fetch his driver who will drive the Gypsy back from BTL.

 While saying goodbye to Faiyaz, he seized my hand and said, "Anthony, I will never forget this spring."

 Back at BTL, Darshan told me that he had done his own thinking on village relocation and showed me the plan on paper in his note book. I didn't need any convincing, but my inclination was further confirmed. The question is: Would Avtar take it on? In fact, upon my direct questioning, Darshan himself doubted it, and asked me what I would do if Avtar would not touch it. I said plainly, "I'd just have to get WCWC to find another partner who would, then hire you." Again, this could be reach Avtar's ears, but do I care? It might even do him some good.

 Faiyaz still has several important meetings here to build a solid case for my proposed "What happened to Sita?" international article. He will be in Delhi till April 3rd, then come back to Bandhavgarh to do the interviews, including the self-professed killer/poacher of Sita, whom others don't seem to be taking seriously. Yesterday, Faiyaz confided to Jane and me that Mohinder said to him that Raman said a flat "No" to Faiyaz coming back to Bandhavgarh, and something about a "new itinerary", which Faiyaz interpreted as a sign of his oncoming dismissal from Tiger Fund. But earlier today, Mohinder told him that when he asked Avtar about Faiyaz's desire to come back to Bandhavgarh to do some more work, Avtar said no problem. Earlier today, Faiyaz called his friends in Delhi about my coming talk at the Habitat House March 29th, 19:30, and not only did his friend say he would bring other friends, but that he had seen this long-haired Canadian conservationist on TV

Omni-Science and the Human Destiny

before.

During the meeting, the DD invited me with genuine sincerity and some eagerness to join in a day-long conference with about three dozen village elders tomorrow (27th, my last day at Bandhavgarh) starting at 12:30. I asked for his permission for me to bring Jane and Darshan with me, Darshan as my translator, and of course as TF operative, and received it. What we worked so hard for and got aborted in sedate Kanha, we are invited to as honoured guests here in troubled Bandhavgarh without even trying.

The Lord works in mysterious ways indeed.

Last night for me was truly a religious experience of the highest order. And tonight, while lying on the observation platform under the stars, I said to Raminothna, "OMNI-SCIENCE shows the order of things in all its purity, simplicity and majesty. It shows us the Way of the Cosmos – the Tao - and thus the optimal Way of Man – Integrative Transcendence. It shows the path for us to achieve world peace, planetary health and beyond – Integrative Transcendence. It even allows us to achieve total intellectual freedom by not only proving that the Inconceivable can be conceived and the Unspeakable can be spoken, but actually conceives the Inconceivable and speaks the Unspeakable – Integrative Transcendence. But it was not until yesterday night when I finally saw how ultimately profound OMNI-SCIENCE really is - philosophically, spiritually, religiously.

Instead of the traditional teaching of God creating us, OMNI-SCIENCE shows us that we create ourselves, and, in conjunction with other sentient beings throughout the Universe, are part and parcel of a Universe-wide cosmic egg in the self-creation of a new infant universal deity.

What you have shown us should make us feel incredibly small and insignificant, but I don't feel this way. On the contrary, I feel incredibly elated and empowered. Though I am ephemeral and infinitesimal, yet I am part of an orderly, universal whole. Though the few decades of my life are but a split-second in universal time, yet I feel part and parcel of an eternity. And though the course of my life may seem mundane, and yet, it is a part of the Universal Masterplan. I will never look at life the same way as I have done before.

Raminothna, I don't think that my gratitude is what you want, and no gratitude can possibly equal the benefit I have reaped over the last two months, in addition to the tiger conservation work that we have done together. And the pain you have suffered in empathy with mine is mine in empathy with Christopher's. I just want you to know that what you have to teach has made a huge and fundamental change in me, and hopefully, through me, in others, up to and including Homo Sapiens in its entirety. It will have a huge impact in the manifestation of the human destiny. I, and Homo Sapiens, owe you something I doubt that we can ever repay"

"Dearest Homo Sapiens, your happiness enhances universal happiness, your transcendence contributes to universal transcendence, for though you are human, often all too human, and yet, you are divine."

Good night, Christopher. Good night Christopher.

❖ ❖ ❖ ❖ ❖

March 27, 1999, Saturday, sunny, 15-38C

Dearest Christopher:

[19:38 @ Rm.12, Bandhavgarh Tiger Lodge]
My last full day at Bandhavgarh.
No safari this morning, but it doesn't matter, because the single hour of 12:30-13:30 made the whole day. As invited by Deputy Director R.P. (Ramesh Prasad) Singh, we (Jane, Darshan and I) went to the training school to attend the Forest/Park Department and villagers meeting. Originally, I thought we'd just be there as observers, but upon arrival there, I was put front and center on the official panel table facing the 150 or so village representatives of some 30 villages, and I was expected to address the assembly, with no mental preparation whatsoever.
Well, not exactly true. I've thought about what speech I would make at the aborted Kanha conference. So I just slightly modified it to suit Bandhavgarh, and let it out. I suppose I did it, because whatever I said, as translated by Darshan, was received with keen interest, full attention, open respect, with positive feedback galore. The raising of park fee and the sharing of revenue were received with many nods from both panel and audience. My promise to go back to Canada and propagate the name of Bandhavgarh as the tiger-viewing capital of the world was received with pride and gratitude, and the solar cooker idea was received with enthusiasm. When I asked how many villages would like to have one solar cooker to try out, 23 villages signed up, and five local people expressed interest in learning how to make solar cookers.
Jane and I exchanged glances to say that this is almost exactly what we had in mind for the Kanha All-Panchyats Conference. In Bandhavgarh, with all its bad

Omni-Science and the Human Destiny

reputation, it is a breeze, but in Kanha, an abortion.

So, what we now have taken on is to supply one solar cooker to each of 23 villages free of charge, and train 5 villagers to make solar cookers, and make arrangements for more cookers if the initial ones succeed, this time at a cost. I will let Faiyaz, Darshan and Jane work the logistics out. My job is to commit Avtar to the task.

This late evening, I climbed the "watch tower" one last time.

"Raminothna, if you know, please let me know. Are we going to make it or not?"

"If I told you yes, you would be happy, and stop striving; if I told you no, you would be sad, and stop striving. So, why should I tell either? But I can tell you this. It depends on where the transcendence limit of the key species is, which in Earth's case is of course the species Homo Sapiens."

"What is 'transcendence limit'?"

"Tell me. If you put a thousand termite mounds of the species Macrotermes Bandhavgarhansis in a plain, do you think they would specialize and cooperate to form a society of mounds?"

"No, they would not. They will stay identical and continue to mutually compete as they have done for millions of years."

"Thus the transcendence limit of the species Macrotermes Bandhavgarhansis is on the Citian level, and no higher."

"Yes, I see. They just cannot transcend any higher than they already have, no matter what."

"Now, if you put a thousand human cities on a plain, would they integratively transcend on to higher levels?"

"Evidently, since we have cities and nations."

"So, again, the question is: Where is the transcendence limit of Homo Sapiens? If it is on the National level and no higher, then your species is a dead-end, and the Earth is doomed."

"I hope not."

"On the other hand, if you could transcend nationalism, Homo Sapiens, then you may one day fulfill Earth's Shining Destiny – among the stars."

Good night, Christopher. Good night, Christopher.

Anthony Marr

March 28, 1999, Sunday, sunny, 16-34C

Dearest Christopher:

[18:39 @ Rm.507, Habitat World Hotel, Habitat Centre, Delhi]

Back in Delhi again. In another 5 days, I'll be back home in Vancouver. Then what?

We (Jane, Mohinder and I) left Bandhavgarh Jungle Lodge for Khajuraho early in the morning (05:00) in a diesel Mahindra jeep driven by its own driver. Darshan couldn't come because of arriving tourists, but he insisted on getting up at 04:15 along with us, just to say good-bye. When walking me to the jeep, he said in his trademark way, "Please feel free to write to me. If you find yourself in Agra, I would be honoured if you would come to our home to stay. Please treat me like a young brother." Yesterday night, I asked him to submit to me a proposal of what could be done at Bandhavgarh for about C$30,000. I will look it over, then form a plan for next year.

By 11:30, we arrived at Khajuraho. The procedure to get the plane ticket reserved took half an hour at the agent's. After that, Jane had the option to go to the erotic temple for a long visit or come with me to the airport first, then go to the temple for a short visit. She elected to come to the airport first to say goodbye.

I said to her, "That's mushy." Then added, "Mushy first, erotic later?"

We shared a last laugh. At the airport, Mohinder asked respectfully to have a picture taken with me. Jane and I hugged goodbye, and off I went to go through security.

The near new Boeing 737 of Jet Airways landed in Delhi around 16:00. First thing that happened was that I got swindled by the prepaid taxi at the airport terminal. When I asked how much to the Habitat Centre, the woman at the counter said, with a sly smile (I should have known right there and then), that it would cost Rs.550 (C$22). When I got to the hotel and asked the people there how much it should have cost, they said Rs.150, no more. I was furious, not as much for the money, but for my being taken for a fool, yet again.

[19:32]

I called Faiyaz this afternoon at his sister's place. He was not in. I left a message. He called me back from the university. It took him two hours to come by public bus. He got here about half an hour ago. I told him about yesterday's government-panchayat meeting at Bandhavgarh, complete with solar cooker orders and five people wanting to learn how to make the device. We exchanged mutual congratulations. He asked me about Latika. I suggested that he and Jane go and visit her one day. I also talked about village relocation, which in my mind, along with anti-corruption and anti-poaching, has become the first major item on the agenda to preserve Bandhavgarh National Park and the Bandhavgarh tigers. I also suggested that he work with Darshan on a field proposal for Bandhavgarh and Kanha commensurate with the CIDA grant. I don't want Tiger Fund, but I want Faiyaz and Darshan.

[01:34 (1999-03-29) @ Rm.507, Habitat World Hotel, Habitat Centre, Delhi]

I went to sleep early for once, but was awakened about an hour ago by a swaying motion of the bed. In the stupor of semi-sleep, I moved to the other bed and it too was swaying, and thought that the building was being buffeted by high winds. Or was it an earthquake?

Now, again, I can't sleep. Another room, another ceiling to stare at. Excruciating psychic pain of Christopher suffering. Seething impotent rage. Next to the Devil himself, Christine is everywhere.

"Dearest Homo Sapiens, has the 'inconceivable' been conceived?"
"Oh, Raminothna. You are as good as the cavalry. What did you say?"
"I asked you whether the 'Inconceivable' had been conceived."
"Yes, I believe that it has."
"And has the 'unspeakable' yet been spoken?"
"No, not yet, not publicly."
"Is it ready to be spoken?"
"Yes, it is."
"Then, Homo Sapiens, speak. What is this 'Inconceivable' 'Way of the Cosmos', this 'Unspeakable' Tao?"
"The yin-yang of: Transcendent Integration and Integrative Transcendence."
"What then is the optimal 'Way of Man'?"
"The Tao Teh Ching says, '… Man accords his way to that of the Earth, the Earth to the Sky, the Sky to the Tao…' Therefore, the optimal Way of Man is also the yin-yang of Transcendent Integration and Integrative Transcendence."
"Amen."
"Amen."
"Dearest Homo Sapiens. My work on Earth is now done. Other transcending planets beckon and I now must go to them, as I heeded your beckoning and came to you. The time has come to bestow upon you the gift I

bring, a gift of hope, of joy, of love and of peace. And now, I want you, Anthony Marr of Homo Sapiens, to receive it, on behalf of the transcending planet Earth."

"I am ready to receive it, in the name of Homo Sapiens, on behalf of the Earth, for the sake of Christopher."

"When you invoke the name of Christopher, there is more solemnity than when you invoke the name of God. So in this I can trust. This gift is in the form of a book. A universal book. The Earth Edition of this universal book. Titled: Omni-Science and the Human Destiny."

"I am ready to receive it," I said, solemnly, holding out both of my palms.

"They will be filled as soon as the book is written."

"When will it be written?"

"As soon as *you* have written it."

Good night, Christopher. Good night, Christopher.

❈ ❈ ❈ ❈ ❈

March 29, 1999, Monday, sunny, 19-35C

Dearest Christopher:

[09:33 @ Rm.507, Habitat World Hotel, Delhi]

The frontpage article of the Times of India this morning was titled "100 feared killed as quake hits Garhwal". The epicenter was not far NE of Delhi. The quake registered 6.8 on the Richter scale. If it struck Delhi, how many would have perished? Hundreds of thousands I should think. Would this very building I'm in be able to withstand a 6.8 quake?

[23:28 @ Rm.507, Habitat World Hotel, Delhi]

I called on Raminothna many times through the day, but there was no answer.

This afternoon, I went to the Tiger Fund Delhi office to check and send email. Nothing from Christine. Nothing from Christine's friends. Nothing from even my friends – that contains any good news about Christopher.

My last performance in India this time round. Habitat House introduced Avtar, Avtar introduced me, again with much praise. In the end, it was "the best presentation on conservation I've ever witnessed", said Sarita's husband Raheed. Faiyaz, who has translated the show many times, said that he has never imagined that my unilingual presentation could be so "different and powerful". A young man came to me and said that the presentation "changed his life". Several journalists wanted to interview me, one will call me at the hotel tomorrow and set an appointment. Not bad for a last hurrah.

I just called Raminothna's name again. Still no answer.

Good night, Christopher.

❖ ❖ ❖ ❖ ❖

March 30, 1999, Tuesday, sunny, 18-35C

Dearest Christopher:

[23:26 @ Rm.507, Habitat World, Delhi]
I called on Raminothna through the day. Still nothing.
The significant events today are two.
The first is the hour-long interview by Rohit Nair, Press Trust of India, who came to my hotel room at 08:30, instead of 10:30 as earlier agreed, at my request. I have something to do out of town. He wanted a good photo of the campaign at Kanha or Bandhavgarh, which I promised to send to him within 10 days.
I also spoke with Ashok Kumar and Belinda Wright by phone and arranged to have lunch with them tomorrow 13:15 at the restaurant at the India International Centre.
Avtar issued me an invoice containing every single rupee spent on my behalf during my stay. He has the gall. I wonder if it is also inflated.
As soon as I was free, I went to the train station and took the earliest train to Ranthambhore. I arrived in the late afternoon. There, I hired a jeep to take me back to the dam in that desertified valley behind the park. My heart was pumping hard when I topped the rim of the depression on top of the hill, only partly due to the physical exertion. My first sight of the inside of the depression made my blood boil and my tears flow. The Raminothna tree was indeed gone. Its stump was still weeping. But not a branch remained. I collapsed on to the carpet of its discarded

leaves, which were still green. I stroked the leaves, mourning their passing, and then, my fingers felt a clump of something. I looked. It was a cluster of berries. I had an inspiration. I fished out a plastic bag from my knapsack, and filled it with the few berries that I could find. I will take them back to Vancouver and plant them in my garden. If the climates are too different, I'll grow them indoors.

    I called on Raminothna again just now, and of course there was no answer. I was sorely tempted to eat the berries, but I resisted. Instead, I began to think about writing the book, which I will dedicate to Christopher.

Good night, Christopher.

※ ※ ※ ※ ※

March 31, 1999, Wednesday, sunny, 18-35C

Dearest Christopher:

[18:19 @ Rm.507, Habitat World, Delhi]
    Last day here in India this time. Leaving with no regrets, but much to miss and remember and work out. Flight at 23:25.
High point today is our 13:45-15:15 luncheon meeting with Belinda Wright and Ashok Kumar. I invited Faiyaz along. Good time shared and vague plans made.
    Avtar finally agreed to pay my hotel bills. Probable rationale: "Anything to get Anthony out of here."
    Farewell, India!

Good night, Christopher.

※ ※ ※ ※ ※

May 4, 1999

[22:27, @ home, Vancouver]

Christopher's fourth birthday, itself a minor miracle. But there is another. I spent close to three hours with him. The fact that Christine watched our every move did not even bother me, if that's what it takes to see Christopher just one more time.

Where Christopher is concerned, I basically did nothing when I came back from India. I went to see Tasha and Wilhelmina and Donna, but their receptions were less than warm. I did not call Christine. If she does not want to talk to me, it does no good to call. If she wants to talk to me, she would call me herself. I did send Christopher a few cards with tigers and other animals on them. At least they were not returned. In the whole month of April, all I could think of was May – Christopher's birthday. Meanwhile, I immersed myself into writing the book, or at least working on writing it.

Yesterday, purely on faith, I bought a child's bicycle. This morning, I put it in my car and drove to work. Mid-morning I knocked on the office door of my colleague and friend, the darkly beautiful Roxanne Stillwell. She is close enough of a friend to me to be aware in some detail of the situation.

"Rox, I need to ask you a favor. Please feel free to decline if you don't feel comfortable with it."

"What is it?"

"I need someone to make a phone call on my behalf."

"To Christine, I presume?"

"Good guess."

"Sure. No problem. What would you like me to say?"

"Well, today is Christopher's birthday. I have a present for him. I would like to give it to him in person. Failing that, I'll get a taxi to deliver it."

This afternoon I had to go for a jury selection session. When I returned to the office, Roxanne gave me a big smile and an all-systems-go sign. "She said yes, but just for this once. They're having a birthday party for Christopher in the afternoon. Be there at 6:30, after the party."

"Thanks, Rox, I owe you one."

"Good luck. And enjoy."

"I'll try."

Now, about our beloved Christopher. When the door opened, he was standing there next to Christine, looking up at me, like almost every time previously when I went visiting. Usually, he would cry out excitedly, "Uncle Tony! Uncle Tony!", bouncing on his feet a little and raise his arms up inviting me to pick him up and hold him. This recurrent scene has haunted me on many a night when I could not sleep. This was the moment. I could not believe my eyes even when I was looking at him.

But it also did not escape my notice that he was much more subdued and hesitant. His eyes said volumes, although what they were saying I could not quite read. I took the liberty and risk to pick him up. He let me, but seemed unsure. "Christopher, I missed you very much."

"I missed you too, Uncle Tony," he suddenly burst out in tears.

He is noticeably taller, his face a little less baby-like, his vocabulary has increased, his pronunciations more precise, and distinctly more mature in a mental sense – or is it his innocence lost?

Then, I made the mistake of hugging Christine. It was like hugging a tree trunk. No, more like a rock.

The place was in a bit of a disarray, with the aftermath of the birthday party after everyone had left. I offered to help Christine clean up.

At one point, when Christine went down to the basement to attend to laundry – a total of 10 seconds – I said to Christopher quietly, "Christopher, I missed you very much."

He whispered back to me, "Uncle Tony, why are you a bad man?"

I meant to say, "Christopher, I want you to listen very carefully. Your Uncle Tony is not a bad man. When you grow up, you will understand." But we heard Christine's footsteps coming up the stairs. He glanced over his shoulder, then looked back at me, put his index finger to his lips and said, "Shhh." I have never seen him do this before. Three months ago, he wouldn't have done this. In those brief 10 seconds, we were 100% with each other.

After some formalities in the kitchen, we went down to the basement playroom – memory lane big time. All his old toys still there – his castles and dinosaurs and ogres. We had to reinvent the games. And like before, he got right into it, as if it were only yesterday we had last played together. Christine just sat there and watched, expressionless, or should I say monitored. She did not encourage conversation. On my part, I was so focused on Christopher that her presence or absence seemed beyond the event horizon. But in the back of my mind, I fleetingly wondered: What is she afraid of? That I might kidnap Christopher? That I might do him harm? Of course not. But what Christopher and I might say to one another? Definitely.

The doorbell rang. Christine went up to answer it, and called Christopher after her. He went up and I stayed behind. A moment later, I heard him exclaiming excitedly to whomever was at the door, "Uncle Tony is here! Uncle Tony is here!" When they came down, it was Wilhelmina. She tried to sound cheerful, but her eyes were sad. We had played dozens of games of chess over pots and pots of tea, but now she felt almost like a stranger, and presumably me to her too. We knew that we too would never again meet.

Soon after that, the thought began to intrude, that I shouldn't overstay my welcome. I asked Christine if I could present the gift to Christopher. She asked me what it was.

"A child's bicycle, with training wheels."

She nodded her approval. I excused myself and went to my car to get the bike. When I brought it down to the playroom, Christopher's eyes lit up. It was shining green and purple, reminiscent of the woman at the river. Christine liked it too and thanked me more than once for it, saying what a lovely gift it was.

I got Christopher to stand astride the bike and adjusted the seat height for him. "You have to do as mommy says about where and when you can ride, okay, Christopher? This is very important. Otherwise you might get hurt, okay Christopher?" I said while dropping some 10-40 on the chain.

"Okay, Uncle Tony. Thank you, Uncle Tony."

Christopher was allowed to overstay his bedtime by 1.5 hours, perhaps for my sake. Time to do a graceful exit. We all walked out to my car, Christopher holding hands with both Christine and me. At my car, I picked him up and hugged him close, and he reciprocated. We did not mention further visits. But I promised to write him and send him cards. I told him about the cards I had bought for him – the one with the ram, and the one with the otter, and parrot… He listened with bright eyes, then asked me something I couldn't catch. I looked at Christine.

"He was asking you if you had a card with an owl on it," said Christine.

"Tomorrow, I will go looking for a card with an owl for you," I told him, and drove away.

On the way home, I stopped at Oscar's Books on Broadway near Granville, and lo and behold, on the rotary rack, staring me in the face, was a great horned owl on the cover of a leftover 1999 calendar, with each month featuring a different owl. I'll mail it to Christopher tomorrow first thing.

1999-05-10-1   *The Vancouver Sun*   **by Alex Strachan**
[Discovery show wins early Leos]

… In television awards, Andrew Gardner won best writing in an informational series for a segment of Champions of the Wild featuring conservationist Anthony Marr and his efforts to draw attention to the plight of India's Bengal tiger. Champion's cinematographer Rudolf Kovanic was also cited for a segment about elephants…

1999-05-16-7 *The Province*, Vancouver by Jason Proctor
[Whale escapes after shrugging off harpoon]

Makah whalers in Washington's Neah Bay struck their prey yesterday, but the whale escaped, (hurt, but alive).

"The Makah harpooner threw the harpoon at the whale from about 10 feet away," said Anthony Marr… who was watching from about 600 meters. "The harpoon entered the left flank of the whale, who did a nose dive, carrying the harpoon and the attached float with it. But the harpoon soon got duslodged and the whale disappeared."

Activists opposed to the hunt earlier scared away several whales. Some protesters were arrested and the rest were prevented by authorities from nearing the whales (on grounds of harassing them)…

"The whale is a warrior, just like our Makah men are warriors," said Joddie Johnson, a member of the Makah band. "He wants to die in honour."

1999-05-18-2 *The Vancouver Sun* by Craig McInnes
[Native leaders condemn Clark for 'colonial' position]

… Anthony Marr… said that the anti-whaling campaign is not aimed at aboriginal rights. "We're not pointing fingers at the native people. We are just against whaling."

Marr said it was "ludicrous" to describe Monday's whale killing as a revival of tradition. "First they towed their ceremonial canoe out to the whale with a power boat. Then, after ceremonially harpooning the whale, they used a .50 calibre gun to finish it off."

Marr said the Makah's whale hunt has little to do with the band's food needs. "It's something they've chosen as a vehicle to assert themselves as a self-determined people. If they want to stand up and be counted, fine, but not on the back a whale that they kill."…

1999-05-22-6 *Times Colonist*, Victoria, BC by Anthony Marr
[Tradition should end like slavery]

… On May 17, the day the whale died - sacrificed in a vain and vainglorious attempt to revive an obsolete tradition… To many in the environmental movement, it is a day that will go down in infamy…

Should native cultures with whaling traditions have special rights to whale? In my opinion, no, just as I say no to the Chinese culture having special rights to use bear gall bladders, tiger bone and rhino horn in traditional medicine, nor European

Omni-Science and the Human Destiny

cultures having special rights to practice their bloody trophy hunting tradition. To integrate myself into the Canadian society during the last three decade since I became a Canadian, I've had to retrain myself many times in just about everything in life; I can't see why ex-whalers can't do the same…

1999-06-02-3 *The Daily New*, **Nanaimo, BC** **by Valerie Wilson**
[Students learn plight of the tiger]
… Anthony Marr… warns tigers are disappearing at an alarming rate. He is in Nanaimo this week to ask area school children to save the tiger from extinction. "Your voice is important and you must speak out," Marr told students of Uplands Park Elementary Tuesday. "You are very powerful if you want to make some changes in the world."

Marr has been back in BC for about a month, after a 10 week working stint at tiger reserves in India. He brought home with him a breathtaking slideshow of the country's landscape, tree and plant life, birds and animal life, and of course, photographs of the tiger he viewed at India's Kanha, Bandhavgarh and Ranthambhore tiger reserves.

"A question I am asked often by adults is there are no tigers in Canada, so why should we be bothered.," Marr told student. "Somehow, children never ask that."

"Very simply, the tiger is one of most beautiful animals in the world. If it becomes extinct, our world would be a much less beautiful place. We all lose."…

1999-06-07-1 *Nanaimo News Bulletin* **by Erin Fletcher**
[A tale of 4,000 tigers]
Children hold the key to the survival of the endangered tiger, says tiger conservationist Anthony Marr…

To spread the word about the plight of tigers, Marr was visiting Nanaimo schools last week with a slideshow presentation, video, and a discussion in the hopes to stimulate an interest in tiger preservation among local youth.

Marr has been involved with tiger conservation since 1994. His passion takes him into the depths of India where he works to educate and promote the preservation of tigers…

❖ ❖ ❖ ❖ ❖

Most unfortunately, the birthday visit proved to be only a momentary reprieve.

Anthony Marr

In the ensuing weeks, I sent Christopher several cards, in which I wrote him messages, which would have to be read to him, presumably by Christine. This was like trying to send a letter to some loved one in Communist China from the free world. You have to watch every word you write. I may have let my heart rule my head and gone a little over the line once or twice too often, with phrases like "Do not lose hope, Christopher, we will one day meet again." After five or six cards, the ensuing ones began being returned-to-sender, unopened. Four or five more of these, and I stopped. By then, it was mid-June, and I turned to my last resort. I looked into the Yellow Pages for a family lawyer.

The agony took on a new twist. Did Christine tell Christopher about my cards being returned, or did she not? Both alternatives have their agonizing aspects, and so have their sub-alternatives. If she did tell Christopher that he would not be receiving any more cards from me, did she tell him that it was her or it was me? In all cases, it would kill his last lingering hope, and he would finally fall into despair. But if she did not tell him anything, it could be even worse. Christopher would be waiting, day after day, until his heart wilts. And, as always, every time, my agony turns to rage.

In regards to a lawyer, all I was thinking about at first was to have a lawyer mediate between Christine and me, beginning with writing a letter to her asking her to lift the ban in the best interest of the child. In June, I interviewed four lawyers, all women, in hopes that Christine would read the letter more kindly. Of the four, I found three to be so jaded and money oriented that Christopher's suffering and emotional damage seemed not a factor in their equations. The fourth, an energetic woman in her early thirties, named Margo E. Bryant, made me think, "She has heart." So we talked further, in the course of which we explored the option of launching a civil suit for access to Christopher. A custody case would be different of course, but Ms. Bryant was of the opinion that I had a good chance of winning an access case, even though I was not the biological father of the child. She suggested that I should accumulate a few character references from my friends, and to put together a photo album featuring Christopher, Christine and me.

On June 27, I wrote the following letter to several of my friends:

Dear friends:

Your names are included in this letter because you are the ones with whom I have shared my personal plight in regards to Christopher (which I have not told even my parents). I want first of all to thank you for your emotional support over the last four very difficult months. I have no idea where my sanity would be today without your understanding and sympathy.

Omni-Science and the Human Destiny

As you know, I have been driven to contemplate taking legal action for access to Christopher, or, closer to the truth, for Christopher and I to have access to each other. I have already retained a family law lawyer for this action. Her name is Margo Bryant. It is her opinion that not only do I have a legal leg to stand on, but that my grounds are solid enough to promise a high probability of success.

As far as I can follow Ms. Bryant's legal jargon, it would be a four-stage process, as follows:

She will write a letter to Ms. Mason (Christopher's mother) informing her of our intent;

In the event where Ms. Mason fails to respond or responds negatively, Ms. Bryant would start the legal application towards an enforceable "interim Order of Access";

Should Ms. Mason contend this Interim order, Ms. Bryant would apply for a "Final Order";

Should Ms. Mason still contend this, the case would go to trial.

In order to initiate this process, Ms. Bryant requested that I ask my friends to each write her a letter essentially addressing the question "Why should Christopher be allowed to see his Uncle Tony again?" These letters will serve as basis for the judge's Court Orders in stages 2 and 3, which in itself would cost in the region of $6,000. Of course, the fewer the stages needed to bring forth a decisive outcome, the better for all concerned, especially for a four year old child for whom each day of waiting would seem an eternity.

Since this legal action is a "one shot deal", it would have to be conducted as strongly and solidly as possible from Square One. I am sure you know that my decision to take this course of action was due to the exhaustion of all other options. If there ever is once in my life I have to ask for concerted support from my friends, this is it. It is understood that this support, if given, will be given voluntarily and I will not hold it against anyone for not extending the help requested. On the other hand, I would be forever grateful to anyone whose signature will appear on his/her version of such a letter. Ms. Bryant asks that the letters be written within the next ten days or so, since in her opinion I have already waited too long…

In closing, I would like to emphasize that this action is taken primarily in the best interest of the child.

Yours very sincerely,
Anthony Marr

June 28, 1993

I had lunch with my friend James Taft. We had the following conversation:

JT: "I'm concerned about your reputation."

AM: "My reputation versus Christopher's emotional and psychological integrity? No contest."

JT: "In that case, you'd better be prepared to fight dirty, because I'm sure she's going to."

AM: "She will, but I won't."

JT: "Oh, come on, Tony, drop this Victorian honor crap."

AM: "It's not honor, it's Christopher. I don't want to use dirty tactics on *his* mother."

JT: "Don't you want to make her suffer just a little, for what she's done to you?"

AM: "No. I don't want to make her suffer at all. All I want is for Christopher and I to be able to see each other again. Making her suffer will just act against this objective."

JT: "I don't understand you. I've seen you turning your cheek week after week. Are you going to do it till your head falls off?"

AM: "It's all for Christopher. She is holding him hostage. So don't call me a saint. And she doesn't have to thank me. And, oh, one more thing. I pride myself to be Christopher's male role model. What kind of a model would I be if I used dirty tactics on anyone?"

JT: "What about, say, fighting fire with fire then?"

AM: "What do you mean by that?"

JT: "Holding something of hers hostage. Maybe blackmail her with some secret in her life. Threaten her with damaging something important to her if she doesn't stop what she is doing."

AM: "Strange as it may seem, even though she has deliberately put Christopher through hell, the most important thing in her life is him. So, tactically, I should threaten to harm Christopher if she doesn't comply. Is this what you mean?"

JT: "I didn't say that."

AM: "No. I know you didn't. But if I want to fight dirty, this is what I would have to do."

JT: "She's fighting dirty, whatever you do."

Omni-Science and the Human Destiny

AH: "Yes. But I don't have to stoop down to her level. Offer me a million dollars to harm Christopher, a billion, and see what I would say."

JT: "I know. I know. Okay, I'll write a letter for you, but you're gonna lose, my friend."

AM: "So be it."

JT: "Good luck, old man."

❖ ❖ ❖ ❖ ❖

I received four letters of support from my friend, including one from Roxanne, one from James, one from my housemate Imogen, and one from my long time friend Diana. Following is Diana's, as a sample.

July 16, 1999.

To whom it may concern:

I first met Anthony Marr in 1977. Since that time, I have always found him to be scrupulously honest and dedicated to making positive changes in the world. He is a principled man who really lives what he believes. He is an exceptional human being.

Although Anthony often mentioned Ms. Christine Mason in conversion, I do not recall anything derogatory or disrespectful said about her. I did not meet Ms. Mason until 1986 or thereabouts. I first met Christopher when Anthony first brought him to our house. This was when Christopher was less than one year old. Since then, Christopher and Anthony have visited our family on a regular basis. Frequently, they joined my family (myself, husband and two children, 6 & 9 years) on outings. My children always looked forward to seeing Christopher. Anthony regularly spent one day each weekend, plus weekdays, with Christopher.

I remember Anthony giving Christopher his bottle and changing his diapers. A child's car seat became a permanent fixture in his car. He showed tremendous dedication to Christopher and on occasions when he visited our home on his own, he would use our phone to call and say goodnight to Christopher.

Anthony is also a special friend of my children Crystal and Dylan. His visits to our home are always filled with laughter and fun. My children are always excited to see Anthony and there are few people I would trust so totally with them.

On several occasions Ms. Mason also joined Anthony and Christopher on outings with my family. On one occasion, we went to the Game Farm in Aldergrove and all returned to my home afterwards for dinner. We also met one day at Playland. Ms. Mason and Christopher joined Anthony on a working holiday last summer and my family met them at Cranbrook. We traveled together to Banff where we spent the weekend together. During this time, Anthony and Ms. Mason jointly cared for Christopher.

Anthony has always been concerned for Christopher's safety and on a number of occasions checked to see if I had also put sunscreen on my children. He also convinced me of the importance of having my children wear sunglasses with the proper UV protection when going outdoors. Of course Christopher would always arrive at our home fully attired in sunscreen, hat and sunglasses.

In addition to physical care and supervision, Anthony also spent a lot of time playing with Christopher, exploring with him, and teaching him how to do things. On our outings he would hold Christopher's hand and carry him if he became tired. He always set clearly explained consistent limits fro Christopher with very positive results. On one occasion Christopher had a frustration tantrum which Anthony handled calmly, sticking to his limits and not giving into Christopher's tears. Afterwards, he expressed respect for Christopher and empathy for his feelings. During all my times with Anthony, I have never seen him become impatient with Christopher. Christopher always followed Anthony wherever he went and always came to him when needing anything. On a number of occasions Anthony stated that he believed a male role model was particularly important to Christopher since Christopher's father is an alcoholic and has been estranged from him by Ms. Mason. Anthony said that he saw his role as filling that void in Christopher's life. He felt his input would significantly enhance Christopher's development. He began this relationship with Christopher's needs in mind, but the results are much more precious as Anthony and Christopher are very bonded and share a special and pure love with each other. "Uncle Tony" has always been there cheering Christopher's first steps, his first words, and joining in the discovery of his world.

Christopher's world has always included "Uncle Tony". Anthony has been one of Christopher's prime caregivers since birth. Christopher has been accustomed to virtually daily contact with Anthony. Anthony is not Christopher's father, but is a strong role model and a "father figure" in Christopher's life. Although we may see a clear distinction between father and "father figure", the distinction would not be so clear to Christopher, and the effect of unilaterally terminating this relationship will be virtually the same.

I believe severing Anthony and Christopher's relationship must have been a shocking and painful loss to Christopher as it was for Anthony.

Yours Truly,
Diana McNeil-Buckingham*

* *Ms. McNeil-Buckingham is an elementary school counselor in the Greater Vancouver Area.*

❖ ❖ ❖ ❖ ❖

July 29, 1999

Dear Ms. Mason:

We have been consulted by Mr. Marr, who advised us that until recently, he has spent a great deal of time with your son Christopher who we understand was born on May 4th, 1995.

Mr. Marr advised us that, since Christopher's birth, he has visited with your son 2 to 3 nights a week after work and usually one day per weekend. We understand that Mr. Marr has taken Christopher to a number of places, such as the Science World, the Game Farm and Playland, and that you and he have taken several trips with Christopher. In other words, Mr. Marr has acted as a surrogate father to Christopher since your son's birth.

We are further advised that, unhappily, Mr. Marr has been barred from seeing Christopher since February 3, 1999, save and except for a few hours on Christopher's birthday in May, with your permission. It is not clear to Mr. Marr why you made this decision as apparently you have never expressed any concerns about Mr. Marr's relationship with your son or his care for him.

Mr. Marr is, understandably, most distressed that this relationship has been severed, and wishes to resume his visits with Christopher as soon as possible. He would prefer to settle this matter as amicably as possible, but, if we have not heard from you or a lawyer on your behalf on or before August 13, 1999, we will be seeking instructions to commence Court proceedings in this regard.

Anthony Marr

Hopefully that will not be necessary.

We look forward to hearing from you.

Yours very truly,
Margo E. Bryant
Attorney at Law

❖ ❖ ❖ ❖ ❖

August 10, 1999.

Dear Ms. Bryant:

<u>Re.: Mr. Anthony Marr's access to Christopher Mason</u>

Please be advised that I have been retained by Ms. Christine Mason, mother of Christopher, in the above matter. I have received your letter to Ms. Mason dated August 3, 1999.

In a nutshell, Ms. Mason does not wish Mr. Marr (or Mr. Ma, as his real name may be) to have *any* access to Christopher. Further, Ms. Mason wishes Mr. Marr to have no contact with her or with the day care centre to which she sends Christopher which Mr. Marr has telephoned.

Mr. Marr is a long time family friend of the Mason family. Many years ago, Ms. Mason supported him financially when they lived together. However, Christopher does not regard Mr. Marr as a father of any kind. Christopher knows who his father is, namely Mr. Charles Gordon. Christopher calls Mr. Gordon "dad" and calls Mr. Marr "Uncle Tony", the term "uncle" being used for adult male friends of the family. Mr. Marr is at best a friend (although no longer wanted) and, at worst, a pest; he is definitely *not* a surrogate father.

Mr. Marr is middle-aged, unmarried and lives among people half his age. Until February, Mr. Marr tried to insinuate himself into Ms. Mason's life. She often gave in, because it was difficult to resist his persistent efforts, including long distance phone calls. By now, she has an unlisted phone number. If Mr. Marr had spent money on Christopher, this money only reciprocated for meals that Ms. Mason provided for Mr. Marr when he showed up for dinner.

Mr. Marr seems to seek the pleasures of (surrogate?) fatherhood without the daily responsibilities. His obsession borders on the unhealthy. If he persists in contacting Ms. Mason, I have instructions to seek a restraining order.

Tim Ebner
Attorney at Law

❖ ❖ ❖ ❖ ❖

**1999-08-02-1   Associated Press, New York City   by Katherine Roth
[Despite tougher laws, tiger bone still widely available in Chinatown]**
… As of Monday, the products were still prominently displayed on the shelves of some pharmacies and grocery stores (in New York City's Chinatown)…

"It's very popular and is good for people with bad backs," a smiling clerk at Kam Man Food Products on Canal Street told shoppers on Monday. "I don't take it, because I don't have a bad back, but a lot of people do," said the man, who declined to give his name or comment further…

(Tiger preservationist) Anthony Marr… said that of the 37 traditional Chinese pharmacies visited in Chinatown recently, nine were openly selling products listing tiger bone as an ingredient. He is calling for stiffer penalties for sellers and importers who break the law…

But the US Fish and Wildlife Service… says it doesn't have enough resources to stop the brisk trade…

"We have 93 inspectors and 230 special agents for the entire country. They're stretched pretty thin," said Patricia Fischer, a spokeswoman for the agency. "The sheer volume of wildlife products coming into this country present a monumental task…"

More than 50,000 over-the-counter tradition Chinese medicines containing, or purporting to contain, tiger bone and parts from other critically endangered species are sold in the United States each year to people of all ages and ethnic groups…

**1999-08-03-2   *Daily News*, New York City   by Laura Seigel
[Tiger bone Rx selling in the city despite ban]**
At a cramped grocery in Chinatown yesterday, a casually dressed man plunked down $3.95 and was handed an alleged arthritis cure - tiger bone bills.

Anthony Marr, the Chinese-Canadian tiger campaign director of WCWC in Vancouver, said the purchase proved a grim fact that he had traveled to New York to demonstrate:

The law against selling medicine made from the bones of tigers, an endangered species, is not being enforced.

"I'm here in New York to persuade the government to enforce the law," said Marr. "Tigers will be extinct within 10 years unless things change."

A spokeswoman for the federal Fish and Wildlife Service, which is responsible for monitoring the sale of tiger bone medicine, conceded the agency could do a better job. "But we don't have the staff," Patricia Fisher said. "We only have 230 special agents for the entire country."

She said the agency has tried to control the sale of tiger bone by teaching Asian communities about endangered species, rather than by enforcing the law without explaining it. "This is a tradition in Oriental medicine that goes back centuries," Fisher said…

1999-08-03-2   *World Journal* (Chinese, global)
[The 'Long March' of a Chinese-Canadian conservationist]

… Marr arrived in New York City last Friday. On Saturday, he conducted a reconnaissance of Manhattan's Chinatown district with some local help. In one sizzling afternoon he investigated 37 medicinal stores, and found at least nine that still openly displayed tiger bone medicines for sale…

Yesterday, after a brief media conference in which Marr gave a slideshow on tiger conservation, he led the media present to three of the nine stores to perform demonstration live-purchases…

Shop keepers interviewed seemed aware of the illicit nature of the product, but said since most tigers in China have been killed off, the tiger bone medicines they sell probably contain no real tiger ingredient…

The new Rhino and Tiger Product Labeling Act of 1998, however, ban any product claiming to contain tiger or rhino parts, whether or not they actually do…

1998-08-12-4   Reuters News Agency   by Manuela Badawy
[Import of tiger bones a problem in U.S.]

…"At today's rate of poaching tigers will be extinct in a decade. Tigers don't have the time to wait for the Chinese community to change its habit," said Marr, who is of Chinese descent and has taken heat from other Asians for his campaign.

On a recent day, he led journalists to New York's Chinatown, which has one of the largest concentrations of people with Chinese background in the United State, to buy supposedly banned tiger elixirs.

At the Golden Spring pharmacy on Bowery in Lower Manhattan, Marr walked right in and bought a vial of Tiem Ma tiger bone pills for $3.95. Tiem Ma pills, made by Guiyang Chinese medicine factory in China, listed 6.8 percent ground tiger bone as one of its ingredients and claimed to treat rheumatic neuralgia, lassitude of tendon and back pain.

When journalists and photographers went into the store after Marr purchased the pills, clerks became visibly anxious, removing the pills from the counter and shoved them into a box. They refused to answer journalists' questions...

1999-08-21-6 *The Toronto Star* **by Manuela Badawy, Reuters**
[A helluva town for tigers]
... Under the 1998 Rhino and Tiger Products Labeling Act ...people caught with these products face a fine of $5,000. Business owners pay $10,000 and/or get six months in jail. In comparison, fines for seal penises are $100,000 for individuals and $200,000 and/or one year in jail for business owners.

Marr says the fines for tiger violations should at least equal that for seal violations, if only because the tiger is critically endangered...

1999-09-10 **by Wetland Preserve**
[Wetlands and Western Canada Wilderness Committee Expose Illegal Chinatown Trade in Tiger, Jaguar, Seal, Endangered Species Parts]
"At today's rate of poaching to supply the traditional Chinese medicinal market with body-parts of tiger, rhino and bear, among others, the tiger will be extinct within a decade, and the rhino and bear species thereafter." - Anthony Marr

In response to a report in the tiger conservation publication TIGERLINK that a survey of 47 Chinese pharmacies in New York's Chinatown, 63% (30 shops) still offer tiger parts or products containing, or claiming to contain, tiger parts, Anthony Marr, Biodiversity Campaign Director of the Western Canada Wilderness Committee (WCWC), conducted a reconnaissance of Chinatown in conjunction with Wetlands and Animal Defense League activists during the first weekend in August.

What they found shocked them. Not only were pills claiming to contain ground tiger bone openly on display, but leopard bone, seal penis, and pangolin (an African endangered animal species), were also available! Upon making these discoveries Wetlands issued a press release announcing a press conference to be held the following Monday morning to present the findings.

After the media conference, which was held in Wetlands downstairs lounge, Marr led journalists into Chinatown for a sting operation. While photographers and videographers positioned themselves out of sight, Marr went to purchase endangered species products. However, as he was about to make the purchase, the store clerk saw the journalists and began clearing all endangered species parts from the shelves. But it was too late: the journalists had the proof they needed.

What resulted was huge media splash, as the first wave of journalists, including the Associated Press, Daily News, Reuters, World Journal (the New York area's largest Chinese-language paper), ran their stories, resulting in a second wave of coverage from journalists who saw the initial coverage, including a French-based world news agency, Fox News Channel, Radio Free Asia, and others.

In 1996/97, Marr conducted a similar investigation into the Chinatowns of Vancouver, Toronto and Ottawa, which made national news resulting in quick government response and a near-total elimination of these medicines from Chinatowns country-wide. As a person of Chinese descent, Anthony is able to investigate the sale of endangered species parts in Chinese herb shops and traditional pharmacies without raising suspicion. In traditional Chinese medicine, it is believed that consuming the parts of an animal acclaimed for its strength will pass that strength on to the consumer.

Wetlands and WCWC are currently pursuing this campaign to the next stage, working with the NY State Division of Fish and Wildlife Enforcement Division to prosecute business selling endangered species parts.

1999-09-27

One month ago, due to disagreements between Anthony Marr and WCWC regarding Tiger Fund, Anthony Marr and WCWC parted company.

Today is the day of birth of HOPE-GEO - Heal Our Planet Earth Global Environmental Organization. Founder – Anthony Marr.

1999-10
Open letter to the President of the United States of America

Dear President of the United States of America:

On February 11, 1997, you wrote a letter to the U.S. Congress citing Canada as having "conducted whaling activities that diminish the effectiveness of a conservation program of the International Whaling Commission", regarding the granting of whaling licenses to the Canadian Inuits without IWC approval. We as Canadians take your point well, and pledge to pursue the matter with our government. This letter, however, concerns the killing of a Grey whale by your

Omni-Science and the Human Destiny

own Makah tribe.

In the same letter to Congress, you also wrote: "I understand the importance of maintaining traditional native cultures, and I support aboriginal whaling that is managed through the IWC." On this, we beg to differ, and hope that you will reevaluate the basic philosophy behind this statement.

First, we question the word "traditional". Obviously this is a key word distinguishing aboriginal whaling from non-aboriginal whaling, and must itself therefore be clearly defined. In particular, should traditional whaling employ definitely non-traditional equipment such as motorized watercraft and armor-piercing firearms? We believe that the vast majority of Americans and Canadians would say a resounding "NO!"

More basically, and especially applicable to the Makah, is the question of traditional need, namely food, clothing and fuel. The Makah have done without whale-derived food, clothing and fuel for over seven decades. High on their list of reasons is to use the killing of whales to solve their people's alcohol and drug abuse problems. Kindly show us the traditionality of this reason.

Even more basic than this is whether all elements of traditional aboriginal culture are to be held sacrosanct. If so, then even slavery should be revived. If not, then why should killing whales be so unquestionably honoured?

Ultimately, we believe that as civilization advances on to a new millennium, killing sentient, intelligent, peaceful and trusting creatures like whales and dolphins can no longer be justified, for any reason, by anyone, be they Japanese, Norwegian, Russian, American (Makah), or, yes, Canadian (Inuit). This means that within or beyond IWC parameters, whaling must end.

We ask you to please re-examine the basis of your thinking, which the vast majority of your citizens, judging by their overwhelming opposition to the hunt, obviously have done.

Yours sincerely,
Anthony Marr
Founder, HOPE-GEO

1999-11-18   *Hornby-Denman Island Grapevine*   by Fireweed
[Marr to Speak on OMNI-SCIENCE]

Vancouver-based conservationist Anthony Marr will be making an intriguing new presentation in Courtenay and on Denman Mon., Nov. 22nd & Tues. the 23rd respectively.

Many islanders will remember the engaging speaker as the driving force behind

Western Canada Wilderness Committee's high-profiled Bear Referendum Campaign a number of years ago. Others will recall his fabulous slideshow presentation here in '97 on the plight of the world's dwindling tiger population. Millions of Discovery Channel, PBS and the Knowledge Network viewers have since applauded his efforts as celebrated in the award winning television documentary series Champions of the Wild.

Marr is currently on a cross-country tour under the banner of HOPE (Heal Our Planet Earth) with a thought provoking talk titled [Earth's Shining Destiny]. This original millennium vision, based upon Marr's own "Omniscientific Cosmology", has won the accolades from professors in a diverse range of scientific disciplines.

"Omni-Science," explains Marr, "is a new model of the Universe built not on the physical sciences alone, but the life and social sciences as well. It is a cosmology that can answer the great philosophical questions such as the purpose of humanity, the meaning of life, the destiny of Earth, the Way of the Cosmos, the Masterplan of the Universe, even the nature of 'God'."

Dissuading quick dismissal of such a grandiose claim, Marr's impressive list of supporters (including dozens of distinguished academics), encourages thoughtful attention to the writer's concepts. For example, Stanford University Professor of Geology W.R. Evitt's comments read, "sincerity, imagination, intellectualism, scholarship… meticulously thought out… majestic in scope but intrinsically simply, satisfying and optimistic… broad appeal… important ideas with great potential for lessening the conflicts in a troubled world." Adds Dr. William Kimbel, President, Institute of Human Origins, Berkeley, "… no amateur populariser… a dedicated scholar whose theory makes a profound contribution to the fundamental definition of humankind in relation to the broader universe… too important to be ignored."

While no stranger to controversy as an activist, the praxis of Marr's ideology is bound to enjoy broad appeal. His current HOPE initiative is primarily concerned with collecting signatures on a bold worldwide petition destined for the United Nations. It requests the redirection of ten percent of international military expenditures into a UN administered global ecology/environmental fund.

Courtesy of Denman's Community School, the captivating Marr will be speaking Tuesday evening at 7 pm in the School library.

※   ※   ※   ※   ※

From the journal of Margo E. Bryant on

Omni-Science and the Human Destiny

Marr vs Mason

… In the ensuing months, motions and counter-motions went back and forth, with Anthony stating benignly that he and Christopher had a strong bond and that severing this bond would cause Christopher serious psychological harm, and thus, letting them see each other again would be in the best interest of the child. On the other hand, Christine's is a campaign of character assassination against Anthony, which progressively escalated.

Christine's onslaught culminated in early December in a voluminous package comprising a thick affidavit from her and several one-page affidavits from her several women friends and relatives. Christine affidavit contained one hundred points, no more, no less, against Anthony's character, most of which being petty, and many being demonstrably false. There was also a letter of support from Christopher's father Charles Gordon whom Christine temporarily recalled from his intoxicated exile for the purpose.

"He is not even Christopher's father," wrote more than one of Christine's friends in their affidavits. Charles' letter of support basically said that Christopher did not need a father figure, since he already had a father.

One example of the hundred points in Christine's affidavit that was both petty and untrue had to do with Anthony's refusal to go through with a church ceremony to become Christopher's godfather. This was proof, so concluded Christine, that Anthony lacks conviction in fulfilling the responsibilities of being Christopher's spiritual guide.

Anthony responded, "'Godfather' is just a word, and one with a dubious connotation at that. Our love for each other is the reality, pure and simple. Christopher and I have already made a covenant with each other, and with God if you wish, that cannot be surpassed. The ceremony is not only meaningless to me, but a little demeaning – that I would need some institution to commit me to my own words and my own heart. I also did not go to my own convocation ceremony when I graduated from university. The love in my heart and knowledge in my mind were what counted, not a ceremony or a ritual. For the same reason, I do not celebrate my own birthdays."

Christine also stated that the motive for Anthony to offer to be Christopher's guardian in the event of her death was that Anthony was after Christopher's money. Anthony's reaction to this was a bitter laugh.

Christine also stated that Anthony "free loads" on her, dropping by her place for dinner, and this is in spite of Anthony paying for every weekly outing without exception.

Another point against Anthony's character in Christine's affidavit was his buying high quality toys for Christopher, such as an upholstered rocking horse when Christopher was one year old, and more expensive dinosaur models than those she bought of Christopher. Christine's accusation was that Anthony bought Christopher expensive things for the prime purpose of showing her up, since she could not afford to buy them. Anthony said, "All I want is for Christopher to have the best that I could afford."

An example of an accusation which may seem petty, but is not, is Christine saying that Anthony found pregnant women "repugnant". Anthony's response: "I love children and admire the courage of those women who would dare to go through the birthing process, including Christine herself. If I were a woman, I would be scared shitless."

Yet another accusation is that Anthony told Christopher that Christine had wanted a girl and not a boy. Anthony said, "I have never once touched upon gender comparison in any context with Christopher."

"How can you be so sure? Sometimes people say things they later forget."

"I'm very conscientious of this, because I have been annoyed for years by Christine's anti-male bias. I doubt even her friends could deny this bias in Christine. If Christopher got the idea, it would be from Christine, not from me."

"How does Christine express this bias? Overtly? Subtly?"

"I'd say both," said Anthony, pondering. " In fact, I would be surprised if Christopher did not get that notion somewhere along the line. Through the years, at every opportunity, such as, for example, when a report comes out comparing the performance of schoolboys and schoolgirls, Christine would enthuse about how much smarter and superior girls are than boys. She has a basic dislike and disrespect for men. All her close friends are women. With her women friends, she is sweetness and light. Not so with men. Three years ago, she had two close male friends – Charles and myself. Up to February this year, she had one – me. Now, she has none."

An example of an accusation which was decidedly not petty is a quotation from the psychiatrist that Christopher had been seeing, that Christopher told her that Anthony threatened to shoot him with a "blue gun" if Christopher told Christine a certain "secret".

"I threatened to shoot Christopher?!" cried Anthony, almost in tears. "What kind of mental twisting would make him think that of me and say something like that about me?!"

Other accusations open doors for attacks against Christine's credibility. One was that on Christopher's fourth birthday, Anthony crashed Christopher's party in the afternoon, without permission, behaved rudely and upset everyone. Anthony suggested that we could call Roxanne Stillwell to verify that Christine did give me permission, and also Wilhelmina to verify that he was there at Christine's place in the mid-evening when she arrived. And that further, we could also call those who went to Christopher's party to asked them if what Christine wrote did happen.

One accusation that Christine repeatedly made in her various affidavits over the months was that Anthony on numerous occasions parked his car outside of her condo, spying on her.

"Did you?" I asked him.

"I know one thing without a shadow of a doubt."

"What's that?"

"I can tell you right now that she has never once called her friends, or the police for that matter, telling them that I was right there and then in the process of spying on her, and if she did, and if they did come to investigate, they had never once found me there."

"The absence of proof is not the proof of absence," I quoted, just to test him.

He just plowed on, "Further, I also know without a shadow of a doubt that she has never taken a single photo or a single second of video of me and my car sitting outside her window."

"How do you know all these? Have you spoken with Christine's friends or the police about it? You certainly haven't spoken with Christine about any photos or video."

"The point here is that I don't have to, simply because I have never once been there to be videoed or reported on."

Ah, now, *this* is good. He's got even *me* convinced.

There were other false accusations that could be easily disproven by legal documentation. After Anthony graduated from university, he worked in real estate. After a few years, he left the industry, mostly out of sheer boredom and a sense of meaninglessness, he told me. In Christine's affidavit she stated that Anthony was barred from the Real Estate Board for unethical conduct.

"So, what did you do that was unethical?"

"Why don't you ask the Real Estate Board?" he answered, almost defiantly.

"Tell me and I'll verify," I played back.

"Nothing."

"Have you already checked?"

"No, I haven't. There is nothing to check."

I did. There was indeed no such record.

Christine grossly overplaed her hand. Her blalantly false accusations are all on record. She's too smart for her own good. She would be a vulnerable and not-too-credible witness. Cross examination would be fun.

Shortly before Christmas, nearing the court date, Anthony received a phone call from Diana McNeil-Buckingham, Anthony's prime character witness. Diana told Anthony that she received a telephone call from Christine. Christine was charming and friendly, and apparently very caring. At one point during their conversation, Christine said to Diana, "If you value your children, NEVER, EVER, let them be alone with Tony."

"What are you implying?" Diana asked Christine. "That he is a pedophile?! A child molester?!"

"Just be very careful with what he does with your children, for their own good. That's all I want to say,"

Since then Diana has shown hesitancy in her previously wholehearted support. I no longer consider her a prime witness. Not only has Christine successfully manipulated her own friends, she is succeeding to manipulate Anthony's friends as well.

As an opponent, overextended as she is, this woman is not to be underestimated, inside or outside the courtroom, during and after this conflict.

All in all, however, with or without Diana's support, I feel that we have a strong case. Although the law would favor Christine on account of her being Christopher's biological mother, this is not a custody case but an access case. Anthony has the fighting spirit. He will see Christopher yet.

※ ※ ※ ※ ※

1999-12-23　　　Special to *The Capitol Times*, U.S.A.　　by Anthony Marr
Omniscientific Cosmology: A new millennium vision

A **cosmology** is a model of the Universe. It is essentially a tool for our self-understanding. Why? Because the part cannot be fully understood without an understanding of the whole and its part in this whole. Throughout human history, many cosmologies have been advanced, most being in the form of **mythologies** (incl. Creationism), and all, unless viewed as metaphors or allegories, are far from the truth - except one. The only cosmology that stays true to fact when taken

Omni-Science and the Human Destiny

literally is **scientific cosmology**. Unfortunately, as so far developed, involving only the **astro-chemo-physical sciences**, it is incomplete. **Omniscientific Cosmology** completes it by incorporating the **bio-socio-ecological sciences**, the reason being that the biosphere is a part of the Earth, which is a part of the Cosmos. And since Homo sapiens is a part of Earth's biosphere, the omniscientific cosmology is needed for human self-understanding, which therefore makes it also a system of omniscientific cosmological **philosophy**.

The omniscientific cosmology builds upon the physical structure and processes of the Cosmos as per conventional scientific cosmology by adding the following as integral parts: the original inorganic molecules of the primordial Earth gave rise to the cells ~3.5 billion years ago, which gave rise to the metabionts (multicellular organisms) ~600 million years ago, which gave rise to animal societies (initially the insect societies) ~100 million years ago, which gave rise to the human-based nations ~about 10,000 years ago.

The cell, the metabiont, the "city" (including all animal societies), and the nation are all demonstrably bona fide **organisms**, or "**living systems**", each on its own **level of organization**. Today, the physical matter of planet Earth is organized in five levels of organization: the **Molecular**, the **Cellular**, the **Metabion**, the **Citian** (derived from "city") and the **National**. In contrast, all other Solar System planets have only one level of organization – the Molecular.

The phenomenon by which a lower level gave rise to its adjacent higher level is **Integrative Transcendence (I.T.)**. The process by which I.T. is achieved is **Transcendent Integration (T.I.)**, which essentially involves **differentiation** and **cooperation**. By means of T.I., the social organisms of level (X) formed societies; and by means of I.T., the advanced societies of Level (X) became the original organisms of level (X+1). Thus, a cell is a "society" of its own "social molecules", a metabiont is a society of its own social cells, a city is a society of its own social metabionts, and a nation is a society of its own social cities.

Interlevel Parallelisms exist, and are of predictive value, e.g.: 1. On every level of organization, there are non-social and social units. 2. For every living system, on any level, there are 20 "subsystems" (see the book for details). 3. Evolution occurs on all levels simultaneously, although, by **Translevel Progression**, the lower levels are dominated by **Darwinian evolution**, and the higher levels by **Lamarckian evolution**. There are many other interlevel parallelisms.

By far the most monumental of all interlevel parallelisms is the **O.S.E.S. Cycle**. O.S.E.S. represents the four quadrants of a cycle of the **T.I./I.T. Spiral**, namely: **Organismization, Speciation, Ecosystemization** and **Socialization**. And, by the resultant societies organismizing into the first organisms of the level above, they start a new and next higher O.S.E.S. Cycle on the ever-ascending T.I./I.T. Spiral.

Consciousness is matter-based, and is therefore a physical phenomenon. It, too, is a result of T.I./I.T., by which the **proto-consciousness** or consciousness of the units of a certain level gives rise to that of the level above. Thus, the T.I./I.T. spiral is in fact a **matter/consciousness T.I./I.T. Twin-Spiral**.

The planet Earth is an egg, literally. First, a universal definition of "egg" – a physical entity containing an embryo destined to develop into a full organism. A bird egg, for example, is a specific case of a universal egg, as is a **planetary egg** like the Earth. The planetary egg Earth does contain a **planetary embryo**, namely, the **biosphere**. The main difference between a bird egg and a planetary egg is that a bird embryo is on the inside of the egg, whereas a planetary embryo is on the outside of the egg, which nonetheless is enclosed by the atmosphere. The development of a planetary egg does follow a definite **planetary gestation period**. Specifically, Earth's planetary embryo has hitherto undergone four stages of **planetary metamorphosis** – from molecules to cells to metabionts to cities to nations. In other words, it has successfully progressed through four O.S.E.S. Cycles of Earth's T.I./I.T. Twin-Spiral; and the T.I./I.T. Twin-Spiral itself has ascended through four levels of organization pertaining to life on Earth. The development of Earth's planetary embryo follows a preset **metamorphic schedule** as predetermined by the planet's original physical and chemical properties, which follows an accelerating exponential timeframe. This timeframe appears to accord to the Fibonacci numbers series applicable to the many spiraling forms found in nature.

The metamorphosis of Earth's planetary embryo has currently progressed on to the Socialization quadrant of the O.S.E.S. Cycle of Earth's T.I./I.T. Twin-Spiral on the National level of organization. If the T.I./I.T. Twin-Spiral would continue to unfold as it has over the last 4.6 billion years of Earth's history, the next step would be **planetary organismization**. This would involve the nations transcendently integrating into a harmonized **international society** involving differentiation and cooperation, and to integratively transcend from the geo-embryo to the full-fledged **Planetary Organism Earth**. Of course, it could also fail and, at the crucial juncture, Earth's biosphere might spontaneously regress back down to the lower levels, with the National, Citian or even Metabion levels terminated.

Once the Planetary Organism Earth has organismized into being, it will be the original organism on the **Planetary level of organization** within the Solar System. After a period of maturation, it will reproduce, begetting offspring planetary organisms on other Solar System planets and their satellites, or in interplanetary space.

Omni-Science and the Human Destiny

Earth's "seeds" will be space colonies - citian organisms in their own right, which will contain the genes and memes of Earth. Once landing on other planets and their satellites, or stabilized in orbit, these citian level "Earth seeds" will quickly form national organisms, and eventually planetary organisms. Thus, yet a new O.S.E.S. Cycle, on the Planetary level of organization, will unfold. Like the lower-level organisms before them, these planetary organisms will speciate, form a **multi-planetary ecosystem**, and eventually **inter-planetary society**, which, if all go well, will become the **Stellar Organism Sol** - on the **Stellar level of organization**.

A further extrapolation of the Earth's T.I./I.T. Spiral beyond the Solar System may find it joining the T.I./I.T. twin-spirals of other integratively transcended planetary systems in the interstellar realm. Especially if light-speed could be exceeded by some yet unknown technology, there will likely be three levels of organization from the stellar organism to the **Galactic Organism**, and another three levels from the galactic organism to the ultimate and singular **Universal Organism**.

What would this Universal Organism be like? Comparing the physical and mental powers of a human being (a metabion organism) against those of an amoeba (a cellular organism), the difference is of course immense. And yet, they are but one level of organization apart. By the above reckoning, the Universal Organism is ten levels above the human being, and eight levels above the United States (a national organism). Within the Cosmos, the Universal Organism will be everywhere. Its knowledge will encompass that in every library on every planet endowed with civilization. Its physical and mental powers will be virtually infinite. A traditional theologian would have no choice but to describe it as being virtually "omnipresent, omniscient and omnipotent".

But two things he would have to concede: 1. There is nothing supernatural about this Universal Organism; it is entirely natural. And 2. It certainly did not create us; on the contrary, we will have participated, in however miniscule a capacity, in creating *it*.

The above assumes that we can survive our current planetary crisis. According to the Omniscientific Cosmology as conceived by the author, the key to success is T.I./I.T..

❖ ❖ ❖ ❖ ❖

From the journal of Anthony Marr:

1999-12-31

Snow is falling heavily outside the mountain cabin. Millennium fever is sweeping the globe, but up here in the Coastal Mountains of British Columbia, Canada, surrounded by rock and ice, this could be the Pliocene era for all I know. Even my friends the bears have withdrawn into their wintry refuges, enjoying their annual oblivion from human evils and follies. If Apocalypse were now, if Armageddon were here, if the End-of-the-World descended, I'd be the last to know.

I just had the most excruciating Christmas of my life. One without Christopher. One in which I could not even send a Christmas card to Christopher. One where I could not even share my joy with him for my discovery of the Tao. One when my very best gift to Christopher would be rejected, and was.

The fact that I did not fight tooth and nail to see him he might consider cowardice. This is a painful concept to contemplate.

So now, do I fight tooth and nail to win this court case? Would anyone understand if I say that I am more afraid of winning than of losing? Does anyone even care?

"My dearly beloved, I do understand, and I do care."

"Raminothna! Is that you?!"

"Yes, it is I."

"Where've you been?"

"Among the stars."

"So what are you doing here?"

"I feel your distress, and your need for counsel. Besides, my seeds in your sun room have germinated."

"Oh, have they? I will take good care of them. Don't you worry. So, you said you understood. What do you understand?"

"Why you are more afraid of winning than of losing."

"Why?"

"If you lose, you lose nothing other than what you have already lost. But if you win, Christine would wage a campaign to turn Christopher himself against you, until he himself hates you and despises you."

"Oh, please, don't! I can stand the thought! That would screw him up for good!"

"Or perhaps she won't, in the best interest of the child."

"I wish."

"Upon a very lucky star, I know."

"What *should* I do, Raminothna? What should I *do*?!"

"I could invoke the Cosmic Hand of Destiny, if you like."

"Whatever, if you think it would help."

"It could. Just one thing. The Cosmic Hand of Destiny can be effectively invoked only once in a lifetime. You have to choose your subject matter with all due care."

"Sure. I'll try anything once. And I cannot think of a better thing to use it on, whatever it is."

"Very well, then. Go outside and bring in five boulders, each one about the size of a bowling ball, and arrange them in the form of a pyramid - in your fireplace."

"Done," I said after a few minutes, a little breathless, my hands wet and gritty and my shirt soaked with melting snow.

"Write on a piece of paper the following: 'I will fight to the bitter end.'"
"Done"

"Crunch the piece of paper into a ball and insert the ball into the pyramid."
"Done."

"Now listen carefully. If you are destined to fight and win, nothing will happen to the paper ball. But if you are meant to lose or surrender, a cosmic hand of destiny will reach into the pyramid, and reduce the paper ball to ashes – before the stroke of midnight tonight."

To make a long evening short, just before midnight, a cosmic hand of destiny did reach into the pyramid, and reduced the paper ball to ashes. The means was a simple match. The hand was mine.

❖ ❖ ❖ ❖ ❖

Dear Homo Sapiens:

On January 1, 2000, Anthony faxed the following letter to Margo Bryant's office: "… Where this case is concerned, I am more afraid of winning than of losing. If I lost, or surrendered, Christine may hopefully halt her campaign of hate against me and of devastation against Christopher. But if I won, she would assuredly make Christopher himself hate me and despise me and abhor me to the extent where he himself would refuse to see me. This would result in the final breaking of Christopher's heart and the total devastation of his emotional integrity. I cannot allow this to happen, nor even bear the thought… So, in the name of my love for Christopher, I capitulate and agree never to see him again…"

On January 12, 2000, Anthony received a visit from a sheriff, who delivered to him a court restraining order against him seeking contact with Christopher ever again. Anthony did not contest it.

In March 2000, while driving to visit his parents, Anthony saw half a block away a woman walking with a child. He thought they were Christine and Christopher. Upon circulating the block, he saw that he was not mistaken. He drove to within 100 feet of Christopher, but he did not stop.

Not only would Anthony find it harder and harder to recognize Christopher's physical appearance as time goes by, he would likewise find it harder and harder to recognize Christopher's mind. That Christopher would say that Anthony threatened to shoot him with a gun tells volumes of how his mind had been altered. If mere months of leading questions and manipulations through incompetence or malice had turned Christopher into thinking of his devoted friend and guardian angel as a threatening and evil villain, who knows what years of such influences would do. Here then is another test for Anthony's love.

I ask him, "What if Christopher one day turns against you, would you still love him?"

"I will never stop loving him, no matter what."

"How much will you love him?"

"Wholeheartedly, unconditionally, as always."

"Even if he accuses you of the vilest of crimes?"

"Like what?"

"Whatever Christine manipulates him to believe."

"Whatever. 'Wholeheartedly and unconditionally' is what I said."

"What if he becomes even more of a villain than Christine herself?"

"If he becomes a villain, it would not be due to him, but to whomever made him that way. He would be the victim, as he already is. Nothing is a factor in the equation of my love for Christopher exeept love itself. You be my witness."

"And Christine?"

"What about her?"

"Will you ever forgive her?"

He said nothing.

I have just one last question for him. "Now that you can no longer do anything for Christopher personally, how will you use this miraculous power of yours?"

He did not think long before answering, "I will devote myself to working for all the children of the world, of whom Christopher is one. If I benefit children in general, I benefit him. Nobody, not even Christine, can keep me from doing that."

At this moment of his reverie of tragedy and determination, Tears In Heaven flow out of his car radio. Eric Clapton wrote it to commemorate his small son who fell out of an 18th floor window and died. It was a poignant and gentle song, but it hit Anthony like a sledgehammer in his solar plexus. He had to pull his car off the road, to cry his heart out.

Homo Sapiens of Earth, sometimes, I cannot help but abhor you, but always, I cannot help but adore you.

I remain
Raminothna
the Fortunate and the Called Upon
at your service

THE END

About the Author

Anthony Marr is an internationally recognized wildlife preservationist who was featured as the "Champion of the Bengal Tiger" in the award winning TV wildlife documentary series "Champions of The Wild" aired in 20 countries worldwide (1998). He served for four years as a campaign director for the 25,000 members-strong Western Canada Wilderness Committee. He travels extensively to conduct his campaigns, including an intense 8-week road tour throughout British Columbia against grizzly bear hunting in which he was constantly harassed by large groups of trophy hunters (1996), three sojourns in deep rural India where he worked closely with the villagers living around two tiger reserves (1997, 1998, 1999), and the 40-states-and-4-provinces-in-7-months Compassion for Animals Road Expedition (CARE) throughout Canada and the United States (2003-2004). He appears regularly on media, has participated in dozens of in-hall and on-air debates, has been guest of honor as a public speaker on hundreds of occasions, and has had numerous articles published in newspapers and magazines. He has a science degree (physics major) from the University of British Columbia and has worked as a field geophysicist and an environmental scientist. **Omni-Science and the Human Destiny** is his first major work (2003), which took him 25 years to accomplish. He was born in China, raised in Hong Kong, has never been married, and lives in Vancouver, Canada.